Critical Studies
in Teacher Education

Its Folklore, Theory and Practice

For Lori and Dina as they consider professional careers

Critical Studies in Teacher Education

Its Folklore, Theory and Practice

Edited by

Thomas S Popkewitz

University of Wisconsin-Madison

 The Falmer Press

(A Member of the Taylor & Francis Group)
London, New York and Philadelphia

UK   The Falmer Press, Falmer House, Barcombe, Lewes, East Sussex, BN8 5DL

USA   The Falmer Press, Taylor & Francis Inc., 242 Cherry Street, Philadelphia, PA 19106-1906

First published 1987

Library of Congress Cataloging in Publication Data

Teacher education.

   1. Teachers—Training of. I. Popkewitz, Thomas S.
LB1715.T395   1987   370′.7′1   86-29353
ISBN 1-85000-153-7
ISBN 1-85000-154-5 (pbk.)

Jacket design by Caroline Archer
Illustration by Kerry Freedman

Typeset in 11/13 Garamond by
Imago Publishing Ltd, Thame, Oxon

Printed in Great Britain by Taylor & Francis (Printers) Ltd, Basingstoke

Contents

v

Contents

Preface

One of the most dramatic shifts in the focus on school reform in the past few years has been the attention given to teacher education. The aftermath of the American government report, *Nation-at-Risk*, has produced a variety of proposals to improve the quality and standards of teachers who are being trained in Schools of Education. The demography of the profession-at-large is also changing as new graduate school specialties in teacher education emerge, school districts create positions in teacher training, and research in supervision is given support through federal grants. In Great Britain as well, the organization and control of teacher education has been under continual pressure as the government monetarist policies are applied to the university and school sectors.

Contradictions of current reforms are embedded in the political strategies to change teaching. At one layer, there is a general discussion in the United States about the federal government reducing its role in educational policy making. The rhetoric of reform is concerned with developing local community initiatives to determine the scope and boundary of the changes. While the general tenor of debate focuses attention on communal problem-solving, the actual strategies to alter the control mechanisms of educational systems involve a continuum of elements of centralization, decentralization and devolution of decision-making.[1] Strengthened procedures of accountability through standardized testing procedures and revised certification programs have been introduced in teacher education to provide greater control by the state. At the same time, local authorities and universities have been called upon to develop alternative curricula for teacher education, reflecting demands for decentralization and, in some instances, devolution of decision-making.

The seemingly contradictory reform strategies may, in fact, strengthen particular state interests for a more rational, and hence controllable, educational apparatus that responds to particular economic and social interests. Certain themes, for example, appear in both state and local school reforms: business interests have been more directly involved in school policy making; policies for teacher reform challenge union influence in setting curriculum and work policy; and state control over policy and content of teacher education curriculum is more pronounced, an area previously determined by university communities.

The contradictions and tensions within teacher education suggest that educational reform may involve deeper institutional tensions than those identified in the public discourse. There are a number of ideological, cultural, economic and administrative factors that influence the scope and direction of reform. Changes in professional programs in the United States are coupled with a number of structural issues. These issues include an economic crisis in government, a conservative political shift, the development of an ideology that more clearly integrates industrial needs with educational policy, and a belief that the previous era of centralized social and educational reforms has failed. The latter belief has a consequence of uniting both American conservatives and liberals in the argument for school reform.

While structural issues provide a horizon to institutional practice, it is also evident that reforms are mediated by the interests of bureaucratic and professional groups. In the United States, professional educational associations and research communities have called for expert leadership in program development and evaluation of community-based reforms. These groups have succeeded in redirecting policy through lobbying for federal research funds and creating professional centers of power which are sometimes in conflict with legislatively defined monitoring agencies, such as the State Departments of Instruction.

Underlying the public criticism is an acceptance of the folklore and myths of institutional life. The discourse of our teacher education is a celebration about existing institutional patterns. The discussion takes for granted that the problems of teacher education are improving the relation between theory and practice, facilitating communication between university and school, extending practical experiences, and providing more training in science, computers and mathematics. The discourse of administrative change, efficient procedures and rational planning is made to seem as progressive, yet the practices conserve the power arrangements of schooling.[2]

The public discourse should be distinguished from the actual reform practices. The public language functions as a slogan system to develop a consensus about an agenda for schooling. The language is often built upon popular social and political beliefs which call attention to the need for innovation and change. In the case of the current American reform, the public language contains images of schooling as fulfilling a mission in which liberal hopes of individualism and democracy are tied to a millennial promise of material affluence and national destiny.[3] The public language, however, may have little relationship to the actual values that shape practice, the latter reflecting the working out of specific networks of power in the organization of institutions.[4]

The current slogans about quality, excellence, school effectiveness and professionalism are categories of the power relations of institutional life. The discourse of reform is not simply a formal instrument for describing events but a part of the events that structures loyalty and solidarity. The public discourse is a source of sanction for social participation. It defines the nature, causes, consequences and remedies for institutional practices. Conditions are set for interpretation which give objectivity to the topics, forms, and textualities of the ongoing relations; exercising control is over what knowledge is relevant and the structure by which certain issues are made legitimate for public consideration. At the same time, a bias is mobilized that filters out certain issues, making them seem as existing beyond the possibilities of the existing definitions and organization of social life.

To borrow from Michel Foucault, the French social philosopher/historian, the categories of the discourse form a 'regime of truth'. Power is exercised through the ability to assign categories that provide identity to those to whom the categories are to be applied. The techniques of sorting, classifying and evaluating of people enable the exercise of sovereignty.

The public discourse dulls one's sensitivity to the complexities that underlie the practices of teacher education. There is a filtering out of its historical, social and political assumptions. Issues of class, ethnicity, and gender are transformed into questions about liberal arts course requirements, merit pay and more student-teaching experience. Excellence and effectiveness in schooling become slogans that signify elite agendas for defining teacher training and school study. The slogans obscure how policies and practices are related to specific groups' economic requirements for science, technology and bureaucratic mechanism of control.

The volume brings together major scholars who are concerned with the 'regime of truth' that emerges in teacher education. The essays draw upon critical traditions in political science, sociology, anthropology, philosophy and history. The patterns of teacher education are located in larger issues of cultural contractions, economic structures and social transformation. The categories of teaching, learning and competency are transposed into questions of labor, ideology, power and gender. The call for professionalism in teaching is defined as a dynamic of social transformation, serving as an institutional ideology which legitimates existing power arrangements and the assumptions of teacher labor. The essays are concerned with the structure by which certain questions of power become omitted from public consideration, obscuring the social and political complexity of professional life.

Thomas S. Popkewitz
March 1986

Notes

1. For general issues of decentralization and power in education, see, for example, POPKEWITZ T., (1979) 'Schools and the symbolic uses of community participation', in GRANT, C. (Ed.) *Community Participation in Education*, Boston, MA, Allyn and Bacon Inc; POPKEWITZ, T. (1978) 'Change and the social structure of schooling', in WILLIS, G. (Ed.) *Qualitative Research*, Berkeley, CA, McCutchan.
2. See, for example, POPKEWITZ T. (1985) 'A comparative perspective to teacher education', *Journal of Teacher Education*, 36, 5, October/November, pp. 2–10.
3. POPKEWITZ, T., PITMAN, A. and BARRY, A. (1984b) 'Educational reform and its millennial quality, the 1980s', *Journal of Curriculum Studies*, 18, 3, pp. 267–84.
4. See, for example, DICKSON, D. (1984) *The New Politics of Science*, New York, Pantheon.

Introduction

1   Ideology and Social Formation in Teacher Education[1]

Thomas S. Popkewitz

The language, rituals and behaviors of teacher education are realized in an institutional context. Conduct is structured by codes of culture which govern the ways in which people think, feel, 'see' and act toward the practices of schooling. Two important dynamics of American life shape and fashion these codes of culture. First, the professionalization of knowledge gives certain occupations cultural and social authority in controlling institutional realms of meaning and definitions of reality. Second, the codes of teacher education respond to the social predicament of schooling. We live in a society in which there are differences in social class, gender, race, ethnicity and religion. In significant ways, methods of teaching, theories of instruction and practices of student teaching are part of a discourse that responds to tensions and power arrangements underlying these two dynamics of our social conditions.

The issues of professionalization and cultural/social formation are often obscured in the discourse of teacher education. This process is especially the case when the discourse is concerned with efficiency, management or effectiveness. Not understanding administrative problems as existing with contexts of power and authority removes from scrutiny the social assumptions and implications of professional actions. Teacher education becomes a legitimating mechanism. The categories of curriculum, learning and research are made to seem objective and unrelated to political agendas.

Institutional Qualities of Schooling

To consider the problem of teacher education, let me state what might seem an obvious 'fact' about occupational preparation.

Teacher education exists and is historically related to the institutional development of schooling. As schooling evolved as a social form to prepare children for adulthood, there also developed a specialized occupational group with control and authority to work out the charter of its everyday life. The occupational group developed certain specialized bodies of images, allegories and rituals which explain the 'nature' of schooling and its division of labor. The conduct of teacher education can be understood, in part, as a mechanism for legitimating occupational patterns of labor to new recruits.

The potency of the social patterns of teacher education can be understood more adequately when we consider the difference between the surface and underlying layers of meaning in institutional life. The surface layer of meaning is provided by publicly-accepted criteria or standards by which people judge success or failure. Writing a lesson objective, doing microteaching or working in a team teaching situation might provide such criteria. The underlying layer of meaning directs attention to the assumptions, presuppositions and 'rules of the game' that give plausibility and legitimacy to the ongoing actions. Student-teachers learn not only the academic subject-matter but also the appropriate forms in which to cast their professional knowledge.[2]

The underlying layer of meaning is illustrated by focusing on a lesson in mathematics observed in an American inner city school.[3] The students were black, from families of the industrial poor and unemployed. The public purpose of the lesson was to help students learn subtraction. The teacher approached the instruction as a management problem. She wrote a lesson plan, constructed materials, and evaluated according to the set objectives. The lesson was justified for different reasons: subtraction is an important ingredient of a mathematics curriculum and future lessons depend upon acquiring the presented knowledge. During the lesson, the teacher explained elements of subtraction and students worked with textbooks and ditto sheets.

These surface meanings of the lesson developed in a context of institutional patterns which constitute the underlying meanings. That teachers do not follow 'rational' procedures in teaching is well documented.[4] Only partially studied are the relationship of teacher practices to institutional rules and values.[5] In this particular lesson, mathematics was defined as having a fixed and unyielding definition with which teachers are to 'fill' the minds of students, reflecting what Friere refers to as a banking conception of education. The subject-matter of the lesson, however, was only a part of the content. The lesson carried social messages that were as important as the cognitive considerations. The introduction to the lesson involved a discussion that focused upon the children's academic failures. The discourse reflected the teacher's feeling that the welfare status of the children made it likely that they possessed undesirable 'traits' which needed to be overcome before any achievement could be obtained. Much of the classroom interaction was related to the teacher's belief in the cultural and personal pathology of the children.

We can begin to understand from this lesson that the form and content of schooling are interrelated; they are not only channels of thought and action but reinforce and legitimate social values about authority and control. The achievement of schooling is giving direction to social thought and the formation of intelligence for both those who succeed and those who fail. The banking concept posits knowledge as external to individuals and controlled by those who have power to define and categorize social reality. The social interactions reinforce that notion of power by suggesting that failure to learn is a personal, not institutional, failure.

While the example focuses upon classroom teaching, certain issues about teacher education are raised. It is clear that the focal point of teacher education is schooling. Yet there is not one common school but different types of schooling that respond to the social location and cultural circumstances of the children.[6] In the light of this diversity, we need to ask: How do methods courses, theories of childhood and cognition, histories of education and clinical experiences give definition and rules to our reasoning about diversity? How do the patterns of discourse in teacher education legitimate or make problematic the content and form of schooling? What codes govern institutional discourse and make reasonable the language, behaviors and patterns found in schools?

Codes and Power Relations

How can we think about the institutional codes that underlie teacher education? One approach is offered by Michel Foucault, a French social philosopher and historian.[7] Foucault suggests that there are fundamental codes of a culture that underlie a society at any one time. These codes govern the society's discourse, its exchanges, its techniques, its values and the hierarchy of its practices. The codes become a 'regime of truth'. They shape and fashion what can be said and what must be left unsaid, the types of discourse accepted as true and the mechanisms that make it possible to distinguish between truth and error.

Codes of culture are illuminated by an examination of discourse. In the realm of discourse, Foucault is interested in more than the rules and structure of grammar. Our signs, gestures, routines and behaviors carry rules about what is to be considered normal, reasonable, and legitimate. Discourse sets conditions by which events are interpreted and one's self as an individual is located in a dynamic world. Embedded in codes of culture, Foucault continues, are power relations. The notion of power relates not to ownership but to the understanding of changing social relations and innumerable vantage-points from which power is exercised.

To focus upon the method of analysis, Foucault gives attention to a shift in codes between the seventeenth and nineteenth centuries. Foucault argues that a break-up occurs in the specific epistemological configuration of the classical era. There was a decline in the belief that things and beings had a manifest identity through their representation. Prior to the seventeenth century, for example, art was considered a replica of reality. It was incomprehensible to the 'mind' of the Greeks or the medieval European to consider objects as expressions of the artist's personality or as a medium of personal communication.[8] The new epistemology enabled people to become conscious of themselves, providing a transformation of consciousness in which human beings could be considered ontologically, as objects of knowledge. Foucault traced the relation of knowledge to power in the changing configurations of the penal systems, sexual relations and clinical medicine. New methods of observation, classification and organization increased the authority and legitimacy of certain power relations.[9]

The idea of cultural codes provides a more appropriate way of considering the problem of socialization than is found in much contemporary research. Socialization has been considered in a functional and technical manner. It is equated with the adoption of certain rules of the game, usually related to identified beliefs, attitudes and information. The implicit question is whether individuals in an occupation have met the predefined expectations and demands of a work place; or how they compare to an ideal type of professional. Where the rules are not incorporated, much of the research in teacher education suggests there is incomplete or ineffective socialization.[10] The work of Foucault suggests that the prevailing conceptual view is inadequate. The problem of socialization lies with how the social production of meaning takes place. Rather than incomplete socialization, there are various possibilities for socialization as the intentions and implicit philosophies of our discourse are mediated by our institutional contexts. As people participate in the world, they continually react to the structures of language and practice, adopting a stance to social affairs that can glorify existing institutions or seek alternative or oppositional structures.

If we use Foucault's method for the study of teacher education, two dynamics of social life seem influential. One is the professionalization of knowledge. The second is the set of social and cultural tensions that create a predicament for schooling. These two dimensions interact in a way that produces the codes of the 'culture' of teaching.

Professionalization of Knowledge

The codes of teacher education are part of a larger social dynamic associated with the professionalization of knowledge. Particular occupations have emerged to control certain elements of institutional life. This control, however, is not through overt power or force. Power is exercised through the production and reproduction of knowledge. The quality of knowing is esoteric and scientific rather than commonsensical and related to face-to-face interactions. Professional knowledge is to organize social and private life, with the definitions 'owned' by particular communities of experts.

In this section, I would like to explore problems of the professionalization of knowledge as they relate to teacher education. First, professionalization will be considered as a particular dynamic of a changing cultural consciousness among the middle class in America. Second, the role of science in interpreting institutional life will be discussed; my intent is to consider science as a means by which political agendas are incorporated into professional structures. Third, the use of instrumental reasoning as a logic of teacher education will be discussed. The combining of science with instrumental reason creates an illusion of disinterestedness and objectivity in practices that are socially constructed. The discussion is not intended to deny the possibilities of science or professionalization in improving social life but to point to the social location and ideological implications of these practices in our contemporary situation.

Careers, Social Identity and Middle-class Consciousness

The professionalization of knowledge reflects the change in the material conditions and the cultural consciousness of the middle class after the American Civil War (1865). New specialized communities of experts emerge to give definition to social, political and economic affairs. The knowledge of the expert was to be disinterested and seemingly neutral toward existing political agendas, yet control the cultural symbols that define public and private concerns.

In the same period when teacher education expanded rapidly in normal schools, a general change occurred in cultural sensitivities so as to structure the definitions of American middle class life and influence professional education.[11] Until the American Civil War, the rural image of community and individual efficacy had been an essential part of American folklore and Protestant millennial beliefs. The pastoral image was threatened by the development of corporate capitalism and more complex transportation arrangements that made individual communities interdependent. The image of rural community was in conflict with metaphors of industrialization, the later projected an image of the world as a machine that operated through laws of nature.[12]

Specialized communities of professionals developed, such as those in psychology, economics and political science, to explain the changes and to guide the social reforms that were to reestablish meaning and tradition in society. The importance of the new communities of professionals can be understood by focusing upon the idea of career. Career in the early nineteenth century referred to the course of a race track. By the end of the century, it suggested that one's identity, self-image and material prospects were tied to a pattern of organized activity.[13]

The idea of the sovereign individual was replaced by a belief that an individual's good works and self development were to occur in structured communities. The currency of the professional was words: to be able to categorize social relations was to have power to define, organize and control them.

The new position of the professional was based upon social and cultural authority.[14] Social authority was built upon the recognition that a professional group's definitions are legitimate according to the prevailing rules of the society. Cultural authority was also associated with the professions, assigning the realm of meaning and ideas in which particular definitions of reality and judgment prevail as valid and true. By shaping clients' understanding of their experience, techniques of social manipulation — and also symbols that are to influence moral conduct and direction of will — became part of the professional mandate.

The authority of the intellectual was legitimated by the changing role of the intellectual.[15] Many people who called themselves social scientists prior to the 1900s saw their position tied to the twin tasks of understanding and social agitation. The dual position produced conflict, and an alternative strategy of reform was created. The strategy was that the social scientist would serve as expert consultant to the policy maker. The new role was expressed through an ideology of disinterest to protect the academic from changes in political party or policy.[16] Normative elements were removed from discussions of theory and philosophy of science. The expert, it was argued, was to decide not upon ultimate purposes but upon effective strategies. The Progressive political era in America, for example, defined government and civil reform as problems of efficient administration. The changing meaning of professional authority was reflected in the development of teacher education. The original mandate of teacher education was deeply embedded in religious education and related to the idea of a 'calling'.[17] The early teacher educators were ministers who sought to train those who would inculcate the word of God in children. As teacher education moved into normal schools and universities, its aims were made secular without losing the moral fervor. Teachers were to offer salvation to immigrants, the working classes and more recently, a nation at risk. The moral claims were to extend beyond the soul to the personality of the child in all his or her interpersonal relations, sexual attitudes and work ethics. The moral claims, however, became hidden as professionals assumed a technical stance through the incorporation of positivism into educational sciences.

To understand how the social agendas become defined with schooling we need to focus upon the role of the academic expert. This entails considering how the interests of a few are redefined as universal values of teaching and learning through the canopies of science. While science has an interpretive potential for 'seeing' through the facades of our social existence, science also contains a contradiction by its merging of public and formal languages.

Science: The Merging of Public and Formal Languages

Science has a particular sacred quality in American society. It is believed that science provides society with the knowledge and expertise needed for a better life. The quality of the better life is not restricted to the physical and biological world. An innovation of the past century is the application of scientific thought to social and political institutions.

The idea that science provides the professions with authority needs to be considered in both its formal and public qualities.[18] The formal language of science calls attention to things in the world rather than to the processes by which ideas and activities occur. Images of inner control, respect for rules and proven experience are projected. By affiliating with the rituals and ceremonies of science, occupational life is made to seem objective.

The sciences of teacher education are also part of a public language. The concepts and generalization are not simply formal instruments for describing events but are themselves part of the events, helping to create beliefs about the nature, causes, consequences and remedies of institutional practices. The concepts of teaching, learning, supervision and methods receive definitions from the structure of discourse found in schools. The language of teacher education creates a structure for loyalty and social solidarity through this relationship. The use of scientific language to maintain trust is important because of the ambiguities and controversy that underlie our institutional conditions. The mandate to 'educate' is never straightforward or unidimensional.

The merging of a public and formal language can be illustrated in the history of teaching and teacher education. While there are competing views of science (hermeneutics, empiricism and marxism are three examples), a certain style of scientific discourse came to dominate teacher education.[19] The view was associated with empiricism and positivism. It stressed measurement and testing and involved a preoccupation with practical problems. It had its origins in a number of cross-currents. Among these were the growing importance of utilitarian thought as the practical reasoning of business was to gain dominance in other social institutions.[20] Another influence was the eugenics movements in America and Europe. Scientists and social reformers believed that society could be improved through more rigorous occupational selection and breeding procedures.[21] Also, there was a more active state policy towards schooling as it became a factor in the development of production.[22] A scientific pedagogy was to remove the difficulties of assimilation and socialization of the new immigrants, and to facilitate economic development. Science was to provide ways of understanding teaching, of judging behavior, and establishing purpose.

As empiricism became part of teacher education at the turn of the century, it had an illiberal effect in at least two ways. The first was the overambitious claims and overconfidence in results related to 'the idea that a specifically desired trait could be directly achieved by a conditioning process, and the sublime confidence in quantification . . .'.[23] An oversimplified assumption was produced that major problems of teacher education could be solved by analyzing the traits considered essential to a good teacher or the specific functions involved in a teacher's job. Analyzing the teacher's work was considered analogous to industrial task analysis. The second was the tendency among researchers to assume that professional education was essentially technical. Surveys in the 1920s were conducted in which teachers were asked what courses they thought 'most helpful in teaching', and when teachers responded with courses related to technical aspects of teaching, the researchers argued that 'scientific evidence proved that curriculum should be made more consistently technical'.[24] Both elements of this empiricism are still with research in teacher education.[25]

The new sciences of education also served to obscure the gender and class issues that underlie teacher work and teacher education. Mattingly and Apple (in this volume) argue that professional autonomy was a chimera by the middle 1800s. Women increasingly moved into teaching as the fluidity of the job, the low salary and the redefinition of schooling as a domestic sphere made it a possible occupation. The career, however, had its own contradictions. Women increasingly embraced bureaucratic work conditions as a way to distance themselves from conflicting social pressures of work vs. domestic responsibilities. These conditions incorporated conceptions of labor that were borrowed from industrial organizations which further reduced teacher autonomy. At the same time, new male career tracks in administration and the university as a mechanism of control over school further redefined the work of teachers.

Instrumental Reason as a Discourse of Power:
A Case of Reform

The belief in a scientific pedagogy gave legitimacy to a style of discourse which we can call 'instrumental reason'. It is assumed that there is a common framework of experience for all people and fixed goals. The problem of training is to identify the most appropriate means to attain given ends. Strategies to improve teacher education are to increase effectiveness and coordination of programs. A science of teacher education is to identify the specific effects that influence movement towards the defined goal.[26] The language of instrumental reason is important because it projects an image of rational thought and institutional efficiency. The style of thought creates a view of human activity that is highly specialized, fragmented and impersonal.

The development of instrumental reason is a response to the new role of the professional as a disinterested consultant to the policymaker. The concern is not with ultimate values or institutional purpose but with social administration. The strategy, however, is not without value or interest.

An instrumental quality of reasoning is so pervasive a part of our professional language that we take its values and assumptions for granted. It is an element of our practices of teaching, learning and models of school change. A recent proposal for reform in teacher education is a case in point. 'The Phoenix Agenda', a proposal for reform in teacher education, is offered as a way to symbolize a 'rebirth from a desperate situation'.[27] Yet, the recommendations focus on administrative problems as the task of reform. The discussion is about a balance between technical and liberal education, proposing that teachers 'be connected to the emerging knowledge base', that teacher education is to prepare teacher candidates:

(a) for the lifelong study of the world, the self, and academic knowledge; (b) for the lifelong study of teaching; (c) to participate in school renewal efforts, including the creation and implementation of innovation; and (d) to approach the generic problems of the workplace (the school and classroom).[28]

As we look past the configuration of words, we find linguistic confusion. What does innovation, school renewal or lifelong study mean? Which brand of political economy do we use to talk about 'participation'? Whose notion of society and individuality are we to accept to understand the meaning of 'study' or 'workplace'?

The words are part of the public language rather than a language of enquiry. The words function as slogans to arouse interest, possibly incite enthusiasm or achieve a unity of feeling and spirit about the tasks to be confronted in teaching. The slogans establish a mood or a form with which people can feel that certain contemporary values about schooling are being captured by professional education. The mood is made more powerful by the style of talk which makes the reform proposal seem rational, detached and scientific in posture. A teacher education program is talked about as having a structure, research components, clinical practioners, sequential organization 'knowledge production', and models of teaching.

The style of discourse contains elements of power, giving attention to certain problems while filtering out other elements of practice and value. As we look more closely at what seems to offer intellectual rigor, we find the reform flattens reality and obscures the struggles which fashion and shape our world. The history of schooling involves debates about the organization of pedagogy and teacher-education. Career education, the discipline-centered curriculum, or back-to-basics are not 'merely' pedagogical practices but contain assumptions and social relations that emerge from and are related to structures of power found in the larger society. These debates, some of which are considered below, are often related to more profound issues of social transformations. The organization of school knowledge becomes a central site in which general ideological struggles are given focus.

The instrumental quality also hides fundamental values in the models of teaching. Humanist psychology, subject-matter, behaviorism and social theories are treated as logically distinct and equivalent perspectives for modeling teaching. Yet each of these models can contain positivist assumptions about knowledge and instrumental reason. For example, humanist psychology is an offshoot of industrial psychology, developed to motivate workers and parallel in purpose to behavioral thought.[29] The differences in the models are differences in the facades.

The discourse of the reform proposal is not neutral. The proposal is a part of a discourse that exerts control over what knowledge is relevant and the structures by which issues are defined and solutions sought. By assuming a consensus about goals and values in reform, one reduces reason to the administration of social affairs. The categories and dichotomies of education deny the human debate, social values and power relations that underlie the institutional arrangements of schooling. The reform discourse creates a 'mobilization of bias' that excludes certain relations and problems as they exist beyond the possibilities of the existing order to things.[30]

In fundamental ways, the discourse of instrumental reason becomes part of the myth structure of school.[31] The myths appear as themes of the ongoing relations of schooling, of teaching skills, truth as certainty and taxonomical, and a belief in the evolutionary growth of mind and body. The rituals of science make the myths appear universal and ahistorical, dramatizing ideas and cultural cohesion while, at the same moment, normalizing inequal social relations.

Codes of Professionalization

Three commonplaces in the discourse of teacher education can enable us to pursue the implications of instrumental reason. These commonplaces are (a) the tension between university and schools; (b) the reduction of teaching methods to psychological qualities; and (c) the belief in the value of practice in teacher education. I use the notion of 'commonplace' to make problematic the structure of analysis offered by Schwab[32] and used in much curricular research and planning. The three offered in this paper are not those provided by Schwab. The problem of enquiry is not to 'take' the commonplace but to make the categories subject to analysis *and* critique. The commonplaces are part of a discourse that contains principles of authority, legitimacy and social order.[33] While there is debate about these commonplaces, that debate occurs within a general discourse which reifies existing patterns of power in teacher education.

A Tension Between University and Schools (Theory and Practice)

An essential element of the folklore of teacher education is a tension between university and schools. The tension is usually attributed to differences in purpose between the practices of the academy and those of the practitioner. The dichotomy is given legitimacy through (a) histories of teacher education which focus upon the distinction between the liberal and technical; (b) research on changes in student beliefs as they move through student teaching and into their first year of teaching; and (c) reforms which take up that tension, proposing to improve interactions and communications between the two organizational spheres.[34]

The university-school dichotomy can be scrutinized by enquiring into the historical tensions and social paradoxes of knowledge. The American university, after the American Civil War, underwent a transformation in which programs related to the practical concerns of business, engineering, and commerce were established.[35] Many educators sought to interrelate liberal and technical elements in professional education.[36] In part, the relation of liberal and technical was made possible by the philosophical canopies of positivism. Although developed in Europe, positivism received support in America as a way of explaining the nature and character of science. The focus upon logic and organization of knowledge as the principles of science was important to the early educational psychologists and sociologists. They sought useful knowledge about schools, military selection and industrial relations and the administration of the State.

The notion of liberal in teacher education responds to the utilitarian discourse through the organization of knowledge. One can regard university courses in the liberal arts as providing a strong framing and classification of knowledge.[37] There is thought to be a clear demarcation of one field from another; and content is organized in a discrete, sequential, and hierarchical manner. The style of argument, the manner in which findings are presented, and the form of student evaluations are similar to the detached style associated with the behavioral and experimental sciences. Learning is mastery of the accepted definitions of knowledge in a field. The content of instruction becomes 'objects' to be transmitted. The mysteries, ambiguities, drama and dynamics of change that characterize a discipline are lost. The change in meaning of a textbook reflects this style of reasoning. Once thought of as a book in which a prominent scholar discussed the cutting edge of a field, textbook now means the codifications of knowledge. It contains the consensually accepted and therefore non-problematic knowledge of a field.

Bernstein's conceptual perspective has been modified for the study of professional education by Franke-Wikberg.[38] Principles of power and control are found in the content and organization of university education in psychology, economics, medicine, and engineering. The educational content of a field is organized in a way related to the occupation's position in society. This relation of power and knowledge is illustrated in Schneider's (this volume) study of schools of education. The work situation and values within the schools of education are related to those fields which are considered high status; psychology, a field which has mostly male faculty, has traditionally adopted the norms of utilitarian science and the hegenomy of a science as administration.

The tension between theory and practice, a theme related to the university-school dichotomy, is a false one as well. Practice depends upon theory as it involves implicit visions of social reality. Theory, on the other hand, is a second-order abstraction, built upon our commonsense understanding and cultural sensitivities.[39] Theory and practice are in a dialectical relation in power structures.

The separation of theory and practice, or university and school, does more to mystify current relations than to illuminate the tension. While legitimate distinctions can be made between a critical theory and practice, such as illuminating the contradictions and incompleteness in our choices, actions and utterances,[40] most contemporary research ignores the role of intellectuals in integrating institutional structures. As will be illustrated below, educational researchers provide symbols that give coherence and credibility to existing power structures. The legitimacy is provided, at one layer, by accepting the official language of institutional life as the categories of enquiry. At a different layer of discourse, contemporary theories of schooling contain background assumptions and presuppositions about individualism and political economy.[41] These assumptions create a false impression of consensus and stability that reinforces the position and status of certain groups in society and handicaps others.[42]

The Reduction of Teaching Methods to Psychological Qualities

The belief in consensus shapes the organization of teacher methods. This can be explored by examining the style of reasoning about teacher methods found in textbooks. Knowledge and process are defined as logical and psychological abstractions. The concepts of science and social studies are talked about as if they have clear and fixed definitions.[43] Concepts are definitions. The problem of teaching is to have children learn the correct definitions. The thinking process is defined as consisting of abstract states or qualities un-related to any social or historical context. Enquiry and discovery are considered to be the logical processes of observing, communicating, hypothesizing, experimenting, classifying, generating and predicting. Instructional processes are attributes such as focus on task, the effective use of questioning, or the use of appropriate physical resources in classroom teaching.

The irony of the psychology of teaching is that methods are denuded of social, human and historical elements.[44] The notion of process contains no movement, intentionality or expressiveness. The view of concepts and generalizations is static and unyielding. The interplay of social, communal, political and creative elements that give direction to art, science, and literature is transformed into a set of one-dimensional and disinterested projects. Yet the sciences contain ambiguity, playfulness and conflict as essential elements.[45]

Psychological reductionism introduces the problem of reifica-tion.[46] What are essentially human and social activities seem to exist outside our subjectivity, will and history. Content, process and methods of teaching are seen as external to human agency. While learning was originally a metaphor for thinking about what occurs in schooling, the metaphor is mistaken for reality.[47] Children *are* learners, schools *are* places to learn. The reification of knowledge is related to instrumental reason itself, as the dynamics of life are reduced to problems of administration and control.

The Belief in Practices

A third commonplace of teacher education is the belief in practice. The reasoning is functional: schools are the places where student-teachers will spend their professional lives. The object of prepara-tion should be to enable students to be successful. The best way to learn is by doing.[48] Discussion often involves the ways in which university method courses and practicum experiences can be inte-grated and how the expertise of practising teachers can be used to enhance the university's professional sequence. As in other commonplaces of teacher education, the reasoning about practice seems sensible and, in some instances, laudable. Yet, when the discourse is examined, there is a strong relation between the practices of university and school. This unity is in the instrumental rationality and a reification of knowledge.

The theories and practices of the university serve to legitimate the categories of sorting, classifying and evaluation found in schooling. This occurs through the ways in which methods and 'foundation' courses give theoretical potencies to the dichotomies of knowledge (for example, reading, writing, science, etc.) found in classroom practices. The language of learning, instruction, management and evaluation has a dual function: it makes the ongoing relations of schools seem normal while at the same time desensitizes the new teacher to the social and political contradictions of the curriculum in a differentiated society. From this perspective, the university education is functional. The practice sanctifies and makes psychologically compelling the institutional arrangements in which the student-teacher will work.

This functional relation can be seen in student-teaching. An instrumental rationality guides the practices of students.[49] While the rhetoric of university programs emphasize student-teacher autonomy and reflectiveness about teaching, reflection tends to be tied to utilitarian concerns: how do I get the materials for this lesson? How can I keep order? Given a lesson to teach, how can I organize the time effectively? Most often, the reifications of content found in the method courses guide school instruction. Students teach lessons on inferring or analyzing, with the assumption that each of the discrete skills is related cumulatively to some notion of enquiry. Attention is given to the minute tasks and not the relation of the tasks to the purpose. The language of learning and mastery justifies the ongoing practices. The discourse leaves little room to scrutinize the assumptions, implications or consequences of the work of teaching.

The three commonplaces of teacher education — the dichotomy of theory (university instruction) and practice (schooling), the psychologization of teaching, and the belief in practice — involve fundamental contradictions. While moral in principle and political in origin, the categories are made to seem technical. The conceptions of professionalism ignore the manner in which teaching is a gendered labor process. As ideology, it masks how teachers' labor responds to issues of gender, the reproductions of inequalities in wealth and power and the contradictions in the work of teachers. Densmore and Ginsburg (in this volume), for example, argue that teaching can be considered as a process of proletarianization related to capitalism, with its increased division of labor, separation of tasks, increased volume of work, and ideological and technical control. Ideologies of professionalism make the control mechanism appear reasonable and credible in the everyday patterns of teaching.

Professional Education and the Social Predicament of Schooling

A second dynamic of discourse in teacher education relates to the social predicament of schooling. Schooling is seen by many as part of an American millennial vision. It is the institution on which people place their hope for a good tomorrow. Schools are to promote the improvement of our material conditions by labor training and selection. After World War II, schools became a focal point for responding to issues of social equality, moral development, and political legitimacy. Schools are believed to provide an enlightened citizenry and the route to a meritocratic society.

The predicament of schooling is in its responding to these social pressures. Schools are expected to intervene and correct social inequities, while at the same time contributing to the ongoing dynamics of reproduction and production in society. The history of American schooling shows both its conservative and liberating effects.

One way in which these multiple pressures are addressed is through the use of ritual and ceremony in teacher education. The work of Meyer and Rowan[50] on organizational theory and Edelman[51] on political symbols focuses upon the formal rituals and ceremonies of organizations in creating institutional stability and consensus. The language of national security, the labor negotiations whose outcome 'protects' the public interest, or a school's announcement of a new reading specialist to improve student achievement are rituals which make policies that benefit specific groups seem as policies for the benefit of the 'public' as a whole. The hiring of a reading specialist who works with children once a week, moving from school to school, has little chance of remedying a situation that is often related to complex issues of social class, cultural background, and institutional biases of schooling. The presence of reading specialists enables the school to project an image of responding to all children in an objective manner. The division of labor conveys the workings of an institution that is efficient and rational.[52] The recent reform proposals, such as the *Nation-at-Risk*, can also be viewed as part of a public ceremony that structures policy in ways that legitimate elite agendas.[53] The Report serves to shape public perceptions about economic priorities in science and technology that serve particular segments in the American society.

The manipulation of symbols is an important element in the creation of rituals. The language and theories of teacher education orient us towards our everyday world. We think of theory as describing our daily conversations, as an expression of our hopes, and a conveyance of the facts that surround us; and practice as a means of accomplishment and learning. But educational theories can serve other social functions. The incantations of words become rituals of political affiliation that create a social identity. The language of research and pedagogy can also serve to legitimate interests which seek to establish cultural hegemony. The scientific pedagogy of the early 1920s, for example, was a part of a more general shift in discourse in which social welfare, control of labor in industry and reorganization of government were seen as solvable by a general logic of administration and discovery of empirical principles of efficiency.

The function of theories as rituals of affiliation and legitimation is rarely examined in professional education. Yet these enactments can influence professionals and the publics of schooling. Theories relate individuals to the social order of the occupation. Images are created that can deflect attention from the actual priorities, values and patterns of social control. As argued earlier, our commonplaces of schooling are articulated through social and psychological research. The theories dull critical reasoning by creating illusions of a world as already made, devoid of social interests and unyielding to human interventions. It is to this consequence of educational science that attention is now focused.

Theories as Rituals of Political Affiliation

Theories of pedagogy in teacher education can be viewed as prescriptions for action and rituals of social manipulation. As prescriptions, theories provide ways of considering the complexities and possibilities of classroom activities. Theories also provide symbols of affiliation as people struggle with the changing constellations of their worlds. Theories of totalitarianism of the 1950s justified how enemies of the United States during World War II could become allies and some of the previous allies be transformed into threats to democracy and liberty. The theory of structural-functionalism of Talcott Parsons, as well, can be viewed as a conservative response to the upheavals of the American depression and European turmoil during the 1930s. The theory stressed the 'natural' equilibrium of social systems and the need for evolutionary rather than revolutionary change.

The relationship between pedagogy, research and cultural and social issues has been discussed in histories of pedagogy. Durkheim's important work on the formation of the French secondary school illustrates the manner in which issues of nation-state, religion and social groupings impinge upon the formation of pedagogy.[54] The counter-reformation, for example, produced a new school organization so that the Jesuits could monitor the attitudes and character development of their students. The individualization of instruction was to control the consciousness of the pupils as well as to give organization to curriculum. David Hamilton[55] documents how the interplay of the Scottish Enlightenment, industrial transformations, and material crises become interrelated in the development of the classroom as a 'system' of instruction. The ideologies of pedagogy reflected the transformation of notions of political economy into conceptions of individuality and cognition. The resulting pedagogies were to provide education for the newly formed working classes.[56]

From this perspective, theories are social inventions. The inventions respond not so much to the accumulations of facts, as some argue, but to conflicts, strains, and tensions of the world in which the social theorist lives. Much classical sociology reflects the felt need of the theorist to give definition and direction to the mass upheavals in values and relationships produced by industrialization. Tonnies' *Gemeinschaft und Gesellschaft,* Durkheim's theme of anomie and Marx's view of comodification and surplus value are attempts, albeit different ones, to understand the social, cultural and economic transformations occurring in the nineteenth century.[57]

Pedagogy and research respond as well to their context of social reproduction and transformation. Pedagogy involves various interests seeking to define how change and stability should be articulated in schooling. As discussed earlier, the movement to establish a scientific pedagogy was related to a variety of factors, including the development of utilitarian thought, the rise of a testing and measurement movement and a more active state intervention policy. Pragmatism, an invention of American social thought in the early 1900s, responded to social and industrial change, but in a way different from that of persons interested in social engineering. The pragmatism of Mead and Dewey can be seen as a way of resolving the tension between the pastoral image of nineteenth-century America and industrialization through the creation of symbolic canopies in philosophy, social science, and a pedagogy of progressivism. Problem-solving was to resolve the tensions created by the juxtaposition of industrialization and the rural ideas of American life.

Pragmaticism is also a form of discourse related to the aspirations of social mobility found in the new professional strata of American society.[58] George Herbert Mead's social psychology and John Dewey's pedagogy offered methods that legitimated the interests of the new professionals. The tentativeness of knowledge and ambiguities of roles were important to the professional's claim to authority and to the socialization patterns in schooling that could account for social production.[59]

The reintroduction of progressive ideologies and ethnographic research into the American teacher educational community during the late 1960s was a response to the pressures of an increased division of labor, social conflict and a fragmentation in social institutions.[60] Popular literature of the period continually brought forth an image of the 'organizational man' who had no sense of 'self' except that provided by the company with which one worked. Increased complexity of government and the devaluing of face-to-face interaction through increased bureaucracy created a belief that there was a loss of personal and political efficacy. Ethnographies and open education reassert certain fundamental liberal beliefs about American culture and political life that many middle class Americans felt challenged. Themes of negotiated realities, pluralism and individual efficacy are emphasized, providing a belief that democratic values can be revitalized in an industrial and corporate society.

The conflict between scientific management and progressive ideologies in teacher education provides a way to consider deeper tensions of schooling and society. They point to the different ideologies and social interests that enter into schooling and the preparation of teachers. The two strands of pedagogy and research compel us to realize that schooling involves a site in which larger issues of social interest and power are contested. The conflicting methods of pedagogy and research illustrate how intellectuals affiliate with interests in society and seek to establish moral direction and will. Each pedagogy expresses particular hopes and beliefs held by segments of society. The incorporation of the various pedagogical methods in the conduct of schooling serves to reconcile conflict, obtain social cohesion, and make cultural aspirations possible. Yet the conflict between scientific management, progressive or developmental views of pedagogy exists and is made plausible within a large horizon of social conflict; the mainstream discourse of traditional and progressive education also structured out other pedagogies developed by the socialist movement of the turn of the century,[61] and the social reconstructionist curriculum of the 1930s.[62] One is left with a discourse about pedagogy which contains complementary ideologies: designed for the middle class or by the professional strata of the middle class for the working classes.

Ritual and Cultural Legitimacy

The social predicament of schooling provides a context in which to consider theory as mediating dominant cultural interests. The mediating quality becomes apparent as we return to the category of 'learning' when considering problems of teaching. Earlier, implications of the category of learning were discussed by considering the problem of reification in teacher education. The category, though, also functions politically. It captures certain general values of a pluralistic society. 'Learning' focuses attention upon one purpose of schooling, enabling us to believe that schooling should be equally responsive to particular individuals regardless of social circumstance. The notion of learning identifies the problem of schooling as answered by various strategies of individualization. The imagery is one of institutions responding to human differences. Each child is to achieve according to his or her unique capabilities. The psychology of individual differences is joined with organizational management approaches through the technologies of instructional systems, objective based curriculum and record-keeping procedures.

The psychological abstraction decontextualizes and refocuses social experience in teacher education. The theories of learning and teaching in professional programs are based upon an experience of particular groups in society such as found in the conceptions of time, space, and embodiment of the bourgeois.[63] Schools take the cultural capital (language, knowledge, taste and aesthetic awareness) of the middle class as natural and employ it as if all children have had equal access to it.[64] This occurs in the subject matter of science and literature, but is also an element of the conceptions of aesthetics, taste and talent that are accepted in schooling.[65] The theories of professional education refocus these experiences through abstractions that make knowledge seem universal to all in society and then recontextualize the experiences as part of formal education.[66]

The decontextualization and recontextualization of social interests involves issues of gender as well as those of class. Theories of pedagogy and approaches to research reflect the feminization of teaching.[67] The child-centered pedagogies in elementary teacher education, for example, take the bourgeoisie ideal family life and make that ideal into a universal form.[68] Ideas about identity and moral development in psychology adopt male life as the norm.[69] The theories of Freud, Erickson, Piaget and Kohlberg introduced a bias into teaching that devalues women's experiences and moral development. The cultural differences in development between men and women become a liability for women.

The process of decontextualization and recontextualization gives potency to the reifications of institutional conditions. The relation of individual to society seems devoid of history, human agency, and political interest. While the social organization of schooling does reflect class, gender, ethnic, and geographic differences, the rituals of schooling project an objective image in which we think of school standards as part of a unified, nationwide moral system.

Rituals of differentiation and homogeneity

The movements towards increased testing of teachers and students, and competency-based teacher education in current teacher reforms can be considered as they relate to the social predicament of schooling. Rather than a means to improve quality or standards in teaching and teacher education, standardization serves as a ritual of differentiation and homogeneity. Testing creates patterns of behavior that enable teachers and students to assume that there are universal meanings in experience.

The belief about a consensus on meaning also involves rituals of differentiation. Testing provides ceremonies that define groups and award status. Since the rewards of schooling are limited because of economic and cultural structures, the patterns of competency education enable schools to seem to arrange fair competition for the scarce prizes. Tests, grades, compensatory education, and education for the gifted suggest that diversity is based upon merit, such as that conveyed by the labels, individualization, or scores on achievement tests.

Yet recent critical literary traditions enable us to focus upon our categories, conventions, and strategies of interpretation as a problem of ideology. The structure of communication in a society 'is as often as not a monologue by the powerful to the powerless, or if it is indeed a "dialogue" then the partners — men and women, for example — hardly occupy equal positions'.[70] As the structures of interpretation carried in competencies become a part of teacher education, they legitimate the images, meanings, and ideologies of the school's patterns of communication.

The discourse of instruction enables us to ignore the political agendas which underlie the rituals of differentiation. In part, the problem is related to the professionalization of knowledge. The language of differentiation, such as 'learning style' and 'teaching style', is a quasi-scientific language. It assumes a common school rather than different types of schooling which respond to the social and cultural differentiations in society. Different conceptions of work, patterns of communication, and professional ideologies however, do shape classroom conduct. The differences in schooling can be called technical, constructive, and illusory.[71] The different social conditions in the schools are not differences of the schools themselves. The differences are related to geographical, racial, religious, and class differences of the communities in which the schools are located. The technical language of professionalization in contrast project an organization of experience in which people are objectively and systematically sorted, thus obscuring the particular assumptions and implications of institutional structures.

The pervasiveness of legitimating rituals and discourse extends into current efforts in teacher education reform. There is an acceptance of administrative activity as a definition of change. Proposals for improving teacher education range from increasing admission and graduation requirements[72] to making academic experience more intensive[73] and providing teachers more of a voice in professional programs.[74] The reasoning defines procedures and administrative action as change. The nexus between value and interest in conducting practice and research is defocalized as the reforms assume a consensus on value and purpose. Ignored are the social debates and tensions that underlie institutional life.

Contradictions: Professionalization and Social Interests

Professionalization and the social predicament of schooling have been regarded as analytically distinct yet in practice they have complementary and contradictory elements. This relation can be explored in efforts to impose instrumental reasoning upon specific social relations in teacher education.

While administrative systems are intended to maintain stability in social relations, the application of instrumental reasoning can be seen as working against the interest of certain strata of the middle class. Such is the case of some professionals who seek to use the schools for purposes of social production. Sieber, for example, focused upon the conflict produced in schools in an inner-city neighborhood which has undergone some gentrification.[75] The disagreement was not 'merely' a disagreement about means to the same ends but about the socialization patterns, values, and purposes of schooling itself. Newer, professional parents in the community wanted to establish a more progressive pedagogy that emphasized a tentativeness to knowledge, intra- and inter-personal relations, personal relations and personal authority. These qualities were seen as important to the position of the professional. The professional parents fought against teachers who wanted to maintain the existing, more instrumental approach to teaching. The result of the conflict was two schools within one. A sequence of instruction was organized around the concerns of the professional parents. The existing pattern of instruction was maintained for children who came from the poor and minority families of the neighborhood.

We can also identify contradictions as different interests seek to make teacher education more rational. For the state, competencies are related to the credentialing role. Competency-based teacher education involves identification, and the systematic monitoring of teachers' acquisition of effective teaching practices. In some instances, the state has used competency-based teacher education for social accounting in its efforts to improve the relation of schooling to labor markets. For the profession, competency involves establishing control over institutional life.

Tensions between the development of an autonomous career and state control emerge in the discourse of a competency-based teacher education program.[76] Foundation and methods courses focused upon an image of a professional who has status, upon the location of the teacher in relation to social stratification of wealth and power, and upon the superiority of teachers over the working class. At the same time, the discourse posited the authority of the state in determining work conditions. The contradictory messages were muted by making issues seem impersonal and suggesting a technical role for teachers.

Creating its own paradox, the instrumental quality of teacher education can decrease teachers' control over their labor. Management ideologies, such as competency-based teacher education, draw upon a logic of work that underlies much industrial production in the United States.[77] The concern is to develop labor-saving devices and management control in production. As incorporated into curriculum, this concern leads to systematic and rational organization of what is to be learned and taught, the materials to be used, specific teacher actions and student responses, and diagnostic and achievement tests that define appropriate behaviors and skills.

The separation of planning from execution creates a situation in which teachers are reskilled in the ideologies and practices of management.[78] Where prepackaged materials have been made a part of school culture, patterns of interaction between teacher and student have been reduced to procedural concerns and the discussion of curriculum content has been minimized.[79] The dissociation and fragmentation of knowledge and work produce a definition of professionalism that limits the creative and purposeful quality of teaching. The rationalization also increases the social control over teachers, as overt conflict about purposes and goals is eliminated.

In reflecting upon these changes in labor, Braverman[80] argued that management perspectives destroy the self-organized and self-motivated community. Work is dehumanized. The individual no longer has a conception of how the separate elements of work relate to the total product of labor. The fragmentation and rationalization undermines an individual's capacity to provide for him or herself. A form of dependency is introduced in which people are taught to rely upon professionals to categorize and minister social affairs.

Professionalization, the Social Predicament of Schooling and Teacher Education: Some Concluding Thoughts

The dynamics of professionalization and the social predicament of schooling provide a way of considering the discourse of teacher education. The behaviors, patterns of language, and actions used in teacher education contain codes of culture that have implications for fundamental issues of power in American society. The tensions inherent in teacher education are tensions inherent in schooling and American society. Specialization and fragmentation of knowledge and work exist both as phenomena of teacher professionalization and as a dynamic of the larger context of labor in general. To understand teacher professionalization, the analysis must consider the work, culture, and power in schooling and the interplay between the specific institutional setting and general issues of social structure. In America, where social amelioration is important to intellectual work, relating the behavior and language to the social horizons of professional practice is necessary in order to prevent a vacuous notion of behavior and reform.

Much of the discussion has focused upon the decontextualization of experience provided by an instrumental rationality. Instrumental reason is a dominant way of thinking about, organizing, and evaluating teacher education in America. It asserts professional control of the definitions and meanings of individual life by obscuring the tensions and strains of competing social interests. The instrumental quality of discourse is not without tensions and contradictions. It can deskill teachers, reduce their autonomy, and dull their sensitivity to the issues involved in professionalization.

We must also consider power as relative in discourse. No theory or ideology is brought into practice without modification. There are interests that reject administrative ideologies and vie for control over pedagogical definitions. Scientific curricula and progressive pedagogies have been in continual interaction since the early 1900s within professional programs and the general dynamics of our social and cultural conditions. These traditions of pedagogy also exist in relation to other, radical, traditions which give focus to teacher education.[81] Teachers and student-teachers as well resist the coercive practices of institutional life in a way that allows human agency to find some expression.[82]

One might ask at this point whether considering teacher education in the context of larger issues of social formation may, in fact, debilitate individual and institutional efforts towards reform. If practice seems historically determined and causes lie outside our immediate bounds, how are we to act with integrity? The answer, I believe, lies in the following. Our methods of study should provide a way of considering the constraints of our professional situations. Our world is continually offered as one of ready-made customs, traditions, and order in the things of daily life. Yet the natural order is not natural or inevitable, but constructed historically, socially, and politically. Enquiry should enable us to consider the possibilities of our social conditions by exposing the fragility, to some extent, of the causality in which we live. To make our social situation problematic — not a foreordained order of things but the outcome of the collective actions of men and women — is to make these situations potentially alterable and amenable to human agency.[83]

To engage in strategic actions requires that we understand what constitutes professional education, which elements are bound in larger horizons, and which can be immediately challenged. The 'technical' and practical are intricately bound to the norms, values, and ideologies of our situation. Without a method of understanding how behaviors are structured within culture and social interests, we are left with no theory and, in what is the greatest irony of American utilitarian thought, useless practice but potent ritual.

Notes

1. A version of this chapter appeared in *Teaching and Teacher Education*, 1, 2, (1985) pp. 91–107. I wish to thank Pergamon Press, Ltd. for permission to reprint this essay.
2. This secondary socialization may not be as strong as in professions which have stronger communal elements and economic power, such as medicine or law. The same principles of institutional life and its relation to consciousness, however, are appropriate. This is where much research on teacher socialization needs to be reconsidered. See discussion of socialization in section on codes of culture and power relations.
3. POPKEWITZ, T., TABACHNICK, B. and WEHLAGE, G. (1982) *The Myth Of Educational Reform, A Study Of School Responses To A Program Of Change*, Madison, WI, University of Wisconsin Press.
4. MCCUTCHEON, G. (1981) 'Elementary school teachers' planning for social studies and other subjects', *Theory And Research in Social Education*, 9, 1, pp. 45–65.
5. While studies of student-teacher beliefs are typically different in focus, one could interpret the various responses in the same way. For discussions of teacher beliefs, see FEIMAN-NEMSER, S. and BUCHMANN, M. (1983) *Pitfalls of Experience in Teacher Preparation*, Occasional paper No. 65, East Lansing, MI, Institute for Research on Teaching, Michigan State University. For the relation of beliefs to institutional mechanism of control, see ZEICHNER, K. and TABACHNICK, B. (forthcoming) 'Social strategies and institutional controls in the socialization of teachers', *Journal of Teacher Education*.
6. LIGHTFOOT, S. (1983) *The Good High School: Portraits of Character and Culture*, New York, Basic Books; POPKEWITZ, *et al.*, (1982) *op cit.*
7. FOUCAULT, M., *The Order of Things: An Archaeology of the Human Sciences*, New York, Vintage Books, called this investigation 'an archeology of knowledge'.
8. OSBORNE, H. (1968) *Aesthetics, Art Theory: An Historical Introduction*, New York, E.P. Dutton.
9. FOUCAULT, M. *op cit.* For a discussion of education see, for example, CHERRYHOLMES, C. (1983) 'Knowledge, power and discourse: Social

studies education', *Journal of Education*, 165, 4, pp. 341–58.

10. LORTIE, D. (1975) *School Teacher: A Sociological Study*, Chicago, University of Chicago Press.

11. BLEDSTEIN, B. (1976) *The Culture Of Professionalism: The Middle Class And The Development Of Higher Education In America*, New York, Norton; HASKELL, T., *The Emergence of Professional Social Science: The American Social Science Association And The Nineteenth-Century Crisis Of Authority*, Urbana, IL, University of Illinois Press.

12. MARX, L. (1964) *The Machine In The Garden: Technology and the Pastoral Image In America*, New York, Oxford University Press.

13. BLEDSTEIN, B. (1976) *op cit.*

14. STARR, P. (1982) *The Social Transformation Of American Medicine: The Rise Of A Sovereign Profession And The Making Of A Vast Industry*, New York, Basic Books.

15. HASKELL, T. (1977) *op cit*; CHURCH, R. (1974) 'Economists as experts: The rise of an academic profession in America 1870–1917' in STONE, L. (Ed.) *The University In Society, Europe, Scotland And The U.S. From The 16th Century To The 20th Century*, Princeton, N.J., Princeton University Press, pp. 571–610.

16. SILVA, E. and SLAUGHTER, S. (1984) *Serving Power: The Making of the Academic Social Science Expert*, Westport, Conn, Greenwood Press.

17. MATTINGLY, P. (1975) *The Classless Profession*, New York, New York University.

18. EDELMAN, M. (1977) *Political Language: Words That Succeed And Policies That Fail*, New York, Academic Press.

19. POWELL, A. (1980) *The Uncertain Profession*, Cambridge, MA, Harvard University Press.

20. BLEDSTEIN, B. (1976) *op cit.*

21. GOULD, S. (1981) *The Mismeasure Of Man*, New York, Norton & Company; KLIEBARD, H. (1986) *Struggle For The American Curriculum*, London, Routledge and Kegan Paul; SELDON, S. (1986) *The Capturing Of Science: The Influence Of Eugenics On Education*, London, Routledge and Kegan Paul.

22. LUNDGREN, U. (1983) *Between Hope And Happening: Text And Context In Curriculum*, Geelong, Australia, Deakin University.

23. BORROWMAN, M. (1965) *The Liberal and Technical in Teacher Education: An Historical Survey of American Thought*, New York, Teachers College Press, p. 196.

24. *Ibid.*

25. POPKEWITZ, T., TABACHNICK, B. and ZEICHNER, K. (1979) 'Dulling the senses: Research in teacher education', *Journal Of Teacher Education*, 30, 5, pp. 52–60.

26. PECK, R. and TUCKER, J. (1973) 'Research on teacher education', in TRAVERS, R. (Ed.), *The Second Handbook on Research on Teaching*,

Chicago, Rand McNally; ROBINSON, V. and SWANTON, C. (1980) 'The generalization of behavioral teacher training', *Review Of Education Research*, 50, 3, pp. 486–98.

27. JOYCE, B. and CLIFT, R. (1984) 'The Phoenix Agenda: Essential reform in teacher education', *Educational Researcher*, 13, 4, pp. 5–18.

28. *Ibid*, p. 8.

29. NOBLE, D. (1977) *America By Design: Science, Technology and the Rise of Corporate Capitalism*, New York, Knopf.

30. BACHRACH, P. and BARATZ, M. (1963) 'Decisions and Nondecisions: "An Analytical Framework"', *American Political Science Review*, 57, pp. 632–42.

31. See CORNBLETH in this volume.

32. SCHWAB, J. (1978) 'The practical: Arts of the eclectic', in WESTBURY, I. and WILKOF, N. (Eds), *Science, Curriculum and Liberal Education: Selected Essays*, Chicago, University of Chicago Press.

33. See GINSBURG, DENSMORE, and WHITTY in this volume.

34. WISCONSIN STATE SUPERINTENDENT'S TASK FORCE, (1984) *Teaching And Teacher Education, Final Report*, Madison, WI, Department of Public Instruction, January; BOYER, E. (1983) *High School: A Report on Secondary Education in America*, New York, Harper and Row; JOYCE, B. and CLIFT, R. (1984) *op cit*.

35. CURTI, M. and NASH, R. (1965) *Philanthropy in the Shaping Of American Higher Education*, New Brunswick, N.J., Rutgers University Press.

36. BORROWMAN, M. (1965) *op cit*.

37. BERNSTEIN, B. (1977) *Class, Codes and Control: Towards a Theory of Educational Transmissions* (2nd ed.) (Vol. 3), London, Routledge and Kegan Paul.

38. FRANKE-WIKBERG, S. (1982) 'From ideas on quality of education to ideas as quality of education', paper presented at a conference on the socialization effects of higher education, Klagenfurt, Federal Republic of Germany.

39. POPKEWITZ, T. (1984a) *Paradigm and Ideology in Educational Research: The Social Functions Of The Intellectual*, Philadelphia and London, Falmer Press.

40. CHERRYHOLMES, C. (1983) *op cit*.

41. See, for example, the chapter by ST MAURICE on the notion of clinical supervision in this volume.

42. POPKEWITZ, T. (1984a) *op cit*.

43. POPKEWITZ, T. (1984b) 'Methods of teacher education and cultural codes', in TAMIR, P., BEN-PERTZ, M. and HOCKSTEIN, A. (Eds) *Preservice And Inservice Education of Science Teachers*, Rehovot, Israel, Balaban Publishers.

44. KALLOS, D. and LUNDGREN, U. (1975) 'Educational psychology: Its scope and limits', *British Journal of Educational Psychology*, 45, pp.

111–21.

45. LEWONTIN, R. (1983) 'Darwin's revolution', *The New York Review Of Books*, 30, 10, pp. 34–7.
46. BERGER, P. and PULLBERG, S. (1965) 'Reification and the sociological critique of consciousness', *History and Theory*, 4, 2, pp. 196–211.
47. HEUBNER, D. (1966) 'Curricular language and classroom meanings', in MACDONALD, J. and LEEPER, R. (Eds), *Language and Meaning*, Washington, DC, Association for Supervision and Curriculum Development, pp. 8–26.
48. For critical examinations of the assumptions and patterns of practices, see ZEICHNER, K. (1980), 'Myths and realities: Field-based experiences in preservice education', *Journal of Teacher Education*, 3, pp. 45–55; and BUCHMANN, M. and SCHWILLE, J. (1983) 'Education: The overcoming of experience', *American Journal of Education*, 92, pp. 30–51.
49. GOODMAN, J. (1983) 'An analysis of the seminar's role in the education of student-teachers: A case study', *Journal of Teacher Education*, 34, pp. 34–49; ADLER, S. (1984) 'A field study of selected student teacher perspectives toward social students', *Theory and Research in Social Education*, 12, 1, pp. 13–30.
50. MEYER, J. and ROWAN, B. (1977) 'Institutional organizations: Formal structures as myth and ceremony', *American Journal of Sociology*, 83, 2, pp. 340–63.
51. EDELMAN, M. (1977) *Political Language: Words That Succeed and Policies that Fail*, New York, Academic Press.
52. MEYER, J.W. and ROWAN, B. (1977) *op cit*.
53. WESTBURY, I. (1984) 'A nation at risk', *Journal of Curriculum Studies*, 16, 4, pp. 431–45.
54. DURKHEIM, E. (1938/77) *The Evolution of Educational Thought. Lectures on the Formation and Development of Secondary Education in France*, COLLINS, P. (trans), London, Routledge and Kegan Paul.
55. HAMILTON, D. (1980) 'Adam Smith and the moral economy of the classroom system', *Journal of Curriculum Studies*, 12, pp. 181–98.
56. FRANKLIN, B. (1986) *Building the American Community: The School Curriculum And The Search For Social Control*, Philadelphia and London, Falmer Press.
57. NISBET, R. (1976) *Sociology as an Art Form*, New York, Oxford University Press.
58. MILLS, C. (1967) in HOROWITZ, I. (Ed.) *Sociology And Pragmaticism: The Higher Learning In America*, New York, Oxford University Press.
59. GOULDNER, A. (1979) *The Future of the Intellectual and the Rise of the New Class*, New York, Seabury Press; BERNSTEIN, B. (1977) *op cit*.
60. POPKEWITZ, T. (1984a) *op cit*.
61. TEITLEBAUM, K. (1985) 'Schooling for good rebels', unpublished dissertation, University of Wisconsin.

62. KLIEBARD, H. and WEGNER, G. (1987) in POPKEWITZ, T. (Ed.) *The Formation of the School-Subject Matter: The Struggle for Creating an American Institution*, Philadelphia and London, Falmer Press.

63. LOWE, D. (1983) *The History of Bourgeois Perception*, Chicago, University of Chicago.

64. BOURDIEU, P. and PASSERON, J. (1977) *Reproduction in Education, Society and Culture*, London, Sage.

65. FREEDMAN, K. (1987) 'A mandate for public expressions: Art in American schools', in POPKEWITZ, T. (Ed.) *The Formation of the School Subject Matter: The Struggle for Creating an American Institution*, Philadelphia and London, Falmer Press.

66. While there are certain transcending qualities to science, mathematics, and the arts, those endeavors contain inner contradictions that undermine their claims to universality. It is the dual quality of possibility and pathology that is a necessary part of our cultural consciousness (GOULDNER, 1979).

67. POWELL, A. (1980) *op cit.*; PURVIS, J. (1981) 'Women and teaching in the nineteenth century', in DALE, R., ESLAND, G., FERGUSSON, R. and MACDONALD, M. (Eds) *Education And The State: Politics, Patriarchy And Practice*, Vol. 2, London, Falmer Press.

68. MACDONALD, M. (1981) 'Schooling and the reproduction of class and gender relations', in DALE, R., ESLAND, G., FERGUSSON, R. and MACDONALD, M. (Eds) *op cit.*

69. GILLIGAN, C. (1982) *In A Different Voice, Psychological Theory And Women's Development*, Cambridge, MA, Harvard University Press.

70. EAGLETON, T. (1983) *Literary Theory: An Introduction*, Minneapolis, University of Minnesota Press, p. 73.

71. POPKEWITZ, T. (1982) *et al. op cit.*

72. NATIONAL COMMISSION ON EXCELLENCE IN EDUCATION, (1983) *A Nation at Risk: The Imperative for Educational Reform*, Washington, D.C., U.S. Government Printing Office; ADLER, M. (1982) *The Paideia Proposal: An Educational Manifesto*, New York, N.Y., Macmillan Publishing Co.

73. TASK FORCE ON EDUCATION FOR ECONOMIC GROWTH, (1983) *Action for Excellence*, Denver, Co, Education Commission of the States.

74. JOYCE, B. and CLIFT, R. (1984) *op cit.*

75. SIEBER, R. (1982) 'The politics of middle-class success in an inner-city public school', *Journal of Education*, 164, 1, pp. 30–47.

76. GINSBURG, M. 'Reproduction, contradiction and conceptions of professionalism: The case of pre-service teachers', in this volume.

77. BRAVERMAN, H. (1974) *Labor and Monopoly Capital: The Degradation Of Work In The Twentieth Century*, New York, Monthly Review Press.

78. APPLE, M. (1982) *Education And Power*, Boston, MA, Routledge and Kegan Paul.

79. POPKEWITZ, T. (1982) *et al., op cit*, chapters 2 and 4.
80. BRAVERMAN, H. (1972) *op cit.*
81. GIROUX, H. (1981) *Ideology, Culture and the Process Of Schooling*, Lewes, Falmer Press.
82. GRANT, C. and SLEETER, C. (1984) 'Who determines teacher work: The teacher, the organization, or both?', paper presented at the American Educational Research Association Annual Meeting, New Orleans, April.
83. How a program in teacher education might be theoretically organized towards a critical stance, see GIROUX, BEYER and ZEICHNER, POPKEWITZ in this volume.

Part I
Teacher Education, Class
Relations And Gender:
Historical Perspectives

2   Workplace Autonomy and the Reforming of Teacher Education

Paul H. Mattingly

Current efforts to reform teacher education raise issues of teacher autonomy. These analyses ignore the historical conditions in which teachers' work has been formed. Since the early 1800s, the work conditions of teachers have been continually defined by the pressures of urban growth, class structures, gender relations, ideologies of professionalism and models of social science. These dynamics of the relation of society to schooling served to narrow the autonomy of teaching. The chapter concludes that an adequate perspective to contemporary issues of teaching and teacher education requires that we have historical understanding of occupational development that includes attention to issues of social policy and power.

For most of the twentieth century scholars and policy-makers have energetically discussed teacher education through studies of its presumed failures rather than through its achievements. The recent series of commission reports on American education have beaten out a drum roll of negative judgments about the intelligence and instructional competence of the teaching profession. In the eyes of the US Office of Education, the Carnegie Foundation for the Advancement of Teaching and other prestigious organizations, teachers have become the agents of a proliferating educational mediocrity in America's public schools.[1] Policy-makers' criticisms of teachers and teacher education have not prevented social science analysts from discovering education as an extraordinarily fruitful field of investigation over the past two decades. Economists and historians have approached public school systems as one of the earliest prototypes of modern bureaucratization. Political scientists

have treated schools as ideological arenas, litmus tests for the rise
and fall of theoretical -isms in American life. Psychologists have
continued their extensive studies of the school as the locus of cultural
transfer, crucial to understanding the process of socialization to a
capitalist culture. Sociologists have insisted that the school has been
a strategic key to the actual achievement of social opportunity,
so historically attractive to every racial and ethnic group. Demo-
graphers have assumed the school to be the strategic occupational
bridge for women between the home and non-domestic careers.[2] In
spite of this extraordinary upsurge of both negativism and curiosity
about education, teachers, one of education's central elements, are
treated as peripheral factors in significant social change. For all of
the renewed interest in education as a field of criticism and analysis,
the teacher has not emerged as a factor of significant change or
power. How can the process of education remain so essential to
policy-makers and social scientists and yet, in their analyses, omit
the strategic contribution of the teachers? How can the teacher be
held responsible for the faults of this basic social system, if so little
serious consideration has actually been paid to their relative contributions or autonomy over time?

In this form the question merely underscores some larger
problems that concern the assumptions of policy-makers and social
scientists. It also draws attention to the literature of teachers and
teacher education and its assumptions. The primary characteristic of
this literature is its isolation from discussions of social policy or
social power: it portrays teacher education merely as a matter for
rational debate or else as a response to acknowledged social needs.
Invariably such discussions immediately reduce themselves to
limited questions of curricular design, organizational planning, and
to administrative and psychological accommodations to primary and
secondary levels of schooling. In the proliferating professional
journals this literature further narrows itself into discussions of
personal styles of application and technique. It seldom enlarges itself
into an argument with the conscious, theoretical connections of
teachers to the economic or political realities of American life.
Teacher education becomes thereby merely a subject separated from
the complex historical process by which the very meaning of
'teacher education' changes from generation to generation.

This stereotyped thinking, it is imperative to understand, represents a larger historical process, one that is central to the treatment
of teachers' work in America: over time American teachers have
never experienced control of their workplace sufficient to fulfill

their educational responsibilities. Policy-makers and social scientists now think of teacher education as a static, secondary subject rather than as an ongoing social problem; they never treat their professional training as a precarious process with its own special significance. This mode of analysis has become one of the essential ingredients undermining the teachers' control of their workplace. Such a habit of thought, of course, has developed within its own historical context and within a definable social structure. Historically, these habitual judgments about American teachers and techer education have been distinguished by their repetitiveness rather than by their truth. Precisely when did this habit of thought arise and what sorts of workplace control have teachers exerted earlier?

Before the nineteenth century only a few individuals made their living as full-time teachers in America.[3] In spite of New England's seventeenth and eighteenth century laws that supported town schools, American schools followed the British tradition: schools served those whose families could afford to excuse the young from remunerative work long enough to attend schools, or else they were custodial arrangements for the dependent classes. The schools were generally controlled by the town fathers, a group that often included the town's minister. The minister in turn often kept a school as a part of his ministerial responsibility as well as a strategy to enhance his salary. Whether in the minister's home, a rented space, or in a formal classroom, the school was thought to serve the 'public' and operated seasonally as befitted an agricultural economy. Any preparation for the role of teacher was subsumed into the minister's training. Serious schoolteaching was for the most part but a special moment of denominational didactics, and the minister/teacher experienced a workplace control in direct proportion to his authority in his congregation. Dame schools, though for younger children and primarily custodial, fit into the domestic routines of women and drew their authority derivatively from the family whose essential purpose was educational only in the broadest sense. There were of course other teachers and artisans, often itinerants who hired space to set up temporary schools teaching dance, music, writing and other skills. Before 1800 schooling in America seldom had a distinctive workplace because the work of instruction coincided with the ordinary work of community life.[4]

Even before 1800 many voices expressed the need for a different brand of instruction and different instructors. Benjamin Franklin's famous proposal for an 'academy' argued for a special place where general instruction in basic reading and mathematical skills would be given and where the teacher would take special pains to instill moral discipline.[5] The language of such appeals would not change for several generations. However, the social and cultural contexts in which these appeals were advanced changed markedly over time. In the Middle Colonies and during the revolutionary period appeals like Franklin's did not occur in a social vacuum. Acute as Franklin was, it took no political genius to observe Philadelphia was rapidly becoming profoundly different from its agricultural hinterland. In the city certain forms of technical and cultural training paid rich dividends. Moreover, mercantile success, especially in the Middle Colonies, had flooded cities, like Philadelphia, with an enviable immigrant labor force and with unenviable language and ethnic barriers.[6] By the time of the revolution virtually all the principal colonial cities had experienced the stress of demographic heterogenity.[7] The moral and cultural training of any school in Philadelphia would necessarily be different from schooling in more homogeneous places: the 'moral' instruction of any school could neither be taken for granted nor could it be in any obvious sense denominational proselytizing or political indoctrination. Thus, the social heterogeneity of revolutionary America created a particularly severe problem of moral indoctrination, one that could no longer be left to the relatively informal earlier traditions of public instruction.

The dynamics of the revolution called for a division between the role of the minister and the role of the teacher. However, the economic depressions and readjustments of American Independence dramatically slowed these educational developments as they did other economic and cultural plans of the time. It was left to the first generation of post-revolutionary Americans, those born in the 1780s and 1790s, to create both new institutions and a new ideology for the production of American teachers. The earliest efforts to produce enlightened and morally upright teachers came from ministers themselves. In part, they hoped to stabilize their hard-won gains as representatives of particular denominations. At the same time denominational competition had made these ministers realize the costs of open, public warfare among individuals committed to Christian charity and public peace. Particularly as the threat of Roman Catholicism rose with the arrival of Irish immigrants in the 1830s, these ministers, especially of the New England and middle states, reaffirmed their common Protestantism and the traditional efficacy of evangelical revival techniques. Ministers and many of their female congregants founded a large array of voluntary reform organizations to respond to the social dislocations of America's great economic development in the first half of the nineteenth century.[8]

One of the most enduring of these reforms was the effort in behalf of the American schoolteacher. It was a reform that drew upon a deep-seated evangelical tradition that led to the proliferation of teachers' institutes, which were essentially educational revivals that for a generation carried the work of public awakening and basic teacher preparation to the countryside and to the cities.[9] Nineteenth-century evangelism was, by contrast to eighteenth-century versions, a tempered brand of 'awakening'. It sought to organize and channel the public emotions it stimulated; it was a planned and consciously social endeavor. Although they publicized their central purpose as 'non-denominational', the teachers' institutes drew creatively upon the devices and revival language of specific religious denominations. Educators often used churches for institute meetings, sought to 'quicken' the spirit of the general public in educational matters, and, when successful, 'awakened the moral character' of young men to the 'missionary calling' of Christian education. The architecture of their model schools always resembled places of worship — mission chapels, village churches, Greek temples. Though voluntary, the teachers' institutes extracted extraordinary exertions from individuals who came to believe that their 'profession' produced moral entities, institutions and communities that were greater than the sum of their parts.[10]

The adaptation of a fundamentally religious structure of thought and behavior to the broader public arena was one of the striking achievements of American antebellum reform movements. In education the new ideology of 'public education systems' sustained and transformed many talents that, while not primarily religious, had the effect of investing teachers with a legitimate fervor and a respected public image that they had never had earlier. Of course, this transformation was not a function of mere quasi-religious associations and techniques; it had powerful economic backing. In Boston, for example, recently arrived merchants and bankers such as Francis Calley Gray and Edmund Dwight, supported with their money and active participation new institutions like the American Institute of Instruction (the first and longest-lived professional association of teachers in the nineteenth century) and the first public normal schools.[11] Particularly those business entrepreneurs whose operations went beyond local and state boundaries recognized quickly the economic and cultural importance of a new type of American teacher. This combination of evangelical and financial support was the prerequisite for attracting first-rate professional talents, such as the Whig lawyers Horace Mann and Henry Barnard, into the work of educational reform. In this context of mixed public and private interests the American teacher worked with considerable autonomy and effect until the Civil War.

Antebellum reform movements had enhanced the teacher's workplace and indeed the teacher's lot, particularly in salaries, and by mid-century effectively separated the role of minister and teacher. But the improvement did not bring to the teacher automatic autonomy into his or her workplace. 'Non-denominational' and non-partisan sponsorship made education a powerful new social force, but for that reason many new groups attempted to influence the nature of its educational work, especially in the area of moral instruction. The teacher became saddled with an insupportable burden: the set of public expectations that proper instruction would not only shape the character of each individual but would provide, in Horace Mann's resonant phrase, 'the balance wheel of the social machinery'.[12] Greater claims for the public utility of basic skills substantially inflated the social benefits expected from teaching reading, writing and arithmetic. These heightened anticipations came at the very moment that the teacher necessarily forfeited any powerful, interventionist pedagogy that smacked of factional bias or physical coercion. The teacher, educational thinkers said, should necessarily guarantee more and better educational results by doing less, that is, by indirect suggestion and example. Both teachers and the public agreed that schools should 'inculcate' moral character. No one, however, hazarded any articulate, public definition of precisely what 'inculcation' meant. The omission recognized the multiple pressures on any public school and acknowledged how 'non-denominational' schooling continued to be implicitly political in spite of its public claims. The very conception of the new teacher created a special dependence for the first generation of professional teachers, leaving each instructor responsive more than responsible to a school's board or trustees. In spite of the increased access of American citizens to such schools, the public school systems were neither controlled by the teachers nor by the representatives of the school's democratic constituencies.[13]

The rapid population expansion via immigration, the extraordinary attraction of unsettled Western land, and the great fluctuation of prices and wages maintained conflicting pressures on every public school during the antebellum period. How great an investment of resources were towns to provide for transient populations? What common principles of democracy could be imparted to such heterogeneous ethnic, political and religious populations? What sort of training and what sort of person could respond and satisfy the perceived needs of these different groups? This historical context posed extraordinary difficulties for any school and kept them highly vulnerable to external forces before the Civil War.

This vulnerability, however, helps explain two major developments. First, teachers rapidly embraced bureaucratic systems to distance themselves from conflicting public pressures. These bureaucracies, of course, further narrowed their autonomy. Secondly, the precariousness of the work made teaching accessible to a range of talents. The dislocation of the times ensured that individuals of high and low moral character could gain access to teaching. It was exceedingly rare for any individual to remain for an entire career in schoolteaching, much less in a single school. Male and female teachers alike incorporated in lifetime careers an extraordinary job fluidity, passing in and out of schoolteaching, linking a dozen different work experiences.[14]

These two factors set the stage for the dramatic increase of schoolkeeping women up to and after the Civil War. The feminization of teaching also testified as much as any single factor to the paternalistic place of education in the hierarchy of Victorian values.[15] Mid-century Americans financed their rising school systems with cheap female labor and refined their conception of the public grammar school as a branch of women's special 'domestic sphere'. The rising proportion of females in the educational workforce also tended to undermine the persistent effort to make school teaching a 'profession' in quasi-religious nineteenth century terms. The reliance on women was predicated on the notion that teaching was a more natural gift and was not something for which one could actually train. This distinction solidified into a principle of 'woman's special sphere'. The values of 'domesticity' separated a female spiritual authority from woman's worldly dependent role without acknowledging any implicit contradiction. This set of cultural conceptions rather than any curricular or institutional distinctions made the meaning of 'profession' a debatable problem for teachers into the present century. In practice, the conceptual confusions were far less problematic. Given the choice between selecting and training teachers who could shape moral character, or teachers who would tolerate reduced pay, Americans began to manifest this preference in the earliest choices of newly-formed state boards of education of the 1840s and afterwards. It was a pattern of choice that the Civil War would confirm not only by siphoning off the remaining male teachers into the armies but by creating a qualitatively new economic and cultural context that systematically stratified work by gender and social class.[16] The ensuing problems weakened the primacy of the older moral aspirations, which, in the face of any political competition, seemed to be progressively abstract.

If the American teacher had not achieved workplace autonomy but only an expanding bureaucratic hierarchy by the outbreak of the Civil War, the teaching corps nevertheless had achieved a new legitimacy in the public eye. The distinctive sphere of the teacher was largely a by-product of the specialarena that Victorian culture accorded women and their work. These arenas became increasingly subordinated in every organized workplace. Even by the Civil War both male and female interests of both students and teachers alike were differently served by the insistence that elementary instruction merely extended the domestic sphere and required maternal instincts.[17] Not only untrained teachers but even Massachusetts's prototype, the professionally trained normal school teacher, had become predominantly female. Of the 4400 graduates of the Massachusetts normal schools before 1860 the percentage of females had been 78 per cent and rising fast.[18] The war simply confirmed a pattern already in motion, one in which gender separated the majority of women workers from male administrators and male instructors of academic subjects.

The feminization of teaching did not immediately threaten the modest gains in professional standing that the antebellum teachers had won, for teaching was still a calling rather than a profession (a matter of moral commitment rather than a product of institutional practice), and the shaping of character still resisted close analysis. It was difficult to discern whether prospective teachers had the 'aptness to teach' that nineteenth-century schoolmen sought or whether they could communicate it to others. These ambiguities may have contributed strategic confusion to the teacher's work and training, but it also opened quasi-ministerial work to many young men with evangelical commitments but without the resources to pursue them. The generation of individuals most aggressively recruited to serve as principals and senior staff of the new normal schools and public high schools were men who came from less privileged social classes than those who recruited them. Both generations however agreed that teaching public schools was 'missionary' work. This emphasis kept personal commitments more important than formal training and obscured for many the full implications of gender and class divisions.

Initially, male teachers and second generation superintendents (roughly those born in the 1820s and 1830s) voiced few objections against women who came, like themselves, in disproportionate numbers from the hill farms of New York and New England. Gradually, however, their ambitions for the work of teaching with its quasi-ministerial associations caused problems. Young men who once aspired to the ministry also coveted college study, an opportunity they began to seek through normal schools with more traditional academic orientations, like the State (Massachusetts) Normal School at Bridgewater (f. 1840). However, such ambitions were thwarted by the tradition that made colleges generally male preserves (in spite of a few postwar women's colleges and some coeducational universities[19]). If the admission of females raised questions about the collegiate quality of normal school instruction, the admission of females still in their high school years challenged the professionalism of normal schools even further. Particularly in regions where women had little preparation in classics and the increasingly important subjects of language, mathematics and science, colleges and normal schools both faced the choice of creating special preparatory classes or devising preventative standards of selection. In the older, more influential normal schools the policies of admission, staffing, duration of study, economic support and later job placement became distinctively stratified in the postbellum period and made the curriculum of teacher education a symptom of gender and class divisions.

In spite of these stratifications the most important and distinctive feature of postbellum schoolmen's careers was their remarkable homogenization due to common farming and working-class social origins. The ascendancy of men like Alfred Boyden (1827–1915) in Massachusetts, David Camp (1820–1916) in Connecticut, Richard Edwards (1822–1902) in Illinois, Edward Sheldon (1823–1897) in New York, Francis Parker (1837–1902) in Chicago, William H. Payne (1836–1897) in Tennessee, among others, to normal school principalships and superintendencies of city and state school systems, represented a second generation of professionally oriented (i.e., male) teachers who had careers with similarities of experience that could not and did not occur either a generation earlier or later.[20] These men began their work with commitments to lifetime careers in moral work akin to the ministry. Conceptually they were in accord with the traditions of evangelism and domesticity that Horace Mann's generation had used to make teaching attractive to ambitious young men less privileged than themselves. Before they were done, the second generation exemplars of public schooling had transformed the conception of their role from a calling to a profession. Teachers achieved this shift because of a three-stage sequence of events: a new social class solidarity within the teacher corps, an outbreak of public conflicts between privileged and public schooling, and a temporary acquiescence of women in their subordinate occupational status.

The solidarity of postwar schoolmen was a product of more than their relatively unprivileged social origins; schoolmen began to use their administrative authority to preserve the prerogatives of power, which coincided neatly with the gender divisions sanctioned by the tradition of domesticity. Few men served for long in the elementary school ranks before moving into some administrative responsibility, although the Civil War so reduced the numbers of males that in many high schools women did assume principalship roles and in some smaller districts even superintendencies. Generally however a standard of academic credentialing for administrative posts necessarily put men in these positions. This academic standard also accorded normal schoolmen and collegiate leaders a disproportionate authority in debates over public school. The Civil War had thus solidified a pyramidal old boy network in the decision-making roles of teachers' councils and associations like the American Institute of Instruction and the upstart National Teachers Association (f. 1857), which would become the National Education Association. Their policies seldom discussed the intellectual contribution of women to public education and gradually shifted their attention to the structure and mechanical functions of the workplace. Whenever possible, this cohort of male teachers put available resources, not into the revival-like and adaptable teachers' institutes, but into permanent normal school campuses. Through the spawning of normal schools, private as well as public, the second generation of educational leaders began to compete successfully with the colleges for both the new war-made fortunes as well as state subsidies.[21]

One central aspect of this aggressive postwar competition for resources was the cultivation of an explicitly class conscious argument against private colleges and academies. There had been class competitions before the Civil War but rarely did the evangelical conception of instruction permit open, public clashes.[22] The post-war expansion of the school system and the cultivation of high schools in every major town and city created the economic and institutional base for aggrandizing public schoolmen throughout the Northern, Midwestern and for a time even the Southern states. Accommodating a range of subjects and ages, private academies for some time before the 1870s experienced a substantial downturn. In New York City, for example, private schools taught 62 per cent of the school population in 1829, whereas by 1850 the percentage had dropped to 18 per cent.[23] As public schools extended into less populated regions private schools became less and less the 'public' schools they had once been. Many academies simply became the public secondary school of their region, while others converted themselves into endowed schools for the rich. Post-war public schoolmen sought to attract this more affluent social class by driving private schools out of the competition altogether, though they never acknowledged themselves how selective their own admissions policies had been or continued to be.[24] The upshot was a partial success: some older academies sought endowments and converted themselves in boarding schools that tightened any existing 'feeder' arrangements with prestigious private colleges and universities.[25] Since the public high schools did not cater to the influx of immigrants and urban poor, the private systems of schooling developed by Roman Catholic orders appeared less threatening than they had earlier. By the 1880s the public schoolmen had monopolized the conception of 'public' education and had begun a long-term effort to monopolize the school-going population as well.[26]

There were several historically distinct features to the post-war conditions of schoolwork. The attacks by schoolmen upon private schools and endowed academies as 'undemocratic' tightened the solidarity among rank-and-file public school teachers, male and female. In addition, there is substantial testimony to the enthusiasm women experienced upon entering teaching as an alternative to domestic labor. These three factors — a clear external enemy, a social class esprit, and a sense of new choice about life-planning — combined for the post-war generation of teachers to keep the reduced salary of female teachers from becoming an occupational or a gender issue. Indeed there is mounting evidence that in spite of the unequal pay for equal work women took great pride in contributing sufficiently to family incomes. Often their work made the difference in keeping their families in the middle class.[27] Going into teaching was not, however, a 'liberation' of women, simply because they worked outside the home. There were powerful cultural dynamics that explain why female teachers acquiesced in a paternalistic and stratified system during the second half of the nineteenth century.

Like all gender distinctions, the nineteenth century stratification of men and women teachers gave the greatest workplace autonomy to men. In teaching, men served at a greater and greater distance from the actual work of public instruction. It essentially formalized a division, not only of salary, but of knowledge. The normal schools, even those with practice schools, promoted a theoretical knowledge that had less and less to do with its practical application, especially in urban public school systems. Gender divisions introduced and legitimized a separation between academic discipline and pedagogical methodology that would ultimately have a destructive impact upon teachers of every gender.[28] The female portion of schoolteaching became locked into the lower grades and into progressively narrow, mechanical practices; the male portion purported to make educational administration a comprehensive science whose theoretical underpinnings needed little defense. The result was a workplace divided against itself. And, of course, the gender division introduced curriculum as the arena for articulating and working through problems that went far beyond curriculum alone. In essence, where the first generation had aligned teacher education, if not the public school itself, with moral discipline, its immediate successors aligned teacher education with career tracks. Like virtually all other strategic occupations of the period, teachers' work became intricately inserted into the structures of industrial capitalism.

By the 1880s these institutional paths to advanced salary and preferred teaching positions reflected the broader rationalizations of industrial capitalism in America and exacerbated the gender and class divisions of the post Civil War era. The institutional competition between public school systems and private schooling broadened to every aspect of education. In the debates over curriculum, course arrangements, individual credentialing, and school supervision, teachers, like other occupations of the period, experienced a crisis of professionalism. The debate quickly became ritualized between the 'liberal' and 'technical' factions, which pitted enlightened and well-educated (generally male) individuals against mechanized practices that substituted efficiency for judgment and insight. The distinctions, needless to say, came from one side of the debate and ignored the largely contextual factors that conditioned whatever autonomy most practising (female) teachers had. Particularly in the cities where working-class women teachers, representing local ethnic cultures, constituted an important element in neighborhood solidarity, the elaborate 'educationist' distinction seemed irrelevant and threatening by turns. When salary and labor conditions became heated issues, many female teachers gravitated quickly from debate to alliance with functioning labor organizations.[29] Their actions represented to many mayors and city councilmen, not to mention an older business leadership, *prima facie* evidence of low behavior unbefitting a teacher of children.[30] Such divisions between teachers and city officials documented the breakdown of an older conception of social harmony and the rise of social class and gender stratifications within the occupation of teaching as a whole.

By the turn of the century university presidents, particularly those in institutions whose future was not a fully established certainty, allied themselves against teachers' unions and their labor allies. William Rainey Harper, the first President of the Rockefeller-financed University of Chicago, could openly denigrate the cultural backgrounds and professional competence of unionized women.[31] In one sense, the division stemmed from long-standing conditions; in another sense, it represented a new institutional competition between freshly minted private universities and the older state-supported normal schools for dominance of the public educational systems.[32] These universities began to create graduate levels of professional schools that would produce the leadership of educational and corporate organizations of modern America. They made their bid for this market in the face of a vigorous normal school expansion, primarily composed of women. In the last two decades of the nineteenth century, enrollments in state- and city-supported normal schools increased fourfold, to an estimated 43,000 pupils; in the same period private normal schools increased ten-fold, to 24,000 pupils. 'In 1880', the US Commissioner of Education reported, 'there were 240 normal students in each million of inhabitants; in 1897 there were 936 in each million'.[34] In Chicago, New York and elsewhere, men like Harper sought allies in other university presidents and superintendents to make the bachelor's degree the basis for entry into the teaching profession.[34] At the very least urban development and their attendant conflicts had outstripped every earlier conception of evangelical harmony or non-partisan behavior. It was no accident that some schoolmen advanced the notion of teaching as 'classless', when teachers as a group had become more stratified than they had been at any other time in the century.[35]

At the turn of the century Progressive reformers like William

Rainey Harper of the University of Chicago and Nicholas Murray Butler of Columbia University successfully engineered limitations on teachers' ability to organize and participate in determining the conditions of their own labor. State and city regulations denied teachers minimal controls over the basic conditions of instruction (preassigned teaching materials and textbooks), reasonable job security (maternal leaves, retirement plans, etc), equitable advancement in career (gender discrimination), and peer judgment in cases of professional disagreement (anti-unionization). All these restrictions have become permanent parts of public school teaching in America. Moreover, in the past and the present, social science and policy experts have drawn upon an ideology generated by themselves to accuse teachers of rigidity because of teachers' opposition to 'reforms', like the centralization movement at the turn of the century, that undermined their working conditions. Over time, the rhetoric of Progressive notions about 'change' — with its emphasis on the 'organic', the 'natural', the 'social', and the 'participatory' — has remained, decade after decade, consistently both highly abstract and immediately personal. It has become a habit of thought that consciously evades an examination of its own ideological assumptions. From John Dewey's pragmatism to defenses of the back to basics movement or to the current commission reports, the heirs of Progressivism share a studied resistance to an examination of the full social and political implications of their values.

During the Progressive period America redefined the meaning of professionalism, one which was incompatible with the nineteenth century traditions of non-denominational moral indoctrination and normal school disciplines. The twentieth-century educational professionals reflected less on the transmission of specific values or the cultivation of native talent; they focused more on their own future career ambitions within their respective bureaucracies. Too late the normal school leadership realized how they had abetted this shift through their own adoption of collegiate ambitions. Too late they realized the competitive power of colleges and universities, which sought to build their ties to corporate resources on a student body and curriculum that regularly excluded women. The normal school that made effective compromises with earlier evangelical traditions (usually with multi-track curriculums and other discriminating devices) would ultimately become teachers' colleges or schools of education within the orbits of universities and state systems of instruction. The surviving collegiate ideal within normal schools became far more exclusive than it had been for several previous generations, ensuring with its special academic standards a further distancing from the intellectual needs of America's teachers.[36]

The actual nature of Progressive 'reform' has been subjected to vigorous debate over the past two decades. Few deny that Progressive reform has left Americans with a powerful conceptual inheritance.[37] Not the least of this heritage was the change introduced into the composition of educational leadership. Graduates of the more affluent women's colleges entered graduate programs in education and eventually administrative roles in large urban and state networks. Such surface reforms belied the way these collegiate women were used to defend bureaucracies against the charge of gender bias and to convert protesting female teachers into middle-class compliance with school boards. The school boards themselves reorganized into smaller membership units to avoid sharing power with working-class political appointees. In the larger cities and towns especially they transformed broad-based ward representatives into elected officials who could command funds and associations sufficient for city-wide election campaigns. These more 'democratic' procedures generally selected more affluent individuals on the board, persons who could afford the time and leisure required to oversee a centralized system.[38] Such patterns of preferment have continued well into the late 1960s and 1970s, when a new generation of middle-class women broke into a still wider range of professional and occupational alternatives beyond the schools entirely.

The persistent abstractions of 'pragmatic' discourse about education have obscured how ideologically resonant the professional discussions of teacher preparation and curriculum have always been. There has been no easy cyclical rhythm to the successive teachers' crises in our history. Invariably, however, the attention to crises involving teachers is fundamentally serious and should alert Americans to a range of gender and class issues that have the potential of spilling into genuine public debate. It is an extraordinary commentary on the unthinking persistence of our traditional approaches toward teachers to witness the response to a recent national poll, documenting scandalously low teachers' salaries, a wholesale rebellion against educational working conditions and the immanent risk of losing over a quarter of America's two million teachers within the next five years.[39] Yet, the force of these findings has not been sufficient to breach the long-standing indifference to the teacher's seminal place in our cultural life. In some ways this indifference has historically concealed the ingenuities teachers have brought to the promise of the American school. In other ways the easy willingness of policy analysts and public critics to blame the teachers for institutional failings simply repeats one of the more prominent ideological rituals of modern life in America. It also underscores one of the deeper dilemmas of modern democratic institutions: how can the process of American education be defended as democratic when teachers, one of democracy's central agents of cultural transfer, operate with so little genuine autonomy. In a process of socialization so selective and preferentially structured, the subordination of the teacher unfortunately clarifies much about the school as the 'balance wheel of the social machinery'.

The dilemma leaves us with several important political and historical questions: were teachers to have sufficient autonomy for their democratic and educational responsibilities, how would the education offered differ and whose resources and values would be necessarily transformed?

Acknowledgments

I wish to express profuse thanks to Marcia Carlisle, James McLachlan, Thomas Popkewitz and Daniel J. Walkowitz for their incisive, professional critiques of an earlier draft of this chapter.

Notes

1. BOYER, E. (1983) *High School: A Report on Secondary Education in America*, New York, Harper and Row; and The National Commission on Excellence in Education's report (1983) *A Nation at Risk: The Imperative for Educational Reform*, Washington, D.C., US Government Printing Office. These studies update precedents studies like COFFMAN, L. (1911) *The Social Composition of the Teaching Population*, New York, Bureau of Publications, Teachers College, Columbia University; and the U.S. Office of Education's (1930–35) *National Survey of the Education of Teachers*, 6 Vols.
2. The complete range of this scholarship has appeared in *The History of Education Quarterly, Teachers College Record, Harvard Educational Review* among other scholarly journals. There are several convenient anthologies of this social science literature. See, for example, KARABEL, J. and HALSEY, A.H. (Eds) (1977) *Power and Ideology in Education*, New York, Oxford University Press.
3. SMITH, W. (1966) 'The teacher in puritan culture', *Harvard Educa-*

tional Review, 36, Fall, pp. 394–411; SEYBOLT, R. (1935a) *The Public Schools of Colonial Boston, 1635–1775*, Cambridge, MA, Harvard University Press and (1935b) *The Private Schools of Colonial Boston*, Cambridge, MA, Harvard University Press; CREMIN, L. (1970) *The Americans: The Colonial Experience*, New York, Harper and Row.

4. BAILYN, B. (1960) *Education in the Forming of American Society*, Chapel Hill, University of North Carolina Press.

5. FRANKLIN, B. 'Proposals relating to the education of youth in Pennsylvania [1749]', in (1961) *The Autobiography and Other Writings*, New York, The New American Library, pp. 209–16.

6. NASH, G. (1979) *The Urban Crucible: Social Change, Political Consciousness and the Origins of the American Revolution*, Cambridge, MA, Harvard University Press.

7. HENRETTA, J. (1973) *The Evolution of American Society, 1700–1815* Lexington, MA, D.C. Heath and Company.

8. MATTINGLY, P.H. (1975) *The Classless Profession: American Schoolmen in the Nineteenth Century*, New York, New York University Press; ELSBREE, W. (1939) *The American Teacher: The Evolution of a Profession in a Democracy*, New York, American Book Co.; BORROWMAN, M. (Ed.) (1965) *Teacher Education in America*, New York, Teachers College Press.

9. SINGLETON, G. (1976) 'Protestant voluntary organizations and the shaping of Victorian America', in WALKER HOWE, D. (Ed.) *Victorian America*, Philadelphia, PA, University of Pennsylvania Press; RYAN, M. (1981) *The Cradle of the Middle Class*, Cambridge, MA, Cambridge University Press, chapter 3.

10. MATTINGLY, P.H. (1975) *op cit.*, Chapter 4.

11. Francis Calley Gray (1790–1856) was born into the wealthy Salem (Mass.) family of financier and politician, William Gray. His family connections had opened the way for him to diplomatic service in Russia and to political life via the private secretary's role to John Quincy Adams. He served many cultural reform efforts that included the presidency of the Boston Athaeneum and contributions (money and collections) to a museum of comparative biology at Harvard, his alma mater.

Edmund Dwight (1780–1849) became a powerful cotton manufacturer from Springfield (Mass.) and created an integrated system that eventually became the Chicopee Manufacturing Co. He committed himself as intensely to the development of railroads that connected Massachusetts with the rest of the nation as he did to the creation of the equally effective network of teacher training institutions. He advanced $10,000 for the first normal school on the condition that the state match his offering and quietly increased out of his own pocket the salary of Horace Mann as Secretary of the Massachusetts Board of Education, the organizational prototype of its kind.

Cf also STORY, R. (1980) *The Forging of an Aristocracy: Harvard and the Boston Upper Class, 1800–1870*, Middletown, CT, Wesleyan University Press.

12. MANN, H. (1957) 'Twelfth annual report [1848] to the Board of Education of Massachusetts', in CREMIN, L. (Ed.) *The Republic and the School: Horace Mann on Education*, New York, Teachers College Press, p. 87.

13. KATZ, M.B. (1971) *Class, Bureaucracy and Schools*, New York, NY Praeger Publications; KATZ, M.B., DOUCET, M.J. and STERN, J. (1982) *The Social Organization of Early Industrial Capitalism*, Cambridge, MA, Harvard University Press.

14. MATTINGLY, P.H. (1975) *op cit.*, chapters 2 and 3.

15. DOUGLAS, A. (1977) *The Feminization of American Culture*, New York, Avon Books; COTT, N. (1977) *The Bonds of Womanhood: Woman's Sphere in New England, 1780–1835*, New Haven, CT, Yale University Press; CLINTON, C. (1984) *The Other Civil War: American Women in the Nineteenth Century*, New York, Hill and Wang; PRENTICE, A. (1975) 'The feminization of teaching in British North America and Canada, 1845–1875', *Histoire Sociale/Social History*, 8, May, pp. 5–20.

16. GENOVESE, E. (1984) *The Fruits of Merchant Capital*, New York, Oxford University Press. See also MONTGOMERY, D. (1981) *Beyond Equality: Labor and the Radical Republicans, 1862–1872* 2nd edn, Urbana, IL, University of Illinois Press.

17. SKLAR, K. (1973) *Catherine Beecher: A Study in American Domesticity* New Haven, CT, Yale University Press; WELTER, B. (1966) 'The cult of true womanhood', *American Quarterly*, 18; FIROR SCOTT, A. (1979) 'The ever widening circle: The diffusion of feminist values from Troy Female Seminary, 1822–1872', *History of Education Quarterly*, 19, spring, pp 3–46.

Though widely imitated, the structure and curriculum of Beecher's and Willard's schools were hardly representative of women's schools during the antebellum period. Indeed the geographical variations in schools for men and women prevented any generic prototype until late in the nineteenth century.

18. QUINT, A. (1861) 'The normal schools of Massachusetts', *Congregational Quarterly*, January, p. 18. See also HERBST, J., (1980) 'Nineteenth-century normal schools in the United States: A fresh look', *History of Education*, 9, 3, September, pp. 219–27.

19. FRANKFORT, R. (1977) *Collegiate Women: Domesticity and Career in Turn-Of-The-Century America*, New York, New York University Press; HOROWITZ, H.L. (1985) *Alma Mater*, New York, A. Knope; SOLOMON, B.M. (1985) *In the Company of Educated Women*, New Haven, CT, Yale University Press.

20. MATTINGLY, P.H. (1975) *op cit.*, especially chapter 7; ALLMENDINGER, D. (1979) 'Mount Holyoke students encounter the need for life-

planning, 1837–1850', *History of Education Quarterly*, 19 spring, pp. 27–46.

21. See DILLINGHAM, G. (1970) 'Peabody Normal College in Southern Education, 1875–1909', unpublished PhD dissertation, George Peabody College, for a singularly successful example of such fund-raising efforts. For another example see the manuscript correspondence between Genl Samuel Chapman Armstrong of Hampton [VA.] Normal and Industrial Institute and New York merchant, Robert C. Ogden, in the Robert C. Ogden Papers in the Library of Congress.
    See also ANTLER, J. (1981) 'Female philanthropy and progressivism in Chicago', *History of Education Quarterly*, 21, winter, pp. 461–70.
    It is important to remember that state supported normal schools did not clearly outnumber the private entrepreneurial normal schools until the end of the century. See 'Statistics on Normal Schools', *U.S. Commissioner of Education Report, 1900–1901*, 2, Washington D.C., 1902, pp. 1843–1901.

22. KATZ, M.B. (1967) *The Irony of Early School Reform*, Cambridge, MA, Harvard University Press, especially chapter 1. See also MATTINGLY, P.H. (1975) *op cit.*, chapter 6.

23. KAESTLE, C. (1983) *Pillars of the Republic: Common Schools and American Society, 1780–1860*, New York, Hill and Wang, p. 116.

24. Though the estimates are not definitive, the American public high school did not likely serve more than 10 per cent of the high school age population until sometime between 1900 and World War I.

25. McLACHLAN, J. (1969) *American Boarding Schools*, New York, Charles Scribners Sons, especially Part III.

26. See, for example, the address to the American Institute of Instruction by George Boutwell, 'The Relative Merits of Public High Schools and Endowed Academies', [1857] reprinted in SIZER, T. (Ed.) (1964) *The Age of the Academies*, New York, Teachers College Press. In this same collection one can see the acquiescence of private school leaders into a smaller but more powerful portion of the school-going population. Confer Charles Hammond's address, 'New England Academies and Classical Schools', [1868]. The two viewpoints document the polarities of the social class debate during these years.

27. DANYLEWYCZ, M. and PRENTICE, A. (1984) 'Teachers, gender and bureaucratizing school systems in nineteenth century Montreal and Toronto', *History of Education Quarterly*, 24, spring, pp. 75–100.

28. JOHNSON, W.R. (1975) 'Professions in process: Doctors and teachers in American culture', *History of Education Quarterly*, 15, summer, pp. 185–99.
    These gender divisions were incontestably political and ideological constructs. By contrast to American arrangements it is well to remember that France under the Third Republic looked to male and female teachers as the vanguard of the next generation. The Ferry Laws

of 1882 intentionally introduced regulations that supported the erosion of gender differences in the workplace, like dual appointments of married partners in the same district and maternity leave (1910). Those same laws successfully supported the introduction of secular women -*institutrices*- into the teaching population, partly to displace religious women and partly to appreciate women as a national resource. In 1882 secular women constituted 22 per cent of the teaching corps; in 1910 they reached 57 per cent. If they did not receive absolute parity with men in salary and promotion, the French appreciation of women's singular contribution to schooling went much further than their American counterparts in the same period.

I am particularly indebted to the research of Leslie Moch, presented at the Social Science History Association meeting, Toronto, Canada, 26 October 1984: 'Women teachers — Feminization, the state, professionalization and gender in nineteenth-century France, US, and Canada'. See also KEYLOR, W. (1981) 'Anticlericalism and educational reform in the French Third Republic: A retrospective evaluation', *History of Education Quarterly*, spring, pp. 95–103 and SMITH R.J. (1982) *The Ecole Normale Superieure and the Third Republic*, Albany, NY, SUNY Press. See also MEYERS, P.V. (1985) 'Primary school teachers in nineteenth century France: A study of professionalization thru conflict', *History of Education Quarterly*, 25, spring-summer pp. 21–40.

For comparison with the British experience see Barry Bergen's prize-winning essay, (1982) 'Only a schoolmaster: Gender, class and the effort to professionalize elementary teaching in England, 1870–1910', *History of Education Quarterly*, 22, spring, pp. 1–21.

29. HOGAN, D. (1985) *Class and Reform: School and Society in Chicago, 1880–1930*, Philadelphia, PA, University of Pennsylvania Press, chapter 5. This chapter was co-authored with Marjorie Murphy and is based on her unpublished doctoral dissertation (1981) 'From artisan to semi-professional: White collar unionism among Chicago public school teachers', University of California. See also DOHERTY, R.E. (1979), 'Tempest on the Hudson: The struggle for "equal pay for equal work" in the New York city public schools, 1907–1911', *History of Education Quarterly*, 19, winter, pp. 413–34.

30. WRIGLEY, J. (1982) *Class Politics and Public Schools, 1900–1950*, New Brunswick, NJ., Rutgers University Press. See also LAZERSON, M. (1984) 'Teachers organize: What Margaret Haley lost', *History of Education Quarterly*, 24, summer, pp. 261–70.

31. HOGAN, D. (1985) *op. cit.* p. 196.

32. A. Lodeman of Ypsilanti (Michigan) Normal School, in *The Place and Function of the Normal School* (1887) argued that the universities were attempting to impose a set of castes within the profession. See also, TYACK, D. (1973) *The One Best System*, Cambridge, MA, Harvard

University Press.

33. TORREY HARRIS, W. (1899) 'The future of the normal school', *Educational Review*, January, p. 8. See also MATTINGLY, P.H. (1981) 'Academia and professional school careers, 1840–1900', *Teachers College Record,* 83, winter pp. 219–33.

34. DINER, S. (1980) *A City and its Universities: Public Policy in Chicago, 1892–1919*, Chapel Hill, University of North Carolina Press; URBAN, W. (1976) 'Organized teachers and educational reform during the progressive era: 1890–1920', *History of Education Quarterly*, 16, spring, pp. 53–61.

35. MATTINGLY, P.H. (1975) *op cit.*, especially chapter 7.

36. MATTINGLY, P. (1981) *op cit.*

37. Consult the numerous articles about 'Revisionism' and its opponents in journals like *The History of Education Quarterly*. Witness the powerful conceptual cohesion among scholars of the progressive period in RAVITCH, D. and GOODENOW, R. (Eds) (1981) *Educating an Urban People: The New York City Experience*, New York, Teachers College Press. See also the review of this collection by WALKOWITZ, D. J. (1984) 'Consensus history in hip dress', *History of Education Quarterly*, 24, 2, summer, pp 235–9.

38. COUNTS, G.S. *The Social Composition of School Boards*; VEBLEN, T. (1899) *The Theory of the Leisure Class*, New York, The Macmillan Co.; TYACK, D. (1973) *op cit.*

39. SHANKER, A. (1985) 'Where we stand', *The New York Times*, 15 September, p. E7. Shanker, the President of the American Federation of Teachers, was reporting on the second annual Metropolitan Life Poll of the American Teacher conducted by Louis Harris and Associates.

3   Gendered Teaching, Gendered Labor[1]

Michael W. Apple

Teaching and teacher education, especially at the elementary level, are historically related to the construction of teaching itself as 'women's work'. They are articulated with changes over time in the sexual and social divisions of labor and patriarchal and class relations. By focusing on the United States and England, the chapter demonstrates that as teaching changes from a pre-dominantly male to a predominantly female occupation, the constitution of the job changes as well. It is subject to significantly greater controls over teaching and curriculum at the level of teacher education and in the classroom. It is structured around a different set of class and gender dynamics. The transformation of teachers' work was not accepted passively, however, teachers were active figures in this process, though their actions often had contradictory results.

Introduction

Any attempt at fully understanding teaching and teacher education — especially the current attempts in the United States to nationalize them and bring them under tighter control — must do two things. First, it must be historical. It needs to situate these current tendencies into the considerably longer history of which they are a part. Just as importantly, it should focus its examination around the question of *who* is doing the teaching and what the social relations involved in it are. That is, we can understand the constitution of teaching and teacher education best if we see them as articulated with changes over time in the sexual and social divisions of labor and patriarchal and class relations.

A key element here is seeing teaching and teacher education — particularly at the elementary school level — as being strongly related to the construction of teaching itself as largely 'women's work'. Women's paid work has long been subject to rationalizing logics and to attempts to gain external control over it, and teaching is no different here. In this chapter, I want to enquire into how it came about that teaching became 'women's work' and how the control of teaching has a strong relationship to sexual and class divisions in the larger society. I shall focus historically here on the United States and England, though the arguments presented are not necessarily limited to these countries.

The Structure of Women's Work

As one of the very best historians of women's labor has recently argued, most historical analyses of the rationalization and control of labor have been 'preoccupied with artisans or skilled workers' such as weavers, shoemakers, or machinists or with those people who worked in heavy industry such as miners and steelworkers. Almost by definition this is the history of men's work. Only a relatively few individuals — though luckily this number is growing rapidly — 'have considered the implications of rationalization for women workers, despite the steadily growing number of women in the workforce'.[2]

Let me begin by going into even more detail about what the shape of women's paid work currently looks like. Such work is constructed around not one, but two kinds of divisions. First, women's work is related to a *vertical* division of labor in which women as a group are disadvantaged relative to men in pay and in the conditions under which they labor. Second, such work is involved in the *horizontal* division of labor where women are concentrated in particular kinds of work.[3] Thus, 78 per cent of all clerical workers, 67 per cent of service workers, 67 per cent of teachers (but much higher in the elementary school), and so on are women in the United States. Less than 20 per cent of all administrative, executive or managerial workers in the US, and up to a decade ago less than 10 per cent in England, are women.[4]

The connections between these two divisions, however, are quite striking. Low wage, competitive sector employment contains a large share of women in both countries. In England, 41 per cent of jobs women hold are part time, thereby both guaranteeing lower wages and benefits and less control, but also documenting the linkages between patriarchal relations in the home (it is the woman's place to only work part time and take care of children) and the kinds of work made available in the wage labor market.[5]

We can get an even better idea of the concentration of women in certain occupations in the following data. As of 1979, in England, two-thirds of all women engaged in paid work were found in three occupational groups. Over 31 per cent were working in clerical and related jobs; 22 per cent worked in personal service occupations; and approximately 12 per cent were employed in 'professional' and related occupations in health and welfare. Within nearly all occupations, however, 'women were over-represented in the less-skilled, lower status or lower-paid jobs, while men were over-represented in the highly-skilled and managerial jobs'.[6]

Though showing some differences, the figures are similar in the United States. Clerical work constitutes 35 per cent of women's paid labor, followed by service work at 21 per cent, educators, librarians and social workers at 8 per cent, retail sales at 6 per cent, nurses and health technicians at 5 per cent and clothing and textile work at 4 per cent.[7] Michele Barrett and others have pointed to the close correspondence between the kinds of paid work women tend to do and the division of labor in the family. Service work, the 'caring professions', domestic service, clothing, human needs, and so forth, all remain part of this relationship between work inside and outside the home.[8] As I shall document in my next section, this relationship has a long history in education.

While these statistics are important in and of themselves, what they do not reveal is the working conditions and class dynamics themselves. Historically, women's jobs have been much more apt to be 'proletarianized' than men's. There have been constant pressures to rationalize them. This is brought home by the fact that in our economy there has been a major expansion in positions with little autonomy and control, while the number of jobs with high levels of autonomy has declined. These proletarianized positions are largely filled by women.[9] Evidence of this is given by the fact that the majority of working class positions (54 per cent) in the United States are held by women, a figure that is increasing.[10] These figures actually speak to a complicated and dialectical process. As the labor market changes over time, the decrease in jobs with autonomy is related closely to changes in the sexual division of labor. Women will tend to fill these jobs. Just as importantly, as jobs — either autonomous or not — are filled by women, there are greater attempts to control both the content of that job and how it is done from the outside. Thus, the separation of conception from execution and what has been called the deskilling and depowering of jobs have been a particularly powerful set of forces on women's labor. (The current transformation of clerical work by word processing technologies, with its attendant loss of office jobs and mechanization of those jobs that remain, offers a good example here.)[11]

These points have important implications for the analysis I am presenting. The sex-typing of a job is not likely to change unless the job itself undergoes substantial alteration in some respects. Either the surrounding labor market needs to change and/or the tasks of the job itself are restructured.[12] But sex-typing when it has occurred has had a distinct impact on conflicts in the workplace and on negotiations over such things as the definition of jobs, pay level, and determining whether or not a job is considered skilled.[13]

In general, there seems to be a relatively strong relationship between the entry of large numbers of women into an occupation and the slow transformation of the job. Pay is often lowered and it is regarded as low skilled so that control is 'needed' from the outside. Added to this is the fact that 'those occupations which became defined as female were expanded at a time when the skills needed to do them were [seen as being] commonly held or easily learned and when there was a particularly high demand for labour, or an especially large pool of women seeking work'.[14]

Of course, sometimes the very tasks associated with a job reinforce such sex-typing. Since teaching, for instance, does have a service and nurturing component to it, this reconstitutes in action the definition of it as women's work. And given 'our' association of service and nurturing activity as less skilled and less valued than other labor, we thereby revivify patriarchal hierarchies and the horizontal and vertical divisions of labor in the process.[15] In many ways, the very perception of an activity is often saturated with sexual bias. Women's work is considered somehow inferior or of less status simply due to the fact that it is women who do it.[16] Because of these conditions, it has been exceptionally difficult for women to establish recognition of the skills required in their paid and unpaid work.[17] They must fight not only the ideological construction of women's work, but against both the tendencies for the job to become something different and for its patterns of autonomy and control to change as well.

In my presentation of data to show the progression of teaching from being largely men's work to that of women's work, in many ways we shall want to pay close attention to how teaching may have changed and to the economic and gender conditions surrounding this. In essence, we may not be describing quite the same occupation after elementary school teaching becomes women's work. For jobs *are* transformed, often in significant ways, over time. A good example here is again clerical work. Like teaching, this too changed from being a masculine occupation in the nineteenth century to that of being a largely female one in the twentieth. Yet the labor process of clerical work was radically altered during this period. It was deskilled, came under tighter conditions of control, lost many of its paths of upward mobility to managerial positions, and lost wages during the end of the nineteenth century both in the United States and England as it became 'feminized'.[18] Given this, it is imperative that we ask whether what has been unfortunately called the feminization of teaching actually concerns the same job. I will claim in fact that in some rather substantive economic and ideological aspects it was not. This transformation is linked in complex ways to alterations in patriarchal and economic relations that were restructuring the larger society.

Gender and Teaching Over Time

Where does teaching fit in here? Some facts may be helpful. What has been called the 'feminization' of teaching is clearly seen in data from England. Before the rapid growth of mass elementary education, in 1870, men actually slightly outnumbered women. For every 100 men there were only ninety-nine women employed as teachers. This, however, is the last time men have a numerical superiority. Just ten years later, in 1880, for every 100 males there are now 156 women. This ratio rose to 207: 100 in 1890 and to 287 in 1900. By 1910, women outnumbered men by over three to one. By 1930, the figure had grown to closer to four to one.[19]

Yet these figures would be deceptive if they were not linked to changes in the actual numbers of teachers being employed. Teaching became a symbol of upward mobility for many women and as elementary schooling increased so did the numbers of women employed in it, points I shall go into further later on. Thus, in 1870 there were only 14,000 teachers in England, of which more were men than women. By the year 1930, 157,061 teachers worked in state supported schools in England and Wales. Close to 120,000 of these were women.[20] The definition of teaching as a female enclave

Michael W. Apple

Table 1: Teachers in public elementary schools in England and Wales from 1870–1930

Year	Total number	Number of women teachers per 100 men teachers
1870	13,729	99
1880	41,428	156
1890	73,533	207
1900	113,986	287
1910	161,804	306
1920	151,879	315
1930	157,061	366

Source: Reconstructed from Bergen B, (1982) 'Only a schoolmaster: Gender, class, and the effort to professionalize elementary teaching in England, 1870–1910', *History of Education Quarterly*, 22, spring, p. 4.

is given further substantiation by the fact that these numbers signify something quite graphic. While the 40,000 men employed as teachers around 1930 constitute less than 3 per cent of the occupied male workers, the 120,000 women teachers account for nearly 20 per cent of all women working for pay outside the home.[21]

If we compare percentages of male to female teachers in the United States to those of England for approximately the same time period, similar patterns emerge. While there was clear regional variation, in typical areas in, say, 1840, only 39 per cent of teachers were women. By 1850, it had risen to 46 per cent.[22] The increase later on is somewhat more rapid than the English experience. The year 1870 finds women holding approximately 60 per cent of the public elementary school teaching positions. This figure moves up to 71 per cent by 1900. It reaches a peak of fully 89 per cent in 1920 and then stabilizes within a few percentage points over the following years.

Given the historical connection between elementary school teaching and the ideologies surrounding domesticity and the definition of 'women's proper place', in which teaching was defined as an extension of the productive and reproductive labor women engaged in at home,[23] we should not be surprised by the fact that such changes occurred in the gendered composition of the teaching force. While there are clear connections between patriarchal ideologies and the shift of teaching into being seen as 'women's work', the issue is not totally explained in this way, however. Local political economies played a large part here. The shift to non-agricultural employment in male patterns of work is part of the story as well. Just as important was the relationship between the growth of compulsory schooling and women's labor. As we shall see, the costs

Table 2: Teachers in public elementary schools in the United States from 1870–1930

Year	Number of men	Number of women	Total number of teachers	Percentage of women
1870	—	—	—	59 (estimate)
1880	—	—	—	60 (estimate)
1890	121,877	232,925	354,802	65.6
1900	116,416	286,274	402,690	71.1
1910	91,591	389,952	481,543	81.0
1920	63,024	513,222	576,246	89.1
1930	67,239	573,718	640,957	89.5

Source: Adapted from Elsbree W S. (1939) *The American Teacher*, New York, American Book Co., p. 554 and Foster, E M (1932) 'Statistical summary of education, 1929–30', *Biennial Survey of Education 1928–1930, Volume 2,* Washington, U.S. Government Printing Office, p. 8.

associated with compulsory schooling to local school districts were often quite high. One way to control such rising costs was in changing accepted hiring practices.[24] One simply hired cheaper teachers — women. Let us examine both of these dynamics in somewhat more detail. In the process, we shall see how class and gender interacted within the limits set by the economic needs of our social formation.

Some simple and well-known economic facts need to be called to mind at the outset. In the U.K., although women teachers out-numbered their male colleagues, the salaries they were paid were significantly less. In fact, from 1855 to 1935, there was a remarkably consistent pattern. Women were paid approximately two-thirds what their male counterparts received.[25] Bergen claims in fact that one of the major contributing factors behind the fact that schools increased their hiring of women was that they would be paid less.[26]

In the United States, the salary differential was often even more striking. With the rapid growth of schooling stimulated by large rates of immigration as well as by struggles by a number of groups to win free compulsory education, school committees increased their rate of hiring women, but at salaries that were originally half to a third as much as those given to men.[27] But how did it come about that there were positions to be filled in the first place? What happened to the people who had been there?

Elementary school teaching became a women's occupation in part because men *left* it. For many men, the 'opportunity cost' was too great to stay in teaching. Many male teachers taught part time (for example, between harvests) or as a stepping stone to more lucrative or prestigious jobs. Yet with the growth of the middle class in the United States, with the formalization of schools and curricula in the latter half of the nineteenth century, and with the enlarged credentialling and certification requirements for teaching that emerged at this time, men began to and were often able to look elsewhere.

Strober summarizes these points nicely.

> All of these changes tended to make teaching less attractive to men. When teaching was a relatively casual occupation that could be engaged in for fairly short periods of time, it was attractive to men in a variety of circumstances. A farmer could easily combine teaching in the winter with caring for his farm during the rest of the year. A potential minister, politician, shopkeeper or lawyer could teach for a short period of time in order to gain visibility within a community. However, once standards rose for teacher certification and school terms were lengthened and combined into a continuous year, men began to drop out of teaching. In urban areas, where teaching was first formalized, and then, later, in rural areas, most men found the opportunity cost of teaching was simply too great, especially since although annual salaries were higher once standards were raised and the school term lengthened, the average teaching salary remained inadequate to support a family. Men also disliked losing their former classroom autonomy. And at the same time attractive job opportunities were developing for men in business and in other professions.[28]

Thus, patriarchal familial forms in concert with changes in the social division of labor of capitalism combine here to create some of the conditions out of which a market for a particular kind of teacher emerges. (In England, we should add the fact that a considerable number of men sought employment both there and abroad in the civil service. Many of the men who attended 'training colleges', in fact, did so as a point of entry into the civil service, not into teaching.[29] The 'Empire', then, had a rather interesting effect on the political economy of gendered labor.)

Faced with these 'market conditions', school boards turned increasingly to women. Partly this was a result of a successful struggle by women. More and more women were winning the battles over access to both education and employment outside the home. Yet partly it is the result of capitalism as well. Women were continuing to be recruited to the factories and mills (often, by the way, originally because they would be sometimes accompanied by children who could also work for incredibly low wages in the mills.)[30] Given the exploitation that existed in the factories and given the drudgery of paid and unpaid domestic labor, teaching must have seemed a considerably more pleasant occupation to many single women. Finally, contradictory tendencies occurred at an ideological level. While women struggled to open up the labor market and alter patriarchal relations in the home and the paid workplace, some of the arguments used for opening up teaching to women did so at the expense of reproducing ideological elements that had been part of the root causes of patriarchal control in the first place. The relationship between teaching and domesticity was highlighted. 'Advocates of women as teachers, such as Catherine Beecher, Mary Lyon, Zilpah Grant, Horace Mann and Henry Barnard, argued that not only were women the ideal teachers of young children (because of their patience and nurturant qualities) but that teaching was ideal preparation for motherhood.'[31] These same people were not loath to argue something else. Women were 'willing to' teach at lower wages than those needed by men.[32] When this is coupled with the existing social interests, economic structures, and patriarchal relations that supported the dominance of an ideology of domesticity in the larger society, we can begin to get a glimpse at the conditions that led to such a situation.

Many men, however, did stay in education. But as Tyack, Strober and others have demonstrated those men who stayed tended to be found in higher status and higher paying jobs. In fact, as school systems became more highly bureaucratized, and with the expansion of management positions that accompanied this in the United States, many more men were found in positions of authority than before. Some men stayed in education; but they left the classroom. This lends support to Lanford's claim that from 1870 to 1970, the greater the formalization of the educational system, the greater the proportion of women teachers.[33] It also tends to support my earlier argument that once a set of positions becomes 'women's work', it is subject to greater pressure for rationalization. Administrative control of teaching, curricula, and so on increases. The job *itself* becomes different.

Thus, it is not that women had not been found in the teaching ranks before; of course, they had. What is more significant is the increasing numbers of women at particular levels 'in unified, bureaucratic, and public schools' with their graded curricula, larger and more formally organized districts, growing administrative hierarchies,[34] and, just as crucially, restructuring of the tasks of teachers themselves.

Such sex segregation was not an unusual occurrence in the urban graded school, for instance. At its very outset, proponents of these school plans had a specific labor force and labor process in mind. 'Hiring, promotion and salary schedules were routinized.' Rather than leaving it up to teachers, the curriculum was quite standardized along grade level lines, with both teachers and students divided into these grades. New managerial positions were created — the superintendent and non-teaching principal, for instance — thereby removing responsibility for managerial concerns out of the classroom. Again, women's supposed nurturing capabilities and 'natural' empathic qualities and their relatively low salaries made them ideally suited for teaching in such schools. Even where there were concerns about women teachers' ability to discipline older students, this too could be solved. It was the principal and/or superintendent who handled such issues.[35]

This sexual division of labor within the school had other impacts. It enhanced the ability of urban school boards to maintain bureaucratic control of their employees and over curriculum and teaching practices. The authors of a recent historical analysis of the relationship between gender division and control demonstrate this rather well. As they argue:

> By structuring jobs to take advantage of sex role stereo-types about women's responsiveness to rules and male authority, and men's presumed ability to manage women, urban school boards were able to enhance their ability to control curricula, students and personnel. Male managers in nineteenth-century urban schools regulated the core activities of instruction through standardized promotional examinations on the content of the prescribed curriculum and strict supervision to ensure that teachers were following mandated techniques. Rules were highly prescriptive. Normal classes in the high schools of the cities prepared young women to teach in a specified manner; pictures of the normal students in Washington, DC, for example, show women students performing precisely the same activities prescribed for their future pupils, even to the mid-morning 'yawning and stretching' session. Given this purpose of tight control, women were ideal employees. With few alternative occupations and accustomed to patriarchal authority they

mostly did what their male superiors ordered. [This by the way is partly questionable.] Difference of gender provided an important form of social control.[36]

Given these ideological conditions and these unequal relations of control, why would women ever enter such labor? Was it the stereotypical response that teaching was a temporary way station on the road to marriage for women who loved children? While this may have been partly accurate, it is certainly overstated since in many instances this was not even remotely the case.

In her collection of teachers' writings from the nineteenth and twentieth centuries, Nancy Hoffman makes the point that most women did not enter teaching with a preoccupation with a love of children or with marital plans as the main things in mind. Rather, uppermost in their minds was one major concern. They entered teaching in large part because they needed work. The teachers' comments often document the following:

> Women had only a few choices of occupation; and compared with most — laundering, sewing, cleaning, or working in a factory — teaching offered numerous attractions. It was genteel, paid reasonably well, and required little special skill or equipment. In the second half of the century and beyond, it also allowed a woman to travel, to live independently or in the company of other women, and to attain economic security and a modest social status. The issue of marriage, so charged with significance among male educators, emerges in stories of schoolmarms pressured reluctantly into marriage by a family fearful of having an 'old maid' on their hands, rather than in teachers' accounts of their own eagerness or anxiety over marriage. There are also explicit statements, in these accounts, of teachers *choosing* work and independence over a married life that appeared, to them, to signify domestic servitude or social uselessness. Finally, the accounts of some women tell us that they chose teaching not because they wanted to teach children conventional right from wrong, but in order to foster social, political, or spiritual change: they wanted to persuade the young, move them to collective action for temperance, for racial equality, for conversion to Christianity. What these writings tell us, then, is that from the woman teacher's perspective, the continuity between

mothering and teaching was far less significant than a pay-check and the challenge and satisfaction of work.[37]

We should be careful in overstating this case, however. Not a few women could and did train to be teachers and then worked for a relatively short period. As Angela John puts it, 'Because the dominant ideology argued that woman's place was in the home, it conveniently enabled elementary teaching to be viewed in theory (if not in practice) as a profession for which women could train and work for a limited time.'[38] Obviously, by constructing the image of teaching as a transient occupation, this 'permitted the perpetuation of low wages', since such waged labor was merely a way of 'tiding women over until they were married'.[39] Many women teachers in England, the United States, and elsewhere, however, never married and, hence, the situation is considerably more complicated than conventional stereotypes would have it.[40]

Yet while many teachers in the United States and undoubtedly in the UK approached their jobs with a sense that did not neces-sarily mirror the stereotypes of nurturance and preparation for marriage, this did not stop such stereotypes from creating problems. The increase in women teachers did not occur without challenge. Conservative critics expressed concern over the negative effects women teachers might have on their male pupils. Such concerns increased as the proportion of students going on to secondary schools rose. 'While recognizing the beneficial effects on primary-level pupils, the continuation of the female teacher-male student relation into higher grades was viewed as potentially harmful.'[41] (The longer tradition of single sex schools in England partially mediated these pressures.) That this is not simply an historical dynamic is evident by the fact that even today the proportion of male high school teachers is considerably higher than in the ele-mentary school.

Class Dynamics and Teaching

The general picture I have painted so far has treated the constitution of teaching as primarily a part of the sexual division of labor over time. While this is crucially important, we need to remember that gender was not the only dynamic at work here. Class played a major part, especially in England, but most certainly in the United States as well.[42] Class dynamics operated at the level of who became teachers and what their experiences were.

It was not until the end of the nineteenth century and the outset of the twentieth that middle class girls began to be recruited into teaching in England. In fact, only after 1914 do we see any large influx of middle class girls entering state supported elementary school teaching.[43]

Class distinctions were very visible. While the concept of femininity *idealized* for middle class women centered around an image of the 'perfect wife and mother', the middle class view of working class women often entailed a different sense of femininity. The waged labor of working class women 'tarnished' them (though there is evidence of between-class feminist solidarity).[44] Such waged labor was a departure from bourgeois ideals of domesticity and economic dependence. With the emergence of changes in such bourgeois ideals toward the end of the nineteenth century, middle class women themselves began to 'widen their sphere of action and participate in some of the various economic and social changes that accompanied industrialization' and both the restructuring of capitalism and the division of labor. Struggles over legal and political rights, over employment and education, became of considerable import. Yet because of a tension between the ideals of domesticity and femininity on the one hand and the struggle to enlarge the middle class woman's economic sphere on the other, particular jobs were seen as appropriate for women. Teaching (and often particular kinds of stenographic and secretarial work) was one of the more predominant ones.[45] In fact, of the white women who worked outside the home in the United States in the mid to late nineteenth century, fully 20 per cent of them were employed at one time or another as teachers.[46]

This entrance of women, and especially of middle class women, into paid teaching created important pressures for improvements in the education of women both in the United States and England.[47] Equalization of curricular offerings, the right to enter into traditional male enclaves within universities, and so on were in no small part related to this phenomenon. Yet we need to remember an important social fact here. Even though women were making gains in education and employment, most, say, middle class women still found themselves *excluded* from the professions and other areas of employment.[48] Thus, a dynamic operated that cut both ways. In both being limited to and carving out this area of employment, women 'held on to it as one of the few arenas in which they could exert any power, even at the expense of further reinforcing stereotypes about women's sphere.'[49]

Having said this, we again should not assume that teachers were recruited primarily from middle class homes in the United States or England. Often quite the opposite was the case. A number of studies demonstrate that working class backgrounds were not unusual. In fact, one American study completed in 1911 presents data on the average woman teacher's economic background. She came from a family in which the father's income was approximately $800 a year, a figure that places the family among skilled workers or farmers rather than the middle class.[50]

These class differences had an impact not only on an ideological level, but in terms of education and employment within education as well. Girls of different class backgrounds often attended different schools, even when they both might wish to be teachers.[51] Furthermore, by the end of the nineteenth century in England, class differences created clear distinctions in patterns of where one might teach. While middle class women teachers were largely found in private secondary and single sex schools 'which catered especially to middle class girls' or as governesses, women teachers from working class backgrounds were found elsewhere. They dominated positions within state supported elementary schools, schools that were largely working class and mixed sex.[52] In many ways these were simply different jobs.

These class distinctions can hide something of considerable import however. Both groups still had low status.[53] To be a woman was still to be involved in a social formation that was defined in large part by the structure of patriarchal relations. But again patriarchal forms were often colonized and mediated by class relations.

For example, *what* was taught to these aspiring teachers had interesting relationships to the social and sexual divisions of labor. Many aspiring working class 'pupil teachers' in England were recruited to work in working class schools. Much of what they were expected to teach centered around domestic skills, such as sewing and needlework in addition to reading, spelling, and arithmetic. For those working class pupil teachers who might ultimately sit for an examination to enter one of the teacher training colleges, gender divisions were most pronounced. In Purvis's comparison of these entrance tests, the different expectations of what men and women were to know and, hence, teach are more than a little visible. Both men and women were examined in dictation, penmanship, grammar, composition, school management, history, geography, French, German, Latin and Welsh. Yet only men were tested in algebra, geometry, Euclid and Greek. Only women took domestic economy and needlework.

The focus on needlework is a key here in another way, for not only does it signify clear gender dynamics at work but it also points again to class barriers. Unlike the 'ornamental sewing' that was more common in middle class households, these working class girls were examined on 'useful sewing'. Questions included how to make the knee part of 'knickerbocker drawers' and the sewing together of women's petticoats of a gored variety. (This was one of the most efficient uses of material since less material is needed if the fabric is cut and sewn correctly.)[54] The dominance of utility, efficiency, and cost saving is once more part of the vision of what working class girls would need.[55] As Purvis notes, 'it would appear then that female elementary teachers were expected to teach those skills which were linked to that form of femininity deemed appropriate for the working classes'.[56]

But teaching, especially elementary school teaching, was not all that well paid to say the least, earning somewhat more than a factory operative but still only the equivalent of a stenographer's wages in the United States or England.[57] What could its appeal then have been for a working class girl? In England, with its very visible set of class relations and articulate class culture, we find answers similar to, but — given these more visible class relations — still different from, the United States. First, the very *method* by which girls were first trained in the 1870s to become teachers was a system of apprenticeship, a system that was 'indigenous to working class culture'. This was especially important since it was evident at the time that 'female pupil teachers were usually the daughters of laborers, artisans, or small tradesmen'. Second, and here very much like the American experience, compared to occupations such as domestic service, working in factories, dressmaking, and so on — among the only jobs realistically open to working class women — teaching had a number of benefits. It did increase status, especially among working class girls who showed a degree of academic ability. Working conditions, though still nothing to write home about, were clearly better in many ways. They were relatively clean and, though often extremely difficult given overcrowded conditions in schools, had that same potential for job satisfaction that was evident in my earlier quotation from Hoffman and that was frequently missing in other employment. And, just as significantly, since teaching was considered to be on the mental side of the mental/manual division of labor, it gave an opportunity — though granted a limited one — for a certain amount of social mobility.[58] (This question of social mobility and 'respectability' may have been particularly important to those women and families newly within a 'lower-middle class' location, as well, given the increasing proportion of such people in teaching in England by the beginning of the second decade of this century.)

There was a price to pay for this 'mobility' and the promise of improved working conditions that accompanied it. Women elementary school teachers became less connected to their class origins and at the same time class differences in ideals of femininity still kept her from being totally acceptable to those classes above her. This contradictory situation is not an abstraction. The fact that it was lived out is made clear in the frequent references by these teachers about their social isolation.[59] Such isolation was of course heightened considerably by other lived conditions of teachers. The formal and contractual conditions under which teachers were hired were not the most attractive. As many of you already know, women teachers in the United States, for example, could be fired for getting married, or if married, getting pregnant. There were prohibitions about being seen with men, about clothes, about makeup, about politics, about money, about nearly all of one's public (and private) lives.

It would be wrong to trace all of this back to economic motives and class dynamics. For decades married women were prohibited from teaching on both sides of the Atlantic. While single women were often young, and hence were paid less, the notion of morality and purity as powerful symbols of a womanly teaching act undoubtedly played a large part. The very fact that the above mentioned array of controls of women's physicality, dress, living arrangements, and morals speaks to the import of these concerns. Ideologies of patriarchy, with the teacher being shrouded in a domestic and maternal cloak — possibly combined with a more deep seated male suspicion of female sexuality — are reproduced here.[60] It is the very combination of patriarchal relations and economic pressures that continue to work their way through teaching even to this day.

These controls are strikingly evident in a relatively standard teacher's contract from the United States for the year 1923. I reproduce it in its entirety since it condenses within itself so many of the ideological conditions under which women teachers worked.

TEACHERS CONTRACT 1923

This is an agreement between Miss _____, teacher, and the Board of Education of the _____ School, whereby Miss _____ agrees to teach for a period of eight months, beginning 1 September 1923. The Board of Education agrees to pay Miss _____ the sum of ($75) per month.

Miss _____ agrees:

1 Not to get married. This contract becomes null and void immediately if the teacher marries.
2 Not to keep company with men.
3 To be home between the hours of 8.00 p.m. and 6.00 a.m. unless in attendance at a school function.
4 Not to loiter downtown in ice cream stores.
5 Not to leave town at any time without the permission of the chairman of the Board of Trustees.
6 Not to smoke cigarettes. This contract becomes null and void immediately if the teacher is found smoking.
7 Not to drink beer, wine or whiskey. This contract becomes null and void immediately if the teacher is found drinking beer, wine or whiskey.
8 Not to ride in a carriage or automobile with any man except her brother or father.
9 Not to dress in bright colors.
10 Not to dye her hair.
11 To wear at least two petticoats.
12 Not to wear dresses more than two inches above the ankles.
13 To keep the schoolroom clean
    (a) to sweep the classroom floor at least once daily;
    (b) to scrub the classroom floor at least once weekly with hot water and soap;
    (c) to clean the blackboard at least once daily;
    (d) to start the fire at 7.00 so the room will be warm at 8.00 a.m. when the children arrive.
14 Not to use face powder, mascara or paint the lips.

In many ways, the contract speaks for itself. It is important to note, though, that this did not end in 1923. Many of these conditions continued on for decades, to be ultimately transformed into the more technical and bureaucratic forms of control now being instituted in many areas of the United States.

Let me give one further concrete example. The larger political economy, in combination with patriarchal ideological forms, shows its power once again whenever the question of married women who engage in waged work appears historically. By the turn of the century hundreds of thousands of married women had begun to work outside the home. Yet during the Depression, it was very common for married women to be fired or to be denied jobs if they had working husbands. The state played a large role here. In England, governmental policies and reports gave considerable attention to women's domestic role.[61] In the United States, in 1930–31 the National Association of Education reported that of the 1500 school systems in the country 77 per cent refused to hire married women teachers. Another 63 per cent dismissed any woman teacher who got married during the time of her employment. This did not only occur at the elementary and secondary levels. Some universities as well asked their married women faculty to resign. Lest we see this as something that only affected women teachers, the Federal government itself required in 1932 that if a married couple worked for the government, one must be let go. This law was applied almost invariably to women only.[62]

The very fact that these figures seem so shocking to us now speaks eloquently to the sacrifices made and the struggles that women engaged in for decades to alter these oppressive relations. These struggles have been over one's control of one's labor and over the control of one's very life. Given the past conditions I have just pointed to, these historically significant struggles have actually brought no small measure of success. It is to these activities that I shall briefly turn in the concluding section of my analysis.

Beyond the Myth of the Passive Teacher

Women teachers were not passive in the face of the class and gender conditions I described in the previous sections of this chapter. In fact, one of the major but lesser known stories is the relationship between socialist and feminist activity and the growth of local teachers' organizations and unions in England and the United States.

Even while they worked internally to alter the frequently awful conditions they faced in urban schools on both sides of the Atlantic — such as crowded, unsanitary buildings, a teacher/student ratio that was often incredibly high, and an impersonal bureaucracy that especially in the United States was daily attempting to transform, rationalize, and control their work — a good deal of the unified action teachers took was concerned with their economic well-being. For example, grade school teachers in Chicago worked long and hard for adequate pensions. Out of this experience, the Chicago Teachers Federation headed by Catherine Goggin and Margaret Haley was born in 1897. It soon lead a successful fight for salary increases and succeeded in organizing more than half of the city's teachers in less than three years. Still an organization made up primarily of elementary school teachers, it was quite militant on economic matters. And while the women leaders and rank and file teachers were not necessarily as radical as some other leftist unions in cities such as Chicago, they still actively supported women's issues, municipal ownership of all utilities, popular elections and recalls, and labor solidarity. They did this in the face of middle and upper class resentment of unions. There was a constant struggle between the school board and the CFT, with the school board voting in 1905 to condemn the teachers for affiliating with the Chicago Federation of Labor. Such an affiliation was, according to the board, 'absolutely unjustifiable and intolerable in a school system of a democracy'.[63]

While these teachers were never totally successful in either their economic demands or organizing plans,[64] they did succeed in forcing school boards to take elementary teachers — women — seriously as a force to be reckoned with. In the process, they too partially challenged the economic and ideological relations surrounding women's work.

For many others in England and the United States, the conditions under which they labored had a radicalizing effect. Thus, many of the leaders of feminist groups were originally teachers who traced their growing awareness of the importance of the conflict over patriarchal domination to the experience they had as teachers. Their resentment over salary differentials, over interference in their decisions, over the very ways they were so tightly controlled often led in large part to their growing interest in feminist ideas.[65]

These examples offer us a glimpse at politicized activities. But for a large portion of the teachers in London or New York, Birmingham or Chicago, Liverpool or Boston, they struggled in 'cultural' ways. They developed practices that gave them greater control of the curriculum; they fought to have a much greater say in *what* they taught, *how* they were to teach it, and how and by *whom* their work was to be evaluated. These everyday efforts still go on as teachers continue to defend themselves against external encroachments from the state or from capital.

The history of elementary school teaching (and curriculum in part, as well) *is* the history of these political/economic and cultural struggles. It is the history of a gendered work force who, in the face of attempts to restructure their job, fought back consciously and unconsciously. Sometimes these very battles reinforced the existing definitions of women's work. Sometimes, perhaps more so in England, they led to a cutting off of ties to one's class background. And sometimes they supported class-specific ideals of work and professionalism. Just as often, however, these efforts empowered women by either radicalizing some of them, or by giving them much more say in the actual control of what they taught and how they taught it, or by demonstrating that patriarchal forms could be partially fractured in equalizing both salaries and hiring and firing conditions.

What ultimately shapes how curricula and teaching are controlled at the level of classroom practice is, hence, an *ongoing* process. It involves a complex interplay among the ideological and material structures of control of gendered labor that arise from bureaucratic management, the forms of resistance and self-organization of teachers, and then employer counter-pressures,[66] which once again produce a response by teachers themselves. I have shown one moment in this process. As teaching changes from a predominantly male to a predominantly female occupation, the constitution of the job itself changes as well. It entails significantly greater controls over teaching and curriculum at the level of teacher education and in the classroom. It is structured around a different set of class and gender dynamics. Finally, women are active, not passive, figures in attempting to create positions for women as teachers based on their own positions in the social and sexual divisions of labor. These efforts may have had contradictory results, but they were part of a much larger movement — one that is still so necessary today — to challenge aspects of patriarchal relations both within the home and the paid workplace.

Yet, as I have also argued, the transformation of teaching also led to the job itself becoming a breeding ground for further struggles. Many women were politicized. Some created unions. And others fought 'silently' everyday on their jobs to expand or retain control of their own teaching and curriculum. In a time when the state and capital are once more searching for ways to rationalize and control the day to day work of teachers, these overt and covert efforts from the past are of more than historical interest. For elementary school teaching *is* still gendered labor.[67] It is not too odd to end this chapter by saying that the past is still ahead of us.

Notes

1. This chapter is based on a longer analysis in APPLE, M.W. (1987) *Teachers and Texts: A Political Economy of Class and Gender Relations in Education*, Boston and London, Routledge and Kegan Paul. A briefer version appears in *Teachers College Record*, spring 1985.
2. MELOSH, B. (1982) *The Physician's Hand: Work Culture and Conflict in American Nursing*, Philadelphia, PA, Temple University Press, p. 8.
3. BARRETT, M. (1980) *Women's Oppression Today*, London, New Left Books, pp. 154–5.
4. COOK, A.H. (1978) *The Working Mother: A Survey of Problems and Programs in Nine Countries*, Ithaca, New York State School of Industrial and Labor Relations, Cornell University, p. 11.
5. BARRETT, M. (1980) *op cit.*, p. 155. This is, of course, reproduced in education where substitute teachers in the elementary school are largely women.
6. MURGATROYD, L. (1982) 'Gender and occupational stratification', *The Sociological Review*, 30, November, p. 582.
7. BARRETT, N.S. (1979) 'Women in the job market: Occupations, earnings, and career opportunities', in SMITH, R.E. (Ed.) *The Subtle Revolution: Women at Work*, Washington, DC, The Urban Institute, p. 49. Similar but slightly different figures can be found in COOK, A.M. (1978) *op cit.*, p. 12.
8. BARRETT, M. (1980) *op cit.*, pp. 156–7.
9. This is quite a complicated process, one including changes not only in the division of labor in capitalism, but in the family/household system as well. See BRENNER, J. and RAMAS, M. (1984) 'Rethinking women's oppression', *New Left Review*, 144, March/April, pp. 33–71.
10. OLIN WRIGHT, E. *et al.* (1982) 'The American class structure', *American Sociological Review*, 47, December, p. 723.
11. See for example, BARKER, J. and DOWNING, H. (1981) 'Word processing and the transformation of the patriarchal relations of control in the office', in DALE, R. *et al.*, (Eds) *Education and the States: Politics, Patriarchy and Practice, Volume 2*, Lewes, Falmer Press, pp. 229–56

and CROMPTON, R. and REID, S. (1982) 'The deskilling of clerical work', in WOOD, S. (Ed.) *The Degradation of Work?*, London, Hutchinson, pp. 163–78.

12. MURGATROYD, L. (1982) *op cit.*, p. 591.
13. *Ibid*, p. 575.
14. *Ibid*, p. 588.
15. *Ibid*, p. 595.
16. *Ibid*, p. 581.
17. BARRETT, M. (1980) *op cit.*, p. 166–8. Barrett goes on to say here that the extent to which any job is seen as requiring a high level of skill is often dependent on the ability of the people who do it to have the power to establish that definition over competing ones.
18. BEECHEY, V. (1982) 'The sexual division of labour and the labour process: A critical assessment of Braverman', in WOOD, S. (Ed.) *op cit.*, p. 67. See also DAVIES, M. (1982) *Women's Place is at the Typewriter*, Philadelphia, PA, Temple University Press.
19. BERGEN, B. (1982) 'Only a schoolmaster: Gender, class, and the effort to professionalize elementary teaching in England, 1870–1910', *History of Education Quarterly*, 22, spring, p. 12.
20. *Ibid.*
21. *Ibid*, p. 5.
22. STROBER, M. 'Segregation by gender in public school teaching: Toward a general theory of occupational segregation in the labor market', unpublished manuscript, Stanford University, p. 16. Figures for the eastern cities of Canada are similar (though individual cities — such as Toronto and Montreal — do differ, often for ethnic and religious reasons). See DANYLEWYCZ, M. and PRENTICE, A. (1984) 'Teachers, gender, and bureaucratizing school systems in nineteenth century Montreal and Toronto', *History of Education Quarterly*, 24 spring, pp. 75–100.
23. See, for example, ROTHMAN, S. (1978) *Women's Proper Place*, New York, Basic Books; and BARRETT, M. (1980) *op cit.* The role women were meant to play in upholding the religious and moral 'fiber' of the nation should not go unnoticed here, as well. Native-born Protestant women were often recruited by the National Board of Popular Education to teach on, say, the American frontier to 'redeem' the West. Many women themselves combined this vision with a clear sense both of economic necessity and of the possibilities of independence and adventure. These women were as a rule somewhat older than beginning teachers and were looking for both personal and professional autonomy in conjunction with their 'moral mission'. Attempts at controlling the religious and other content of the curriculum were also visible in these western schools. However, many of these woman teachers were successful in resisting such pressures on their teaching practices. See WELTS KAUFMAN, P. (1984) *Women Teachers on the*

Frontier, New Haven, CT, Yale University Press, especially Part I.

24. RICHARDSON, J. and HATCHER, B.W. (1983) 'The feminization of public school teaching, 1870–1920', *Work and Occupations*, 10 February, p. 84. Following Douglas and others, Richardson and Hatcher also associate this with the relationship between middle class women and religion.

25. BERGEN, B. (1982) *op cit.*, p. 13.

26. *Ibid*, p. 14.

27. HOFFMAN, N. (1981) *Women's 'True' Profession: Voices From the History of Teaching*, Old Westbury, The Feminist Press, p. xix. Conditions in Canada were very similar. See DANYLEWYCZ, M. and PRENTICE, A. (1984) *op cit.*, p. 88.

28. STROBER, M. *op cit.*, p. 18. On the difficulties schools had in keeping male teachers, even in earlier periods, see JENSEN, J.M. (1984) 'Not only ours but others: Teaching daughters of the mid-Atlantic, 1790–1850', *History of Education Quarterly*, 24, Spring, pp. 3–19.

29. See the discussion in WIDDOWSON, F. (1983) *Going Up Into the Next Class: Women and Elementary Teacher Training 1840–1914*, London, Hutchinson.

30. GORDON, D., EDWARDS, R. and REICH, M. (1982) *Segmented Work, Divided Workers: The Historical Transformation of Labor in the United States*, New York, Cambridge University Press, p. 68. Many 'native-born' women, however, fled the factories for other reasons. Not only had working conditions deteriorated, but a significant portion of these women preferred not to work alongside the immigrant women who were being hired to work in the mills. For further analysis of the changing conditions of women's labor and the tension between immigrant and native-born women workers, see KESSLER-HARRIS, A. (1982) *Out to Work: A History of Wage-Earning Women in the United States*, New York, Oxford University Press, pp. 108–41.

31. STROBER, M. *op cit.*, p. 19. See also MELDER, K.E. (1974) 'Mask of oppression: The female seminary movement in the United States', *New York History*, 55 July, pp. 261–79.

32. *Ibid*. This 'willingness' often had *religious* roots. Thus, evangelical religious imperatives, and the history of protestant denomenationalism, may have led to 'moral' reasons for women to teach. See BRUMBERG, J.J. (1983) 'The feminization of teaching: "Romantic sexism" and American Protestant denominationalism', *History of Education Quarterly*, 23, Fall, p. 383.

33. LANFORD quoted in STROBER, M. *op cit.*, p. 21.

34. RICHARDSON, J. and HATCHER, B.W. (1983) *op cit.*, p. 82.

35. STROBER, M. and TYACK, D. (1980) 'Why do women teach and men manage? A report on research on schools', *Signs*, 5, Spring, p. 499.

36. *Ibid*, p. 500. The authors also note that men made it to the top in school systems in part because of the advantages they had over women

in linking schools to the surrounding community. Maleness was an asset in meeting with the mostly male power structure of organizations such as the Kiwanis, Lions clubs, etc. This point was also made much earlier by ELSBREE, W. (1939) in *The American Teacher*, New York, American Book Co., p.555.

37. HOFFMAN, N. (1981) *op cit.*, pp. xvii–xviii. For a general discussion of related points, see MELDER, K.E. (1972) 'Women's high calling: The teaching profession in America, 1830–1860', *American Studies*, 13, Fall, pp. 19–32.

38. JOHN, A.V. 'Foreword' in WIDDOWSON, F. (1983) *op cit.*, p. 9.

39. *Ibid.*

40. See, for example, DANYLEWYCZ, M. and PRENTICE, A. (1984) *op cit.*

41. RICHARDSON, J. and HATCHER, B.W. (1983) *op cit.*, pp. 87–8.

42. On the importance of thinking about the United States in class terms, see HOGAN, D. (1982) 'Education and class formation: The peculiarities of the Americans', in APPLE, M.W. (Ed.) *Cultural and Economic Reproduction in Education: Essays on Class, Ideology and the State*, Boston, Routledge and Kegan Paul, pp. 32–78; and WRIGHT, E.O. (1978) *Class, Crisis and the State*, London, New Left Books.

43. PURVIS, J. 'Women and teaching in the nineteenth century', in DALE, R. *et al.* (Eds) (1981) *op cit*, p. 372. See also WIDDOWSON, F. (1983) *op cit.*

44. See the interesting historical analysis of the place of socialist women here in BUHLE, M.J. (1981) *Women and American Socialism, 1870–1920*, Urbana, IL, University of Illinois Press.

45. PURVIS, J. (1981) *op cit.*, pp. 361–3. See also ROTHMAN, S. (1978) *op cit.* We should not assume that such educational and political struggles by middle class women meant that these gains simply reproduced a 'safe liberalism' and bourgeois hegemony. For an argument that liberal discourse can be progressive at times, see APPLE, M. (1982) *Education and Power* pp. 123–5; and GINTIS, M. (1980) 'Communication and politics', *Socialist Review*, 10, March–June, pp. 189–232.

46. DEGLER, C. (1980) *At Odds: Women and the Family in America from the Revolution to the Present*, New York, Oxford University Press, p. 381.

47. PURVIS, J. (1981) *op cit.*, p. 372. I stress *paid* teaching here, since Purvis also argues that middle and upper class women often worked as voluntary teachers in working class literacy programs. Philanthropy and voluntary teaching could solve the problem brought about by the dominance of bourgeois ideals of femininity. A women *could* work, but only for the highest ideals and without remuneration.

48. STROBER, M. and TYACK, D. (1980) *op cit.* p. 496. See also WALSH, M.R. (1977) *Doctors Wanted, No Women Need Apply: Sexual Barriers in the Medical Profession, 1835–1975*, New Haven, CT, Yale University Press. For England, see LEWIS, J. (1980), *The Politics of Mother-*

hood, London, Croom Helm; and ROWBOTHAM, S. (1974) *Hidden From History*, New York, Random House.

49. ACKER, S. (1983) 'Women and teaching: A semi-detached sociology of a semi-detached profession', in WALKER, S. and BARTON, L. (Eds). *Gender, Class and Education*, Lewes, Falmer Press, p. 134.

50. DEGLER, C. (1980) *op cit.*, p. 380. Paul Mattingly, as well, argues that by the 1890s even many normal schools had become almost exclusively female and had directed their attention to a 'lower-class' student body. See MATTINGLY, P. (1975) *The Classless Profession*, New York, New York University Press, p. 149. The significant portion of teachers who came from working class families in Canada, as well, is documented in DANYLEWYCZ, M. and PRENTICE, A. (1984) *op cit.*, pp. 91–3.

51. Interestingly enough, some believed that upper middle class young women were at an academic disadvantage to working class young women in teacher training institutions in England. See WIDDOWSON, F. (1983) *op cit.*

52. PURVIS, J. (1981) *op cit.*, p. 364. Widdowson claims, however, that in general by the first decade of the twentieth century 'the early education of the nation's children was predominantly in the hands of aspiring ladies recruited mainly from the lower-middle classes'. *Ibid*, p. 79. She also makes the interesting point that the ultimate entry of significant numbers of lower-middle class young women into such positions contributed a good deal to the 'professionalization' and increase in status of teaching.

53. *Ibid*, p. 364.

54. *Ibid*, p. 366. For further discussion of the effect of such needlework on the women teachers of working class girls, see the interesting treatment in COPELMAN, D. (1985a) 'We do not want to turn men and women into mere toiling machines: Teachers, teaching, and the taught', unpublished paper, University of Missouri, Department of History, Columbia.

55. I wish to thank Rima D. Apple for this point.

56. PURVIS, J. (1981) *op cit.*, p. 366.

57. ROTHMAN, S. (1978) *op cit.*, p. 58. For a discussion of how secondary schools grew as 'training grounds' for preparing women for clerical work, see RURY, J.L. (1984) 'Vocationalism for home and work: Women's education in the United States, 1880–1930', *History of Education Quarterly*, 24, spring, pp. 21–44.

58. PURVIS, J. (1981) *op cit.*, p. 367.

59. *Ibid.* See also EATON, W.E. (1975) *The American Federation of Teachers, 1916–1961*, Carbondale, IL, Southern Illinois University Press. The problem of a lack of connection between working class parents and teachers in England is still a serious one. See, for example, C.C.C.S. EDUCATION GROUP, (1981) *Unpopular Education: Schooling*

and Social Democracy in England Since 1944, London, Hutchinson.

60. See BARRETT, M. (1980) *op cit.*, pp. 187–226. See also her discussion of class differences in this section.

61. See WOLPE, A.M. (1974) 'The official ideology of education for girls', in FLUDE, M. and AHIER, J. (Eds). *Educability, Schools and Ideology* London, Halsted Press, pp. 138–59.

62. DEGLER, C. (1980) *op cit.*, pp. 413–4. Degler does point out, however, that the Depression did not ultimately drive women out of the paid work force. Their rates of participation continued to increase. See p. 415. Similar policies were put into effect elsewhere as well. In New South Wales in Australia, married women were dismissed from their teaching jobs during the Depression to protect men's positions. See CONNELL, R.W. (1985) *Teachers' Work*, Boston, George Allen and Unwin, p. 154.

63. EATON, W.E. (1975) *op cit.*, pp. 5–8. In his nicely written study of the history of teachers' organizations in the United States, Wayne Urban argues, however, that most of the membership of these early teachers' organizations were significantly less radical than many of their leaders. Economic, not political, demands were more important for the bulk of the teachers. This, though, needs to be situated within the history of women's struggles over disparities in income, since in terms of this history economic issues may be less conservative than at first glance. See URBAN, W.J. (1982) *Why Teachers Organized*, Detroit, MI, Wayne State University Press.

64. The leadership of the CFT believed that teachers might be lost in an amalgam of other unions and, to be taken seriously nationally, had to form their own national union. The attempt was first made in 1899 and again in 1902 by Haley and Goggin. The National Teachers Federation, an early precursor of the AFT, limited membership to grade school teachers and, while it did attract some national membership, it ultimately failed. See EATON, W.E. (1975) *op cit.*, p. 10.

65. See CLIFFORD, G. (1981) 'The female teacher and the feminist movement', unpublished paper, University of California, Berkeley. Similar struggles occurred in Canada, as well. See, for example, DANYLEWYCZ, M. and PRENTICE, A. (1984) *op cit.*, pp 43–4. For England, see COPELMAN, D. (1985a) *op cit.* Copelman has also analyzed the relationship between women teachers, feminism, and professional struggles in England in her interesting paper, (1985b) 'The politics of professionalism: Women teachers, 1904–1914', unpublished paper, University of Missouri, Department of History, Columbia.

66. LITTLER, C. (1982) 'Deskilling and changing structures of control', in WOOD, S. (Ed.) *op cit.*, p. 141. The importance of class as well as gender dynamics is made visible in Gerald Grace's argument that external control of teaching and curriculum by the state in England was lessened in the 1920s because of fears that a Labour government

would use its power over teachers and curriculum to instill socialist ideas. Though Grace could have made more of gender issues, his points are provocative. See GRACE, G. (1985) 'Judging teachers: The social and political contexts of teacher evaluation', *British Journal of Sociology of Education*, 6, 1, pp. 3–16.

67. For a current statistical portrait of American teachers, see FEISTRITZER, C.E. (1983) *The American Teacher*, Washington, DC, Feistritzer Publications.

Part II
Professional Education:
Forms of Labor and
Ideology

4 Reproduction, Contradiction and Conceptions of Professionalism: The Case of Pre-service Teachers

Mark Ginsburg

This chapter is based on a two-year ethnographic study of a teacher education program in one university. Pre-service teachers are shown to draw upon education, remuneration, power, and individual attitude/behavior themes of the ideology of professionalism both in making claims about whether teaching is a profession and in indicating their perception of the legitimacy of unequal social relations characteristic of societies in which capitalist and patriarchal societies dominate. It is argued that such ideologically informed conceptions of professionalism can function either to mask and thus mediate or illuminate and thus provide the basis for intervening in contradictions associated with unequal class and gender relations.

Introduction

In this chapter I examine the ways in which pre-service teachers conceive of professionalism. This is not undertaken, however, to address the proverbial question: 'Is teaching a profession?'. Too much has already been written on this question[1] informed by a 'trait theory' approach that has been convincingly criticized because of the variation among lists of traits employed, the static and ahistoric assumptions implied, and the overly positive, even apologist, tone exhibited.[2] Rather my focus on pre-service teachers' conceptions of professionalism is designed to illuminate the contribution of the ideology of professionalism[3] to the reproduction of inequalities in wealth and power characteristic of capitalist and patriarchal structures in (at least) the United States.

This is not to argue that class relations or gender relations are solely or primarily reproduced by the ideology of professionalism or even more generally through dynamics at the ideological level.[4] I am not positing an idealist notion that if we just altered people's ways of thinking and talking, a classless and gender-equal society would appear. Certainly, individual and collective human action is shaped by material reality and the extant political economic distribution of wealth and power. This is only to claim that the ideology of professionalism warrants attention as a source of support for unequal and unjust social relations.

It should also be clarified that the approach adopted here does not assume a simple or perfect deterministic process of reproduction. While taking as the major problematic the question of how unequal social relations are perpetuated and legitimated,[5] my approach provides space for human agency, that is, for people's relatively autonomous acts of resistance, contestation and struggle.[6] Thus, I posit a notion similar to what Giddens[7] has termed the 'duality of structure' — that the 'logic' of the macro political, economic and ideological spheres both constrains and enables human action and consciousness, while at the same time this context is reproduced, challenged, or sometimes transformed by human thought and action. Moreover, because human agency is a factor and because social formations (at the societal and world system levels) contain contradictions, the potential for social transformation or change, 'however trivial or minor' is 'inherent in all moments of reproduction.'[8]

The concept of contradiction has been seen as a particularly promising corrective to overly-deterministic models of reproduction — one that does not accord undue weight to voluntarism, which can sometimes occur with overzealous celebration of resistance.[9] It is rather paradoxical, though, that there have been relatively few efforts among critical theorists in education to incorporate systematically the notion of contradiction in their analyses,[10] given 'the centrality of the category of contradiction for any Marxist analysis'[11] or that, as Mao[12] notes, the 'law of contradictions in things, that is, the law of unity of opposites, is the basic law of materialist dialectics'. My approach is based on the marxist notion, here expressed by Mao, that 'contradiction exists in the process of development of all things,'[13] i.e., 'nature as well as social and ideological phenomena,'[14] but that the 'particular essence of each form of motion is determined by its own particular contradiction'.[15] This is not to argue, however, that social structures and ideologies are completely isolated regions of contradiction. It is only to clarify the relative autonomy of, for example, the ideologies of professionalism from extant class or gender relations and to indicate that ideologies and structures may stand (at any historical conjuncture and with respect to any particular aspects) in a relation of correspondence or contradiction.[16]

Teachers as an Occupational Group: Class and Gender

Before turning to a discussion of how a group of pre-service teachers conceptualized professionalism, we need to look briefly at the characteristics and functions of teachers, especially in relation to issues of social class and gender. Although school teaching in the United States initially attracted occupational incumbents who were sons of either middle class professionals or (petit) bourgeoisie, the class of origin of teachers increasingly became working class.[17] The trend toward teachers of working class origin was partly counter-acted by a tendency for daughters of middle and capitalist classes to enter teaching in increasingly greater proportions compared to sons from any social classes. The field of education, especially school teaching, became increasingly femininized[18] as the compulsory school age population expanded, larger schools were organized (and managed by males) in urban areas, and 'state regulations and standardization intensified'.[19] Since the 1960s with the opening of other 'professions' to the daughters of the middle and capitalist classes, however, although school teaching has remained a pre-dominantly female line of work, the teaching labor force has become populated more so by people with working class backgrounds.

Class and gender pertain to teaching and professionalism not only as characteristics and background factors of occupational members. The question of teachers' involvement in class and gender *relations* is even more important. In terms of their participation in class relations, teachers are in some sense members of the middle class(es). From a Weberian, status group perspective, they might be conceived as part of a buffer group, protecting the upper or dominant class(es) from challenges by the lower or subordinate class(es), either as examples of the 'open' contest system of status mobility or as more explicit agents of social control (via physical force or ideological transmission). From a marxist, class conflict perspective, the class location of teachers as intellectuals and situated in the middle class(es) is no less ambiguous and contradictory.[20] Within this viewpoint teachers' economic functions are seen to include, to varying extents, aspects of both the global function of capital and the function of the collective laborer; thus teachers share in part the class relational experience of both the bourgeoisie and the proletariat. Generally, similar to workers, teachers do not own or control the means of production (or even the means of 'educational production'), and work for wages or salary. However, similar to the bourgeoisie, they live (some would argue barely) off the wealth created by productive workers and to some degree operate as managers/socializers of future workers.

This is not to suggest that we can somehow read teachers' political stance from their economic class location.[21] The point is that teachers are intimately and complicatedly involved in class relations (in the context of the state), and, thus, questions of how they act and how they characterize their actions (for example, in terms of professionalism) are important to examine for their political economic consequences.

With respect to gender relations we should first note that district and state level school boards, as well as principals and district/state educational administrators, are predominantly male groups, while (as noted above) school teaching is a predominantly female pursuit. Thus, the social relations of educational work not only represent class relations — employer/manager and workers — but also involve gender relations. Historically, the sexual division of labor enabled school boards and administrators 'to maintain bureaucratic control of their employees and of the curriculum and teaching practices',[22] because 'the managerial aspects of education were removed from the job of teaching and the new solely managerial positions of principal and superintendent were created'.[23]

The connection of these developments with patriarchy and the ideology of domesticity was explicitly made by some of the Victorian era's leading proponents of women entering teaching, Catherine Beecher, Mary Lyon, Zilpah Grant, Horace Mann, and Henry Barnard, who argued that women, because of their 'natural' qualities of nurturance and patience, would be ideal teachers, but not managers; that teaching was an ideal preparation for women's most 'appropriate' role, motherhood;[24] and that women would 'willingly' work for less money than men.[25] It is this historical context as well as subsequent developments in education and in the political economy which leads Acker to conclude that the:

sexual division of labor among teachers contributes to the reproduction of patriarchal and/or capitalist social order, especially in providing models to students of male/female power relations.[26]

As in the case of class relations, however, teachers' involvement in the gender relations of educational work is marked by contradictions. First, we should note the fact that not all school board members or all administrators are male, nor are all school teachers female. Second, there is the expansion of the number of 'supervisors' in school systems. This position, apparently occupied more often by women, is in some sense located above teachers in the educational system hierarchy, but without the attendant formal organizational authority to manage or control teachers. Third, there is the contradiction — a tension of binary opposition — within the practice of teaching itself. In relation to their students (and, to some extent, parents), teachers must often play both a detached, authority role (controller and evaluator) and one of emotional engagement (socializer and motivator for learning). As Connell explains:

> There is a tension here which is more than an incompatibility between two practices. It is a tension about gender itself. Authority, in our society, is felt to be masculine; to assert it is to undermine one's femininity, in other people's eyes and often in one's own.[27]

adding that:

> If teaching has aspects that are not easily reconcilable with traditional femininity, it is not unambiguously masculine either.... The element of emotional engagement, and indeed emotional manipulation, that is inevitable in teaching, is defined as feminine in our culture.[28]

As we examine pre-service teachers' conceptions of professionalism, therefore, we will want to keep in mind how the ideology of professionalism, which they draw upon and reproduce, serves to mask/mediate or expose/challenge the contradictions associated with the class and gender relations operating at the school and broader societal levels.

Pre-service Teachers' Conceptions of Professionalism

The discussion that follows is organized around six themes which emerged from an analysis of a series of interviews with seventeen secondary education students in the University of Houston (Central Campus) Professional Teacher Preparation Program conducted as part of a longitudinal ethnographic study.[29] These themes are: teaching as a profession?, professionalism and the legitimation of inequalities, professionalism and education, professionalism and remuneration, professionalism and power, and professionalism as individual attitudes and behavior. The first two themes are in a sense more general, with the latter four themes illuminating salient dimensions which were articulated by pre-service teachers both to develop their perspectives concerning whether or not teaching is a profession and to legitimate or critique social inequalities.

Teaching as a Profession?

Of the pre-service teachers interviewed at least once after the beginning of their first semester in the program only one ever responded negatively to the question, 'Do you think teaching is a profession?'. This respondent, a masters degree student who became a part of the interview sample during her second semester in the program explained:

> Teachers themselves will not allow it to be considered a profession. Few of them join any organizations. They never want to be accountable for what they do, which is different from a professional. Um, they certainly don't have any advanced educational training that other professions do ... [I]t seems to be looked at as a temporary job. ... Then once you're in teaching ... in the system [the administration] gives you no autonomy and the pay really wouldn't draw you to teaching. ... [And yet] I think that teaching is something that's certainly as vital, in a lot of ways more vital, than doctors and CPAs because you have an opportunity for a year to infiltrate the minds of a lot of people. (Mary, 13 May 1981).

And after completing student teaching she reasserts that teaching is not a profession, adding that 'they don't act professionally' and that 'they don't police themselves' (Mary, 24 January 1983).

Interestingly, some of the same themes (to be discussed in more detail later) were raised by each of the other respondents who affirmed that teaching is a profession. One of these prospective teachers qualified his positive response by terming teaching as a 'younger profession' (Roberto, 4 May 1981) and 'a very low status profession ... a very unappreciated profession ... [and] an unprofessional profession' (Roberto, 28 May 1982). None of the other respondents wavered in their belief that teaching was a profession, although, as they progressed through the program, they began to question whether all teachers were professionals and whether others (for example, the public) shared their view. This doubt about the 'public's' perception of teaching as profession came partly from increasing criticisms in the media — this was the period preceding the 'flood' of reports on the 'rising tide of mediocrity' (as the National Commission on Excellence in Education[30] termed it).

Ironically, however, although many of the college of education faculty were strongly committed to teaching as a profession (see Ginsburg and Spatig, 1985) — a point commented upon by one student in the sample: 'the college here wants so much to impress upon us that teaching is a profession' (Sonia, 28 May 1981), students' doubts about teachers' status as a profession stemmed partly from the issues raised in the formal curriculum of the program.[31] Three respondents discussed this irony most explicitly:

> I had never had to confront the issue of whether or not I thought a teacher was a professional until I started in the education classes.... You know we spent an awful lot of time on it this semester, too. And I thought, well, there must be a question in somebody's mind somewhere, you know, or else we wouldn't be spending so much time on it. (Donald, 15 May 1981)

> I had always thought 'yes' until the question was raised and then, you know, it makes you think more about it. But, um, I still see it as a profession. (Jane, 27 May 1981)

> And the only thing that bothers me about this is that, I've heard this over and over in almost every education course I've taken, and I think we're damning ourselves with faint praise. I think that by talking about it so much we're putting ourselves on the defensive. (Carol, 26 May 1982)

Pre-service teachers interviewed thus presented a strong, almost univocal, message — that teaching is and should be considered a profession, although not a consummate profession. They remained attached to this position, despite encountering questioning about and challenges to it by the 'public', educators in the field, and university faculty.

Professionalism and the Legitimation of Inequalities

As these prospective teachers discussed issues of professionalism and teaching, they also indicated how they perceived the hierarchy associated (implicitly or explicitly) with professions as a segment of the division of labor. Seven of the fifteen interviewed, including the respondent who did not see teaching as a profession, discussed professionalism and never questioned the system of occupational stratification. One of these pre-service teachers noted that teaching is a profession and explained:

> For one thing, you have people in society itself who still look up to a teacher as being a profession. And that right there means a whole lot. . . . Teachers still get, you know, a certain amount of respect, honor and prestige. (James, 7 May 1981)

Another prospective teacher not only referred to status distinctions but also seemed to allude to class (market relations and the mental/manual dichotomy) divisions:

> I think that being a professional is having a set of abilities that most people around don't have ... If you don't strive for that sort of thing, you're sort of like the guy who digs the ditches and, be there tomorrow or not, it's not going to make much difference ... I think there are some jobs that are not professional, uh, although I guess in some sense everything has some sort of professionality, because they all have some sort of abilities that are needed to be performed. But if you wanted to be clear-cut, this is professional [and] this is not, I think you probably could make a distinction. Maybe some of it's status. (Nancy, 18 May 1982)

What about the other eight respondents who did not unambiguously reference as legitimate the hierarchical division of labor and thus may have been challenging the class and gender divisions which are characteristic of (at least) capitalist and patriarchal social structures? We would be surprised if most of these offered a strong critique of the basic assumption of structured inequalities, given that only two prospective teachers in the sample communicated even an incipient radical critique of US society when discussing inequalities and the role of schooling.[32] The pre-service teacher, quoted immediately above, provides an insight into the others' views. Indeed, had she *not* fully clarified her view, she would *not* have been classified as *un*ambiguously conceiving of professions as a part of a legitimate stratification system.

The point is *not* that most of the other eight respondents were *un*ambiguous in critiquing the structured inequalities connected with the concept of professionalism, but that their views, expressed even at different points of the same interview, were contradictory. Five of these pre-service teachers discussed professions as being on top of a legitimate hierarchy, but argued that one could exhibit professionalism in any type of work. For example, during the interview at the beginning of the program, one respondent stated:

> Well, you know, something that is not a profession, maybe the skill of learning how to make shoes or whatever ... [However,] I feel you can be a professional at shining shoes, if you are expert at it, if you know so much about it ... if you are doing well and you are happy doing it. (Sonia, 16 September 1980)

The remaining three interviewees, while at times claiming teaching as a profession deserved higher income than some other workers, argued more forcefully against the invidious status distinctions. One, who was considering whether to pursue teaching or dentistry as his future profession and who dropped out of the pre-service teacher preparation program at the end of the first semester (partly because of a low overall grade point average), commented on the issue raised in class of the mental/manual distinction between professions and other occupations:

> It's not right to separate certain groups by whether they think or not. How does one determine and who determines when someone is thinking? It's like the arm and the brain, how does one weigh one against the other? (Richard, 9 December 1980)

Another student, who dropped out of the program after the first semester (because she learned that she could not use Texas certification to teach in another country), also reacted to class discussions on the topic of teaching as a profession:[33]

> We were talking about why teaching is a profession. I don't agree with the others, because they didn't list (teaching in the column with) doctors and lawyers and engineers and architects. And I was very hurt by that fact, because they listed me in the second column [trades].... It made me feel like I'm something less than someone else.... When the class put a plumber at the very end of the list [of trades as contrasted with professions], or a mechanic, I was very hurt about that, too. It's just like they're lower people. I consider people to be members of a profession if they are all professionals at their jobs, if they are masters at their job. (Rachel, 19 September 1980)

The third, who did complete the program, exclaimed during an interview after one semester as a teacher:

> Professionalism involves a dedication to task ... It's the attitude of the person that's important ... An auto mechanic or an assembly line worker can be a professional ... I sense a distinction, a class distinction ... that a professional is better than someone who isn't ... I resent that distinction.... I don't see any job as non-essential, except for bureaucrats. (Dana, 2 July 1982)

We now turn to examine more thoroughly some of the aspects of the ideology of professionalism which respondents drew upon and reproduced in making their claims about teaching being or not being a profession. We should keep in mind that these aspects were also employed concomitantly to critique and, more frequently, to provide legitimacy for the structured inequalities characteristic of (at least) societies in which capitalist and patriarchal structures dominate.

Professionalism and Education

Ten of the fifteen interviewees identified length of formal preparation or education in explaining why they did or did not view teaching as a full profession and in clarifying how they distinguished professions from lower occupational groups. For many of these pre-service teachers, profession was almost synonymous with work which required a college degree. Perhaps, unlike the individual quoted below, the five respondents who didn't mention education as an aspect of professionalism, took it so much for granted that they left it unsaid.

> Well, what I mean by [teaching is a profession] . . . is the basic meaning in the word: uh, a teacher is a university graduate, has gone to school to prepare for what they're doing. . . . And, oh well, for me I know I couldn't do that, spend this much time trying to do something, if I didn't, I wasn't absolutely sure that I was becoming a professional. (Donald, 15 May 1981)

And for those who questioned whether teaching was fully professionalized, it was suggested that one 'could upgrade it if you required more education' (Allison: 12 September 1980).

Thus, most of these pre-service teachers drew upon and concomitantly reproduced the ideology of professionalism in a manner which Larson claims constitutes 'an important contribution to the ideological denial [and thus the legitimation] of structured inequalities'[34] by 'stressing the apparent fusion between educational and occupational hierarchies,'[35] both of which are represented as part of a meritocracy. As more fully discussed elsewhere,[36] it would seem to be difficult for aspiring teachers to seriously question the legitimacy of the stratification function of schooling. In their eyes, the system must be basically meritocratic: why else would they have 'succeeded' thus far and why else would they want to become part of an education system which, according to one respondent, is 'the backbone of our society . . . responsible for what people grow up to be' (Cindy, 5 January 1982)?

Professionalism and Remuneration

Eleven of the fifteen respondents mentioned issues of remuneration in their discussion of teaching and professionalism. However, unlike the issues surrounding education, the viewpoints expressed were more heterogeneous. This appears to result because of the contradiction within the ideology of professionalism. On one hand, professionalism is identified with high incomes and, on the other, with a 'service ideal' in which remuneration is downplayed in importance, if not completely eschewed.

Six pre-service teachers consistently stated that a high level of remuneration was a central feature of professionalism. This viewpoint was articulated by the one respondent, Mary, who did not believe teaching was a profession (see previous discussion). The pre-service teacher, who referred to teaching as a 'younger' or 'low status' profession, offered as part of his explanation:

> But I think part of the reason that it's hard for even teachers to think that they are a professional group is that we're not getting paid enough ... You usually think of professionals as getting paid more than the average person, and we're making less than a waiter (laughs). I know because I'm a waiter [in a four-star hotel]. So I'm going to be taking a step down in teaching ... [W]hen most unskilled or even un-educated people are making the same kind of money as teachers are making ... it's terribly unfair. (Roberto, 4 May 1981)

He brought up the issue later in the same interview:

> Too many people are doing it for the vacation time. I think that's very unprofessional.... And I think too many women in the profession, maybe not so much today, but I think in the past ... that maybe women that are married tend to use teaching as something to do while their husbands are making the big bucks or whatever. And so they don't take it [the level of remuneration] seriously sometimes.... It's ok, you can call me a chauvinist pig.[37] (Roberto, 4 May 1981)

Another respondent discussed the issue of pay level, not so much to explain a semi-professional label for teachers as to point out an inconsistency or contradiction.

> But the part that they're lacking so far is, you know, the financial part. And that part right there creates a kind of inconsistency for the teacher, uh, and a kind of strain on them, too. Because, you know, they can't keep preparing themselves and wanting to stay with the profession, if they're not given the support ... Like people in say a grocery store ... maybe a cashier or something, but no years of schooling, and come out making more money in one year than a teacher (James, 7 May 1981)

This contradiction caused considerable consternation for other pre-service teachers, sometimes based on comparisons with a sister who was making more without any college education working for Xerox than could teachers (Allison, 12 September 1980). Other times the concern was stimulated by media coverage of labor disputes, for example, the local meatcutters and four major grocery store chains.

> To be perfectly honest, I don't think (the meatcutters) deserved what they got. They shouldn't have struck. Most of the meat they get is prepackaged; therefore, they don't have any kind of preparation for what they do. There's no kind of real physical labor or mental stress that I can imagine; maybe, to some degree. And on top of that they go on strike for more money. And, of course, we saw the results: they got it. And I don't think they were justified in going on strike. Teachers deserve more money. There's a hell of a lot of difference! (Richard, 9 December 1980)

Three of the interviewees, who mentioned financial issues, consistently articulated their viewpoint in relation to the notion of the service ideal. Their emphasizing the notion of an ideal of service, and thus derogating a concern for financial rewards, may also result from their encountering the contradiction (identified by the respondents quoted directly above) of conceiving of teaching as a profession, but one without the monetary rewards. One of these prospective teachers opined that teaching is:

> A profession ... because, I think, I define a profession as something that one devotes time and energy to, and enjoys.... And it's also something you don't get into, I think, just for the money ... I think if you are going into it for the money, it wouldn't be a profession; it would be a job. (Cindy, 14 May 1981)

Another commented on her growing awareness that not all people shared her view of teaching being a profession:

> Maybe they [the public] feel that teaching is not a profession because you don't make the most money in being a teacher. That's obvious; everybody knows that. But the fact that, if you know that and still want to become a teacher, it makes it a profession, because if they don't care about the financial rewards, then, you know, ... [otherwise] you're like skilled labor who's only doing that because of the money you can make. (Sonia, 16 September 1980)

Finally, two respondents dealt with the contradiction, not by emphasizing consistently one aspect or the other, but by incorporating in their statements both aspects, even within the same interview. One of these pre-service teachers discussed (at the beginning of the first semester) why she viewed teaching as a profession:

> Another aspect of it is that the teacher is supposed to care about the process and the result and become very concerned about it ... and spend a lot of energy on the process of teaching that you wouldn't necessarily spend ... in a regular or 8 to 5 job.... [as opposed to not being able to] do anything else ... and ... needing some money. (Dana, 15 September 1980)

Moments later, she emphasized the other aspect of the contradiction in explaining why she favored teacher organizations being involved in lobbying for pay:

> Because teachers, as compared to some of the other professions, are unable to set their own rates of pay ... A person [i.e., a teacher] with that much education and training and dedication is at the mercy of the taxpayer. (Dana, 15 September 1980)

At the end of the semester she reported on a dilemma she had experienced during her school visits: 'The one teacher who seemed the least professional [i.e., dedicated and concerned about students] in the classroom was the one who was most concerned about the future of the profession [for example] ... [and] ... was an active member of the HTA', a local affiliate of the National Education Association (Dana, 15 December 1980). She then commented, without any critical allusion to the relevance of gender relations, that:

> Well, I do know that there are other people who are professionals [nurses and certified professional secretaries] who share the similar situation with teachers in that they are not able to set their own pay or run their own office. (Dana, 15 December 1980)

And a few minutes later she indicated further the complexity of her perspective when she discussed her reactions to the meatcutters' strike:

> My first reaction: it's a strike, well, you know ... management is standing over them holding a whip. And then I saw how much they were making [without a college education] and I saw they were only working a 40-hour week, etc., etc.,

And I became very resentful of the fact that they were asking for 27 thousand and they were being offered something like 22 or 23.... I lost all my sympathy for them. OK, I do feel that people who have jobs on assembly lines or jobs that are tedious, jobs that are repetitious, jobs that don't require any use of their intellect [and] can be psychologically degrading and damaging to the person, ... that giving them a higher pay than certain other people, who might be called professionals, who are doing what they really want to.... But I didn't feel as though they weren't being paid well in the first place. (Dana, 15 December 1980)

The second respondent, who at different times emphasized different aspects of the contradiction connected with professionalism and remuneration, offered the following commentary at the beginning of the first semester in the program:

Another thing, I don't think that teachers have ever been, they haven't been paid like professionals. So, in this materialistic, Philistine society we're living in, you know, you're worth what your paycheck says you are (sarcastic laughter) ... Society has put a lot more emphasis on things with a lot less responsibility, as far as how they are given economic rewards.... Plumbers and construction workers make a lot more than teachers. (Carol, 22 September 1980)

She immediately countered, drawing on the other aspect of the contradiction:

But teaching, on the other hand, has always been something that, in a way, you do it because you love it and because you would do it anyway. And, I think, unless you can say that, then you probably shouldn't, you probably shouldn't be there. (Carol, 22 September 1980)

Then after a clarification probe, 'Does that, does that help make it a profession?', this pre-service teacher raised the issue of the feminization of teaching, one to which she returned in subsequent interviews:

I think so ... I think it was a really valid point that was brought out in the seminar that, uh, too often it's been thought of as a second career and a female-oriented career ... a second job, a second income [for a family] ... Maybe that's where we let ourselves in for getting less money and everything else. (Carol, 22 September 1980)

At the end of the first semester, after relating that her 'father was a union man' and that she opposed collective bargaining and strike action for teachers (at least), she responded to a question about the then recently publicized dispute between local meatcutters and four grocery store chains. Notice how she re-emphasized the aspect of professionalism that identifies remuneration level as the deserved reward of those performing important functions for society.

> I don't remember what they finally agreed on. But I thought, there's really something wrong when you turn the responsibility and the education of your children over to people making, you know, a third as much as a meatcutter. (Carol, 16 December 1980)

And, after commenting that this inconsistency of priorities 'says something about the power of unions', she explained why she feels uncomfortable with that sort of action for teachers — because for her teaching as a profession involves an ideal of selfless service. Note how she revisited the issue of the connection between gender relations and the remuneration of teachers, but this time with a personal illustration.

> The thing is, I have a, if I was totally responsible for my own support and going out, you know, I might have a completely different attitude. But I'm speaking from a comfortable position of knowing that this — I hate to say — but this is, you know, this will be a second income ... I know that's why we get, why teachers often get short-changed because they've been thought of as a female profession and it's a second income. But still, you know, I haven't gotten that individually involved in it because of that. I mean, I can, you know, sit back on my integrity and say, 'Well, no, I'm not going to do that'. (Carol, 16 December 1980)

At the end of the final semester in the program, this same respondent reported on one of several incidents she encountered during the program while attending dinner parties given by her husband's business associates. Notice, however, that this time when she raised the issues of gender and teaching, she focused more on exploitation of women than on how women voluntarily accept lower wages.

> I went to another one the other night. I had a guy who started pontificating about … those who do, do, and those who can't, teach … I have a wonderful talent for running into these idiots. And I gave him my speech about the reason that you maybe don't run across super teachers all the time is because, for one thing, we're not paid enough…
> Also, I like to bring up the point that one of the problems, I think, in teaching is that it's been traditionally a female occupation, and that nursing has had the same problems — because they pay women less and expect more from them and get by with it. (Carol, 26 May 1982)

Thus, as pre-service teachers grappled with one of the contradictions in the ideology of profession — that professionalism involves significant financial rewards for practitioners, but at the same time implies an ideal of service without concern for personal gain — they reached different resolutions on the issues. Some of them emphasized one or the other aspect of the contradiction, while others incorporated in their concepts both aspects, often in a compartmentalized manner that masked the relationship between the remuneration and service ideal aspects. It was also in the context of these discussions that social class and gender stratification emerged explicitly as issues, but not generally in ways that critiqued such unequal social relations.

Professionalism and Power

Thirteen of the fifteen interviewees raised the issue of power in their responses to questions about teaching, professionalism and teacher organizations. In five cases the focus was on the autonomy of the individual practitioner and in six cases collective or organizational power to obtain benefits or to influence policy was stressed; two respondents mentioned both aspects. Of the seven who emphasized individual autonomy in the workplace, one saw this as a negative feature of teaching as a profession, indicating a need for critical consumers with enough power to question what teachers say. Reflecting on some lessons he had taught during his second semester in the program, he stated:

> When I first started ... I taught something that was, that
> was a wrong viewpoint, whatever, you know. I didn't get
> the proper information to the students ... After I finished I
> looked back on it and it kind of made me see how vulnerable
> the students were, you know. They, uh, look up to teachers.
> They respect teachers. They, uh, expect teachers to teach
> them what's supposed to be right, but they'll accept it any-
> way. And that kind of puts them in a vulnerable position
> ... if we force it upon them anyway without them being
> able to have time to critically think about it, whether that's
> what they want to accept or question it. (James, 7 May 1981)

Another pre-service teacher seemed to raise the issue of power in a
similar way, explaining why she did not consider teaching to be a
profession: 'They never want to be accountable for what they do,
which is different from a professional' (Mary, 13 May 1981). However, moments later, she emphasized that power was a positive
attribute of professionalism, although one that so far had eluded
teachers: 'Then, once you're ... teaching in the system [the
administration] gives you no autonomy' (Mary, 13 May 1981). The
others who focused on autonomy shared the latter concern, sometimes faulting teachers:

> Teachers have not wanted to place themselves in a position
> where they're saying, 'what I'm teaching in the classroom is
> right, totally right', like the doctor. Generally a doctor does
> not come out with a diagnosis ... and then change his
> diagnosis (after discussion). But I think a teacher often does
> that. I think if teachers are expert in their field they
> shouldn't have to back down. Who should question them,
> but another expert? (Cathy, 10 December 1980)

and sometimes holding the system or society responsible:

> I consider teaching a profession, but it still isn't treated like
> one, because of all the controls.... [One of the reasons I'm
> dropping out of the program is because] administrators and
> parents are on [teachers'] backs and the state is looking over
> [teachers'] shoulders. It's hard enough to teach without this.
> (Jerry, 15 December 1980)

Of the eight pre-service teachers mentioning collective or
organizational power to influence policy and benefits-related issues
four clearly favored such action for teachers as professionals. For

example, one respondent reported at the end of his second semester in the program on his views on the 'strike' by TAs in the University:

> I think the closest I've come to thinking about teacher organizations is the TA's organizing. I don't know, I think maybe for those purposes it would be a good idea to organize. There's strength in numbers, and for some things it's the only way you will get what you need, in this case, pay. (Roberto, 4 May 1981)

And after completing student teaching, he indicated his plans for joining a teacher organization:

> I plan to be very politically involved in teaching and promoting teacher rights and teacher benefits and that kind of thing, but I don't know how or when or where or which organizations yet.... I want to wait until I start teaching (Roberto, 28 May 1982)

Another interviewee echoed these sentiments at the beginning of the program:

> Probably the NEA, but I haven't done enough research ... But I do know that I want to belong to an organization that lobbies for teachers. I feel that organizations, groups of people, have more effect on the system ... for change, for improvement if it's needed. (Dana, 15 September 1980)

And although she wavered between joining an NEA or AFT affiliate, her positive appraisal of collective action for teachers as professionals remained in place as she progressed through the program. After the first semester, in discussing a teacher collective bargaining bill which had recently been introduced in the State Legislature, she offered:

> I think it's a good idea ... It appears to be the only way teachers can assert their rights, assert their own demands for salary increases or setting their own salaries and their own standards ... You need some kind of consensus somewhere in the system and allowing the school board or the administration to set standards that are used in the classroom ... without giving teachers any input into the system ... doesn't seem to be working ... And teachers, to be able to feel as though they are teachers and they are professionals,

they need to be able to assert themselves as individuals and as teachers ... to have some input into setting the salary ... or gaining input into the way the system is administered and curriculum, etc. (Dana, 16 January 1981)

And after three semesters employed as a teacher and as a member of an AFT local, although anticipating a switch to an NEA local, she made similar remarks in discussing the *Nation at Risk* report:[38]

I think teachers should get more money now. Um, and I think some teacher organizations on a national level should take, should take some kind of control and have more input on a nationwide level like the AMA does for doctors ... to protect teachers, to help set guidelines for competent teachers, to help set curriculum for teacher education ... I believe in teacher testing. Teachers, however, should be able to make up the tests. (Dana, 27 May 1983)

Four other pre-service teachers expressed some ambivalence about the exercise of power by teachers as professionals. For instance, in discussing her reactions to the dispute between the Professional Air Controllers and the Reagan Administration one of these pre-service teachers noted:

I have mixed feelings. On one hand, I can see, well, you know, other people, like other unions, have the right to strike. I mean, you know, that don't threaten, you know, like something like a policeman or fireman would do. Maybe ... [it would] pose a threatening situation. But then I look and see, you know, why is it some groups should have the right to strike and others not? ... [And in terms of teachers?] Uh, that's about the same thing to me. Um, I mean, it seems like, you know, ... why should others have the right? But then I don't know. Teachers, it's difficult for me to say because, I mean, something's missing out then. The students are hurting and it's a touchy subject there again. (Jane, 27 May 1981)

Another of these respondents — who reported (at different phases of the program) that her father was an active union member, that she had friends who were teachers and friends who were on the governing board of a community college where unions had recently been banned from meeting on the campus, and that she 'for the most part' supported the TAs who went out on 'strike' at the

University, expressed her ambivalence about exercising power in this manner:

> Well, I think the time has come for teachers in America, or anywhere ... to get together and make ourselves known. Um, if you're going to be able to have your own way with the rest of society, as far as, not only how much money you're going to get, but in how much, you know, how much input you have in the rest of society ... The idea of being able to be a member of a larger body which would have your concerns [as its primary focus. But] ... as far as going all the way, gung-ho, and becoming a real, you know, adult, organized union, I don't know how I feel about that ... The striking ... that bothers me. Uh, before I decided to go into teaching, right out of high school I decided I wanted to be a nurse. And the same thing bothered me then. You know, is it really ethical to walk out of a hospital full of sick people? ... People can live without their goods being trucked to them ... The ethical part of it bothers me ... I haven't resolved it. (Carol, 22 September 1980)

Her ambivalence was articulated at other times as well. For example, at the end of her first semester in the program she commented:

> I was approached in the teachers' lounge ... [by] one of the union members there ... He had a thing for me to read about what happens to teachers their first year out.... There's a lot of legitimate complaints ... [T]he union is trying to do something about that. And, you know, I think he had a good point, but I can't see myself joining a union ... The strikes still bother me ... I was just a real liberal in the sixties and maybe I'm doing like everybody else and getting more conservative as I get older. And I think that, you know, a lot of economic problems we have are caused by unions ... [However,] I know there's a real power struggle going on, you know ... especially with the economic situation being the way it is. But it's just something I haven't resolved yet ... I think that [teachers] can have a voice, but I don't think it has to be through collective bargaining. (Carol, 16 December 1980)

The power element of professionalism was drawn upon in different ways by the pre-service teachers interviewed. For some it provided the foundation for claims to individual practitioner autonomy, although one respondent commented on the negative implications of such power by professionals. Other pre-service teachers' conceptions evinced another contradiction within the ideology of professionalism — that the use of collective power is a central element of professionalism, while engaging in collective action is 'unprofessional'.

Professionalism as Individual Attitudes and Behavior

Thirteen of fifteen interviewees referred to individual attitudes or behavior of practitioners in their discussion of teaching and professionalism. Here the concern was not with occupational group attributes — for example, prerequisite level of formal education, financial rewards, or power — but with individual level attributes. For instance, one pre-service teacher stated:

> Oh, well, I haven't really thought of it as 'ok, is this a profession?', but I think subconsciously I've been thinking, 'are these people professional? . . . Are they dressing professionally, are they behaving professionally'? (Roberto, 4 May 1981)

The one respondent who did not view teaching to be a profession explained her view in part because 'teachers don't act like professionals . . . they allow colleagues to use improper grammar, an incomplete sentence' (Mary, 24 January 1983). Others, who expressed their belief that teaching is a profession, often qualified this point with reference to some individual teachers' lack of professionalism.

> You know, as far as the education you need to get there . . . I'm sure I would consider it a profession. But as far as other factors like . . . attitude, I don't think so. Because teachers themselves don't act professional, you know, and I don't even think they consider themselves professionals. (Sonia, 9 December 1980)

For many of those interviewed the individualistic notion of a professional is highlighted as the path to professionalization of teaching.[39] As one respondent stated: 'Yes, it is a profession . . . because, I think, I define a profession as something that one devotes time and energy to, and enjoys' (Cindy, 14 May 1981). Unlike the issue of education prerequisites, remuneration and power, about which many pre-service teachers believe they can do little *as individuals*, exhibiting proper attitudes, dress and behavior are perceived to be within the realm of their control. It is an aspect of professionalism which, at least in the case of their individual practice, they can strive to achieve. This point was articulated concisely by the following pre-service teacher:

> I personally think teaching is a profession. I don't think it is seen as a profession by the general public or by many people who are in it. I guess my approach is that I as a teacher . . . think of myself as a professional because I was taking responsibility for what was going on . . . my own attitude makes it a profession . . . I may have restrictions by government agencies [and a relatively low salary] but it's still my responsibility. (Nancy, 5 May 1981)

Interestingly, this emphasis on an individualistic approach was not only provided by those pre-service teachers who were uncomfortable with collective action or who perceived striking to be 'unprofessional' (Mary, 13 May 1981). For example, one of the pre-service teachers, who frequently expressed a collectivist and activist position discussed a contradiction she encountered in her school observations during the first semester of the program:

> I'm not really sure. I don't have any specific criteria for identifying a professional versus a non-professional right now. I can look at behavior and say, 'That's professional behavior and that isn't.' But, uh, for example, the one teacher who seemed least professional in the classroom was the one who was most concerned about the future [status, pay, power] of the profession. And I found that a contradiction, very strange. . . . His attitude towards the students doesn't [seem professional]. . . . Well, I think . . . a teacher's personality, or at least the way they present themselves, is more important than in any other profession, both physically and their personality, their physical appearance and various things like that. (Dana, 15 December 1980)

In their discourse about teaching and professionalism, thus, the pre-service teachers interviewed not only focused on structural features: education, remuneration and power; they also drew upon individual attributes — teachers or other occupational incumbents were 'professionals' if they acted, dressed, and talked 'professionally'. In the next section, I will examine the implications of these conceptions of professionalism — their ideological functions vis-a-vis contradictions contained in capitalist and patriarchal societies.

Implications of the Ideology of Professionalism for Contradictions in Class and Gender Relations

We have seen that these pre-service teachers' conceptions of professionalism were relatively resilient as they encountered messages about professionalism in the formal and hidden curriculum.[40] The one issue that challenged the previously constructed schema involved the public's critique or questioning of the degree of professionalization of teachers. For the most part, the messages encountered were in harmony with the views they brought to the program. Thus, a passive model of socialization, in which pre-service teachers 'absorb' like sponges the messages of the program, is not appropriate, at least in this case.[41]

For some prospective teachers the program messages did provide 'academic' or 'scientific' reinforcement for their conceptions. However, because of the contradictions within the ideology of professionalism and, therefore, within the program messages and interviewees' conceptions, pre-service teachers took on an active, interpretive stance toward the messages encountered; they filtered out or in different aspects of the contradictions in ways that usually sustained the equilibrium of the conception they brought in with them. Pre-service teachers who conceived of professionalism as emphasizing high financial rewards and those who stressed the ideal of selfless service found corresponding (but also contradicting) messages. The same can be said of pre-service teachers whose conceptions of professionalism stressed the exercise of power, individually or collectively, in contrast with those who viewed the exercise of power as 'unprofessional'.

It is nevertheless important to note that the conceptions of professionalism are not just random aggregations of ideas. They are dialectically related to — both constituted by and constitutive of — a broader, less ephemeral ideology of professionalism,[42] which has been constructed during different political economic periods, and which may be seen to both legitimate and challenge contemporary class and gender relations.

As Larson discusses the work ethic and service ideal elements of the ideology have their roots in the pre-capitalist period; the notion of autonomous, educated or credentialed individual practitioners providing services in a market situation have their origin in the period of liberal, competitive capitalism; and during the more contemporary period of corporate or monopoly capitalism the emphasis has been on the organization as the source of legitimate power and on the 'thoroughly modern' concept of expertise to reinforce the exercise of such power. Moreover, the 'great transformation', during which the modern model and ideology of professionalism emerged:

> changed the structure and character of European societies and their overseas offshoots. This transformation was dominated by the reorganization of the economy and society around the market ... The constitution of professional markets which began in the nineteenth century inaugurated a new form of structured inequalities ... the backbone of which is the occupational hierarchy, that is, a differential system of competences and rewards; the central principle of legitimacy is founded on the achievement of socially recognized expertise, or more simply, on a system of education and credentialing.[43]

Pre-service teachers deriving their conceptions from, and at the same time reproducing, the ideology of professionalism can be seen to mask/mediate or expose/challenge fundamental contradictions in (at least) capitalist political economies, for example, that although production is a social activity, the ownership and control of the means of production is privately concentrated. At the same time, their conceptions of professionalism may serve as a source to perpetuate and legitimate or critique and challenge unequal gender relations (and the attendant contradictions) at the school level, for example, that women teach and men manage, but also in society more generally.

The discussion below presents some of the implications of aspects of the ideology of professionalism, first, for class relations and then for gender relations. The four themes that were derived from the analysis of the interview data — education, remuneration/service ideal, power, and individual attitude/behavior — will serve as an organizing frame for the discussion of each form of relations.

Class Relations

Capitalist political economies not only contain the contradiction (as noted above) that although production is a social activity, the ownership and control of the means of production is privately concentrated. They also are characterized by the contradiction that production takes place for profit accumulation by capitalists rather than to satisfy the needs of workers, and that, because of the profit motive to reduce labor costs and increase productivity, many workers experience deskilling/proletarianization and thus become less expensive workers and more easily replaced by other humans or machines, while a few workers undergo reskilling/professionalization as they can be seen to enhance the design or control of the work process.[44] We will now discuss the potential relationships between these contradictions and the ideology of professionalism.

The education theme

Treating professions as synonymous with (highly) educated or schooled workers may help to mediate the social production/private ownership and the profit/worker needs contradictions by lending credibility to the meritocractic notions of the educational system and occupational structure.[45] And as Bledstein observes in his important work on higher education in the United States, *The Culture of Professionalism*:

> Far more than any other types of society, democratic ones require pervasive symbols of authority, symbols the majority of people could reliably believe just and warranted. It became the function of schools in America to legitimize the authority of the middle classes [and elites] by appealing to the universality and objectivity of 'science'.[46]

The point is that if education systems and the occupational structure are meritocratic, then inequalities in control/ownership of the means of production and the profit rewards for few in contrast with workers' needs being left unmet are rendered unproblematic — the 'natural' result of 'open' competition in which the best reap the rewards, while others garner less, but had their 'fair' chance.

It should be remembered that some of the pre-service teachers interviewed did not seem to buy fully into the status, wealth and power distinctions, nor did they seem completely comfortable in justifying such stratification based on inequalities in educational attainment. For them either the ideal of service or the associated individual attitudes and behavior is what made a person a 'professional'. Similar to discourse emanating from the radical movements in the professions,[47] these respondents have begun to develop 'critiques ... directed ... at the ways in which professions articulate and reinforce the class structure'.[48]

The unproblematic fusion of education and occupation evidenced in most pre-service teachers' conceptions of professionalism also may operate to mediate the deskilling/reskilling contradiction. Larson[49] argues that professionalization strategies are experienced as 'effective defenses' against deskilling and other aspects of proletarianization. This occurs because conceiving of one's self as an 'educated worker' sometimes restricts the opportunity to view one's situation as similar to the working class.[50] This perception may be reinforced by the reality that many educated workers (as historically was the case with craft workers) initially only experience ideological proletarianization — the loss of control over decisions of what to do — and only later encounter a press toward technical proletarianization — deskilling.[51] Also, as pre-service teachers observe teachers being deskilled or encounter personally the process themselves, they can rationalize this in terms of the lower education prerequisites of their 'semi-profession'. As some interviewees commented, more education for teachers would justify greater power and financial rewards for them. In addition, increases in education would serve as a partial explanation of why and how some educators will be reskilled.

The remuneration/service ideal theme

The contradictory aspects within the ideology of professionalism — remuneration and an ideal of service as the driving force of professions — were evidenced in the prospective teachers interviewed. Emphasizing the remuneration aspect can help to mediate the contradictions in the economy (outlined above). Inequalities in wealth, and thus private ownership of the means of production and private accumulation of profit, can be rendered unproblematic as 'true' professionals and other significant groups are seen to deserve more because of their rare skill or important and difficult function. At the same time, deskilling may become less visible or of less concern as attention is focused on reskilling of some workers, who are to be financially rewarded.

However, the remuneration aspect of the contradiction within the ideology of professionalism may also serve to highlight contradictions within the economy, and thus perhaps undermine the legitimacy of the extant political economy. One might be moved to question why, if wealth is the result of deserved remuneration, are some social groups wealthy without being highly educated, highly skilled, or performing essential tasks for society? Why are the means of production privately owned and controlled and oriented to creating profits for non-workers, rather than those who labor and deserve to be rewarded? Why are many workers being deskilled and receiving less remuneration; why are fewer workers being reskilled with added financial rewards?

The same can be argued for the service ideal aspect; it can both mediate and highlight contradictions within the economy. On one hand, the ideal of service and the attendant eschewing of financial rewards can operate to deflect concerns of exploitation; dedication to work regardless of personal benefit is an unproblematic given and, thus, who accumulates more money is of peripheral concern. The deskilling/reskilling contradiction is also mediated in that the issue is performing the assigned task as well as possible, not how much skill is involved or how much one is paid for doing the work.

On the other hand, if one stresses an ideal of service one might question why the system is characterized by private ownership and control of the means for performing the various productive and other services? Why are the needs of workers, both those directly and those indirectly involved in the service work, subordinated to the concerns of owners to acquire profit? Where is the service ideal among capitalists? In terms of the deskilling/reskilling contradiction, one might be tempted to ask how are people better served by the process of deskilling which fragments the work process and makes workers cheaper to hire?

The power theme

The element of exercising power being seen as either good/professional or bad/unprofessional could also mediate or highlight contradictions in the political economy. Conceiving that professionals should and deserve (because of their expertise) to be autonomous or authoritative in their work may buttress the domination of workers, including many semi- and 'true' professionals, by political and economic elites.[52] In relation to economic elites, for instance, Larson explains that:

> historically, the core units of monopoly capital show strong
> affinities with experts, on whom their management depends,
> and with professionalism, which tends to be substituted
> for bureaucratic control in multidivisional structures. . . .
> Expertise is implicitly proposed as a legitimation for the
> hierarchical structure of authority of the modern organiza-
> tion; professionalism, in turn, functions as an internalized
> mechanism for the control of the subordinate expert.[53]

Following from this, a positive view of professionalism and power
might even help to mediate the deskilling/reskilling contradiction, in
that decisions about what jobs and which people to reskill or
deskill would be seen to be made by superordinate experts.

Despite the symbiotic relationship between professionalism and
organizational control noted above, for some people, favoring professionals exercising power, individually or collectively, may expose
and facilitate critique of the contradictions in the political economy.
One might be stimulated to ask: Why should non-professionals own
and control the means of production? Why should profit be the
dominating motive of the economy when professionals ought to
determine what the needs of the client are and how those needs are
met?[54] Why are some forms of work being deskilled and thus
reducing the need for experts?

A position opposing professionals' exercise of power, particularly of the collective variety, can also mediate contradictions
within the political economy. If the use of power is conceived to be
'unprofessional', then that potentially leaves the domination by
others, including owners, managers and state elites, unchallenged.
Not only would 'professionals' avoid challenging the status quo
either as 'professional' groups or in concert with other workers/
citizens, but the articulation of this stance would undermine the
legitimacy of other workers'/citizens' exercise of power to transform
existing structural features of society. It may also be, however, that
denigrating the use of power may provide a basis for critiquing the
concentration among a relatively small elite group of control and
ownership of the means of production, benefits from productive
activity, and decisions about reskilling/deskilling. This seems less
likely, though, because elites' exercise of power is less overt, relying
on the existing structures to realize it, and because given the smaller
number of elites (compared to workers/masses) their use of power
might be viewed as individualist rather than collectivist.

The individual attitude/behavior theme

This theme, which is partially linked to the service ideal aspect of another theme, appears to offer a very conservative position. By deflecting or ignoring the social, political and economic structural levels, and by focusing attention on how people should dress, talk, carry out with devotion the tasks assigned as well as what attitudes they should exhibit, this element of the conceptions and ideology of professionalism seem to render as unproblematic, and thus mediate the social production/private ownership and control, profit/worker needs, and deskilling/reskilling contradictions. In a sense, from this vantage point one need not worry about who owns and controls the means of production (or the state apparatus), whether economic activity is governed primarily by a profit motive or by a desire to satisfy human needs, or whether many workers are deskilled while some are reskilled. The concern instead is directed toward oneself and one's colleagues acting in a 'professional' manner and possessing attitudes which are consonant with professionalism. We should note, nevertheless, that given the contradictions within conceptions and the ideology of professionalism, it is not a foregone conclusion whether such professional attitudes and behavior will always buttress existing political economic relations.

Gender Relations

When focusing on patriarchal structures in education, we note the contradiction that although education is predominantly a 'feminine' pursuit — school teachers, especially at the secondary level, are predominantly women — the vast majority of those who control the means and who manage the process of educational production (school board members and educational administrators, respectively) are predominantly men. This contradiction is paralleled in society, in that although the female of the species constitute a numerical majority, political and economic power is concentrated in the hands of relatively few (elite) males. We should also consider the contradiction imbedded in the role of teacher, the 'requirement' of emotional detachment and the 'requirement' of emotional engagement in relation to students as well as their parents. We will examine the potential relationships between these contradictions and the ideology of professionalism.

The education theme

The meritocratic notion that professionals are those workers who have achieved success and attained high levels of education would seem to mediate the female teacher/male manager contradiction in that, at least in the case of educational administrators, those formally in charge of the day-to-day operations of educational institutions normally have additional education — credentials and certificates — than do classroom teachers. From this perspective, educational administrators might be viewed unproblematically as the more able, more highly educated members of the educational profession, who just happen to mostly be men. The fact that many teachers have as much or more formal education as required for entry into administration, however, may render problematic the power and higher earnings of male administrators. A similar point could be made for school board members, to the extent that they have not acquired as high a level of formal educational credentials as teachers.

With respect to gender differences in power, status, and income in society, the education theme of professionalism provides a basis for critique and challenge. One might be moved to question, for example, why is it that even when women have the same level of education (and similar length of job experience) as men, women tend to hold lower status, less powerful jobs and earn less income?[55]

In relation to the detached authority versus emotionally engaged contradiction or dilemma of the teacher's role, the education theme seems to provide a basis for emotional detachment from students and their parents, especially those of the working class who have attained fewer years of formal schooling than teachers or other 'professionals' normally do. The implicit message of this aspect of the ideology of professionalism is that those with less education are less meritorious, that is, less able or motivated, and thus less deserving of the power, wealth and status due to professionals. Such legitimating reinforcement for stratifying people would seemingly either orient teachers to view themselves as superior to some clients (and inferior to others) and/or for their clients to perceive the invidious distinctions and thus reduce the possibility for an emotionally engaged relationship to develop.

The remuneration/service ideal theme

As discussed above some of the pre-service teachers interviewed, both male and female, raised the issue of the relationship between the (semi-) professional status of teaching and the predominance of women in the field — an issue which was reinforced in one of the assigned readings[56] during the first semester of the program. The focus was primarily within the remuneration theme. Drawing on the remuneration issues associated with professionalism, they were able to both argue the legitimacy and offer an emergent critique of the fact that occupations such as teaching, which have a high proportion of women, have lower wages. It seems to depend on whether one assumes that women coming into the field somehow caused the status and remuneration to decline, or as Kelsall and Kelsall emphasize, that 'if this is true, it is a function of the status accorded to women in a given society, not simply to the presence of women'.[57]

The service ideal aspect of this theme also can mediate or highlight contradictions in gender relations. Stressing the ideal of service rather than financial rewards can deflect attention away from, and thus mediate, the contradiction that women workers are paid less. Equally, though, the ideal of service may prompt one to question whether educational administrators, school board members, or other predominantly male occupational groups are sufficiently motivated by a desire to serve the community, clients, etc., as opposed to self-interest or financial issues. Such questioning may lead to queries about the legitimacy superordinate status of such male dominated groups.

In connection with the detached authority versus emotionally engaged dilemma of the teacher's role, the remuneration aspect of the remuneration/service ideal theme appears to encourage an orientation of emotional detachment. Not only is one pursuing a career for economic rewards rather than committed service, one would also be buying into an ideology which operates to distance one from clients, especially of the working class, who are implicitly labelled as not deserving as large financial rewards. The service ideal aspect, in contrast, could reinforce an orientation of emotional engagement or one of emotional detachment, depending on whether the teacher viewed socializing/motivating or evaluator/controller, respectively, as the major aspect of the role in which she or he were serving.

The power theme

To the extent that educational administrators were viewed as consummate professionals, those approving of professionals exercising power might help to mediate the women teach/men manage contradiction, in that the most expert group is seen to be in control. It is here where an examination of the nexus of bureaucracy, professionalism and patriarchy may be helpful. Recall first Larson's[58] claim (discussed earlier) about the symbiotic relationship between professionalism and bureaucratic control.[59] Given the pre-dominance, especially in secondary schools, of male school administrators and female teachers, Larson's observation of how 'professionalism' can be used to subordinate 'professional workers' takes on a more complex meaning:

> Insofar as managers are recruited from the ranks of professional workers ... or if they themselves claim some kind of professional expertise, they are not likely to deny the ideology of professionalism, from which they too can derive legitimation.[60]

This domination of women workers may also be reinforced by drawing on ideological notions, such as that suggested by Simpson and Simpson, 'that women's personality characteristics require bureaucratic organizational control'.[61]

By way of contrast, people who concur with Kanter that 'many so-called sex difference findings about behavior in organizations can be more satisfactorily explained by differences in opportunities, numerical representation, and access to power that often coincide with sex,'[62] and/or those who question whether educational administrators, let alone 'lay' school board members, are professional educators, may tend to expose and challenge this women teach/men manage contradiction. They could ask, why the 'true' professionals, the classroom teachers, are not the ones having the most to say about the content, structure and processes of schooling?

A position opposing professionals' exercise of power, especially of the collective variety, may also mediate contradictions in patriarchal structures. If the use of power is conceived to be 'unprofessional', then that leaves unchallenged the extant gender (and other) relations of domination and subordination, both in schools and society.

The contradiction within teaching — detached authority vs. emotional engagement — is also related to the power theme in the ideology of professionalism. Favoring or opposing the use of power by 'professionals', thus, not only affects perceptions of relations with administrators and school board members; it also affects relations with clients: students and parents. Rather than encouraging people to seek a synthetic resolution in the gender-related contradictory role of teacher, the power theme in the ideology of professionalism may either lead teachers to, respectively, emphasize or de-emphasize the detached, authority aspect depending on whether they view the exercise of power as professional or not.

The individual attitude/behavior theme

As in the case of class relations, this theme in the ideology of professionalism could easily render unproblematic the structural inequalities between men and women in schools and society. With the primary concern about how individuals should dress, talk, carry out their assigned tasks, attention is deflected away from the larger issues of the unequal distribution of wealth and power. That in schools men manage and women teach or that in society men exercise more economic and political power than women is not· a concern; the issue in focus becomes do they do it well, with devotion and in concert with other appropriate attitudes and behaviors.

In relation to the detached authority/emotional engagement contradiction of the teaching role, this theme seems to facilitate people's emphasizing either or both of the aspects of the contradictions. 'Proper' dress and speech may tend to create an emotional distance between teachers and students and parents, particularly those of the working class. But 'proper' attitudes and devotion to work may be translated into greater or lesser emotional attachment to students or parents, depending on what aspect(s) of this dilemma of the teacher's role one stresses.

Conclusions

It has been claimed that in the United States, 'all intelligent modern persons organize their behavior, both public and private, according to 'the culture of professionalism'.[63] While this may be overstated, there is no question that professionalism as an ideology is important to consider at least in English speaking countries.[64] Based on our analysis and discussion here, however, it should be clear that the ideology of professionalism, which is drawn upon and reproduced by people, including pre-service teachers, does not *a priori* have either in mediating or a critical undermining role in relation to the extant unequal class or gender relations.

On the one hand, we identified aspects of the ideology that

appear to provide a foundation of legitimacy for unequal wealth and power between social classes and between gender groups. Similarly, we noted how certain ways in which the ideology is drawn upon in pre-service teachers' commonsense conceptions help to mask and mediate contradictions in both capitalist and patriarchal structures. On the other hand, we described aspects of the ideology of professionalism that could and were drawn upon to raise critical questions if not (as yet) to engender critical praxis. These aspects of the ideology helped illuminate contradictions in capitalist and patriarchal structures, pointing not only to problems, but also to places in which interventions might be attempted.

Some might argue that this type of conclusion — 'on the one hand' and 'on the other hand' — renders the study of the ideology of professionalism as worthless. If the ideology has no consistent impact on class and gender relations, why spend the time theorizing and investigating its implications? In response to this we should first state that the absence of predictability of the relationship between the ideology of professionalism and structural features of society is only a problem if one assumes a non-dialectical account of society, where ideologies and social relations are always in perfect 'correspondence' with each other. Second, the fact that there are contradictory aspects of the ideology of professionalism makes it more worthy of study, as a way to encourage reflection about other contradictions in society. Such contradictions are not only a source of consciousness raising; they also identify regions of social relations toward which progressive transformative action can be directed.

Finally, the contradictory nature of the ideology of professionalism means that those who subscribe to it as a rallying call run the risk of their efforts having unanticipated or opposite consequences.[65] This, of course, can be said of both those who use the ideology to mobilize individual and collective action to challenge unequal class and gender relations, but also those who employ the ideology to keep the proletariat (and the 'professional') in her or his place and/or to subordinate women in paid or unpaid work places. However, given the other ideological and structural resources available to the dominant groups, we should be very cautious even in our critical use of this ideology. The ideology of professionalism may in the immediate struggle help the cause, although in relation to other people's concurrent struggles and in one's own future struggles the one 'success' may translate into a major victory for those who would seek to benefit from the reproduction of unequal class and gender relations.

Notes

1. See for example, Howsam, R., Corrigan, D., Denmark, G., and
   Nash, R. (Eds) (1976) *Education a Profession*, Washington, D.C.,
   American Association of Colleges for Teacher Education; Langford,
   G. (1978) *Teaching as a Profession*, Manchester, University of Manchester Press; Legatt, T. (1970) 'Teaching as a profession', in
   Jackson, J. (Ed.) *Professions and Professionalization* Cambridge, Cambridge University Press, pp. 153–77; Lieberman, M. (1956) *Education
   as a Profession*, Englewood Cliffs, N.J., Prentice-Hall; Lieberman, M.
   (1960) *The Future of Public Education*, Chicago, University of Chicago
   Press; Lortie, D. (1964) 'The balance of control and autonomy in
   elementary school teaching', in Etzioni, A. (Ed.) *The Semi-Professions
   and Their Organization*, New York, The Free Press, pp. 1–53;
   Lortie, D. (1975) *School Teacher: A Sociological Analysis*, Chicago,
   University of Chicago Press; Ruhela, S. (Ed.) (1970) *Sociology of the
   Teaching Profession in India*, New Delhi, National Council of Educational Research and Training; Seymour, F. (1966) 'Occupational
   images and norms: Teaching', in Vollmer, H. and Mills, D. (Eds)
   Professionalization, Englewood Cliffs, N.J. Prentice-Hall, pp. 126–9.
2. See, for example, Collins, R. (1979) *The Credential Society: A
   Historical Sociology of Education*, New York, Academic Press;
   Ginsburg, M., Meyenn, R. and Miller, M. (1980) 'Teachers' concep-
   tions of professionalism and trades unionism: An ideological analysis',
   in Woods, P. (Ed.), *Teacher Strategies*, London, Croom Helm,
   pp. 178–212; Johnson, T. (1972) *Professions and Power*, London,
   Macmillan; Millerson, G. (1964) *The Qualifying Associations: A
   Study in Professionalization*, London, Routledge and Kegan Paul;
   Ogza, J. and Lawn, M. (1981) *Teachers, Professionalism and Class: A
   Study of Organized Teachers*, London, Falmer Press; Roth, J. (1974)
   'Professionalism: The sociologist's decoy', *Sociology of Work and
   Occupations*, 1, pp. 6–23.
3. The ideological nature of professionalism has been discussed by
   various writers. See, for example, Dingwall, R. (1976) 'Accomplish-
   ing profession', *Sociological Review*, 24, pp. 331–49; Finn, D., Grant,
   N. and Johnson, R. (1977) 'Social democracy, education and the
   crisis', in Centre for Contemporary Cultural Studies, (Ed.) *On
   Ideology*, London, Hutchinson, pp. 144–85; Friedson, E. (1970)
   Profession of Medicine, New York, Dodd Mead; Ginsburg, M.,
   Meyenn, R., Miller, H., Khanna, I. and Spatig, L. (1980) 'Teachers'
   conceptions of professionalism: A comparison of contexts in England
   and the United States', revised version of paper presented at the annual
   meeting of the Comparative and International Education Society, Van-
   couver, 19–23 March; Hughes, E. (1966) 'The social significance of
   professionalization', in Vollmer, H. and Mills, D. (Eds.) *op cit*, pp.

62–70; LARSON, M. (1977) *The Rise of Professionalism: A Sociological Analysis*, Berkeley, CA, University of California Press. Professionalism has been referred to by George Bernard Shaw as 'a conspiracy against the laity' and SEYMOUR, F. (1966) *op cit.*, describes it as 'a state of mind, not a reality'. As an ideology, professionalism both distorts or only partially reflects social reality and serves to mobilize or immobilize individual and collective action in ways that support the interests of certain groups in society. More specifically, LARSON, M. (1977) *op cit.*, p. 156 concludes, based on her historical analysis of 'the rise of professionalism' in England and the United States, that professionalism constitutes 'an important contribution to the ideological denial of structured inequalities'. This masking of the structural basis of inequalities in wealth and power is achieved by representing the school system and the political economy as meritocratic (see also, BARLOW, A. (1980) 'Review of M. Larson's *The Rise of Professionalism: A Sociological Analysis*', *Harvard Educational Review*, 50, 3, pp. 427–32) and by characterizing professionals as independent, neutral experts who serve the interests of all people — males and females, capitalists and proletarians, whites and people of color — through their roles as advisors to policy-makers (see POPKEWITZ, T. (1984) 'Social science and social amelioration: The development of the American academic expert', in *Paradigm and Ideology in Educational Research: The Social Functions of the Intellectual*, Lewes, Falmer Press, pp. 107–27). Nevertheless, we should also note, 'even if the idea of professionalism does have some role in maintaining the social system, this does not ... preclude its having some subversive role as well' SCHUDSON, M. (1980) 'A discussion of Margali Sarfatti Larson's *The Rise of Professionalism: A Sociological Analysis*,' *Theory and Society*, 9, 1, p. 227.

4. This conception of ideology is consonant with that of Jameson, who argues that a marxian theory of ideology is not 'one of false consciousness, but rather one of structural limitation and ideological closure' JAMESON, F. (1981) *The Political Unconscious*, Ithaca, N Y., Cornell University Press, p. 52. Jameson illustrates his point by referring to a passage from Marx concerned with petty-bourgeois intellectuals, who 'in their own minds ... cannot get beyond the limits' of the petty-bourgeoisie class location and thus are 'driven theoretically to the same problems and solutions to which material interest and social position drive' the petit-bourgeoisie (MARX, K. (1963) *The Eighteenth Brumaire of Louis Bonaparte*, New York, International Publishers, pp. 50–1).

5. See also, APPLE, M. (1979) *Ideology and Curriculum*, Boston, Routledge and Kegan Paul; BOURDIEU, P. and PASSERON, J.C. (1977) *Reproduction in Education, Society and Culture*, Beverly Hills, Sage; BOWLES, S. and GINTIS, H. (1976) *Schooling in Capitalist America*, Boston, Routledge and Kegan Paul; GINSBURG, M. and ARIAS-

GODINEZ, B. (1984) 'Non-formal education and social reproduction/transformation: Educational radio in Mexico', *Comparative Education Review*, 28, 1, pp. 16–27; GINSBURG, M. and GILES, J. (1984) 'Sponsored and contest modes of social reproduction in selective community college programs', *Research in Higher Education*, 21, 3, pp. 281–300; GINSBURG, M. and NEWMAN, K. (1985) 'Social inequalities, schooling and teacher education', *Journal of Teacher Education*, 36, 2, March/April, pp. 49–54; SHARP, R. and GREEN, A. (1975) *Education and Social Control: A Study in Progressive Primary Education*, London, Routledge and Kegan Paul; YOUNG, M. (1971) *Knowledge and Control*, London, Collier-Macmillan.

6. See also, ANYON, J. (1981) 'Social class and school knowledge', *Curriculum Inquiry*, 11, 1, pp. 3–42; ANYON, J. (1983) 'Interactions of gender and class', in WALKER, S. and BARTON, L. (Eds), *Gender, Class and Education*, Lewes, Falmer Press, pp. 19–38; APPLE, M. (1982a) *Education and Power*, Boston, Routledge and Kegan Paul; APPLE, M. (1982b) 'Reproduction and contradiction in education: An introduction', in *Cultural and Economic Reproduction in Education*, Boston, Routledge and Kegan Paul, pp. 1–23; EVERHART, R. (1983) 'Classroom management, student opposition, and the labor process', in APPLE, M. and WEIS, L. (Eds) *Ideology and Practice in Schooling*, Philadelphia, Temple University Press, pp. 169–92; GRACE, G. (1978) *Teachers, Ideology and Control*, London, Routledge and Kegan Paul; KARABEL, J. and HALSEY, A. (1977) 'Educational research: A review and interpretation', in *Power and Ideology in Education*, New York, Oxford University Press, pp. 1–86; MALMSTAD, B., GINSBURG, M. and CROFT, J. (1983) 'The social construction of reading lessons: Resistance and social reproduction', *Journal of Education*, 165, 4, pp. 359–74; WEIS, L. (1983) 'Schooling and cultural production: A comparison of black and white lived culture', in APPLE, M. and WEIS, W. (Eds) *op cit.*; pp. 235–61; WEIS L. (1985) *Between Two Worlds*, Boston, Routledge and Kegan Paul; WILLIS, P. (1977) *Learning to Labour*, Farnborough, Saxon House; WILLIS, P. (1981) 'Cultural production is different from cultural reproduction is different from social reproduction is different from reproduction', *Interchange*, 12, 2–3, pp. 48–67.

7. GIDDENS, A. (1979) *Central Problems in Social Theory: Action Structure and Contradiction in Social Analysis*, Berkeley, University of California Press, p. 30.

8. *Ibid*, p. 114.

9. See APPLE, M. 'Reproduction and contradiction in education', but also GINTIS, H. and BOWLES, S. (1980) 'Contradiction and reproduction in educational theory', in BARTON, L., MEIGHAN, R. and WALKER, S. (Eds) *Schooling, Ideology and the Curriculum* Lewes, Falmer Press, pp. 51–65.

10. But see ANYON, J. 'Social class and school knowledge'; BERNSTEIN, B. (1975) 'Aspects of the relation between education and production', in *Class, Codes and Control*, Vol. 3, *Towards a Theory of Educational Transmissions*, London, Routledge and Kegan Paul, pp. 174–200; CARNOY, M. (1982) 'Education, economy and the state', in APPLE, M. (Ed.) *Cultural and Economic Reproduction in Education*, Boston, Routledge and Kegan Paul, pp. 79–126; CARTER, M. (1976) 'Contradictions and correspondences: An analysis of the relations of schooling to work', in CARNOY, M. and LEVIN, H. (Eds), *The Limits of Educational Reform*, New York, Longman, pp. 52–82; WEXLER, P. (1979) 'Educational change and social contradiction: An example', *Comparative Education Review*, 23, 2, pp. 240–55.

11. JAMESON, F. (1981) *op cit.*, p. 94.

12. MAO TSE-TUNG, (1971) *Selected Readings from the Works of Mao Tse-Tung*, Peking, Foreign Language Press, p. 85.

13. *Ibid*, p. 91.

14. *Ibid*, p. 96.

15. *Ibid*, p. 96.

16. BERNSTEIN, B. (1975) *op cit.*

17. See LORTIE, D. (1975) *op cit.*; MATTINGLY, P. (1975) *The Classless Profession: American Schoolmen in the Nineteenth Century*, New York, New York University Press.

18. LORTIE, D. (1975) *op cit.*

19. STROBER, M. and TYACK, D. (1980) 'Why do women teach and men manage?,' *Signs*, 3, pp. 494–503.

20. See CARCHEDI, G. (1975) 'On the economic identification of the new middle classes', *Economy and Society*, 4, pp. 361–417; GINSBURG, M. et al., (1980) *op cit.*; HARRIS, K. (1982) *Teachers and Classes: A Marxist Analysis*, London, Routledge and Kegan Paul; JOHNSON, T. (1977) 'What is to be known: The structural determinism of social class', *Economy and Society*, 6, 2, pp. 194–233; NADEL, S. (1982) *Contemporary Capitalism and the Middle Classes*, New York, International Publishers; POULANTZAS, N. (1975) *Classes in Contemporary Capitalism*, London, New Left Review Books; SARUP, M. (1984) *Marxism/Structuralism/Education*, Lewes, Falmer Press; WRIGHT, E. (1979) 'Intellectuals and the class structure of capitalist society', in WALKER, P. (Ed.) *Between Labor and Capital*, Boston, South End Press, pp. 191–212.

21. CONNELL, M. (1985) *Teachers' Work*, Boston, Allen and Unwin, appropriately criticizes those who engage in 'the trigonometrical exercises of calculating a "location" on an *a priori* set of theoretical axes, and reading off the political consequences.' I concur that examining the class location or economic functions of teachers does not lead to an unambiguous determination of what role they will take in the class struggle (see also SARUP, M. (1984) *op cit.*, p. 117). How-

ever, if we juxtapose teachers' class position with their role as intellectuals, having a special connection to producing and reproducing ideas (and thus ideologies), we can discern more clearly to what extent teachers' actions can be shaped by (hegemonic or counter-hegemonic) ideologies. Regardless of whether one concurs that dominant ideologies primarily function to consolidate the capitalist class (see for example, ABERCROMBIE, N., HILL, S. and TURNER, B. (1978) *The Dominant Ideology Thesis*, London, Allen and Unwin, and (1978) 'The dominant ideology thesis', *British Journal of Sociology*, 29, 2, pp. 149–70), or that such ideologies have their most important impact in fostering acceptance of the status quo among the proletariat (see for example, ROOTES, C. (1981) 'The dominant ideology thesis and its critics', *Sociology*, 15, 3, pp. 436–44), it seems very clear that dominant ideologies (even with their contradictory nature) are crucial to understanding the thoughts and actions of the middle class(es), and particularly, intellectuals such as teachers. Not only do teachers constantly work with ideas, but given their contradictory economic functions, ideologies are especially important in shaping their current and future action. If their economic position was more clearly constructed, ideologies could serve primarily to reinforce this position, even if the position was antithetical to their interests. With an ambiguous economic class position, teachers and others in the middle class(es) have less strong structural constraints on their consciousness and action and thus ideology may have more of an influence in swaying them toward coalitions with either the bourgeoisie or the proletariat.

22. APPLE, M. (1984) 'Teaching and "women's work": A comparative historical and ideological analysis', in GUMBERT, E. (Ed.) *Expressions of Power in Education*, Atlanta, Center for Cross-Cultural Education, Georgia State University, p. 37.

23. STROBER, M. and TYACK, D. (1980) *op cit.*, p. 499.

24. In this regard, it is interesting to note the following links between class position, individualism, patriarchy and professionalism: 'Even the virtual confinement of nineteenth century married middle class women to the home was seen as a consequence of individual choice: such women merely chose to develop their special gifts and sensitivities in the professionalization of domesticity' (ACKER, S. (1983) 'Women and teaching: A semi-detached sociology of a semi-profession', in WALKER, S. and BARTON, L. (Eds) *op cit*, p. 132).

25. APPLE, M. (1984) *op cit.*, p. 36; STROBER, M. and TYACK, D. (1980) *op cit.*, p. 496.

26. ACKER, S. (1983) *op cit.*, p. 134.

27. CONNELL, M. (1985) *op cit.*, p. 152.

28. *Ibid*, p. 155.

29. Tape-recorded interviews (see for example, SPRADLEY, J. (1979) *The Ethnographic Interview*, New York, Holt) — focusing on a variety of

topics, including conceptions of professionalism — were conducted individually with a sample of students enrolled in the course observed each semester. A random sample of ten students in the first semester class (in which I informally enrolled as part of the ethnography) were interviewed at the beginning and eight of them were interviewed at the end of that semester. Due to a high dropout rate after the first semester, a new interview sample was identified consisting of ten students: three of whom had been in the first semester sample, the only other five students from the first semester class who continued in the program, and two students who had been in another section of the first semester course. All ten of the members of the reconstituted sample were individually interviewed at the end of the second semester. Nine were interviewed after their student teaching experience and three after their first semester employed as a teacher (as late as May 1983); one respondent dropped out of the program between the second semester and the student teaching semester. To ascertain how the fifteen pre-service teachers, who were interviewed at least once after the beginning of the program, conceived of professionalism and its relation to teaching I drew primarily on comments made in response to two sets of questions asked during each interview:

(i) Do you consider teaching a profession? Why do you say this? (and sometimes) What do you mean when you speak of profession, professional, and professionalism?

(ii) Do you plan to join (or have you joined) a teacher organization? (If yes) Which one(s)? Why?

A variety of probes for clarification and probes to encourage respondents to elaborate on comments they had made during the relevant semester were also used. In addition, interviewees were asked to express their views on relevant events which had received media attention during the semester. These events consisted of three 'labor disputes' — between the Houston area meatcutters/meatwrappers and four supermarket chains, between University of Houston teaching assistants and the campus administration, and between the Professional Air Controllers and the Reagan Administration — as well as a bill to authorize collective bargaining for teachers which was introduced in the Texas Legislature. Two magazines, *Texas Monthly* and *Time*, which during the research period had cover stories dealing critically with education and teachers, also provided stimuli for comments during the interviews. (For further details, see GINSBURG, M. (forthcoming) 'Reproduction, contradictions and conceptions of curriculum in pre-service teacher education', *Curriculum Inquiry*; GINSBURG, M. (1984) 'Reproduction and contradictions in pre-service teachers' encounters with professionalism', paper presented at the American Educational Research Association annual meeting, New Orleans, 23–27 April; GINSBURG, M. (1985) 'Teacher education and ideologies of social mobility and social reproduction', paper presented at the American Educational Studies Association annual meeting, Atlanta, 6–9 November; GINSBURG, M. and NEWMAN, K. (1985) *op cit.*

30. NATIONAL COMMISSION ON EXCELLENCE IN EDUCATION, (1983) *A Nation at Risk*, Washington, DC, US Department of Education.

31. For more details see GINSBURG, M. (1984) *op cit.*

32. See GINSBURG, M. and NEWMAN, K. (1985) *op cit.* Interestingly, James, one of these two 'incipient radicals', who discussed inequalities and schooling from a perspective focusing on institutional and societal structure, had no reservations about hierarchically differentiating professions from other occupational groups (see above). The other, Dana, began with an ambiguous view on the issue of professionalism — a view that, as she moved into teaching, became more clearly critical of the invidious status and class distinctions associated with certain notions of professionalism (see below).

33. For details on class session, see GINSBURG, M. (1984) *op cit.*

34. LARSON, M. (1977) *op cit.*, p. 156.

35. *Ibid*, p. 219.

36. GINSBURG, M. and NEWMAN, K. (1985) *op cit.*

37. See Carol's comments (quoted later) which raise the issue of the impact of the feminization of teaching, at times from a more critical perspective.

38. NATIONAL COMMISSION ON EXCELLENCE IN EDUCATION, (1983) *op cit.*

39. For a discussion of a similar emphasis in the formal and hidden curriculum of the teacher education program, see GINSBURG, M. (1984) *op cit.*

40. For additional details, see *ibid.*

41. For elaboration on this point, see BUCHER, R. and STELLING, J. (1977) *Becoming Professional*, Beverly Hills, Sage; LACEY, C. (1977) *The Socialisation of Teachers*, London, Methuen; LeCOMPTE, M. and GINSBURG, M. (1986) 'How students learn to become teachers: An exploration of alternative responses to a teacher training program', in NOBLIT, G. and PINK, W. (Eds), *Understanding Education: Qualitative Studies of the Occupation and Organization*, New York, Ablex; OLESON, V. and WHITTAKER, E. (1968) *The Silent Dialogue: A Study in the Social Psychology of Professional Socialization*, San Francisco, Jossey-Bass; POPKEWITZ, T., TABACHNICK, R. and ZEICHNER, K. (1979) 'Dulling the senses: Research in teacher education', *Journal of Teacher Education*, 30, 5, pp. 52–60; REINHARZ, S. (1979) *On Becoming a Social Scientist*, San Francisco, Jossey-Bass; SPATIG, L., GINSBURG, M. and LIBERMAN, D. (1982) 'Ego development as an explanation of passive and active models of teacher socialization', *College Student Journal*, 16, pp. 315–25.

42. For details on issue of the ideological nature of professionalism, see note 3 above.

43. LARSON, M. (1977) *op cit.*, pp. xvi–xvii.
44. See BRAVERMAN, H. (1974) *Labor and Monopoly Capital*, New York, Monthly Review Press; CARTER, M. (1976) *op cit.*; GINSBURG, M. (1984) *op cit.*; GINSBURG, M. and SPATIG, L. (1985) 'The proletarianization of the professoriate? The case of producing a competency-based teacher education program,' paper presented at the American Educational Research Association annual meeting, Chicago, 31 March–4 April.
45. See discussion above in reference to LARSON, M. (1977) *op cit.*
46. BLEDSTEIN, B. (1976) *The Culture of Professionalism: The Middle Class and the Development of Higher Education in America*, New York, Norton, pp. 123–4.
47. See for example, PERRUCI, R. (1973) 'In service of man: Radical movements in the professions', in HALMOS, P. (Ed.) *Professionalization and Social Change*, University of Keele, Sociological Review Monograph No. 20, pp. 179–94.
48. ESLAND, G. (1980) 'Professions and professionalism', in ESLAND, G. and SALAMAN, G. (Eds) *The Politics of Work and Occupations*, Milton Keynes, The Open University Press, p. 217.
49. LARSON, M. (1980) 'Proletarianization of educated labor', *Theory and Society*, 9, 1, pp. 131–75.
50. See COLLINS, R. (1979) *op cit.*, p. 172; GRACE, G. (1978) *op cit.*, pp. 55–56; LARSON, M. (1977) *op cit.*, p. xvi.
51. See DERBER, C. (1982) *Professionals as Workers: Mental Labor in Advanced Capitalism*, Boston, G.K. Hall.
52. See BARLOW, A. (1980) *op cit.*, p. 431.
53. LARSON, M. (1977) *op cit.*, p. 193.
54. See JOHNSON, T. (1972) *op cit.*
55. See TREIMAN, D. and TERRELL, K. (1975) 'Sex and the process of status attainment', *American Sociological Review*, 40, 2, pp. 174–200.
56. See HOWSAM, R. *et al.*, (1976) *op cit.*
57. KELSALL, R. and KELSALL, H. (1970) 'The status, role and future of teachers', in KING, E. (Ed.) *The Teacher and the Needs of Society in Evolution*, Oxford, Pergamon, quoted in ACKER, S. *op cit.*, p. 131.
58. LARSON, M. (1977) *op cit.*
59. See also GINSBURG, M. *et al.*, (1980) *op cit.*
60. LARSON, M. (1980) *op cit.*, p. 161.
61. SIMPSON, R. and SIMPSON, I. (1969) 'Women and bureaucracy in the semi-professions', in ETZIONI, A. (Ed.), *The Semi-Professions and Their Organization*, New York, Free Press, quoted in ACKER, S. *op cit.*, p. 131.
62. KANTER, R. (1977) *Men and Women of the Corporation*, New York, Basic Books, quoted in ACKER, S. *op cit.*, p. 132.
63. BLEDSTEIN, B. (1976) *op cit.*, p. ix.
64. See GINSBURG, M. and CHATURVEDI, V. (1985) 'Teachers and the

ideology of professionalism in India and England: A comparison of cases in colonial-peripheral and metropolitan/central societies', paper presented at the Comparative and International Education Society, Stanford University, 16–20 April.

65. See GINSBURG, M., WALLACE, G. and MILLER, H. (1982) 'Teachers, economy and the state: An English example', revised version of paper presented at the 10th World Congress of Sociology, International Sociological Association, Mexico City, 15–21 August.

5 Professionalism, Proletarianization and Teacher Work

Kathleen Densmore

The pedagogical options available to teachers are products of a complex series of factors, including the cultural/ideological, economic context within which schools are located. A key interest is the teaching process as it relates to the more general labor process under capitalism. Specifically, there appears to be a strong basis for the argument that the proletarianization of the occupation is occurring. Case studies about two first-year female teachers illustrate these concerns. These teachers were more vulnerable to the specific operating procedures of their schools than prevailing understandings of professional work suggest; hence the argument for a conceptualization of teachers as workers vs. teachers as professionals. Ideological considerations and gender relations are critically important for understanding various influences and constraints on the teaching process. While the ideals of professionalism are shown to bear little relationship to the circumstances of teachers' practices, as an ideological construct, professionalism informs teacher actions.

Introduction

American public education is characterized by conflict in many areas. Critics of the left and right argue that a crisis exists in the institution, though they differ on the nature of the problem and its causes. Issues raised by critics include: the use of property taxes to finance schooling; the decline in test scores; the impersonal bureaucratization of the school; the proliferation of courses; 'lowered' academic standards; curricula that promote values that are in opposition to those of students' parents; vandalism in the schools; integration and the resulting 'white flight'; the low prestige of the teaching profession; and the inadequate training of teachers.

Some of the most serious questions currently being raised concern teachers — their competence, autonomy, salaries, possibilities for advancement, and evaluation. Some have argued that teachers are being made scapegoats for problems that pertain more fundamentally to how their work is organized and job requirements. Others claim that if teachers were held more accountable for their teaching, many of the problems would disappear. In this vein, attempts to develop 'scientific' curricula and means for managing schools have increased.[1] Serious questions have been raised about the interests that lay behind many of these efforts and their actual effects.[2]

Questions have also been raised about the quality of teacher education programs at universities. These questions differ according to various conceptions of the aims of the field. Educational researchers, tending to view teacher education as a form of applied science, offer an increasing supply of research instruments, models, styles of teaching and data on effective teaching.[3] Their intention is to 'train' better teachers. Others emphasize conceptual matters, such as the ethics of teaching and the role and nature of schooling in our society. In this view, teacher education should engage prospective teachers in serious thinking about, and understanding of, issues pertaining to curriculum and instruction so that they will be able to make reasoned judgments once in the classroom.

Teacher education has long been recognized as facing difficult problems. The enduring nature and complexity of these problems is not surprising once we view teaching as occurring within a context that includes professional organizations, teachers' unions, universities, public schools, and the society at large. Many factors influence and constrain teachers' development, and these comprise diverse social arenas. Therefore, these problems must be understood as interrelated, arising from a number of factors.

One such factor, about which little is known, is the context of teachers' work. This factor is critical, given the prevailing assumption that teachers learn how to teach predominantly from classroom experience as opposed to critical inquiry and study — an assumption evident in proposals to improve teacher education by giving prospective teachers a longer 'apprenticeship' in the schools.[4] However, little attention is given to the quality and character of work life that this apprenticeship entails. A better understanding of the conditions under which teachers teach is necessary to understand actual educational processes and outcomes as well as the circumstances behind the current crisis.

The purpose of this chapter is to offer an interpretation of teaching by investigating the nature of the relationship between the objective working conditions of specific teachers and their subjective experiences of these conditions. Drawing on relevant research and two case studies of first-year teachers, I will examine a number of aspects of teachers' work, including teacher autonomy, skill level, conceptualization and planning.[5] In addition to issues of control and skill, I will examine other aspects of teachers' work situation, such as the organizational structure of schools, in order to describe the various institutional factors that bear upon teachers' practices. Thus, I will consider specific ideological and institutional factors as they combine to influence teaching outcomes. Throughout this account my references to the subjective experiences of teachers are based on the case studies of teachers I observed and interviewed.

These teachers perceive themselves, generally, as professionals — or potentially as professionals. I will question that perception and propose that teachers' working conditions are becoming more like those of industrial workers. My concern is to examine the objective features of the teaching occupation. As it is organized under contemporary institutional arrangements, teaching practice is predominantly characterized by conventionality and passivity, not by professional autonomy or creativity. Viewing teachers as workers may help us to understand teacher acquiescence or ambivalence to the structural conditions within which they occupy a subordinate position. That position, I will argue, has critically diminished teachers' involvement in the educational process. Viewing *themselves* as workers may help teachers recognize both the sources of the troubles schools face and potential means of effective action.

The Received View of Teacher Work

Teacher Professionalism

Conventional wisdom in education typically conceives of teachers as professionals or semi-professionals. This view is generally held by teachers themselves. It is advanced by the leadership of the two national unions. In order to gain some understanding of this claim, we can turn to the sociology of the professions. First of all, there is no theoretical or methodological consensus on the definition of 'a professional' nor of 'the professions'. Typically, professions have been defined as occupations that require practitioners to undergo a long period of special training during which they acquire a broad theoretical knowledge base.[6] Their technical expertise is presumed to be based upon this knowledge. Attributes such as high levels of skill based on theoretical knowledge and altruistic 'public' service are offered as explanations for social and job related privileges, such as relatively high social status and financial remuneration. Autonomy on the job is taken as the cornerstone of professional working conditions since it is through freedom from supervision and external controls that professionals are best able to apply their expertise.

This traditional view of professionalism is held as an ideal-typical description of teachers' work.[7] Accordingly, educators assume that teachers possess pedagogical expertise (knowledge and skills) and significant autonomy in the classroom, even when the type of knowledge, degree of skill, or form of autonomy are disputed.[8] Due to a lack of empirical studies and definitional consensus on these matters, it is difficult to assess the expertise teachers actually do possess or the degree and nature of autonomy they wield. Furthermore, surface appearances in teachers' work processes and work conditions give credence to a number of different interpretations. Self-contained classrooms, for example, suggest substantial freedom for teachers. University degrees imply pedagogical expertise. New patterns of administrative management and organizational forms have emerged that ostensibly allow for a greater degree of teacher participation in school affairs and for significant classroom autonomy. Yet, a number of studies belie these beliefs, identifying limits on teacher authority over both curricula and classroom operations that are less readily apparent.[9]

Teacher Professionalism and Bureaucratization

In sociological literature, neither empirical studies nor theoretical analyses have adequately resolved the question of professional subordination to bureaucratic authority. Among educators, while it is generally understood that the degree of bureaucratization of schools will influence teacher discretion, many are divided on the degree to which, and the precise mechanisms through which, a bureaucratic organizational structure affects teachers' practices. Nevertheless, the dominant assumption is that teachers, as professionals, are accorded classroom autonomy even though they work within bureaucratic settings. Meyer and Rowan, for example, frame the issue in this way:

> educational organizations ... lack close internal coordina-
> tion, especially of the content and methods of what is pre-
> sumably their main activity — instruction. Instruction tends
> to be removed from the control of the organizational
> structure.[10]

Similarly, Warren, after an examination of both formalized and unstructured control processes which operate within schools, concludes:

> While a teacher's public behavior is the object of continuing
> and effective cultural surveillance, his classroom behavior is
> relatively immune to control processes generated either
> within or outside the formal structure and operation of the
> school.[11]

As we shall see, the belief that teachers retain job autonomy and control over their immediate labor process, despite bureaucratic structures, needs to be severely questioned.

Challenges to the Received View

Professionalism as an Ideology

New critical analyses of the professions focus on the social, histori-
cal, and political context in which claims to professionalism are made. The concept of 'professionalism' is viewed as a term that has changed over time. In education, for example, professionalism is seen not as an ideal type, nor as an actual or idealized description of work conditions, but as an ideology that influences teachers' practices.[12] Larson has examined the changing basis of professionalism under capitalism.[13] Larson argues that professional qualities that were fostered in an earlier historical period, under specific structural conditions, persist even when those conditions no longer exist. For example, most professionals today are salaried employees of bureaucratic organizations and are often required to work extra hours without pay (this is frequently true of teachers). Yet these workers are exhorted by management (and the public) to

be motivated by altruism and 'public service'. Such exhortations appeal to anachronistic conceptions of professionalism, despite changing conditions and expectations of work. Larson persuasively argues that the significance of professionalism today lies in its ideological content and not in its description of actual work conditions. Professionalism is an ideal to which individuals and occupational groups aspire that distinguishes them from other workers. However, this aspiration obscures actual job functions, work practices, and social relations. In its contemporary usage, 'professional', according to Larson, refers primarily to a concern with status and privileges vis-a-vis other employees — a concern that obscures professionals' actual lack of power, their subordination, and their commonalities with other workers. The belief by teachers in the professional or semi-professional status of their occupation has, I will argue, had precisely the sort of effect Larson describes.

Proletarianization

Sociologists have recently developed a thesis concerning labor processes based upon the concept of 'proletarianization'. This thesis is advocated by scholars who question the usefulness of the concept 'professionalism' in analyses of the work situation of contemporary 'professionals', including teachers.[14] Proletarianization refers to certain tendencies in work organization and work processes under capitalism: an increased division of labor; the separation of conception from the execution of tasks, including the tendency to routinize high level tasks; increased controls over each step of the labor process; increased volume of work; and the downgrading of skill levels. This pattern of change has been found to characterize even the work of professionals.[15]

The proletarianization of professional work suggests that despite presumed differences between professionals and other workers, the conditions for professional autonomy are being eroded as professionals become increasingly subject to management controls. One reason given for this change is the increasing number of professionals who work for others and who are employed in bureaucratic institutions. That is, there has been a shift from self-employment to being a salaried employee, with implications for control over both the means and ends of one's work. Thus the rhetoric of professionalism appears more 'ideological' as the organization of work actually reduces the autonomy and immediate control over the work process of employees, bringing professionals closer to other workers.

The benchmark for much of the work by proletarianization theorists is Braverman who, in analyzing the division of labor under monopoly capitalism, argued that there is a tendency for decreasing employee autonomy on the job, as skill is increasingly removed from work.[16] The tendency is for both jobs and people to become deskilled and for employees to lose control over the work process through rationalization, fragmentation, and mechanization/technology. While this thesis has been applied primarily to studies of industrial work, proletarianization can be seen as a long-term trend in all work under capitalism, including professional work. In this view, the form of work under capitalism is a product of attempted and contested solutions to problems of fiscal crisis and capitalist development. The need for capital to increase profit levels continually is behind the process of proletarianization.[17] Scholars argue that, in times of economic crisis, various means of capital accumulation will be explored.[18] Thus, for example, increasing sectors of the working population will be incorporated into the wage labor/capital relation, and the labor process of even professional workers will become increasingly subject to rationalization. In this sense, proletarianization is a class phenomenon. Professional working conditions subsequently conform less and less to ideal-typical conditions as they become more routinized and standardized.

Interesting and important work has studied the extent to which the proletarianization of professionals parallels the deskilling of manual craft workers earlier this century. Scholars such as Larson, Edwards and Burawoy correctly point out that the processes of proletarianization are historically specific and uneven in development.[19] That is, proletarianization need not be strictly equated with the process described by Braverman; it will affect different occupational groups in different ways at different times in history. For example, the strength or weakness of workers' responses to management controls can influence the developments that actually take place. This is frequently seen in management attempts to implement technology.[20] Workers' responses in turn are conditioned by such factors as their level of class consciousness and the current level of unemployment. Further, who is available to work is based on racial and gender relations in capitalism. Job segregation, for example, channels women into certain jobs rather than others.[21] One consequence of the 'feminization' of an occupation is an active process of lowered wages and deskilling (again, this has been specifically claimed of teaching).[22] In this way the sexual division of labor can be viewed as a structural feature of modern capitalism.[23]

Charles Derber distinguishes two forms of proletarianization: ideological and technical.[24] A failure to make this distinction, Derber suggests, has resulted in theoretical confusion among proletarianization theorists. Ideological proletarianization refers to the worker's loss of control over decisions concerning the goals and objectives of her/his work. Technical proletarianization signifies the loss of control over decisions about how the technical aspects of her/his work will be carried out. Like Larson, Derber argues that professionals are not being managed exactly like industrial workers (for example, through traditional forms of regimentation); nor does he think this will transpire. Specifically, he argues that professionals are primarily subjected to ideological proletarianization; technical proletarianization is not necessary to the control of professional labor. This position is contrary to that of proletarianization theorists who see impending proletarianization at the technical level, making even professionals subject to the routinization and rationalization that industrial workers know so well. Derber explains his perspective on professional proletarianization:

> At its core is the notion that the ideological proletarianization of professionals reflects fundamentally new systems of labor control that are emerging in advanced or post industrial capitalism. These systems seek to achieve labor discipline and productivity not by stripping from workers the technical knowledge and discretion that potentially allows them to obstruct management's goals, but rather by encouraging technical skill and autonomy and, in so doing, leading the worker to ideologically identify his or her own interests with those of the firm and to develop internalized motivation and discipline.[25]

The ideology of professionalism can be viewed as a construct that both obscures the reality of one's work situation and secures the internalization of the motivation and discipline that Derber refers to.

Thus, according to the proletarianization thesis, trends in the economy contain problems that result in specific pressures on teachers and schools. The job of teaching has structural features that are consistent with patterns in other work places (for example, deskilling, intensification) and that are tied to the current economic crisis. Teaching, then, can be viewed as part of the more general labor process under capitalism in which there is a need both to coordinate work and to control the labor process. The tendency toward proletarianization reflects these needs.

A review of critical sociological and educational research suggests that the organization of teaching can be examined and considered from the standpoint of (a) the proletarianization thesis; and (b) professionalism as an ideological construct.[26] The basic thesis of this chapter is that the process of proletarianization in teaching has undermined the basis of such professional characteristics as job autonomy; hence the ideology of professionalism represents, primarily, a defensive response by teachers to what are objectively alienating work processes and work conditions.[27] This response, I will argue, has been manipulated by various groups as a means of *further* control over the teaching process. Later on I will discuss Derber's concepts of 'ideological desensitization' and 'ideological cooptation' as they help to illuminate the source and nature of defensive teacher reactions.

Forms of Control

Management control can be seen in the specific forms of control on teachers, the types of decisions teachers do and don't make, and the implications of the system of labor control for teachers' professional ideology. Like Derber, Friedman distinguishes between management strategies of control that allow for 'relative worker autonomy' and those that impose more severe constraints.[28] Their work suggests that effective control of professionals depends first and foremost upon the ideological identification of employees with the goals of their workplace. If this identification is secured then the possession of technical expertise is less of a threat to management than would otherwise be the case. In a discussion of management's role in the development of the capitalist mode of production, Friedman identifies two basic managerial strategies that are used to promote employee identification with the loyalty to a job: direct control and responsible autonomy. With the former, workers are given minimal independent responsibilities and are under close supervision. The latter is a strategy whereby workers are given some degree of status, authority, and responsibility in an attempt to win their loyalty to the firm. This strategy is more likely to be used with 'white collar' workers who expect some creativity and flexibility in their work. The goal of this strategy is to channel creative impulses and to structure employee responsibility and autonomy so that the existing organization of work is not threatened, usually to the benefit of the firm. While Friedman's analysis concerns industrial workers, the concepts of responsible autonomy and direct control are useful for understanding organizational structures of schools, such as the calls for various forms of 'teacher input' into the operations of our schools (for example, teacher participation on school committees).

Professionalism and Proletarianization as They Apply to Teaching

Overview

Based on this brief analysis, one can offer three possible characterizations of teaching. First, there was a previous period in history when teachers experienced full control over their work. One interpretation of the proletarianization thesis implies that teachers are currently undergoing a loss of control and autonomy at work *in comparison with* a previous 'golden age' of teacher professionalism. Second, teaching is a quasi-profession. This view maintains that teaching is at least potentially a full profession, and that teachers should pursue its complete professionalization. This is the dominant view in the current literature, and among educators themselves. Third, teaching has never been a 'profession', yet is currently undergoing serious changes, such as an increased use of rationalized curriculum materials, a relative decrease in salaries, etc. that parallel other forms of 'white collar' work. My research favors the third characterization, though given the lack of relevant studies this remains an open question. I will argue here that the content and organization of teaching can be best explained using the proletarianization thesis together with considering professionalism primarily as an ideology. My analysis is of the contemporary structural features of teachers' labor process, rather than on historical precedents. Changes have occurred in the aims and mechanisms of constraint that further subordinate teachers to the dictates of their workplace, despite the efforts of advocates for professionalism. These changes do not necessarily imply an earlier 'golden age'. Admittedly, a complete understanding of teaching cannot be developed apart from historical context. This context is critical given, for example, in the creation of teaching as a mass occupation, coinciding with its feminization and bureaucratization in the mid-nineteenth century. The ideology of professionalism developed later during the twentieth century.[29] The scope of the present analysis is thus admittedly limited.[30]

The discussion that follows focuses on the relation between teachers' labor process and the ideology of professionalism. My claim, that professionalism is best understood as an ideological response to degraded work conditions in teaching, is based on the observation that teachers are undergoing a serious loss of control and autonomy at work. Of course, schools vary with respect to the degree of bureaucratization and organizational innovations that constrain the teaching process. Thus I will identify specific institutional practices that produce and sustain the constraints within which teachers work.

Schools as State Institutions

Schools are structured to a significant extent by being state institutions. A pluralist theory of the state views the state and its institutions as neutral and as distributing power at all levels to different groups seeking to influence the state. In contrast, a Marxist theory of the state emphasizes class conflict. The state is conceived as having a structural role in securing and maintaining conditions that are necessary for the perpetuation of capitalist social relations. Since the survival of capitalism is problematic, the state functions to provide conditions of both accumulation and legitimation. The processes by which this occurs are inherently contradictory and conflict laden.[31] For example, in addition to maintaining the general conditions for capital accumulation, the state promotes social welfare. Schools, like other state institutions, and like the state itself, should be viewed in the context of pressures and social processes involving the current crisis in capital accumulation and legitimation. In present times, the governments of capitalist states are seeking to cut costs, reduce inefficiencies, and increase productivity in a host of social institutions. Work processes and work conditions in public institutions subsequently come under scrutiny with these concerns in mind — schools being no exception.

There are political as well as economic pressures on the state. For instance, as state employees, teachers are held accountable by the public for the services they are to perform. Yet, these services are to be of a 'professional' nature. Tensions and contradictions in the teacher's role become obvious once we appreciate a work context including: (i) pressures to satisfy the public; (ii) expectations to exercise professional discretion; and (iii) positions as both state and bureaucratic employees. Calls by the public for accountability, for example, are frequently answered via the imposition of standardized, prefigured curricula — yet these undermine 'professional' prerogatives. Teachers are expected to interpret and apply specialized knowledge — yet are *rewarded* (for example, under many merit plans) for *different* behaviors. Their employee status signifies a work context with hierarchical authority relations, bureaucratic forms of control, and conditions of limited time and information — yet they are burdened with *increased* expectations in terms of the number (and kinds) of learning activities they should offer.

Expectations for individual teacher discretion and authority exist together with various constraints on teaching. These expectations derive in large part from prevailing notions of professionalism that are promoted not only by the public but by teachers themselves. Together with the autonomy that teachers actually have in their classrooms, these expectations give rise to a general school ambience of professionalism.

General School Ambience and Professionalism

Changes in the teaching process can be understood in the context of various forms of control. Generally speaking, the belief in, and apparent reality of, individual discretion and autonomy are important characteristics of the organization of work within schools. In fact, maintaining the appearance of significant job autonomy legitimates existing constraints on teachers' work. This claim can be illustrated by the teaching experiences and socialization of two first-year teachers — Sarah and Beth. Sarah taught in Cherry Grove Elementary School. Beth taught in Gershwin Middle School.[32] There were differences, however, between the two schools in how the appearance of job autonomy was sustained.

One difference lies in the architectural design: in Gershwin Middle School teachers worked in teams of three, in adjoining modular classrooms called 'pods' with seventy to eighty students. Teachers in Cherry Grove Elementary School worked in separate classrooms. In addition to their individual teaching responsibilities, Gershwin teachers were expected to coordinate their work with the other pod teachers. Ostensibly this physical design allowed for a measure of teacher collectivity and cooperation in classroom affairs. In practice, however, teachers engaged in little genuine collaboration with one another, due to a highly specified curriculum program and a heavy teacher workload. The expectation for coordination among teachers was one officially acknowledged restriction on an individual teacher's autonomy. A second difference between the two schools was that in Cherry Grove, lines of authority and mechanisms of control were less obvious and more thoroughly mediated (for example, through parents) than in Gershwin, where they were more direct and explicit. At the same time, in both schools rules and operating procedures took the form of 'shared understandings' and 'preferences'; harsh and rigid controls were avoided. A third difference in how the overall ambience was maintained can be seen in the different usages of the concept of 'professionalism'.

The meaning given to professionalism in Cherry Grove was more akin to its traditional conception — an emphasis on individual teacher autonomy and the absence of explicit controls. Separate classrooms and a relatively less rationalized curriculum lent credence to this conception. In contrast, professionalism in Gershwin coincided more with the claim to a scientific knowledge base for curriculum and instruction and strict adherence to the performance-based educational program. While official school rhetoric claimed that teachers 'individualized' the standardized curriculum, in practice individualization only took place with respect to the pace at which students moved through common lessons. Even this variation was limited since clear limits were placed on employees' responsibilities for their particular program of curriculum and instruction, as I will discuss below. Despite the appearance and rhetoric of responsible autonomy, one can see a managerial strategy of direct control at Gershwin in both the instructional program in use and the close supervision of employees: the principal toured the building several times daily. His observations were facilitated by the open pod structure. Thus teacher autonomy was actually decreased by both an architectural design and a 'progressive' curriculum.

Deskilling and Bureaucratic Personnel

The functions of ideological and economic reproduction are combined as the state attempts to maintain the necessary conditions for capital accumulation. Given the current crisis in accumulation these functions influence schools in particular ways, since the state must find ways to reduce the costs of schooling and make schooling more productive that will be accepted by both the public and school personnel. It is here that we see one explanation for the tendency toward proletarianization: it grows out of an attempt to 'rationalize' and make more efficient schooling and teachers' work. This tendency can be seen, for example, in the increasing fragmentation of subject matter through the ever-popular prepackaged curriculum units. Discretely measurable performance objectives satisfy calls for accountability and cost-efficiency. This curricular trend increasingly separates the conception and planning of the teaching process from its execution, thereby diminishing the skill components of the work itself.[33]

In the two schools under consideration teachers distributed a received curriculum. Frequently tasks were specified for the teacher. Curricular control was centralized as coordinative and creative activities, such as determining and prioritizing subject matter content, were beyond teachers' purview. This does not mean that Sarah and Beth, for example, refrained from modifying the information they were responsible for relaying to students. But the possession of content knowledge was not critical for their work: even if Sarah and Beth did have a high level of expertise, the expectations for their teaching required few sophisticated pedagogical skills, scant knowledge of content areas, and little detailed knowledge about their students. This was especially true in Gershwin, which had a performance-based program in all subjects. In Cherry Grove this was true in mathematics and reading more than in social studies and science.

The belief in professionalism, as I mentioned previously, can itself be viewed as a form of control. Teachers in the two schools considered their administration of the prescribed curriculum as a 'professional' activity. In both schools, principals as well as teachers reasoned that specialists ('experts' who were professionals in their own right) had designed the curricular programs, and therefore independent judgments as to their value and appropriateness were largely unnecessary. That is, in their minds teacher professionalism did not necessitate the design of learning activities but the execution of programs predesigned by *other* 'professionals'. This was, in fact, the teaching situation, although slightly less so in Cherry Grove, where upwardly mobile parents effectively pressured teachers to supplement the curriculum with 'enriching' learning activities. But if professionalism implies (i) individual teacher authority; (ii) a theoretical knowledge base; and (iii) the exercise of related skills and techniques, teachers at neither school could be viewed as professionals. The contradiction between the expertise that teachers are exhorted to exercise and the relatively rare occasions that they are given to exercise it is strikingly apparent.

It can be argued that teachers have never been in a position to develop professional goals separate from a public school system's objectives — that their professional mandate has always been tied to the school and community within which they work. Yet, appeals to professionalism continue to characterize the occupation. Teacher education programs, for example, while increasingly focusing on a narrowly conceived technical expertise, simultaneously convey the message that teachers should draw upon their independent judgments for curricular and instructional decisions. On-the-job experience, such as student teaching and early 'apprenticeships' tend to reinforce the former, and not the latter message.

Beth, for example, learned during the course of the year not to expect sophisticated conceptual pedagogical work or much control over her work process or situation. 'Professionalism' for her increasingly denoted adherence to accepted institutional norms and often depended on what was required by the immediate situation. Thus, contrary to common assumptions and the ideal-typical construct of professionalism, teachers' professional aspirations are usually not in conflict with bureaucratic controls that in fact subordinate them. For these reasons, professionalism — as traditionally understood — fails to illuminate the critical dimensions of Beth's teaching practices. Her status as a bureaucratic employee tells us much more.

Similarly, for Sarah, being a professional meant, in part, being a school representative (for example, explaining and justifying curricular programs to parents). The organization of teaching in Cherry Grove — including the curriculum — removed from Sarah's work responsibility, skills, and knowledge. Sarah, nevertheless, invoked the concept of professionalism as a claim to pedagogical expertise in an attempt to keep parents and their demands at a distance, fearing otherwise an even greater loss of control over the teaching process. By invoking notions of autonomy and control on the basis of professionalism, Sarah (like other teachers) maintained a tension between herself, the occupation, and parents.[34] This particular tension was less present in Gershwin. There, parent involvement in the educational process also met with disapproval, but the parents intervened less, and efforts by the school to convince parents that their involvement was unnecessary had reportedly been successful. Parents in Gershwin apparently accepted the idea that their children's education was in the hands of experts. They may not have felt able or willing to question professionals: fewer of them were professionals themselves than the parents in Cherry Grove.

Thus professionalism, as an ideological construct available to teachers, contains diverse and contradictory elements. Elements of the ideal-typical view of professionalism co-exist in teachers' world views with incompatible bureaucratic elements and expectations. This is not altogether surprising given the tensions that exist between the teacher's 'professional' role and the teacher's position as a state and bureaucratic employee. Teacher ideology then is mediated by their social position and work situation. Additionally, 'professionalism' is invoked selectively for varying purposes as was evident in Sarah's use of the term to keep parents at a distance, and by her principal's use of the term to promote a commitment to their jobs and schools which teachers should have — regardless of whether there was an organizational basis of support.

A variety of institutional measures also constrained teachers' practices in Gershwin school. For example, charts were displayed on corridor walls comparing classrooms' achievement test scores, having the effect of placing teachers in competition with one another. Additionally, teachers feared being easily substituted for: the principal's hiring criteria had little to do with the unique contributions an individual could make. Structured competition among employees and the perception of employees as interchangeable units are key features of the intensified and deskilled labor process in capitalism at large, as is the absence of formal provisions in the workplace for employees to examine and pursue their collective interests.

Teacher Collectivity and Teacher Professionalism

If teachers are to exert greater influence over the direction of educational change they will need to act collectively. The specific types of action and nature of collectivity, however, are in conflict with many teachers' 'professional' concerns. A preoccupation with individual teacher autonomy, for example, leaves many teachers uncomfortable in discussions of collective challenges to working conditions. Additionally, collective action, including unionism, is considered inappropriate to their professional status — particularly as state-employed 'public servants'.

The two schools under study differed in opportunities for collective interaction among the teaching staff. In Cherry Grove there were few. Teacher association meetings were infrequently held and poorly attended. There were no regularly scheduled faculty meetings. When occasional meetings were called they consisted primarily of reports from the principal. Because of an architectural design in which teachers worked in separate classrooms, and a workload in which many teachers had to remain in their rooms during lunch in order to stay abreast of their work, teachers tended to feel isolated, powerless in their situation, and under the control of the dictates of their workplace.

At the same time, teachers made some efforts to turn this situation to their own advantage. For example, the organizational expectation for teachers to adhere to a common curriculum produced informal opportunities for teachers to meet with one another. That is, by adhering to the practices of co-grade level teachers, teachers had a basis from which to interact with one another. For a new teacher, like Sarah, in particular, such interaction was essential for 'learning the ropes'.

In Cherry Grove a lack of formal provisions for interaction among teachers also influenced the form and weight of parental influence in the school. Although parents wanted creative professionals in the classroom, there were no systematic means whereby teachers and parents could work together. Teachers were inhibited in making discretionary decisions that might meet the disapproval of influential parents. They were in the difficult position of trying to retain what control they had within their classrooms while simultaneously entertaining parents' ideas and demands. Yet teachers only coped with this situation as individuals: the teacher association had low status; the Parent-Teacher Association met during the school day (when teachers could not attend); and there were no teachers on the PTA board!

Teachers' lack of leadership is a consequence of their general failure to act collectively despite their numerical dominance. Sometimes, by conforming to common lessons and teaching strategies, teachers can relate their activities to other teachers as a defense and buffer, as for example when Cherry Grove teachers felt challenged by parents — or anticipated such a challenge. This was particularly evident with Sarah, who was inexperienced in dealing with parents. Here we see the effect of a specific political influence (parents) on teachers' work — one instance of the influence of the political sphere on the labor process. Parental pressures for creative pedagogy reinforced a managerial strategy with the appearance of responsible autonomy and created problems for teachers who were expected to conform to a common curriculum.

In Gershwin, on the other hand, there were some institutional provisions for collective interactions among members of the staff. Yet such interactions served mainly to improve the efficiency of Gershwin's operations, while maintaining existing work processes. Teachers were inhibited from engaging in critical questioning of such matters as the existing parameters on staff meetings, the goals of the curriculum, the division of labor within the school, or their workload. However, participation in meetings tended to make teachers *feel* that they possessed real responsibility for their school's program and helped to secure teachers' identification with the institution. It reinforced the perception of a common 'professional' identity and conduct. For example, while the scope of teachers' decisions on matters of curriculum and evaluation was narrow, the very act of participating in making these decisions reinforced teachers' commitment to institutionalized arrangements within which they occupied a subordinate position.

While the scope of decisions was narrow, the *number* of decisions teachers made within those limits was considerable. Thus the important effect of the choices and decisions that teachers made lay in winning teachers' loyalty and tying them more closely to Gershwin's school program and organizational structure, but not in significantly guiding or directing school policy. Teachers' sense of professionalism was enhanced by their participation in these frequent and varied meetings, in which they had some limited control over certain aspects of their job, such as the definition of student 'needs'. In other words, the ideology of professionalism was partially grounded in, and reinforced by, the teachers' real daily experiences.

Intensification of Work and Teacher Professionalism

The sheer volume of work performed by the teachers can be understood as an intensification of teachers' labor. Intensification has been explained as a means by which the employer (in the case of public school teachers, the state) can extract surplus labor from workers thereby cutting costs while increasing productivity, and a means of diminishing various work privileges of non-manual workers.[35] Intensification can be seen as another means of control over teachers' practices. An important aspect of this intensification is its implicit and gradual development; hence even the fact that it is occurring is often not apparent to the workers themselves.

For example, in Gershwin and Cherry Grove, intensification was achieved through job fragmentation and an increasing number of specialists. In Cherry Grove intensification also arose from parental pressures for creative pedagogy. This translated into projects in addition to the standard curriculum. Additionally, teachers frequently had only ten-minute lunch periods. In Gershwin the many committee meetings, together with the responsibilities that teachers were given during these meetings, took time and added to the teachers' workload. Out of a sense of professional dedication teachers often *volunteered* for additional responsibilities. In both schools, teachers performed a variety of tasks in addition to instruction, such as participating in after-school and evening activities. Participation in such activities was either explicitly required or 'strongly encouraged'.[36] The fact that this 'encouragement' came from a male principal to female teachers, and that teachers accepted it, suggests a congruence between: (i) an appeal to the 'public servant' conscience of the teacher as 'professional'; (ii) the traditional gender role of women as members of 'helping professions'; and (iii) the more general societal pattern of women being subject to the control of men. Thus women are subject to two forms of control: bureaucratic administration and patriarchy.[37]

The ideological construct of professionalism legitimates and rationalizes labor intensification. In Gershwin, handling an increased volume of work enhanced teachers' sense of professionalism, because it enhanced their sense of importance and 'responsibility'. Minimally, an increased volume of work was accepted as part of the teachers' role. In Cherry Grove, ideological conflicts did arise when teachers were required to attend school carnivals and festivals; while it was not accepted by teachers as a professional activity, it was accepted as part of their responsibilities as a teacher. Within the classroom, Sarah worked quickly and efficiently so that she could include creative supplementary lessons once required lessons were finished. Her own sense of professionalism, together with parental pressures for additional effort, propelled her to increase the quantity of lessons taught. Thus the ideology of professionalism for teachers legitimates and reinforces features of proletarianization, such as intensification.

Survival and success at work depend on some degree of acceptance of the objectives and operating procedures in one's workplace. When the professional ideal comes into conflict with the day-to-day reality of teaching, for example, teachers develop strategies that enable them to do the best they can under the circumstances. Taken together, Beth's and Sarah's responsibilities proved to be more than they could satisfactorily handle. Consequently, Sarah learned to 'cut corners' with required material. Beth concluded that personal knowledge about what she was teaching was not necessary and that covering required material was more important than whether or not students fully understood what they were being exposed to. Half-way through the school year, teaching for Beth had become a 'job', requiring little involvement of self. Previously it had been more of an expression of her ideas and interests as these related to her sense of professional responsibilities. Her teacher education program had raised such expectations, and her student teaching experience had afforded some such opportunities. But the real teaching conditions of Sarah and Beth demanded defensive accommodations to a labor process in which they generally had insignificant control and responsibility.

While teachers do have a heavy workload, this does not include a role in making significant determinations about the education they are providing. Their pace and work volume, instead, create duties in addition to their instructional responsibilities. The quantity of work performed by teachers does not tell us anything about the quality of that work; typically, a high work volume increases their dependence upon prescribed materials. That is, they simply do not have the time to create many of their own lessons or to do much beyond distributing predesigned curricular materials.

Professionalism as a Teacher Ideology

The ideal-type of professionalism bears little relationship to the circumstances of teachers' work. Autonomy and the claim to expertise, for example, are weakened as teachers' 'professional' functions are of an increasingly technical nature. The accepted ways of doing things in a particular school patterns teachers' practices to a greater extent than does theoretical, specialized 'expert' knowledge.

A concern with professionalism is similar in some respects to a concern with craft. Prospective teachers are often viewed as 'apprentices' who will eventually become autonomous by acquiring expert knowledge and skills. As we have seen, these notions do not correspond to the work situation of many teachers. If professional expertise is conceived as involving the possession of knowledge about alternate teaching and learning processes, content knowledge, and the ability to create and design learning activities on the basis of the needs and interests of a particular group of students, then teaching as a job requires little professional expertise. For example, neither Beth nor Sarah possessed such knowledge or capabilities, nor were they engaged in processes structured to allow the development or expression of such expertise. Pedagogical expertise appears to be a marginal job requisite; hiring criteria stress much more a teacher's ability to get along and fit in with both the staff, students and sometimes parents, and upholding school norms, particularly those pertaining to school and classroom management.

There is some variation in the degree and nature of classroom autonomy that teachers have. Similarly, there is variation in forms of control. For example, in Cherry Grove, the implicit norms that guide behavior, are less visible than those found in Gershwin: the principal did not visit classrooms himself, however, he encouraged teachers to report on one another. Nevertheless, as Ryan points out, 'the teacher cannot shut his classroom door on the rest of the world, professing to merely teach and care for his children. General school and social policies have their consequences at the classroom level, for example, advocacy or criticism of particular texts or pedagogical approaches, overcrowded classrooms'. [38] While it is widely believed that teachers have significant classroom autonomy and concomitant control over the teaching process, the situations of many teachers, such as Sarah and Beth, do not support this contention.

Because to some extent teachers do expect autonomy and the exercise of a craft-like approach to teaching, problems surface. For example, while Beth and Sarah entered the teaching occupation with little sense of purpose or professional identity, they did hold similar expectations for classroom autonomy at the start of the school year. [39] As the year progressed, however, they learned to adjust these expectations downward, such as preparing for and administering tests in lieu of covering material to their personal satisfaction. While they were aware and somewhat critical of these pressures, being a good employee meant doing what the situation required of them, despite contrasting elements in their ideological make-up.[40] This obscured the nature of the work relations and expectations within which they were enmeshed. As Burawoy has shown, such adjustments act as mechanisms through which employees come to accept existing work arrangements as natural or inevitable.[41] This occurs in large part through choices employees make. Beth and Sarah's accommodations did not preclude some independent initiatives with respect to curriculum and instruction; in fact, these initiatives reinforced their acceptance of the prevailing organization of their work. An awareness of these tensions and ambivalent accommodations is central to an understanding of teaching practices, despite whatever transient resistances individual teachers may mount.

Teacher acceptance of the constraints on their work situation must be understood by looking at the choices and decisions that teachers actually make *in relation to other choices and decisions that teachers have no collective voice over.* Both Burawoy and Derber argue that one common employee response to a loss of control over decisions pertaining to the form and purposes of work is to deny that such control is really of any value. Correspondingly, the significance of the decisions that one can and does make is exaggerated. Derber relates this insight to his concept of 'ideological desensitization' — an historically evolved defensive response to ideological proletarianization.

At the heart of ideological desensitization is a feeling of having little or no responsibility for the uses to which one's work is put and a feeling of detachment from the social context of one's work — feelings common to the labor force as a whole. While employees may subjectively experience this as a form of independence from their workplace, objectively it helps them avoid important moral and social questions. The conflict here with the ideology of professionalism is clear, given, for example, traditional professional claims to a service ideal and moral calling. Derber argues that this conflict has led professional workers to adopt a second accommodative response to management objectives — 'ideological cooptation'. This refers to the process by which employees come to identify with their workplace as an organization and thereby redefine their own goals so that they do not conflict with the organization's. This is done, for example, by perceiving one's workplace as being committed to one's own purposes and objectives. We see this process of ideological cooptation with Sarah and Beth, when they rationalized having to 'teach to the tests'.

Conclusion

When analyzed in relation to critical sociological and educational scholarship, the experiences of Sarah and Beth illustrate how the proletarianization thesis is relevant to an understanding of the specific nature of teaching. The theory of the proletarianization of professional and other 'white collar' work offers a significant and controversial way of thinking about teachers. Clearly, the role of the economy in the tendency toward proletarianization in industry is more direct and more easily discernable than it is in the sphere of state employment, such as schooling. This is a problem that merits explicit study. As state employees in a capitalist society, teachers are vulnerable to the particular organization of their workplace and the control and direction of management, despite prevailing under-standings of professionalism. Hence I have stressed the relevance of a conceptualization and investigation of *teachers as workers.*

We can examine the current structure of teachers' work in order to discern the kinds of decisions teachers actually make together with the forms of control to which they are subjected. We have seen, for example, the following organizational and ideological features of teachers' work functioning as controls: architectural design; curricular programs; staff norms; elements of the ideology of professionalism; the frequency and agenda of meetings; parental pressures; the role of the principal; the absence of opportunities for genuine teacher collectivity; and a heavy work volume. From this perspective, both the data in the study under consideration together with relevant literature suggest that teaching is determined to a significant degree by the standard operating procedures within specific schools — which are connected to larger structural relations. Further, a look at the increased number of school administrators and curricular and instructional specialists suggests *increased* technical and organizational subordination. Job specialization, frag-mentation, deskilling and intensification also place limits on the range of decisions teachers can make as well as the decisions that teachers themselves feel competent to make. Along with increased use of prescribed or 'recommended' curriculum materials and pre-specified learning outcomes (reflecting an increased rationalization of teachers' work) the above job features provide strong justification for considering teaching as a proletarianized occupation, rather than as a 'profession'.

However, the proletarianization of 'educated workers' is signi-ficantly different from that of industrial workers.[42] There is some room, for example, for teachers to interpret the information they are required to distribute to students. Teachers have some limited control over their general work conditions, work processes and the ends towards which they work. In fact, some studies suggest that while professionals are being proletarianized, they are not being deskilled.[43] Derber suggests that this difference may be central for understanding the difference between professional and industrial workers:

> Professionals may be becoming workers, but in this period they appear to be a new type not adequately conceptualized in existing Marxist theory; unlike industrial workers, they maintain their 'craft' skills and their relative autonomy over the technical aspects of their work.[44]

A lack of empirical evidence contributes to differing views among radical scholars on whether effective control of professional activities requires the removal of skill, knowledge and discretion. However, the present study does not support Derber's proposition as applied to public school teaching. To the contrary, my findings clearly suggest proletarianization at the technical level. Derber's separation of ideological from technical proletarianization is over-drawn, because the key forms of proletarianization — job speciali-zation, fragmentation, deskilling and intensification — necessarily have both ideological and technical aspects. Ideological and technical proletarianization are, for teachers, intimately linked. The technical division of labor among educators occurs within a hierarchical context in which fundamental control over the teaching process rests with the upper levels of the hierarchy, not with teachers themselves. This implies the integration of both a social and technical division of labor. Further, the distinction between ideological and technical proletarianization rests upon an overly narrow definition of skill. Skill is more appropriately conceived as including some under-standing of and involvement with the means and ends of one's work. In this view, ideological proletarianization implies technical proletarianization.

Professional expertise, when defined in predominantly technical terms, ties teachers more strongly to the basic objectives of their schools and further integrates them into the hierarchical structuring of their labor process. Professionalism and bureaucracy are actually compatible forms of organization. As we have seen, belief in profes-sionalism does not necessarily imply autonomous professional goals for the bureaucratic employee. For teachers, the definition of 'professional expertise' reflects a situation in which they have already been excluded from the potential for full exercise or development of content knowledge and related teaching skills. Thus, while the ideology of professionalism is supported by certain aspects of teachers' work, the conflicted and contradictory nature of this ideology effectively promotes proletarianized forms of teaching.

While the present study does not support the notion that teachers possess or exercise a broad range of sophisticated pedagogical skills and knowledge, nor that they are free from technical controls, teachers can, and do, make choices and decisions on the job. Here an understanding of the system of control over the teaching process involves ideological considerations. First, exercising some discretion on the job helps teachers maintain a sense of the importance of their individual abilities and to support the ideology of professionalism. Second, through such mechanisms as organization and management initiatives, teachers' control over students, and defensive teacher reactions to their proletarianization, teachers come to identify with the goals and interests of their particular school. Third, by relying on traditional notions of professionalism, including a high value placed on individualism, teachers ignore their changing work situation and the underlying structural conflicts that they commonly face.

It has been argued that teachers' objective work conditions are likely to result in the erosion of teachers' professional self-image and lead them to the conclusion that their interests can best be served by collective organization against the state.[45] Indeed, particular contradictions do surface, for example, between a teacher's expectations and actual job opportunities, or between a teacher's responsibilities and corresponding lack of authority. However, because of their ideological and practical orientations, teacher responses are generally quite consistent with administrative interests. Further, teachers do not comprise a homogeneous group. Particular elements of the ideology of professionalism retain vitality for at least some teachers, particularly elements that pertain to status and the value assigned to individualism. The individualism of most teachers is reinforced by working in separate classrooms or the belief in the importance of their technical skills. Even Gershwin's 'pod' structure did not alter this, in large part because of the mandated performance-based curriculum. Due to the intensification of their labor teachers have few opportunities for association with one another. They simply lack the time. Hence teacher definitions of autonomy and control are frequently of a narrow scope and do not encompass a role in determining educational content and purpose.[46]

While public school teachers are likely to have more individual autonomy on the job than do industrial workers, neither this nor the nature of the discretion that they wield should be exaggerated. Many teachers maintain an identity as independent professionals despite their objective work situation, and perceive themselves as extensions of management rather than as workers. Their experience of control over students helps to secure this perception. With its emphasis on individualism (for example, individual responsibility) the ideology of professionalism prevents teachers from recognizing that their problems are shared by other teachers, and other workers; consequently, they tend to view failures and problems in personal terms, and do not seek social or institutional structural changes. The Marxian literature on the labor process, to the extent that it is based upon an ideal of the independent craftsperson, and to the extent that it either implicitly or explicitly encourages a return to that form of work organization, actually reinforces conventional notions of professionalism.[47] Hence we find even 'radical' critics encouraging teachers to view themselves as 'professionals'.

The ideology of professionalism distracts teachers from recognizing and turning to their advantage current tendencies in the organization of work in our society. For example, by working as individuals, teachers are less able to share in the benefits that accrue from *genuine* team teaching and the *collective* development of curricular materials. Similarly, to the extent that the general public expects teachers as 'professionals' to provide quality educational experiences for the young, they fail to recognize and press for changes in the existing institutional arrangements within which teachers work necessary for improving the quality of education that students receive. It is therefore important to clarify how traditional conceptions of professionalism do not serve teachers' interests.[48]

We should consider the intersection of the questions concerning educational control and purpose. We need democratic means for defining educational problems, and must broaden the terrain of debate. The development of mechanisms to ensure more democratic educational control has critical implications. The problems that are inherent in the extant organization of teachers' work cannot be solved simply by the reunification of conception and execution. For individual teachers such reunification *is* necessary if their work is to afford opportunities for the expression and development of human potential, but in itself this will not address broader social issues. Schooling cannot be transformed in the absence of larger social changes. Just as an understanding of education necessitates an understanding of capitalist society, efforts to change it must be part of broader efforts to transform exploitative social relations. Collective organization and action by teachers are needed in order to give teachers as workers more power in their place of work, but more inclusive alliances between teachers and non-teachers are also critical if a new educational politics is to take root. Educators alone cannot correct our educational problems because these problems are not usually confined to educational institutions. The issue of democratizing control over schools challenges its bureaucratic dimension; provides opportunities for debate about, and public involvement in, defining educational purposes; and helps to counteract the isolating and individualistic features of teacher professionalism (for example, hostility or suspicion toward parents and community involvement).

The current economic crisis encourages state policy directives toward greater control of, and reduced skill requirements for, state employees, including teachers. Changes in teachers' work situation are related to similar transformations in the work processes of other employees, especially employees in the public sector. The ideology of professionalism must be challenged because it fosters a feeling of superiority over other workers. It interferes with a recognition of the proletarianization of teaching, and ignores the origins of proletarianization in class conflict.[49] Given the cultural baggage of this ideology together with its interdependent elements, it is unlikely that particular aspects can be separated out from the rest and 'capitalized upon'. The ideology serves neither the interests of teachers nor of the public — nor, for that matter, of students.

Teacher education, which encourages the ideology of professionalism, must also be challenged. The belief that imparting specialized 'expert' knowledge and skills will itself enable teachers to exercise greater initiative in the public schools is mistaken, given what we know about teachers' labor process. Further, imparting this belief to new teachers inhibits teacher collectivity. The fact is that teacher education actually plays a minor role in promoting the vitality of public school systems. It is to the existing structure of teachers' work and its relation to broader social forces that we must turn our attention and collective efforts.

Acknowledgments

I am particularly grateful to Nick Burbules and Tom Popkewitz for their comments on earlier versions of this chapter.

Notes

1. See APPLE, M. (1979) *Ideology and Curriculum*, Boston, Routledge and Kegan Paul, especially chapters 4 and 6.
2. See, for example, RYAN, B. (1982) 'Accountability in Australian education', *Discourse: The Australian Journal of Education Studies*, 2, pp. 21–40.
3. For a reasoned critique of this perspective, see BARROW, R. (1984) *Giving Teaching Back to Teachers, A Critical Introduction to Curriculum Theory*, Totowa, NJ, Barnes and Noble Books.
4. Fifth-year programs tend to promote this way of thinking.
5. DENSMORE, K. (1984) 'An interpretation of teaching: Two case studies of beginning teachers', unpublished PhD thesis, University of Wisconsin, Madison.
6. The literature on the sociology of the professions conventionally employs a set of traits against which occupations are measured to assess the nature of the work involved and thereby determine the degree to which an occupation constitutes a profession. See, for example, GREENWOOD, E. (1957) 'Attributes of a profession', *Social Work*, 2, 3, July, pp. 45–55; and WILENSKY, H. (1964) 'The professionalization of everyone?', *The American Journal of Sociology*, 70, 2, September, pp. 137–58.
7. See, for example, DARLING-HAMMOND, L. (1985) 'Valuing teachers: The making of a profession', *Teachers College Record*, 87, 2, winter, pp. 205–18.
8. See, for example, BIDWELL, C. (1965) 'The school as a formal organization', in MARCH, J.G. (Ed.) *Handbook of Organizations*, Chicago, Rand-McNally; and WEICK, K. (1976) 'Educational organizations as loosely coupled systems', *Administrative Science Quarterly*, 21 pp. 1–19.
9. See, for example, APPLE, M. (1983) 'Curricular form and the logic of technical control', in APPLE, M. and WEIS, L. (Eds) *Ideology and Practice in Schooling*, Philadelphia, PA, Temple University Press.
10. MEYER, J. and ROWAN, B. (1978) 'The structure of educational organizations', in MEYER, M. (Ed.) *Environments and Organizations*, San Francisco, CA, Jossey Bass, pp. 78–109.
11. WARREN, R. 'The classroom as a sanctuary for teachers: Discontinuities in social control', *American Anthropologist*, 75, 1–3, pp. 280–91.
12. WHITE, R. (1983) 'Teachers as state workers and the politics of profes-

sionalism', unpublished PhD thesis, Department of Sociology, Australian National University.
13. LARSON, M. (1980) 'Proletarianization and educated labor', *Theory and Society*, 9, 1, pp. 131–75; and LARSON, M. (1977) *The Rise of Professionalism — A Sociological Analysis*, Berkeley, CA, University of California Press.
14. WHITE, R. (1983) *op cit.*
15. See, for example, JOHNSTON, D. (Ed.) (1982) *Class and Social Development, A New Theory of the Middle Class*, Beverly Hills, CA, Sage Publications, especially chapters 8–11, where the development of the teaching profession is discussed in relation to the deprofessionalization of the middle class.
16. BRAVERMAN, H. (1974) *Labor and Monopoly Capital*, New York, Monthly Review Press.
17. See, for example, GORDON, D., EDWARDS, R. and REICH, M. (1982) *Segmented Work, Divided Workers: The Historical Transformation of Labor in the United States.* Cambridge, MA, Cambridge University Press; BOREHAM, P. and DOW, G. (Eds) (1980) *Work and Inequality, Vols. I and II*, South Melbourne, Australia, Macmillan Press; and WRIGHT, E. (1978) *Class, Crisis and State.* London, New Left Books.
18. JOHNSON, D. (Ed.) (1982) *op cit.*
19. LARSON, M. (1980) *op cit.*; EDWARDS, R. (1979) *Contested Terrain: The Transformation of the Workplace in the Twentieth Century*, New York, Basic Books; BURAWOY, M. (1979) *Manufacturing Consent, Changes in the Labor Process under Monopoly Capitalism*, Chicago, University of Chicago Press; and BURAWOY, M. (1978) 'Towards a Marxist theory of the labor process: Braverman and beyond', *Politics and Society*, 8, 3–4, pp. 267–374.
20. COOLEY, M. (1980) *Architect or Bee? The Human/Technology Relationship*, Boston, MA, South End Press.
21. STROBER, M. (1982) 'Segregation by gender in public school teaching: Toward a general theory of occupational segregation in the labor market', paper prepared for National Academy of Sciences, National Research Council, Committee on Women's Employment and Related Issues, Workshop on Job Segregation by Sex, 24–25 May, Washington, DC.
22. APPLE, M. (1982) 'Class, gender, and teaching in the United States and England', unpublished paper.
23. Scholars continue to examine the issue of why patriarchy is so persistent in capitalism. For a treatment of this issue in relation to the deskilling process, see GAME, A. and PRINGLE, R. (1983) *Gender at Work*, Boston, MA, Allen and Unwin.
24. DERBER, C. (Ed.). (1982) *Professionals as Workers: Mental Labor in Advanced Capitalism*, Boston, MA, G.K. Hall.
25. *Ibid.* p. 200

26. DENSMORE, K. (1984) *op cit.*

27. I thank David Hamilton for helping me think this through.

28. FRIEDMAN, A. (1977) *Industry and Labor: Class Struggle at Work and Monopoly Capitalism*, London, Macmillan Press, Ltd. 'Relative autonomy' is similar to Edwards' 'bureaucratic control'.

29. I thank Harvey Kantor for his help on these issues. For a discussion on the rise of the ideology of professionalism, see LARSON, M. (1977) *op cit.*; see also WRIGLEY, J. (1982) *Class Politics and Public Schools*, New Brunswick, Rutgers University Press; and URBAN, W. (1982) *Why Teachers Organized*, Detroit, MI, Wayne State University Press, for analyses of the political struggles involved in the growth of schooling and teacher professionalism.

30. The absence of a gender analysis and a more thorough conceptualization of the relationship between bureaucratization and proletarianization are serious limitations to theories of proletarianization in general and to the present essay in particular.

3¹. See, for example, O'CONNOR, J. (1973) *The Fiscal Crisis of the State*, New York, St. Martin's Press.

32. For a more complete description of these schools and teachers, see DENSMORE, K. (1984) *op cit.* Despite the fact that Sarah and Beth are first-year teachers, I would argue that their working conditions are basically typical of teachers at large. The significance of their being first-year teachers is that their *expectations* for their work stand in sharp contrast to the reality of their work situation. The analysis of their teaching is descriptive and illustrative in nature, it is an attempt to provide a condensed account of specific control mechanisms in the two schools under study, including the ways in which teachers' conceptions of professionalism interacted with these control mechanisms.

33. If we conceive of skill as involving the unification of conception and execution, teaching may never have involved much skill. This is a clear example of where analyses of gender, professionalism and the labor process of teachers must be integrated. Female-dominated occupations tend not to be credited with requiring high skill levels. See GAME, A. and PRINGLE, R. (1983) *op cit.* for their insights into how the deskilling hypothesis fails to adequately deal with the complexities of both class and gender.

34. While teachers have been reported to be capable of distancing themselves from various social pressures (for example, parents) by asserting their claims to professional expertise (for example, WHITE, R. (1983) *op cit.*), the data on this school do not support this contention.

35. WHITE, R. (1983) *op cit.*; and LARSON, M. (1980) *op cit.*, respectively.

36. In many school districts this is attempted through various 'merit pay' schemes.

37. One typical feature of teacher education programs is that male professors are generally teaching female students. In this situation,

relations between professors and students parallel students' future relations with principals. The historical relations among the bureaucratization, proletarianization, and feminization of teaching are in need of further study. To some extent, control of teachers has been achieved through bureaucratic authority structures that parallel relations in the domestic sphere. For instance, in moving from the home to the workplace, female teachers typically move from one restrictive environment to another. In addition, the job itself encourages mothering qualities, especially elementary teaching. Further research must consider how the movement of men into the occupation influenced these developments. Some scholars have implied that the primary reason teachers have not achieved full professional status is because of the predominantly female composition of the workforce. See, for example, LORTIE, D. (1975) *Schoolteacher: A Sociological Study*, Chicago, University of Chicago Press. Women lack, it is suggested, a serious commitment to teaching — commitment being a critical feature of the professional ideal. It is debatable whether in teaching women have been permitted to enter the occupation because of its low prestige or whether teaching has low prestige because most teachers are women. Both factors may operate.

38. RYAN, B. (1982) *op cit.*, p. 28.
39. TABACHNICK, B., ZEICHNER, K., DENSMORE, K. and HUDAK, G. (1983) 'The development of teacher perspectives', AERA, Montreal, April; and DENSMORE, K. (1983) 'The world of work: The development of teachers' and students' perspectives', AERA, Montreal, April.
40. For a good analysis of how bureaucratic employees tend to cope with job pressures, see LIPSKY, M. (1980) *Street-level Bureaucracy, Dilemmas of the Individual in Public Services*, New York, Russell Sage Foundation.
41. BURAWOY, M. (1979) *op cit.*
42. LARSON, M. (1980) *op cit.*
43. See, for example, SPANGLER, E. and LEHMAN, P. (1982) 'Lawyering as work', in DERBER C. (Ed.) *op cit.*
44. DERBER, C. (Ed.) (1982) *op cit.*, p. 195.
45. See, for example, OZGA, J. and LAWN, M. (1981) *Teachers, Professionalism and Class: A Study of Organized Teachers*, Lewes, Falmer Press.
46. GRACE, G. (1978) *Teachers, Ideology and Control*, London, Routledge and Kegan Paul.
47. I thank Jerry Lembke for discussions on this matter.
48. For a contrasting perspective and critical discussion on why we should retain elements of the ideology of teacher professionalism, see CARLSON, D. (1984) 'Teachers, class culture, and the politics of schooling', unpublished paper.
49. The denial of class conflict is attempted, for example, through stressing educational opportunities and hence the supposed accessibility of professional states to everyone.

6 Ideology and Control in Teacher Education: A Review of Recent Experience in England

Geoff Whitty, Len Barton and Andrew Pollard

Just as in nineteenth-century England teachers were often seen to occupy a crucial role in the maintenance of social order but one which potentially they might abuse[1], so in recent years have successive governments looked to possible weaknesses in the teaching force as an explanation for what they perceive as broader failings within English society. In Mrs Thatcher's Conservative government of the 1980s, Sir Keith Joseph, as her longest-serving Secretary of State for Education to date, has seen the improvement of 'teaching quality'[2] as a crucial element of a wider strategy to produce 'better schools'[3] which would serve that government's vision of the future of English society more effectively. Though the improvement of teaching quality is partly to be achieved through the introduction of appraisal schemes for serving teachers, the most tangible effects of the strategy have so far been felt largely within initial teacher education. While teacher education has been, in many ways, the cinderella of the English higher education system, it has also been subjected to more changes in public policy than virtually any other section of that system. In a recent paper, Reid has characterized teacher education over the past twenty-five years as a series of 'hoops, swings and roundabouts'.[4]

This extreme susceptibility of teacher education to changes of policy partly results from section 62 of the 1944 Education Act which vested in the Minister of Education, subsequently the Secretary of State for Education and Science, the power to 'make such arrangements as he considers expedient for securing that there shall be available sufficient facilities for the training of teachers'.[5] In practice, political expediency has frequently overshadowed rational forward planning in this field, producing periods of crash expansion followed by periods of equally rapid contraction. However, even if demographic trends, together with changing priorities in public expenditure, may have been the major influences on the pattern of post-war teacher education, it is quite clear that the present government is determined to use the powers of the Secretary of State to further its own ideological purposes. It is upon this aspect of recent developments in teacher education that we shall concentrate in this chapter. The three authors share a commitment to studying the relationship of education to social reproduction and transformation, but we bring to the task rather different backgrounds in teacher education, having come to our present positions from a university, a college of higher education and a polytechnic respectively.

Developments in Teacher Education since 1945

Until recently, changes in government policy have had their major effects on the practice of teacher education only within the so-called public-sector colleges, maintained by local education authorities or various voluntary (usually religious) bodies. The training of mainly secondary teachers on the one-year postgraduate certificate in education courses in the universities had continued relatively untouched by government policy. The availability of places on such courses was increased to meet student demand, rather than the demand for teachers, and only in the last few years has the University Grants Committee (UGC) clearly chosen to reflect government planning priorities within its funding policies in this field. For much of the post-war period, following a recommendation of the McNair Report[6] implemented in 1947, the universities also had a large measure of control over the content of teacher training for non-graduate entrants to the profession, largely destined to teach in primary and secondary modern schools. Though such teachers received their preparation for teaching in public sector teacher training colleges maintained by local education authorities and religious bodies, the award of the teacher training qualification (or Certificate in Education) was the responsibility of Area Training Organizations (ATOs) based, in all cases except one, upon university institutes or schools of education[7].

The expansion of teacher education in the 1950s and 1960s also brought some limited enhancement of its status within higher education as a whole. Within the universities, departments of education[8] increasingly became centres of research and advanced study rather than merely undemanding finishing schools for graduates wishing to enter teaching or centres for the administration of courses taught elsewhere. Meanwhile, most of those training college courses themselves were extended from two years to three years in 1960 and, in the post-Robbins reforms,[9] many students had the opportunity to remain for a further year to gain a Bachelor of Education (BEd) or Bachelor of Education (Honours) degree. Subsequently, after the James Report[10] of 1972, certificate courses were virtually abandoned altogether to be replaced by three-year BEd or four-year BEd (Hons) degree courses which were intended to make teaching ultimately an all-graduate profession. Though the Robbins proposal to integrate the colleges fully into the university sector was never implemented, the 1960s had seen a significant change in name from teacher training colleges to colleges of education and the content of the professional and educational studies elements of their courses had shifted markedly from the purveying of 'tips for teachers' to heavy doses of academic philosophy, psychology, history and sociology of education. The emphasis became increasingly on teacher education in a wider sense, rather than merely teacher training, though there were those who felt that the new academic content might detract from the development of teaching skills. Indeed, the relationship between theory and practice has been a constant theme of the house journals of teacher educators ever since.[11]

Alongside these changes, the 1970s saw some reduction in the universities' domination of the validation of the courses offered within the colleges of education. This came about for a variety of reasons, many of them associated with the massive rationalization and diversification programme for teacher education embarked upon in the mid-1970s[12] which located most of the institutions in which teacher education courses were provided more firmly than ever on the non-university side of the 'binary line'.[13] Although this association with the public rather than the university sector had been resented in the mid-1960s, by the mid-1970s it offered a much-needed lifeline for teacher education. As time went on, the aspirations of the public sector system of higher education for parity of esteem with the universities increasingly pointed (in the absence of self-validation as an option) in the direction of validation of all courses by the Council for National Academic Awards (CNAA) rather than remaining under the tutelage of local universities. The demise of the ATOs in the mid-1970s and the voluntary withdrawal of certain major universities from the validation of courses in colleges of education exacerbated this process. The National Union of Teachers (NUT) was also keen to reduce university influence over teacher education as it had long been far from enthusiastic about the influence of universities over BEd courses[14]. The end result was a rather ad hoc system of teacher education, with the majority of surviving institutions becoming diversified local authority or voluntary colleges of higher education or incorporated into local polytechnics. However, a few teacher education colleges remained essentially monotechnics and a handful did now become completely incorporated into universities, thus making the latter significant providers of undergraduate as well as postgraduate courses in education.[15] A growing majority of public sector institutions chose validation through CNAA, though a few continued to receive course validation from local universities.

Though mourned by many at the time, the abolition of the ATOs was seen by some teacher educators, particularly those who espoused socially progressive ideals, as a liberation from the rather archaic and over-academic orientation of at least some of the universities. Though, in its procedures, the CNAA often appeared as an all-powerful and (by comparison with local universities) distant institution, it provided a model of course validation which few who experienced it could regard as less rigorous than that employed by universities. As it gained in confidence, the CNAA made a creditable effort to assist colleges to pioneer the development of rigorous but professionally-relevant teacher education courses which could support progressive practice within schools. However, public sector higher education has so far failed to attain parity of esteem with the universities and the CNAA remains associated in ministerial and, to some extent, public eyes with low academic standards and even perhaps student unrest in the polytechnics. It has therefore perhaps proved a less effective buffer against political interference in the content of teacher education than the old university-dominated ATOs.

Be that as it may, the present Conservative administration has shown itself more willing than any of its predecessors to intervene directly to control the nature of teacher education, not only within the public sector but also within the universities themselves. Though the granting of Qualified Teacher Status (QTS) to individual teachers has traditionally been the prerogative of the Department of Education and Science, the approval of courses by the old ATOs was effectively taken as a guarantee of the quality of their products. Though there have been a number of changes of procedure over the years,[16] a similar practice was continued in respect of courses validated by the CNAA and by individual universities. However, the 1983 White Paper on *Teaching Quality* and the issuing of DES Circular 3/84 has lead to the establishment of the Council for the Accreditation of Teacher Education (CATE), a quango which is responsible for professional accreditation whilst CNAA and the universities remain responsible for academic validation.[17] Academic validation of courses has thus become clearly separated from the assessment of the suitability of courses to give their graduates QTS. The new body enhances the government's capacity to control directly the nature of teacher education by scrutinizing courses of initial teacher training in all sectors and advising the Secretary of State of their appropriateness in terms of criteria defined by central government. In its work it is advised by a strengthened central government inspectorate (HMI), whose visitations to university departments of education have effectively breached some of that sector's traditional autonomy, even though, unlike the visits to public sector institutions, they are not termed inspections and even though their reports are made public only with university agreement.[18]

In other respects, central government influence on university based teacher education has remained, at least hitherto, far less obvious than that on the public sector. Thus, for example, the government has not chosen to challenge university autonomy to the extent of overturning UGC decisions on the funding of teacher education places in specific university institutions, even if it is clear that the UGC has itself moved to safeguard its autonomy by not repeating the apparent disregard of governmental priorities displayed in its general distribution of grant in 1981. Meanwhile, the government has rejected the advice on the distribution of teacher education places given by its own much less autonomous nationally advisory body for public sector higher education (NAB). Though the advice of NAB has not always been accepted in other fields either, the Secretary of State's peculiar responsibility for the allocation of teacher training numbers has recently been invoked to initiate a further full-scale review of the location of teacher education in the non-university sector, utilizing criteria of cost-effectiveness, resilience and quality which, when taken together with the advice of CATE, place firmly in the hands of government decisions about what styles of teacher education (increasingly, once again, termed teacher training) should survive into the 1990s.

When one looks at teacher education over the past forty years and the various half-hearted and abortive attempts to reform it, there is a superficially attractive case for the sort of intervention being attempted by central government. There are so many variations in the pattern of teacher education that, in some ways, it is now as difficult to speak of a coherent national system of teacher education as it was to speak of such a system of secondary education in the 1970s. While the task of secondary reorganization is virtually completed, though now being complicated by tertiary systems and possibly voucher schemes, teacher education remains an obvious case for rationalization by anyone attracted by tidy solutions. With the universities, CNAA, local education authorities, voluntary bodies, as well as myriad pressure groups all seeking to speak on behalf of teacher education or particular sections of it, it has proved more difficult for governments to exercise any direct control over its nature and its output than the terms of the 1944 Education Act might seem to suggest. When, however, one looks both at the detail of this government's attempts to exercise control and at the broader context within which these attempts are being made, it is difficult not to be suspicious of its motives and anxious about the outcome of the exercise.

At first sight, one would not have expected the present Conservative government to be committed to tidy solutions. The previous rationalization exercise,[19] which has left us with the present untidy situation despite the earlier recommendations of the James Report,[20] was, after all, begun when Mrs Thatcher was Secretary of State for Education. Arguably, though, the present exercise could be regarded as a return to 'unfinished business'. At a more philosophical level, however, one might have expected this government to defend either a variety of local solutions (as the previous Conservative administration did in relation to secondary reorganization) or a free market solution in which only the fittest survived. Equally, one might have expected the latter preference to be accompanied by a distrust of centralized state control and state bureaucracy. In practice, though, what this government has objected to is the existence of intervening political arenas in which attempts can be made to contest or frustrate central government policies which alone it regards as responding to the will of 'the nation'. Where necessary, it has even created or strengthened alternative intervening power bases more responsive to its own will even if the price has been an extension of state bureaucracy. The abolition of the metropolitan counties and the increasing use of the Manpower Services Commission to carry through policies that the local education authorities have been reluctant to pursue are examples of this trend, while the establishment of CATE as a challenge to the power of all those groups with a traditional interest in teacher education is as much a local reflection of this broader policy as it is a specific attack on those involved in teacher education.

Having said that, there can be no doubt that this particular government has little affection for teacher educators in either the university or the public sector, though the former have some staunch supporters in the upper reaches of the Inspectorate. The concern that teachers have sold the country short, a constant theme of the Black Papers,[21] has remained a potent rallying cry for Conservative politicians despite James Callaghan's attempt to hijack it for the Labour government in the mid-1970s.[22] In the eyes of those right-wing commentators whose views have a particular appeal to the Thatcherite wing of the Conservative Party, teacher trainers (and especially sociologists of education) are implicated along with trade union leaders, Trotskyite teachers, social workers, etc. in the economic and moral decline of the nation. In other accounts, educationists are seen as academics who could not have made it in any other field.[23]

The attempt to control teacher education is not thus merely an attempt at control for its own sake, even if it often appears that way, but control that has at its root a vision of a desirable social order, whose realization is at least partially being frustrated by the present state of teacher education. Though Maclure may have been correct to say, in an address to the Universities Council for the Education of Teachers (UCET) in 1983, that 'the actual details of the [government's] new proposals and the precise educational nuances which will be expressed in the criteria for accreditation are much less important than the assertion of control and the declaration of a readiness to exercise responsibility for it', it was his subsequent observation which was more significant:

> This is to be responsibility of a different order from the more familiar obsession with numbers and subject balances — this could go to the basic content and shape of courses.[24]

Indeed, as in other areas of current Conservative education policy, an analysis of this government's curricular prescriptions reveals an uneasy coexistence between advocacy of traditional Tory conceptions of a supposedly detached academic style of education and an unashamed desire to utilize education to foster a politically partisan view of the world, with a marked shift in the latter direction.[25] This is all the more ironic in that the Conservative attack on the left within higher education has itself often involved criticism of just such a shift.

A Critique of Current Policies

Let us then examine in more detail the current government's attempts to improve teaching quality through the reform of initial teacher education. It is worth pointing out, of course, that much of the research evidence suggests that initial teacher education has only limited effects on the performance of teachers even in their first posts[26] and that it is the form as much as the content of their college courses that is influential.[27] However, both government policy and the misgivings of its critics reflect a belief that initial teacher education is, or at least could be, more influential than the available evidence suggests it has been in the past. Of the various criteria set out in Circular 3/84, those concerning the subject backgrounds of students entering one-year postgraduate courses and the subject content of four-year degree courses, together with that requiring that teachers of pedagogy should have or be given recent, relevant and successful experience of school teaching, have proved the most contentious. They have also been the criteria which CATE has seemed determined to maintain despite misgivings not only amongst teacher educators but also amongst large sections of the teaching profession as a whole.

The subject study criterion set out in Circular 3/84 imposes the requirement that 'the equivalent of at least two full years' course time [should be] devoted to subject studies at a level appropriate to higher education'. This refers to the study within education degrees of academic subjects that students are likely to teach. An implicit questioning of the academic quality of work in the professional and educational studies elements of these degrees is evident here, but the major opposition to this criterion has arisen because of the way it will affect the balance of courses — particularly those designed for the professional education of teachers for primary schools. It is felt by many teacher educators that necessary professional work, and especially critical reflection upon professional practice, will be squeezed to a damaging extent by the operation of this criterion. Indeed, in many courses, professional work formerly occupied about two thirds of course time, whereas in future it can comprise no more than half — which must still include adequate practical work in schools. Although this requirement has been slightly mitigated by the clarification that, for primary students, a quarter of subject study time can be used to explore the application of subjects to young children's learning,[28] it has still led to unprecedented resistance amongst those engaged in the preparation of teachers for primary schools. An organization called the Undergraduate Primary Teacher Education Conference (UPTEC) has been established to campaign against it and has been joined by several teacher unions and the National Association of Primary Education (NAPE).

The criterion that staff engaged in teaching pedagogy should have recent, relevant and successful teaching experience has met with less outright opposition, though there is considerable controversy about what sort of experience is appropriate. Nevertheless, it is based on a debatable assumption that successful school teaching experience can be directly translated into effective teaching in higher education and, as Reid points out, it is not a criterion employed in the appointment of Secretaries of State for Education or even Her Majesty's Inspectorate of Schools.[29] However, most staff and institutions have tried hard to accommodate themselves to this criterion, leading to significant changes in practice, and many staff now receive relief from course teaching to go and work in schools. Nevertheless, Reid rightly suggests that teacher educators also need to maintain recent, relevant and substantial experience of research[30] and it is likely that, in a context where resources for higher education are diminishing, especially in the public sector, students will find themselves taught by tutors who are given time for school experience but who have little opportunity to engage in the analytic study of educational policy and practice. Meanwhile, staff recruitment policies have reversed the trend of the past twenty years or so, with recent school experience again beginning to overtake research background and educational qualifications as the dominant criterion for appointment to posts in teacher education.

When looking at government policies as a means of achieving greater control over teacher education, such changes can be seen to have significant consequences. They appear to have been designed so that, at one and the same time, the status and importance of experience is increased and that of analysis is decreased. The scale is thus tipped away from those who might ask questions towards those who will 'get on with the job'. It is undoubtedly the case that those education staff who identify themselves with the study of education via disciplines such as philosophy, sociology, psychology and history are finding themselves in retreat, whilst the populism of 'being an experienced teacher' takes over. Such developments may, however, be double-edged for the possibility exists that those with critical insights derived from these disciplines may sharpen them through their renewed contacts with schools. In doing so, their insights may actually acquire greater radical effectivity, especially as the staff concerned will be in a position to form alliances with practising school teachers to an extent that was inconceivable during the period when educational studies and classroom practice often lacked direct points of contact.

Many of the other criteria merely reinforce existing practice or introduce changes which few would regard as undesirable. Some of them (such as the extension of all one-year postgraduate courses to 36 weeks) can nevertheless be criticized both as tokenistic responses to major problems and as largely ineffectual in view of the fact that few additional resources are attached to the requirements. Others (such as the establishment of local committees for teacher education involving representatives of the wider community) may be motivated by a desire to limit professional autonomy but could ultimately have a potential quite at variance with the present government's intentions and with the current practice of most institutions. However, it is within some of the less celebrated, and surprisingly less controversial, criteria that one finds some of the most worrying indications about the sort of teaching force that this government desires. Indeed, we would argue that implicit within some of these criteria is clear confirmation that the present government's intention is that colleges should be back in the business of teacher training (if not teacher indoctrination) rather than teacher education.

Thus, the central thrust of recent interventions within teacher education seems to be concerned with producing a teaching force which is characterized by specific forms of subjectivity, which it is hoped will, in turn, lead to a style and content of teaching in schools that is more in line with government thinking. This attempt to influence prospective members of the profession is taking place in a context where changing the ways in which teachers and pupils think about the world has become an open and acknowledged task of the present government. It is informed by a narrow and instrumental view of schooling, increasingly concerned with evaluating the quality and effectiveness of schools in terms of how successfully they meet the needs of industry.[31] Wider pressures for accountability, teacher appraisal, cost effectiveness and a vocational orientation to schooling are all expressions of an historical period in which economic priorities are calling into question the appropriateness of the values currently espoused by teachers and educationists. Of course, the active involvement of the state in education is not new, but the modes of control being employed and the haste with which change is being attempted is virtually without precedent within the English educational system.[32]

For example, the overtly political orientation of the government on curriculum issues is in stark contrast to the approach of all parties during the post-war period of social democratic consensus, when such issues were treated as matters of professional judgment.[33] In the present government, as a radical teachers' magazine has put it:

> All Tory ministers seem to have been enlisted for the fight. Keith Joseph has tried to muzzle science teachers; Tebbit to restrict youth training schemes; Heseltine to intervene in the content of classroom resources [for peace education]. All are concerned about the social content of the curriculum and are trying to ensure that it never raises questions about the status quo. A thorough going application of their awareness of social context, relationship and process marks out this Tory government.[34]

More recently, Norman Tebbit, now Chairman of the Conservative Party, has suggested that anti-racism, anti-sexism and peace studies may be contributing to pupil disaffection and truancy. Approaches to education which give prominence to such concerns are therefore seen as a destabilizing influence in society and, ironically, as an unwarranted politicization of education.[35]

When, therefore, Circular 3/84 states that students on courses of initial teacher education will:

> also need to have a basic understanding of the type of society in which their pupils are growing up, with its cultural and racial mix, and of the relationship between the adult world and what is taught in schools, in particular, ways in which pupils can be helped to acquire an understanding of the value of a free society and its economic and other foundations[36]

such sentiments need to be interpreted within the context of the government's broader concerns about what is and is not taught in schools. The nature of the understanding being advocated here is of a very specific kind. It is understanding for society, and one particular vision of society at that, rather than about society. Though couched in terms which may not appear objectionable, and indeed in terms which may be open to other interpretations, courses informed by such requirements are clearly intended to strengthen support for the sort of competitive, free-market society to which the present government is committed.

Important as such relatively rare positive statements on the specific content of teacher education are, the silences of Circular 3/84 are even more revealing of the limited nature of the understanding of society which student teachers are expected to attain. For example, as Reid observes, it warns of the need to 'guard against preconceptions based on race or sex of pupils'.[37] Though this is, in itself, a rare and welcome official recognition of the importance of race and gender in structuring educational experience, the omission of social class as a dimension for analysis is almost certainly a convenient rather than just a negligent one.[38] Historically, class has been a key tool for identifying and explaining structural inequalities and their expression in different institutional settings. By its omission, particular issues and questions may not be raised and alternative forms of explanation may not be examined. Fortunately, the terms of the Circular do not actually preclude the raising of such issues and many teacher educators will find it impossible to help students 'to cope with a full range of pupils ... with their diversity of ability, social behaviour and ethnic and cultural origins' or assist pupils 'to acquire an understanding of the value of a free society'[39] without reference to, amongst others, those modes of analysis in which class is a central organizing category.

Equally disturbing in the government's approach is the absence of any suggestion that social critique might be an important part of a teacher's role and thus of a course in teacher education. Clearly the 'adult world' with which education is expected to enter into a closer relationship is not one towards which most teachers would want their pupils to have an uncritical orientation. It is a world characterized by increasing divisions, discriminations and tensions. The impact of unemployment and underemployment in English society is being felt in terms of the increased number of people living below the poverty line and being dependent on social security benefits.[40] Also, many young people, a disproportionate number of whom are blacks, are becoming pessimistic and distrustful of the state. Being wageless and apparently futureless, they view the state as being 'concerned with regulation and control, rather than help and support'.[41] These are not examples of temporary aberrations or surface problems, they are endemic to the nature of our society and deeply rooted in economic and structural inequalities. Teachers who are not prepared to confront critically these features of the 'adult world' will find it increasingly difficult to engage meaningfully with the children of such a society.

Meanwhile, the education system itself is witnessing serious upheavals. The demoralization of large sections of the teaching force is evident to all, with teacher unionism under attack and individual teachers facing redundancy or redeployment. The curriculum is both contracting and being redefined and the teaching force is facing ever increasing, but often contradictory, demands. In this situation, student teachers need to explore the nature of the pressures they will face in schools and certainly should not be expected to accept uncritically the government's own approach to improving teaching quality.[42] Yet, not only is serious consideration of such issues not being encouraged, the whole notion of criticism, surely an essential precondition of social change, is itself being challenged. In these circumstances, it is tempting to see such developments merely as evidence of the futility of seeking to foster a meaningful and critical approach to educational practice within the institutions of the capitalist state. In this vein, Sharp has recently written of 'the concerted attempt by the capitalist state to incorporate each [transformative] initiative, thereby subverting and dissipating their progressive potential' and 'the extraordinary effeteness of educational liberals, given their professed commitment to critical rational enquiry, in the face of a government determined to undermine even *their* concerns'. She also derides 'left academics caught up in professional education in a context where critical debate and fundamental appraisals of the ideological nature of state education are being progressively muzzled by a spurious commitment to professional standards'.[43]

Contradictions and Opportunities

Nevertheless, we would argue that the reality is somewhat more complicated than Sharp claims[44] and that we should certainly resist the temptation to treat recent developments as merely a sign of the times that we have to grin and bear. Like other elements of current education policy, government initiatives in teacher education are often contradictory and are far from monolithic in their effects. Although it is far from easy to foster socially progressive alternatives within contemporary teacher education, as elsewhere in the education service, our own experience has not been as uniformly negative as

Sharp's appears to have been. Though there are certainly aspects of the current economic and ideological climate that foster a rather instrumental attitude towards training amongst student teachers, it is only part of the story. It is still possible (even, we suspect, within CATE guidelines) to foster a spirit of critical reflection amongst student teachers. Indeed, their experience on teaching practice of declining material conditions and teacher morale generates a positive demand for critical reflection not only upon their own practice but also upon the ways in which state policy impinges upon it. This style of critical reflection upon experience may even contain rather more radical potential than the purely theoretical radicalism that dominated courses in the sociology of education for much of the 1970s.

Meanwhile, even members of HMI seem to retain a degree of independent thinking about the form and content of teacher education. Though they too are constrained by the CATE criteria, they often display a willingness to support approaches that are at variance with the narrowest interpretations of government intentions.[45] Certainly, our own recent experience of an HMI inspection was by no means entirely negative in this respect. Even though HMI have clearly suffered from ministerial incursions into their traditional professional autonomy, the notion of teacher education rather than teacher training is actually far from dead even within the Department of Education and Science. Rather than merely accepting, however reluctantly, the trends outlined above, there is therefore a strong case for capitalizing upon contradictions within government policy, and conflicts amongst those involved in its implementation, to argue that other models of teacher education should be placed on the agenda.

In another sense, too, recent developments in teacher education offer an opportunity for socially progressive teacher educators as well as a threat. Traditionalists within teacher education have only come to realize the seriousness of what is happening when it is already well under way. Initially, their reaction was typical of mainstream academic culture in Britain, which has been well characterized by Williams in the following terms:

> it acts as if today would be better if it were more like yesterday, but as if in any case tomorrow will be broadly similar to both. To support this belief, it has a formal sequence of responses, at both trivial and serious levels. These are: (a) it is not a problem; (b) it may well be a

problem but it is being exaggerated; (c) it is indeed a problem but it is being badly expressed; (d) it is certainly a problem but it is being grossly/obsessionally/hysterically formulated; (e) it is of course a problem but it is already well known and everything likely to solve it has already been tried; (f) it is a problem but it is (has become) boring.[46]

This 'old, tired, basically defensive culture, steeped in habits of privileged disparagement' has certainly used most of the weapons in this armoury in response to recent government attempts to reform teacher education, just as it has used them in the past to disparage proposed reforms from the left.[47] To the extent that government initiatives have forced it to recognize that there is a problem in teacher education and that, boring as it may be, it will not go away, they may even contain some benefits for those who have battled against such reactions from a different perspective. Thus, for example, attempts to redefine the relationship between theory and practice in teacher education may be less easily frustrated by vested interests in the new situation. It may then prove possible to foster discussion of alternatives not only to government initiatives but also to the traditional conceptions of teacher education which they challenge.

For example, enquiry oriented courses such as those discussed by Zeichner and Teitelbaum[48] may have considerable potential here. In a recent paper,[49] Zeichner offers a typology which distinguishes four orientations to the content of school experience programmes — 'behavioristic' and 'apprenticeship' models in which teaching skills and a received curriculum dominate, 'personalistic' approaches in which each student teacher's individual effectiveness and personal reflexivity are emphasized and his preferred 'enquiry oriented' approach in which teachers are conceived as professional decision-makers whose judgments are based on informed enquiry and socially aware reflection. Elsewhere,[50] Zeichner argues that most school experience programmes have treated educational issues narrowly. The consequence of this is that periods of professional practice in schools have been separated from the consideration of the moral, ethical and political issues which are implicit in them. In contrast, enquiry-oriented courses are designed to encourage what can be termed 'reflective teaching'.

We would suggest that there are four important features which are likely to be found in courses designed to encourage such reflective teaching. First, such courses will emphasize a concern with educational aims and consequences as well as having regard to means, technical skills and efficiency. It is assumed here that it is the responsibility of all teachers to consider such ethical and value-based issues and to contribute to the formation of policy, whether it be at classroom, school, local or national levels and students should therefore be prepared carefully for this role. A second characteristic of courses designed to support reflective teaching is that they seek to combine certain skills and attitudes. These skills are those which are involved in classroom enquiry, practical action and classroom competence and the attitudes are those of open-mindedness, wholeheartedness and responsibility.[51] Open-mindedness is used here in the sense of being willing to reflect upon oneself and to challenge one's own assumptions, prejudices and ideologies, as well as those of others. It does not, however, imply a lack of commitment to pursuing particular goals. Hence the necessity of wholeheartedness, in the sense of having a genuine enthusiasm and commitment to the quality of the teaching-learning process and the pursuance of social justice, and responsibility, by which we mean being socially aware and prepared to take action in respect of wider social issues. As Zeichner puts it in arguing this point:

> Because of the intimate relationships between the school and the social, political and economic contexts in which it exists, any consideration of the consequences to which classroom action leads must inevitably take one beyond the boundaries of the classroom and even of the school itself and beyond the consideration of educational principles alone ... An exclusive focus on the level of the classroom and on educational principles alone does not enable the student teacher to contemplate the kinds of basic structural changes that may be necessary for his or her responsibility to be fully exercised. The attention of student teachers remains focused on the amelioration of surface symptoms in individuals and not on an analysis of the social conditions that stand behind, and at least partially explain the existence of those symptoms.[52]

The third characteristic of courses designed to produce reflective teaching is that they are likely to emphasize a process model in which teachers monitor and evaluate their own practice reflexively. This cyclical process provides the fundamental dynamic of teacher action and relates to the more socially progressive strands of the action research and teacher-as-researcher movement. The final feature of such courses is that they attempt to relate educational disciplines and research to the teacher's own thinking. In such an approach, it is accepted that 'theory' should not be imposed, for, as Tom puts it:

> The effective teacher ... is not the one who has been pro-grammed with theory-based answers to many discrete teaching situations but instead is one who is able to conceive of his [or her] teaching in purposeful terms, can size up a particular teaching situation, chooses a teaching approach that seems appropriate to that situation, attempts the approach, judges the results in relation to the original purposes and reconsiders the original purposes.[53]

Teaching is thus treated as involving theorizing from the start and the nature of 'reflection-in-action' is recognized.[54] However, educational disciplines are not abandoned, as they tend to be in those approaches which celebrate experience to the exclusion of analysis. Rather, the disciplines are used to complement, extend, refine and, indeed, criticize the teacher's practical theorizing. Utilized as a resource in reflection upon experience, they can help the teacher to explore the interplay between ideologies, structures and specific contextual practices. The reflective teacher thus has not only the quality of classroom learning as his or her object of enquiry, but also the social meaning and consequences of the teaching and learning processes. Continuous and wide-ranging school experience within teacher education is welcomed by advocates of this model, because reflection in and on action is not abstracted from the activity of teaching itself.

Of course, such enquiry-oriented courses, with their focus on fostering reflective teaching of this sort, are unlikely to have been quite what the present government had in mind when it embarked upon its policies to reform teacher education. Yet there is nothing explicitly to prevent the emergence of such courses and, because CATE criteria regarding course design have been couched largely in terms of the number of hours for various elements, important details regarding specific content and processes, and the relationship between the various elements have been left for local determination. In some ways, government policies have actually made such courses more likely to emerge than they were before. The requirement to increase contact time in schools, combined with the squeeze on professional and educational studies caused by the two years of subject study criterion, makes it more likely that these areas of study will be merged into enquiry activities in school. In some cases, such school-based activities could replace not only professional and educational studies as conventionally conceived, but also the traditional teaching practice with its implicit apprenticeship model.

We have already intimated that the fact that the traditionalists within teacher education have been placed on the defensive is a positive side-effect of government policy. So is the fact that, as a result of the activities of CATE, successive rounds of resource cutbacks and the uncertainties generated by moves to 'rationalize' the number of institutions engaged in teacher education, many more teacher educators have themselves become aware of the social, political and economic issues surrounding education than otherwise might have been the case. The possibility of generating support for alternative approaches to teacher education is arguably greater than it has been in the past — a situation created, in no small part, by the contradictions that follow from the government's own initiatives. There are, however, those who argue that is unnecessary or unwise to pursue active alternatives too vigorously at the present time. They suggest that demographic forces are anyway working in our favour and that, in a period of relative expansion over the next few years, socially progressive teacher educators will be in an increasingly better bargaining position. Though there are some senses in which teacher educators may well find themselves in a relatively strong bargaining position compared to teachers of other disciplines within higher education, they are unlikely to be exempt from the central thrust of state policy, especially once they have shown themselves willing to concur with it. The optimism of the 1960s was anyway no defence against the attack on public sector provision in the 1970s. This is why it is important to recognize not only that policies in relation to teacher education have common features with other aspects of social policy, but also that successful resistance to those policies requires not only mobilization around coherent alternatives but also the building of alliances with other groups undergoing similar experiences.

At a professional level, this is already beginning to happen. The perceived threat from CATE has stimulated an unprecedented degree of cooperation between interest groups, such as the various teaching unions, universities, polytechnics, colleges and LEAs, who in the past have jealously defended their own particular roles in professional preparation and membership of the profession. Discussions about the formation of a General Teaching Council, which amongst other functions would take on some of the responsibilities of the DES and CATE, are more advanced now than they have ever been in the long history of such negotiations.[55] However, socially progressive teacher educators should be looking beyond a merely professional response to current initiatives and to one which goes well beyond the defence of professional autonomy for its own sake. If the prevailing system of teacher education, like the education service more generally, is seen as responding inadequately to the present government's priorities, it also responds inadequately to the interests and experiences of what are often termed the 'popular constituencies' — the working class, women and blacks, for example — and their political movements.[56] There is even a sense in which Thatcherism represents a welcome politicization of questions which have traditionally been regarded as apolitical. Just as the present government seeks to develop a model of teacher education which will further its own vision of a future social order, it is time that socially progressive teacher educators developed their own alternative models in collaboration with those groups whose needs have been neglected by traditional practice and will continue to be neglected by the government's approach to reform. This was a task that was seriously neglected by teacher educators in the previous period of expansion in the 1960s and one which urgently needs to be addressed today.

Acknowledgments

We are grateful to Jennifer Bone of Bristol Polytechnic and Neils Brouwer of the University of Utrecht for some helpful comments on an earlier version of this chapter.

Notes

1. GRACE, G. (1978) *Teachers, Ideology and Control*, London, Routledge and Kegan Paul; LAYTON, D. (1973) *Science for the People*, London, Allen and Unwin.
2. Secretary of State for Education and Science and Secretary of State for Wales (1983) *Teaching Quality*, London, HMSO.
3. Secretary of State for Education and Science and Secretary of State for Wales (1985) *Better Schools*, London, HMSO.
4. REID, I. (1985) 'Hoops, swings and roundabouts in teacher education: A critical review of the CATE criteria', paper presented to the Teacher

Education Study Group of the Society for Research into Higher Education, October.

5. Education Act, 1944, section 62.

6. McNair Committee (1944) *Teachers and Youth Leaders*, London, HMSO.

7. Cambridge University declined to establish an Area Training Organization. The Cambridge Institute of Education was therefore not a university body, although representatives of the University of Cambridge were included in its membership.

8. Some of these departments (UDEs) were termed schools or institutes of education, though in most cases the term 'institute' referred only to the Area Training Organization to which the departments belonged along with other local colleges.

9. Robbins Committee, (1963) *Higher Education*, London, HMSO. The recommendation that teacher education should be fully incorporated into the universities was, however, not implemented.

10. James Committee, (1972) *Teacher Education and Training*, London, HMSO.

11. See particularly the journal of the Association of Teachers in Colleges and Departments of Education (ATCDE), *Education for Teaching* and its successor, *Journal of Further and Higher Education*, produced by the National Association of Teachers in Further and Higher Education (NATFHE).

12. This followed a rather misleadingly entitled White Paper (1972) *Education: A Framework for Expansion*, London, HMSO. Some public sector colleges of education were closed completely, others became colleges or institutes of higher education offering diversified courses, while others merged with local polytechnics. A few were incorporated into universities — see note 15 below.

13. The idea that the 'binary line' between the universities and the public sector colleges would be a permanent feature of English higher education dates from a speech by Anthony Crosland at Woolwich in 1965. This was the precursor of the establishment of the 'new polytechnics' and it also ended any possibility that the Robbins proposal for the absorption of the colleges of education into the university sector would be implemented. See ROBINSON, E. (1968) *The New Polytechnics*, Harmondsworth, Penguin Books.

14. In an executive statement as early as June 1968, the NUT had complained that the universities were not fulfilling the recommendation of Robbins that a BEd should be 'a degree gained in a distinctive way, and characteristically based on the study of education'. We are grateful to Jennifer Bone for this point.

15. The universities involved were Exeter, East Anglia, Durham and Warwick.

16. See Department of Education and Science, Circulars 10/71, 11/73

and 7/82 (1982) *The Qualification of Teachers* and *The Education (Teachers) Regulations* London, HMSO.

17. See (1983) *Teaching Quality,* London, HMSO and Department of Education and Science, Circular 3/84 (1984) *Initial Teacher Training: Approval of Courses.* London, HMSO.

18. Group visitations by HMI to university departments of education are technically by invitation of the Vice-Chancellor and are subject to principles laid down in a concordat reached between the universities and HMI in 1960. Only as this chapter was going to press did the universities agree that reports on such visitations could be made public. Though HMI has clearly wished to take an increasingly interventionist role in both sectors, there have been far more constitutional hurdles to this in the traditionally autonomous university sector.

19. White Paper (1972) *op cit.*

20. James Committee (1972) *op cit.*

21. See, for example, Cox, C.B. and Dyson, A.E. (Eds) (1969) *The Fight for Education: A Black Paper,* London, Critical Quarterly Society; Cox, C.B. and Boyson, R. (Eds) (1975) *Black Paper 5: The Fight for Education,* London, Dent.

22. See Callaghan, J. (1976) 'Towards a national debate', *Education,* 148, 17. For discussion of the ensuing 'Great Debate', see Whitty, G. (1985) *Sociology and School Knowledge,* London, Methuen, chapter 5.

23. On these themes, see, for example, the publications of the Social Affairs Unit and the column in *The Times* by right-wing philosopher Roger Scruton.

24. Maclure, S. (1983) 'Teacher education: Whose responsibility?' address to a conference of the Universities Council for the Education of Teachers, November.

25. For a discussion of recent Conservative education policy, and some of its contradictions, see Wolpe, A.M. and Donald, J. (Eds) (1983) *Is There Anyone Here from Education?* London, Pluto Press; and Dale, R. (1983) 'Thatcherism and education', in Ahier, J. and Flude, M. (Eds) *Contemporary Education Policy,* London, Croom Helm.

26. See, for example, Shipman, M.D. (1967) 'Theory and practice in the education of teachers', *Educational Review,* 9, pp. 208–12.

27. See, for example, Bartholomew, J. (1976) 'Schooling teachers', in Whitty, G. and Young, M. (Eds) *Explorations in the Politics of School Knowledge,* Driffield, Nafferton.

28. See paragraph 7 of Annex to Circular 3/84 and subsequent clarification in CATENOTE 3, Subject Studies. London, Council for the Accreditation of Teacher Education, August 1985.

29. Reid, I. (1985) *op cit.*

30. *Ibid.*

31. Finn, D. (1982) 'Whose needs? Schooling and the needs of industry', in Rees, T. and Atkinson, P. (Eds) *Youth Unemployment and State*

Intervention, London, Routledge and Kegan Paul.

32. SIMON, B. (1984) 'Breaking school rules', *Marxism Today*, September, pp. 19–25.

33. Centre for Contemporary Cultural Studies (1981) *Unpopular Education*, London, Hutchinson.

34. Editorial (1983) *Teaching London Kids.* no. 21.

35. 'Tebbit blames ILEA's teaching policy for truancy'. Report in *The Guardian*, 14 March 1986.

36. Circular 3/84.

37. REID, I. (1985) *op cit.*

38. Reid leaves both possibilities open in his account.

39. Circular 3/84.

40. See special issue of *New Society* on Poverty, 18 April 1986.

41. Wolverhampton Borough Council (1985) *The Social Condition of Young People in Wolverhampton in 1984*, Wolverhampton, Wolverhampton Borough Council.

42. BARTON, L. and WALKER, S. (Eds) (1984) *Social Crisis and Educational Research*, London, Croom Helm. Introduction.

43. SHARP, R. (1986) 'Review of G. Whitty's *Sociology and School Knowledge*' in *British Journal of Sociology of Education*, 7, pp. 95–101.

44. WHITTY, G. (1985) *op cit.*

45. 'Inspectors find criteria hard to apply', *Times Educational Supplement* 21 February 1986, p. 12.

46. WILLIAMS, R. (1983) 'Intellectuals behind the screens', *Times Higher Education Supplement*, 21 January, p. 11.

47. Reactions to Maclure's address to UCET in 1983 were evidence of a similar range of responses to current developments amongst university-based teacher educators.

48. ZEICHNER, K. and TEITELBAUM, K. (1982) 'Personalised and inquiry oriented teacher education: An analysis of two approaches to the development of curriculum for field-based experiences', *Journal of Education for Teaching*, 8, pp. 95–117.

49. ZEICHNER, K. (1986) 'Content and contexts: Neglected elements in studies of student teaching as occasions for learning to teach', *Journal of Education for Teaching*, 12, 1, pp. 5–24.

50. ZEICHNER, K. (1981/82) 'Reflective teaching and field-based experience in pre-service teacher education', *Interchange*, 12, pp. 1–22.

51. DEWEY, J. (1933) *How We Think: A Restatement of the Relation of Reflective Thinking to the Educative Process*, Chicago, Henry Regnery Co. Although the terms derive from Dewey, our own usage is not identical to his.

52. ZEICHNER, K. (1981/82) *op cit.*, pp. 6–7.

53. TOM, A.R. (1980) 'The reform of teacher education through research: A futile quest', *Teachers College Record*, 82, pp. 15–29.

54. SCHON, D.A. (1983) *The Reflective Practitioner*, London, Temple Smith. A fuller indication of the relevance of such ideas to teaching can be found in POLLARD, A. and TANN, S. (in press) *Reflective Teaching in the Primary School*, London, Cassell.
55. See *Times Educational Supplement*.
56. Centre for Contemporary Cultural Studies. (1981) *op cit*.

Part III
Myths and Rituals of
Control

7 The Persistence of Myth in Teacher Education and Teaching

Catherine Cornbleth

Against a background of the sociohistorical nature and role of myth in society, I sketch three prevailing myths that I find especially problematic and then explore their persistence in teacher education and teaching. My purpose is to explain the appeal of these myths on the assumption that such understanding can prompt the modification of old myths or the construction of new ones more compatible with the professed goals of schooling in democratic societies. Making problematic what has been taken-for-granted in teacher education and teaching creates possibilities for their reform.

Myth is integral to modern as well as ancient societies. In contemporary curriculum and school discourse, it is not uncommon to find disparaging reference to this or that as myth as if the label were sufficient to discredit the belief and accompanying practice by associating them with times past, fantasy, or false consciousness. Yet, they persist, both shaping and reflecting school practice. Of particular interest here is the holding power of myth. How might we account for the persistence of myth in teacher education and teaching?

After briefly examining the sociohistorical nature and role of myth, I draw on earlier work to sketch three prevailing myths that I find especially problematic.[1] They are the myths of thinking skills, the right answer, and stages and styles of cognition and learning. Although primarily associated with schooling, these myths can be seen as manifestations of more encompassing themes in U.S. culture and its institutions, related to what Berger, Berger, and Kellner call modern technological consciousness.[2] Against this background, I then explore the persistence of these myths in teacher education and teaching with a focus on the social function of myth. My purpose is to explain their appeal, the assumption being that such understanding can prompt the modification of old myths or the creation of new ones more compatible with the professed goals of schooling in democratic states, for example, to promote the acquisition of valued knowledge and to contribute to social justice.

This kind of attention to myth is particularly appropriate in the light of recent calls for the reform of teacher education in the United States and elsewhere. The mid-1980s have spawned another school of critics and prophets of doom and salvation. Their cries of crisis and calls for reform seem to be little more than essentially conservative, ritualistic activity that reiterates myth and directs attention to outward appearances and away from questions of purpose, substance, and value.[3] Those who would reform teacher education and teaching might well attempt to better understand what is to be reformed, how it came to be, and why it persists.[4] That understanding necessitates probing beneath surface appearances and questioning the prevailing language, assumptions, and practices, including sustaining myths. Making problematic what has been taken-for-granted in teacher education and teaching creates possibilities for their reform.

From True Stories to Scientific Fables

Myth is a widely held belief with tenuous connections to pertinent evidence or circumstance. Sometimes myth is elaborated as a theory or story, sometimes it is simplified as a proverb or slogan. In ancient societies, myths were 'true' stories about historical origins as distinguished from false stories or legends.[5] Today, we tend to think of myth as false belief and to assume that we have rid ourselves of such vestiges of a pre-scientific age. All cultures, however, have their guiding myths although we may not think of our own myths as such.[6] Like the ancients, we see these beliefs as 'truths' — as common sense, empirically established fact, or natural law.[7] Myth is an integral, often unexamined part of our contemporary culture, including our professional discourse in teacher education and teaching.

Ancient myths were historical and particularistic, a rich narrative of 'real' events in times past. Most often, they concerned the role of supernatural beings in creating or bringing about events and institutions. The history sustained through myth was considered sacred because it was the work of supernaturals. The myths provided models for human behavior and gave 'meaning and value to life'.[8] In primitive societies, according to Malinowski,

> myth expresses, enhances, and codifies belief; it safeguards and enforces morality; it vouches for the efficiency of ritual and contains practical rules for the guidance of man. Myth is thus a vital ingredient of human civilization; it is not an idle role, but a hard-worked active force.[9]

Knowing the myths of one's culture also carried social and political import insofar as knowledge of the myths meant knowing about the origins of phenomena and thus having control over them.

Modern myths, in contrast, tend to be abstract and trans-historical, general principles of learning, for example.[10] Through repetition and reification, the abstraction then comes to be treated as 'real' or natural.[11] Principles of learning become *the way people learn* or *learning* itself, and students who do not observe these principles are typically considered deficient or recalcitrant. In some instances, myths can become self-fulfilling as when the presumably deficient or recalcitrant student is treated as such and begins to respond in kind, thus confirming the teacher's expectation and perpetuating both the myth and 'non-learning'.

A number of contemporary myths seem to have their origins in descriptive or explanatory metaphors, that is, in efforts to understand new or puzzling phenomena in terms of other, more familiar ones.[12] Problems arise when metaphors (for example, the mind is a machine) are taken literally and thus turned into myth.[13] Conceptualizing the mind in terms of a machine, for example, makes the non-observable phenomenon manageable and offers a heuristic for further enquiry. While highlighting some aspects of mind, the machine metaphor obscures others. To treat the mind as if it *were* a machine is to abuse the metaphor and distort the concept of mind. It is to engage in reification and consequent mystification, which yield conceptual absurdity and similarly absurd and often dehumanizing practice. An irony of such reification is that something that has been reified (for example, the machine mind) cannot exist on its own as an entity apart from the human activity that created and maintains it; yet, we often act as though necessarily constrained by our own creations.[14] The mythic reification of belief and accompanying practice is a prevalent but not inevitable aspect of human existence and institutions.

The abstractions and metaphors that give rise to myth in modern society tend to be distinguished by claims to a scientific character. Claiming a basis in science is intended to, and often does, bestow legitimacy given the awe with which science is held in contemporary Western societies. Scientific myths, according to Toulmin, are created when scientific concepts or scientifically obtained data are employed for other than scientific purposes or to answer non-scientific questions.[15] They often result from over-interpretation such as generalization beyond the bounds of available data. The link with science, however strained, lends an aura of authority. A prime example is the belief in some kind of social or cultural evolution. Another is the assumption that observed right-left brain differences should be accommodated in teacher education and teaching. To identify differences does not mean, in any scientific sense, that they *should* be responded to in general or in any particular way.

Related to the abstract quality and scientific veneer of modern myth is the appearance of universalism. What is created in particular social and historical circumstances is decontextualized and made to seem universal. Myth 'transforms history into nature', thus 'giving an historical intention a natural justification, and making contingency appear eternal'.[16] For example, bourgeois representations and 'relations between man and the world' have become '"normalized" forms' such that 'bourgeois norms are experienced as the evident laws of natural order'.[17] The myths of thinking skills and the right answer can be seen as manifestations of Western middle class world views and values that have been made to appear universal.

Myth serves multiple, interrelated social functions. Among these are to explain phenomena and direct action, to justify particular interests or practices, to dramatize ideals, and to provide cultural cohesion. Myth offers both description and prescription, an account of things and a model for action, be it a myth of rainmaking or a myth of stages and styles. Even when expectations remain unfulfilled, the myth and associated practices tend to prevail. We are, perhaps unavoidably, creatures of myth insofar as human experience encompasses much that cannot be explained by other means.

The justification function of myth is closely related to its explanatory role. To explain and direct action not only makes something plausible but also legitimates it. The myth of stages and styles, for example, is seen as explaining observed differences among individuals and calling for differentiated treatment of students. Different learning opportunities and outcomes are thus justified by the myth. (That the myth labels more than it explains and diverts attention from efforts to teach 'slow' or otherwise 'different' students is considered in the next section.) Justification of particular interests or practices via myth also serves to obscure or mask others. The individual focus of the stages and styles myth, for example, deflects attention from the influence of culture and social structure on individuality.

Myths also serve as ideals that orient a culture. For example, in the United States, 'We hold these truths to be self-evident: that all men are created equal, that they are endowed by their Creator with certain unalienable rights, that among these . . .'. Myth thus inspires and guides individual and collective action.

Finally, myth provides cultural cohesion. By offering meaning, legitimacy, and ideals, myth perpetuates a shared corpus of belief and thus provides a reassuring degree of security. That myth seems to be pervasive and indispensable to society, however, ought not to lead to unquestioning acceptance of particular myths as inevitable. Just as myth is socially constructed, so it can be reconstructed.

Illustrative Myths[18]

The three myths examined here reflect and contribute to the pervasiveness of technological consciousness in teacher education and teaching. The myths of thinking skills, the right answer, and stages and styles are powerful, widely held, and held sacred by many educators and laypersons alike. They have come to be promoted by experts and institutionalized in teacher education and teaching. Yet, in one way or another, they contradict democratic ideals such as equity and enlightenment or subvert attempts to realize them.

The Myth of Thinking Skills

This is a double-barrelled myth, one part of which asserts that thinking is composed of a number of discrete cognitive skills or steps. The second asserts that these skills or steps are content-free or generic. Together, they direct us to teach 'thinking skills' apart from thinking and subject matter as can be seen in methods texts that offer separate skill development teaching sequences with little or no attention to their integration or relation to subject matter. The problems of the first part of this myth are largely conceptual; the weaknesses of the second are both conceptual and empirical.

Skill A + B + C = thinking

There are at least three interrelated problems with the position that thinking consists of the sum of any list of skills or steps. One is that, without being offered some conception of the nature of thought, we cannot tell whether the skills or steps might add up to thinking or something else or nothing at all. A second is that lists and steps imply that thinking is, or should be, linear, which it rarely if ever is or could be. Instead, thinking tends to be recursive. A sequence of skills or steps is not a logic-in-use but a reconstructed logic that misrepresents what occurs while one is thinking.[19] It also ignores the dispositional quality of thought.

The third and more serious problem concerns the reductionist assumption that thinking can be cut into pieces and reassembled without damage. This reductionist assumption destroys the substance and spirit of thought; you cannot dissect a live frog. Further, when thinking is conceived as raising and pursuing questions about the ideas one encounters, the questions raised and the means needed to pursue them will depend to a large extent on the situation, including the ideas encountered, the social context of the encounter, and the prior knowledge and values of the questioner. Even given a general orientation or disposition to think critically, particular aspects of thinking are situation dependent and cannot be predetermined or specified out of context.[20]

If thinking consisted of a number of skills or a series of steps, one might expect considerable agreement as to the constituent skills or steps. However, there appears to be little or no such agreement; there is not even consensus as to what constitutes a skill.[21] One might also expect that students who had mastered a given set of skills would demonstrate sound thinking. To my knowledge, however, there is no such evidence. Students who have mastered one or another skill have done just that. It does not necessarily follow that the skills will result in or be used in the service of thinking. It is also conceivable that preoccupation with skills might dull one's critical capacity.

No list of skills is either necessary or sufficient for thinking. Any or all possible skills, however, may contribute to thinking in a given case. This position is similar to Dewey's description of the interdependent phases of reflective thought as dependent on, but not equivalent to, diverse skills such as observation and inference.[22]

Thinking cannot be reduced to a universally applicable formula of skills or steps to follow except by conceptual or empirical alchemy. The seeming rationality of specifying thinking skills and sequencing them in a logical or psychological order for instruction is appealing. But that rationality is illusory. Analytically distinguishable elements are interdependent in practice, and logical or psychological order bears little resemblance to the organization of practice. Despite claims to the contrary,[23] there is no reason or evidence to expect that further efforts to specify and sequence supposedly generic skills will be any more productive than previous ones.

Drawing on Aristotle, Wiggins makes a similar case with respect to 'practical reasoning'. According to Aristotle, 'the openness, indefiniteness and unforeseeability of the subject matter of *praxis*' resists codification. Wiggins suggests that those who seek 'a system of rules' hope 'to spare themselves some of the agony of thinking and all of the torment of feeling and understanding that is actually involved in reasoned deliberation'.[24] From a psychological perspective, Shulman and Carey have also argued against reductionism and the assumption of universality with respect to reasoning and rationality.[25] Formulaic approaches to reasoning and thinking are increasingly eschewed in both philosophical and psychological work.[26]

Skills and strategies are content independent

This second part of the myth of thinking skills follows from the first. If thinking consists of a number of skills, the underlying assumption is that these skills are independent of the subject matter content to which they might be addressed. Thinking skills and strategies (patterned combinations of skills) are assumed to be knowledge free or generic and transferable from one situation to another. However, the evidence regarding transfer is mixed at best.[27] There is no 'set of supervening skills' that can replace substantive knowledge of the field in question.

Increasing evidence indicates that the development of thinking and associated skills is highly knowledge-dependent.[28] In other words, we cannot think about ideas we encounter unless we know something about the area in question. With the possible exception of metacognition, skills that contribute to thinking tend to be domain specific.

The conceptual argument for the domain specificity of thinking is well presented by McPeck,[29] drawing particularly on the earlier work of Toulmin.[30] The knowledge in which thinking is embedded is more than empirical and conceptual. The various fields of knowledge have different logics or modes of reasoning. While not mutually exclusive, the standards of judgment for what counts as sound knowledge and argument differ from one subject area to another. What constitutes good reason and evidence for belief in history differs from that in economics, law, and chemistry. 'Just as there are different kinds of knowledge, so there are different kinds of reasons, evidence, and modes of justifying them.'[31] The domain knowledge that is crucial to thinking is procedural and normative as well as empirical and conceptual. Consequently, the separation of subject matter content and thinking process is arbitrary and misleading.

Because each area of knowledge has its own distinctive logic, the criteria or expectations for thinking vary from one to another. The legitimacy of these differences has been well argued by Toulmin. Toulmin's additional argument that the natural sciences are distinguished 'not by the types of objects with which they deal, but rather by the questions which arise about them'[32] seems equally apropos of the social sciences. There are also intra-field differences in questions raised and acceptable grounds for belief such as those between behavioral and cognitive psychology. The differences in questions raised and means of pursuit between and within fields point to a further distinction that cuts across subject matter or disciplinary boundaries. This is the paradigmatic distinction. A paradigm is a world view or framework of knowledge and belief through which we 'see' and investigate the world. Scientific paradigms consist of working assumptions about the world and how it is to be studied, understood, and acted upon, i.e., interrelated concepts and values, questions, procedures, and actions. Commitment to a particular scientific paradigm involves affiliation with a community of scholars who share, sustain, and shape the paradigm.

Thinking, then, varies with the domain investigated and the paradigm adopted. To argue that thinking is neither absolute nor universal is not to suggest that it is either idiosyncratic or individual. Thinking is a social as well as a cognitive activity, shaped by the setting and the norms of the community in which it occurs, for example, Marxist, empirical-analytic. The complexity and pluralism of the knowledge underlying thinking renders generic thinking skills illogical and impotent.

The empirical evidence for the domain specificity of critical thinking and associated skills and strategies comes largely from recent studies of reasoning and problem solving in math, science, and social science.[33] The conclusion to be drawn from this research is that while general skills and strategies can be identified, they are relatively weak and useful only when one does not know much about the field or problem in question.

As inferred cognitive or intellectual processes, skills are important to thinking but not a proxy for thought. By misrepresenting thinking, the 'skill A + B + C' part of the myth of thinking skills tends to mislead curriculum designers, teachers, and teacher educators into psychologizing thought and teaching skills in lieu of thinking. The generic part of the myth tends to further mislead by focusing attention and effort on weak, rather than strong, skills and strategies. Yet, the myth persists as evidenced by the attention to thinking skills in many teaching methods texts and the numerous generic thinking skills materials for classroom use.

The Myth of the Right Answer

According to this myth, a correct student response to a teacher or textbook question is evidence of student thought and learning. Right answers are sought by teachers and rewarded with praise and points that add up to good grades in elementary, secondary, and teacher education. They tend to be valued regardless of the question or the means by which students produce them. Right answers do not necessarily demonstrate student learning. Students may just be repeating what they already know. Nor do right answers necessarily demonstrate subject matter knowledge or thought. They may just be the result of a lucky guess, figuring out 'what the teacher wants', or other survival strategies.[34]

The right answers that are valued by this myth are typically answers to simple knowledge recall or memory questions. The myth of the right answer tends to encourage rote memorization rather than thinking things through. Rote memorization can also be seen as a myth. The memorization myth asserts that information must be acquired (i.e., memorized) before one can use it for thinking or any other purpose and that rote memorization is an effective means of information acquisition. Learning by rote refers to rehearsal, drill, or 'saying it over', none of which necessarily involve knowledge comprehension, integration, or application. Once again, the evidence does not support the claim. Instead, we find that rote memorization is usually an inefficient means of information acquisition and that it does not provide a functional knowledge base for further thought or action.

How information is elaborated and organized in memory appears to affect its accessibility and usefulness. Rote elaboration strategies do not foster the organization and integration of information that enables retrieval and use in new situations. According to Simon, 'rote memorization, as we all know too well, produces the ability to repeat back the memorized material but not to use it in solving problems'.[35] The same applies to concepts, procedures, and other kinds of knowledge. Unless they are appropriately interrelated in memory, they are not likely to be useful to critical or other thinking.[36] Thus, the myth of the right answer and rote memorization fosters an illusion of knowing that subverts construction of a functional knowledge base for thinking and teaching.

The Myth of Stages and Styles

This, also, is a composite myth, encompassing various beliefs about the existence and implications of stages of cognitive development and styles of cognition or learning. Whereas stages usually refer to presumed abilities of one sort or another, styles usually refer to preferred modes of information processing or learning, i.e., cognitive and learning styles. There are similar problems with stage and style forms of differentiation and categorization of students. Both tend to have a negative effect on expectations regarding students' ability or disposition to learn and their 'readiness' to develop desired knowledge or reasoning skills. They might also negatively affect expectations regarding whether and how something can be taught. For example, if critical thinking is assumed to be dependent on having reached the formal operations stage in Piaget's hierarchy, then one would not expect students assigned to the concrete operations stage to be capable of critical thought or of learning how to think critically.

There seems to be a 'catch-22' in this line of reasoning that limits the possibilities of teaching and learning. If students have reached the appropriate stage, they can do it, and either could benefit from instruction or do not need it; if not, they cannot do it, and are not 'ready' to be taught. Yet, there is evidence of instruction 'bringing children who were not even on the verge of acquiring a particular logical form of thought to complete mastery of tasks that supposedly require that form of thought'.[37]

Beyond questions of teaching and learning, there are questions about the consistency of developmental stages, specifically the assumption that an individual at a particular stage functions at that level across tasks and subject areas. According to this interpretation of stage theory, one would not be at a formal operational level in one domain, say history, and at a concrete operational level in another, say mechanics. The empirical evidence, however, is to the contrary: 'careful reviews of the research literature do not support the picture of homogeneity of cognitive activities at particular ages assumed by the Piagetian stage model'.[38]

Task-relevant knowledge, rather than developmental stage or capability, may better explain identified age-related differences in students' reasoning. For example, how well students categorize a given set of items depends not simply on their stage of development or 'categorizing ability', but also on their knowledge of the items and the kinds of categories into which they might be sorted.[39] Ortony suggests a similar interpretation of studies of children's comprehension of metaphor, many of which did not control for 'world-knowledge'. The reported developmental trends, he argues, 'seem to be consistent with the view that, as children grow older and learn more about the world in which they live and the words used to describe it, so their ability to understand metaphors increases'.[40] Prior content knowledge is also important to problem-solving. Whether and how a problem is solved is dependent on the knowledge one brings to the situation.[41] In sum, it increasingly appears that 'changes in such [domain] knowledge may underlie other changes previously attributed to the growth of capabilities and strategies'.[42]

As with the stages myth, there are contrary data and alternative explanations of observed differences attributed to cognitive or learning style. A major challenge comes from studies showing that styles are context-dependent, i.e., they vary with the learning task.[43] Given more than one kind of task, students demonstrate more than one style. Interestingly, many studies purporting to show individual differences in cognitive or learning style employed only one task or kind of task. There was no opportunity for students to demonstrate task-related differences.

So-called style seems to be less an inherent characteristic of individuals than a function of contextual factors such as the nature of the task, subject matter content, teaching mode, and expected kind of test. Research reviewed by McConkie indicates that 'students seem quite willing and able to change their learning strategies in response to task structure characteristics', particularly the nature of the test they expect to take.[44] Thus, students adjust their 'style' of information-processing depending on whether recall, comprehension, reasoning, or critical thinking is anticipated. Similarly, Chi and Glaser note that the task characteristics of a problem solving situation are a major determinant of problem-solving behavior.[45] The evidence strongly indicates that identifiable styles do not exist in the individual, but, if at all, in the interaction of individual and situation.

Stages can be imposed on anything that changes over time; styles can be imposed on anything that varies. The danger in categorizing students according to their presumed developmental level or their presumed learning or cognitive style is two-fold. It lies both in the category labels and in the school practices that are based on such labelling. First, the labels are neither neutral nor helpful to teaching or learning. Not only do they obscure the individual, but they tend to be explanatory fictions whose undesirable social consequences have been well noted.[46]

Pedagogical consequences include negative teacher expectations for many students and the formal or informal tracking of students with the concomitant denial of opportunity to those students deemed unready or incapable of certain kinds of learning.

Teacher education incorporates and perpetuates the myths of stages and styles primarily in education psychology and methods courses. Teacher education programs that attempt to meet prospective teachers' 'needs' through some form of 'personalization' tend to further sustain the myth.[47] Instead of assuming that students *are* 'this way' or 'that way' as an inevitable consequence of their inherent cognitive or learning style, consider the possibility that they have or have not learned to approach given tasks in particular ways. If students have not yet developed the requisite knowledge and reasoning skills for critical thinking, for example, then opportunity and instruction should be provided, not denied.

From Skill in Thinking to Thinking Skills

Examining the emergence of the myth of thinking skills and its incorporation in teacher education and teaching in historical context is intended to serve two purposes. One is to illustrate how myth comes into being in professional education discourse. Consideration of historical context also illustrates how education myths are related to broader cultural themes. What follows is, necessarily, a partial and retrospective account. Although it is neither comprehensive nor causal, it can be seen as plausible and suggestive of further lines of enquiry.

The language of thinking skills and its underlying assumptions are common place in the contemporary discourse of teacher education and teaching. Exceptions include some of the philosophically-oriented literature and discourse within a critical perspective. These exceptions have been overshadowed by the predominantly psychological orientation of teacher education and teaching, which was well established by the 1950s.[48] This psychological orientation, behavioral and now increasingly cognitive, together with the social efficiency and scientific management movements earlier in this century, and the anti-intellectualism that has characterized US history and society for more than two centuries, seem to have been major factors in the transformation of skill in thinking to thinking skills.

At the turn of the century, the language was one of skilled performance where skill referred to proficiency at a task, usually a physical activity that was seen as practical or useful, for example, the skilled worker. By the 1920s, there is reference to skill subjects such as reading, arithmetic, and writing, which were earlier called 'common branches' and later became 'basic skills'. It is not until the 1950s that intellectual activity and thought are referred to as skills, i.e., thinking skills. The 1940s appear to have been a decade of transition and the 1950s one of consolidation such that by the 1960s thinking skills were largely taken-for-granted.

Since the 1920s, social efficiency by means of 'scientific management' has been a watchword of US schooling.[49] The 1980s language of excellence and effectiveness can be seen as a restatement of the social efficiency theme. It is assumed that measurably effective teaching and schooling practices can be identified and implemented to yield more and better informed individuals who, collectively, will strengthen and improve society at large.

Key features of the scientific management that is to provide efficiency have been measurement and task analysis. Earlier in this century, measurement took the form of individual aptitude and achievement tests, teacher rating scales, and school surveys, resulting in what Rugg decried as 'an orgy of tabulation'.[50] Subsequently, these measurement forms have been augmented by behavioral observation and quantification and extended by sophisticated computers that make feasible larger data bases and more complex analyses. Measurement was to enable determination of efficiency and, later, accountability such that less efficient practices could be identified and eliminated in favor of more efficient ones.

Psychometric technology demanded what became known as task analysis, that is, the decomposition of complex acts into presumably discrete elements amenable to quantification.[51] Task analysis also contributed to scientific management by facilitating the pre-specification and control of teaching and learning that was to enhance efficiency. It was not only assumed that tasks such as reading and thinking and teaching could be meaningfully decomposed, but also that the identified elements could be best taught and learned one at a time and then assembled to create the desired whole.

Illustrative of these assumptions and practices is the curriculum work of Bobbitt, Charters and later Tyler (who was a student of Charters). Bobbitt, a leading advocate of scientific management in education, and Charters, adopted a task analysis approach to curriculum construction. For example, in his works *The Curriculum* (1918) and *How to Make a Curriculum* (1924), Bobbitt emphasized the precise specification of 'particularized' objectives derived from activity analysis as the central task of curriculum construction. Appropriate learning experiences and means of evaluation, he believed, would routinely follow from such analysis and specification. The 'Tyler rationale' with its 'production model' of teaching and learning and behavioral objectives can be seen as an extension of this earlier work[52] as can more recent 'rational management' models of curriculum construction.[53]

Thus, the demands of curriculum, teaching, and particularly evaluation for specification of what was to be taught, learned, and measured strongly influenced the redefinition of skill in thinking to thinking skills. It is more difficult to observe and measure thinking or its products, for example, than one's response to a multiple-choice test item that purports to measure a component element or skill such as determining whether a conclusion logically follows from given premises.[54] Reporting on the Cooperative Study of Evaluation in General Education, Dressel and Mayhew noted that available definitions of critical thinking

all proved too abstract for evaluation or teaching purposes. The only recourse was to define critical thinking as the sum of certain rather specific behaviors which could be described and which could be inferred from student acts.[55]

By the 1950s, 'the only recourse' was to cast thinking as skills in order to satisfy psychometric demands.[56]

Decomposition of thought into skills occurred in a political context of demands for accountability and efficiency, supported by psychologists and professional measurement specialists who promised the desired data and outcomes. This context seems to have been forgotten while thinking as skills has come to be taken-for-granted as the correct interpretation or the natural state of affairs. The decontextualization of the transformation and the subsequent recontextualization of thinking as skills in teacher education and teaching tends to obscure the political and professional interests that contributed to and continue to benefit from the transformation (for example, standardized test developers and publishers, education policymakers).

In addition to the psychologizing of education evident in the measurement and task analysis efforts associated with social efficiency and scientific management, the pervasive anti-intellectualism of American society contributed to the redefinition of thinking as skills. While Americans traditionally have been anti-intellectual, being skillful has been an integral part of American traditions and values.[57] Skill is useful and practical and therefore highly valued in the American context. Intelligence and thought have gained acceptance in this milieu in part by transformation to a collection of skills. Making the intellectual technical has made it acceptable. Thinking as skills is manageable; it is compatible with prevailing values and functional within teacher education and teaching. The skills language implies the utility of thinking. Not only are skills socially useful, but they can be specified in ways that enable their sequential arrangement for teaching and learning and their measurement for purposes of efficiency. A psychological construct, skills, thus became a pedagogical imperative. Taking the skills construct literally, as if thinking skills were 'real', reified an abstraction and contributed to the creation of a myth with considerable holding power.

The myth of thinking skills entered into the practice of teacher education and teaching through the medium of professional discourse. Journals, books, and school materials can be seen to gradually adopt the skills language and assumptions. For example, in 1940, the National Council for the Social Studies (NCSS) published a bulletin entitled *Selected Items for the Testing of Study Skills*. In 1957, a third edition was published as *Selected Items for the Testing of Study Skills and Critical Thinking*.[58] In their preface, the authors noted increased attention to the teaching and testing of critical thinking since the American Council on Education's Cooperative Study of Evaluation in General Education, 1950–53[59] and the twenty-fourth NCSS yearbook, *Skills in Social Studies*.[60] The language of the 1957 edition is mixed with respect to thinking and skills. One finds reference to the 'skill of thinking critically and clearly', 'critical skills', and 'skills of critical-mindedness'.[61] With the fifth edition, the language is unequivocally the language of critical thinking skills.[62] The multiple editions of this bulletin indicate its wide appeal and potential impact on teaching and testing in social studies education. The changing language can be seen as reflecting changes in the larger education community and responding to compelling social mandates.

Parallel changes were occurring in teacher education as skill in teaching was reduced to teaching skills and then to effective teacher behaviors.[63] The myth of thinking skills was comfortably incorporated into teacher education texts and practices as both teaching and thinking increasingly became largely technical operations, devoid of reflection and judgment.

Myth Persistence

Examination of how the myth of thinking skills came into being and entered into teacher education and teaching is suggestive of reasons why such myths persist despite contrary evidence, alternative interpretations, and abuse in practice that contradicts professed goals of schooling. One is that myth becomes such an integral part of day-to-day activities that it is taken-for-granted. No longer seen or heard, it is unlikely to be questioned, challenged, or changed. A second, related reason for the appeal and persistence of a particular myth is its congruence with broader cultural themes or aspects of consciousness. Such myths 'make sense' in their cultural context and may be either taken-for-granted or overtly cherished. Further reasons for myth persistence to be considered here are related to the social functions of myth noted earlier: to explain phenomena and direct action, to justify particular interests or practices, to dramatize ideals, and to provide cultural cohesion.

Like the myth of thinking skills, the myths of the right answer and stages and styles have become integral to the language and activity of teacher education and teaching. These beliefs and their accompanying practices are so taken-for-granted that many educators would be astonished to find them questioned and cast as myth. The embeddedness of myth in daily practice renders it barely visible. The visibility of myth is further diminished to the extent that the myth is congruent with overarching aspects of consciousness.

Berger *et al*'s conceptualization of modern consciousness is helpful to integrating and understanding these reasons for the persistence of myth.[64] The three myths of concern here can be seen as manifestations of a particularly modern consciousness whose primary sources and carriers are technological production and political bureaucracy. Berger *et al* define consciousness as the historically and socially located and constructed meanings formed in people's interactions with each other and their institutions. This shared consciousness or 'symbolic universe' encompasses interrelated cognitive and normative dimensions, an organization of knowledge and an orientation toward knowledge and action. The organization of knowledge and orientation derived from technological production and political bureaucracy carry over into other areas of life, including education, to form modern technological-bureaucratic consciousness. This 'symbolic universe of modernity', consisting of a 'network of cognitive and normative definitions of reality', provides a common 'frame of reference shared by most members of a society'.[65]

Among the major themes of the symbolic universe of modernity delineated by Berger *et al* are: functional or technical rationality, componentiality, makeability, and progressivity derived from technological production; and orderliness and taxonomization derived from political bureaucracy. Each of these themes can be seen to make the myths of thinking skills, the right answer, and stages and styles plausible in the context of teacher education and teaching.

Technical rationality represents the generalization of an engineering mentality to the manipulation of cognitive and social as well as material objects. It carries assumptions of machine-like functioning, reproducible linear process (for example, interchangeable parts in assembly line production), and measurability of output. Technical rationality is also dependent upon the assumption of componentiality, i.e., that 'everything is analyzable into constituent components, and everything can be taken apart and put together again in terms of these components'. These components are seen as 'self-contained units' that are 'interdependent in a rational, controllable and predictable way'.[66] Clearly, both thinking and teaching have been deeply affected by the widespread adoption of technical rationality in American life, and not surprisingly, a skills approach to teaching and teaching thinking has been incorporated into teacher education.

The theme of makeability follows from technical rationality and componentiality. It refers to a 'tinkering attitude' and a 'problem-solving inventiveness' that seeks to maximize output or results, usually on criteria of quantity or cost-effectiveness.[67] Progressivity refers to 'an "onward and upward" view of the world' that expects and favors continuing change and improvement.[68] It can be seen as underlying and reinforcing the makeability theme and contributing to the plausibility of the myths of thinking skills and developmental stages.

From political bureaucracy, modern consciousness derives the complementary themes of orderliness and taxonomization. Bureaucracy creates and maintains order and predictability through rationalized procedures, i.e., normal channels. Bureaucratic systems of procedures are typically 'based on a taxonomic propensity' similar to but more arbitrary than the componentiality of technological production.

> Phenomena are classified rather than analyzed or synthesized. The engineer puts phenomena into little categorical boxes in order to take them apart further or to put them together in larger wholes. By contrast, the bureaucrat is typically satisfied once everything has been put in its proper box.[69]

The myths of the right answer and of stages and styles can be seen to persist in part as a consequence of their congruence with these bureaucratic themes of modern consciousness. They also gain plausibility from themes more specific to the US experience.

The myth of the right answer is also sustained by its compatibility with a Christian religiosity. Compatibility is evident in their shared assumption of known 'truth' residing in a sacred text (bible, textbook) as interpreted by authorized experts (clergy, teachers). Further, the desired truths are to be learned by repetition (catechism, drill and practice). Whether in church or in school, youth are to accept, remember, and recite the right answers of their elders.

The myth of stages and styles reflects a particular liberal

ideology of individualism as well as the general modern conscious-ness. Its assumptions of discrete categories and linearity (for example, concrete operations are distinct from and precede formal operations) are consonant with technical rationality, componen-tiality, and taxonomization. The assumption that individuals 'have' a particular stage or inherent style reflects not simply attention to individuality but a 'possessive individualism', which assumes indivi-duals to be the proprietors of their capabilities and characteristics, owning them much as one might possess an automobile or a green sweater.[70] It is an American conception of the individual that can be traced to early Protestant beliefs in progress, liberal democratic political theory (for example, the seventeenth century political philosophy of Locke and the eighteenth century political economy of John Stuart Mill), and the ideology of laissez-faire capitalism. In the twentieth century, it finds expression in psychological approaches to measurement and task analysis intended to further scientific management of schooling for purposes of social efficiency. The compatibility of this conception of individualism with technical rationality and other themes of modern consciousness helps to sustain both and give credence to the myth of stages and styles.

The social functions of myth also contribute to explanation of its persistence. Insofar as particular myths exemplify cultural themes, they not only derive support from those themes but serve to dramatize them as cultural ideals and to orient individual and collec-tive action toward their realization. Thus, myth becomes an integral, sustaining element of everyday life. It is difficult to imagine, for example, teacher education and teaching stripped of the myth of the right answer. What would school classrooms be like without the recitation and the worksheet?

The cultural cohesion provided by myth is closely related to myth's orienting function. Shared ideals and beliefs offer a feeling of community and a comforting measure of security in that com-munity. Myth also serves to promote the interests of particular sub-groups, professional educators in this case. Myths such as those examined here contribute to professional identity and claims to expertise. Educators are the official proprietors and interpreters of myths to which the uninitiated have neither direct access nor the right of appeal.

Myth also persists in teacher education and teaching because it provides an illusion of explanation that serves to direct action and thereby to justify particular social interests and professional practices. The descriptive-prescriptive function of myth has already been touched upon. The description that myth offers is often taken as explanation, as if to name or label a phenomenon such as cognitive stage or style is to comprehend and perhaps to control it. Upon close examination, however, the illusion of understanding disappears and the tautology emerges. The myth of thinking skills, for example, explains neither the nature nor the development of thought.

The labels and their mythic elaborations do direct practice, for example, the admonition that teachers adapt their teaching and/or expectations for learning to the identified stages and styles of individual students. They also contribute to an aura of professional expertise both by providing a language that is incomprehensible to most people outside the profession and by suggesting that professionals have the knowledge and capacity to deal with the problems they have identified. Myth thus justifies professional claims and school practices such as ability grouping or tracking; it makes differentiation of students seem reasonable and appropriate.[71] Myth is perpetuated in part because it supports the political, economic, or cultural interests of groups that are dominant in the wider society, justifying what might otherwise be viewed as discriminatory practices. Myth thereby diverts attention from difficult problems of teaching or provides excuses for not attempting to resolve them.

Reconstruction of Myth

To see the myths of thinking skills, the right answer, and stages and styles in relation to modern consciousness, cultural themes specific to the US experience, and the historical social functions of myth is to begin to understand the social construction and persistence of myth in teacher education and teaching. If teacher education and teaching are to be reformed in ways that affirm cultural ideals, guiding myths must be recognized and challenged.

This is not to call for the exorcism of myth. To do so would be futile, for myth is integral to social life. Myth is probably inevitable, and not all myths are pernicious. In teacher education and teaching, our myths need not obscure social conditions that impede school learning by psychologizing or otherwise masking them. Neither need they foster practices contrary to espoused purposes. Instead of limiting students' opportunities, our myths might expand possibilities for all students and means of their attainment.

The particular myths examined here are neither neutral nor inevitable. They have been created out of US history and culture and the particular experiences and interests of professional educators and researchers within that context. As myths become incorporated into the everyday practice of teacher education and teaching, however, their original purposes and underlying values are gradually lost, and the myths acquire a universal quality that tends to deter challenge. We ought not to be so intimidated.

The reconstruction of myth, however, is neither simple nor straightforward. It requires modification of beliefs and accompanying practices in education and concomitant modification of the institutional conditions that sustain modern consciousness. Such change is not without precedent, and countermodernizing trends are now evident in other institutional sectors; examples include modification of assembly line and business management practices and the revival of 'holistic' medicine. The challenge is to cultivate skepticism and a critical stance that renders both myth and institutional arrangements fragile and susceptible to reconstruction.

Notes

1. CORNBLETH, C. (1985) 'Critical thinking and cognitive process', in STANLEY, W.B. (Ed.), *Review of Research in Social Studies Education*, Boulder, CO, Social Science Education Consortium.
2. BERGER, P., BERGER, B. and KELLNER, H. (1973) *The Homeless Mind: Modernization and Consciousness*, New York, Vintage.
3. CORNBLETH, C. (1985) 'Ritual and rationality in US school reform', paper presented at the Fifth Augsburg-Pittsburgh University Seminar, Augsburg, Federal Republic of Germany.
4. REID, W.A. (1978). *Thinking About the Curriculum*, London, Routledge and Kegan Paul.
5. ELIADE, M. (1963). *Myth and Reality*, New York, Harper and Row.
6. LAKOFF, G and JOHNSON, M (1980). *Metaphors We Live By*, Chicago, University of Chicago Press.
7. TOULMIN, S.F. (1982) *The Return to Cosmology: Postmodern Science and the Theology of Nature*, Berkeley, University of California Press.
8. ELIADE, M. (1963) *op cit.*, p. 2.
9. MALINOWSKI, B. (1926), *Myth in Primitive Psychology*, New York, W.W. Norton, p. 19.
10. Also, whereas ancient myths tended to be anthropomorphic, witness Zeus, for example, the myths of the twentieth-century are more likely to be 'mechanomorphic' (TOULMIN (1982) *op cit.*, p. 24).
11. See, for example, BARTHES, R. (1957/1972) *Mythologies*, New York, Hill and Wang; BERGER, P. and PULLBERG, S. (1965) 'Reification and

the sociological critique of consciousness', *History and Theory*, 4, 2, pp. 196–211.

12. On metaphor in everyday life, see LAKOFF, G. and JOHNSON, M. (1980) *op cit.*

13. HESSE, M. (1980) *Revolutions and Reconstructions in the Philosophy of Science*, Bloomington, IL, Indiana University Press.

14. BERGER, P. and PULLBERG, S. (1965) *op cit.*

15. TOULMIN, S.F. (1982) *op cit.*

16. BARTHES, R. (1957/1972) *op cit.*, pp. 129 and 142.

17. *Ibid*, p. 140.

18. Elaboration of the arguments and evidence provided here can be found in CORNBLETH, C (1985) *op cit.*, pp. 18–32.

19. KAPLAN, A. (1964) *The Conduct of Inquiry*, San Francisco, Chandler.

20. MISHLER, E.G. (1979) 'Meaning in context: Is there any other kind?', *Harvard Educational Review*, 49, pp. 1–19.

21. BEYER, B.K. (1984). 'Improving thinking skills — Defining the problem', *Phi Delta Kappan*, 65, pp. 486–90.

22. DEWEY, J. (1910/1933) *How We Think*, Chicago, Henry Regnery.

23. See, for example, BEYER, B.K. (1984) 'Improving skills — Practical approaches', *Phi Delta Kappan*, 65 pp. 556–60.

24. WIGGINS, D. (1978). 'Deliberation and practical reason', in RAZ, J. (Ed.), *Practical Reasoning*, New York, Oxford University Press, p. 150.

25. SHULMAN, L.S. and CAREY, N.B. (1984). 'Psychology and the limitations of individual rationality: Implications for the study of reasoning and civility', *Review of Educational Research*, 54, pp. 501–24.

26. For a particularly detailed and devastating critique, see McPECK, J.E. (1981). *Critical Thinking and Education*, New York, St. Martin's.

27. BELMONT, J.M. and BUTTERFIELD, E.C. (1977). 'The instructional approach to developmental cognitive research', in KAIL, R. and HAGEN, J. (Eds), *Perspectives on the Development of Memory and Cognition*, Hillsdale, NJ, Lawrence Erlbaum Associates.

28. GLASSER, R. (1983). *Education and Thinking: The Role of Knowledge*, Pittsburgh, Learning and Research Development Center, University of Pittsburgh; GREENO, J.G. (1980) 'Trends in the theory of knowledge for problem-solving', in TUMA D.T. and REIF F. (Eds), *Problem Solving and Education: Issues in Teaching and Research*, Hillsdale, NJ, Lawrence Erlbaum Associates; Voss, J.F. (forthcoming). 'Problem solving and the educational process' in GLASER, R. and LESGOLD, A. (Eds), *Handbook of Psychology and Education*, Hillsdale, NJ, Lawrence Erlbaum Associates.

29. McPECK, J.E. (1981) *op cit.*

30. TOULMIN, S. (1958). *The Uses of Argument*. Cambridge, Cambridge University Press.

31. McPECK, J.E. (1981) *op cit.*, p. 23.

32. TOULMIN, S. (1977) *Human Understanding*, Princeton, Princeton University Press, p. 149.
33. For excellent reviews, see GLASER, R. (1983) *op cit.*, and VOSS, J.F. (forthcoming) *op cit.*
34. For examples in elementary classrooms, see ANDERSON, L.M., BRUBAKER, N.L., ALLEMAN-BROOKS, J. and DUFFY, G.G. (1984). *Making Seatwork Work*, Research Series No. 142, East Lansing, MI, Michigan State University, Institute for Research on Teaching; for illustration in a teacher education context, see LACEY, C. (1977). *The Socialization of Teachers*, London, Methuen.
35. SIMON, H.A. (1980) 'Problem solving and education', in TUMA, D.T. and REIF, F. (Eds) *op cit.*, p. 87.
36. NORMAN, D.A., GENTNER, D.R. and STEVENS, A.L. (1976) 'Comments on learning schemata and memory representation', in KLAHR, D. (Ed.), *Cognition and Instruction*. Hillsdale, NJ, Lawrence Erlbaum Associates.
37. CASE, R. (1981). 'Intellectual development: A systematic reinterpretation', in FARLEY, F.H. and GORDON, N.J. (Eds), *Psychology and Education: The State of the Union*, Berkeley, McCutchan, p. 144.
38. ESTES, W.K. (1978). 'The information-processing approach to cognition: A confluence of metaphors and methods', in ESTES, W.K. (Ed.), *Handbook of Learning and Cognitive Processes, Vol. 5: Human Information Processing*, Hillsdale, NJ, Lawrence Erlbaum Associates, p. 13; also see CASE, R. (1981) *op cit.*; and MANDLER, J.M. (1983). 'Representation', in FLAVELL, J.H. and MARKMAN, E.M. (Eds), *Handbook of Child Development, Vol. III: Cognitive Development*, New York, John Wiley & Sons.
39. CHI, M.T.H. (1983). *Interactive Roles of Knowledge and Strategies in the Development of Organized Sorting and Recall*, Pittsburgh, Learning Research and Development Center, University of Pittsburgh.
40. ORTONY, A. (1980). 'Metaphor', in SPIRO, R.J., BRUCE, B.C. and BREWER, W.F. (Eds), *Theoretical Issues in Reading Comprehension*, Hillsdale, NJ, Lawrence Erlbaum Associates, p. 353.
41. CHI, M.T. and GLASER, R. (1983). *Problem Solving Abilities*, Pittsburgh, Learning Research and Development Center, University of Pittsburgh.
42. SIEGLER, R.S. and RICHARDS, D.D. (1982). 'The development of intelligence', in STERNBERG, R.J. (Ed.), *Handbook of Human Intelligence*, Cambridge, Cambridge University Press, p. 930.
43. LAURILLARD, D. (1979). 'The processes of student learning', *Higher Education*, 8, pp. 395–409.
44. McCONKIE, G.W. (1977). 'Learning from text', in SHULMAN, L. (Ed.), *Review of Research in Education*, 5, Itasca, IL, F. E. Peacock, p. 27.
45. CHI, M.T. and GLASER, R. (1983) *op cit.*
46. See, for example, APPLE, M.W. (1975) 'Commonsense categories and

curriculum thought', in MACDONALD, J.B. and ZARET, E. (Eds), *Schools in Search of Meaning*, Washington, DC, Association for Supervision and Curriculum Development.

47. ZEICHNER, K. (1983). 'Alternative paradigms of teacher education', *Journal of Teacher Education*, 34, 3, pp. 3–9.

48. BORROWMAN, M.L. (1965). *Teacher Education in America: A Documentary History*, New York, Teachers College, Columbia University.

49. CALLAHAN, R.E. (1962) *Education and the Cult of Efficiency*, Chicago, University of Chicago Press.

50. RUGG, H. (1926) 'Curriculum-making and the scientific study of education since 1910', in RUGG, H. (Ed.), *The Foundations and Technique of Curriculum Construction: Twenty-sixth Yearbook of the National Society for the Study of Education, Part I, Curriculum-making: Past and Present*, Bloomington, IL, Public School Publishing Company, p. 71.

51. Also see FREDERIKSEN, N. (1984). 'The real test bias influences of testing on teaching and learning', *American Psychologist*, 39, pp. 193–202.

52. KLIEBARD, H.M. (1975). 'Persistent curriculum issues in historical perspective', in PINAR, W. (Ed.), *Curriculum Theorizing: The Reconceptualists*, Berkeley, McCutchan, p. 45.

53. CORNBLETH, C. (1985) 'Reconsidering social studies curriculum', *Theory and Research in Social Education*, 13, 2, pp. 31–45.

54. See DRESSEL, P.L. and MAYHEW, L.B. (1954). *General Education: Explorations in Evaluation*, (The Final Report of the Cooperative Study of Evaluation in General Education of the American Council on Education) Washington, DC, American Council on Education; SMITH, E.R., TYLER, R.W. and the EVALUATION STAFF (1942). *Appraising and Recording Student Progress*, Adventure in American Education, Vol. III. New York, Harper and Bros.

55. *Ibid*, p. 37.

56. A related development contributing to the redefinition of thinking as skills was the refinement of mental measurement and statistical analysis techniques, especially the work of Thorndike (for example, his 1904 *Theory of Mental and Social Measurements*), Terman (the 1916 Stanford-Binet intelligence test with its multiple subtests), and Thurstone (his work in factor analysis in the 1930s). By the 1930s, a differentiated rather than a unitary view of intelligence predominated, compatible with a component skills view of thinking.

57. HOFSTADTER, R. (1963) *Anti-intellectualism in American Life*. New York, Vintage.

58. MORSE, H.T. and McCUNE, G.H. (1957). *Selected Items for the Testing of Study Skills and Critical Thinking* (3rd ed) Washington, DC National Council for the Social Studies.

59. DRESSEL, P.L. and MAYHEW, L.B. (1954) *op cit.*

60. CARPENTER, H.M. (Ed.) (1953). *Skills in Social Studies*, Washington, DC, National Council for the Social Studies.
61. MORSE, M.T. and McCUNE, G.H. (1957) *op cit*, pp. 3, 8 and 25.
62. MORSE, H.T., McCUNE, G.H., BROWN, L.E. and COOK, E. (1971). *Selected Items for the Testing of Study Skills and Critical Thinking*, (5th edn) Washington, DC, National Council for the Social Studies.
63. See, for example, BORROWMAN, M.L. (1956). *The Liberal and Technical in Teacher Education*, New York, Bureau of Publications, Teachers College, Columbia University; KILPATRICK, W.H. (1933) 'Professional education from the social point of view', in KILPATRICK, W.H. (Ed.), *The Educational Frontier*, New York, D Appleton-Century.
64. BERGER, P., BERGER, B. and KELLNER, M. (1973) *op cit*.
65. *Ibid*, pp. 108–109.
66. *Ibid*, p. 27.
67. *Ibid*, p. 30.
68. *Ibid*, p. 113.
69. *Ibid*, p. 49.
70. POPKEWITZ, T.S. (1983). 'The sociological bases for individual differences: The relation of solitude to the crowd', in FENSTERMACHER, G. and GOODLAD, J. (Eds), *Individual Differences and the Common Curriculum* (Eighty-second Yearbook of the National Society for the Study of Education, Part I), Chicago, University of Chicago Press.
71. POPKEWITZ, T.S. (1985). 'A comparative perspective on American teacher education: Being a stranger in one's native land', *Journal of Teacher Education*, 36, 5, pp. 2–10.

8 Tracing the Provenance of Teacher Education

Barbara L. Schneider

Research and scholarly productivity in schools of education is reputed to be viewed as somewhat suspect by the university academic community. A recent study of forty-two schools of education which involved a series of questionnaires, interviews and on-site visits with administrators, faculty, students and alumni indicates that certain program areas closely resemble other social science departments with prodigious faculty productivity, rigorous program requirements, and extensive student research activities. Some program areas, however, such as teacher education do not exhibit these characteristics. Results reveal that the differences between teacher education programs and other program areas reflect more on the organizational structure of the schools of education and the university communities in which they are located than on the goals and behaviors of faculty members who work in this area.

To understand the current problems of teacher education, one needs to examine the past and present institutional context in which teacher education departments were created and exist. This chapter briefly reviews the history of teacher education in research universities, traces some of the problems that have plagued teacher education departments since their establishment in schools of education, and links present concerns of low prestige, power and research productivity among teacher educators to the institutions in which they work.

Today's questions over the quality of teacher education, reflect its provenance and history in American higher education. To understand fully the current problems of teacher education, one needs to examine the past and present institutional context in which teacher education departments were created and exist. This chapter reviews the history of teacher education in research universities, traces some of the problems that have plagued teacher education departments since their inception in schools of education, and links present concerns of low prestige, power and research productivity among teacher education faculty to the universities in which they work.

Schools of education, particularly in research universities, have been a perpetual target for criticism among the academic community. Reproved for low admission requirements, technical rather than liberal arts focus, and questionable commitment to scholarship, schools of education have been labeled by some to be the 'slums' of the academic campus.[1] However, a recent study of forty-two schools of education in major universities indicates that criticisms toward schools of education are not directed towards the schools themselves but to certain areas of specialization, most notably, teacher education.[2] There are areas of specialization within schools of education, such as educational psychology, which are viewed by university administrators, deans, and faculty as 'high quality'. Educational psychology departments, in schools of education, are frequently cited as having rigorous program requirements, prodigious faculty productivity, and extensive student research activities.[3] In contrast, teacher education departments are often chastised for not exhibiting these same characteristics.

Reasons for the discontinuity between teacher education and other areas of specialization have been attributed to such matters as: utilitarian rather than liberal arts focus of the course content,[4] socioeconomic characteristics of those who elect to become teacher educators,[5] nature of the work responsibilities of teacher educators[6], norms and expectations of teacher educators toward research,[7] low research productivity[8] and perceived value of the knowledge base of teacher education courses, activities and research among the university community.[9] Problems of teacher education are not a recent phenomenon, they have been embedded in this field since its incorporation into the university community nearly 100 years ago. The cultural tradition of teacher education in American universities has been one of controversy, hostility, and sexism.[10] This cultural tradition has influenced how the university community acts, thinks, feels about pedagogical training.[11]

A current frequent criticism of the academic community is that teacher education is not rooted in a substantive knowledge base. As Kroner states, education has poor credentials, it has relied on other fields, especially psychology, for its principal substance, it has not yet developed a corpus of independent knowledge and techniques of sufficient scope and power to warrant the field's being given full academic status.[12] Although this may be the history of teacher education, it does not represent the tradition of pedagogical studies. Pedagogical study has had a central place at least in foreign universities, from their earliest beginnings.[13] For example, in Germany in the late 1600 and 1700s pedagogical training was a vital component of the preparation of theologians in several universities. Philosophical pedagogical seminaries existed with the special aim of preparing students of theology to be teachers. Students in such programs were required to participate in practical experiments in giving instruction.[14]

This traditional study of pedagogy, characteristic of European institutions of higher education carried over to the United States, and several universities offered courses in pedagogy in the 1840s and 1850s.[15] Several important factors distinguished the study of pedagogy in the 1800s from the study of teaching as it was later defined and developed in universities. First, students taking courses in pedagogy considered themselves as philosophers who were learning the art of didactics to improve their theological pursuits. They did not identify themselves primarily as teachers. Second, the professors who taught the courses in pedagogy were for the most part philosophers, whose expertise was in philosophy and psychology, as these two disciplines were joined together at this time. Status was not an issue, because these professors were associated with a substantive core of the liberal arts program. Third, pedagogics was a substantive knowledge area. Students were expected to learn the art of didactics, rather than utilitarian concepts of discipline or material selection which has tended to characterize the substance of teacher education today.[16] Thus, linking the study of pedagogy with the study of teaching is perhaps merely wistful thinking on the part of some, to authenticate the place of teacher education in universities.

The Development of Teacher Education in Universities

Establishment of teacher education in universities was not derived from a movement to institutionalize pedagogy as a fundamental area of study in the liberal arts curriculum, but rather out of a societal need to upgrade the professional status of secondary school teachers.[17] Through the 1800s the majority of training for elementary and secondary public school teachers was the responsibility of the normal schools.[18] As high school education became available to more than a select group, many more teachers were needed in the schools. Normal schools could not accommodate all those individuals aspiring to be teachers. Colleges and universities moved into the teacher training market, with the blessings of the state departments and the vituperations of the liberal arts faculty.

Teacher education departments were started in universities without the approval of the academic community. College presidents and liberal arts faculties resisted the establishment of a teacher training department. They opposed the creation of teacher education programs primarily on intellectual grounds, that is, from their perspective there was no such subject as 'education'. Professional education courses were not only criticized for lacking substance but some critics went so far as to conclude that exposure to education courses was potentially injurious to the student's intellect, 'any attention given to professional education could only dilute the student's interest in knowledge for its own sake', Professor J.P. Sewall addressing the New England Association of Colleges and Preparatory Schools in 1889.[19] Methods courses were viewed as the responsibility of the subject matter professors, as the President of Yale, writes in 1876, to Henry Barnard, '. . . I am convinced that special instruction upon methods of teaching would come with the best effect from professors in several departments — as Latin, Greek, Mathematics and several physical sciences'.[20]

Questions concerning the substance of teaching literature could be raised without much of a rebuttal because of the vulnerable position of pedagogy following the split of psychology from philosophy in the 1900s. When pedagogical study was considered an integral part of philosophy, pedagogical literature received no more or less criticism than other disciplines. However, when the split between philosophy and psychology occurred, the study of didactic thinking moved into educational psychology, the moral and ethical components of pedagogy into philosophy.[21] Neither discipline was concerned with questions of 'how to teach', which left teacher education with having to grapple with the most technical aspect of pedagogy. Consequently, since teacher education's inauspicious beginnings, it has been faced with trying to define a legitimate substantive knowledge base focused on training.[22]

Although controversy continued to surround the establishment of teacher education in universities, economics finally won out. By the 1890s it was apparent that great numbers of teachers and administrators were needed to educate America's rapidly growing school age population. This demand for teachers increased the likelihood that more individuals would consider teaching as a career option. Given this expanding market, criticisms of teacher education took a different form. Rather than dismissing teacher education as intellectually inconsequential, faculty members in universities stressed the need for teacher training programs that were academically demanding and grounded in the liberal arts tradition.[23] Focusing on normal schools, studies were undertaken to examine the quality of teacher training in these institutions.[24] Several studies by faculties in major universities criticized normal schools for having wide variations in requirements, low standards, and narrow technical intellectual focus.[25]

Once universities became intent on capturing the teacher training market, the demise of the normal school was a certain reality. Universities first attempted to increase their enrollments by lowering their admissions requirements in hopes of drawing students away from the normal schools.[26] They also offered courses of inferior standards which were tolerated for similar reasons.[27] However, after the normal schools were driven out of existence, standards in teacher training did not improve. Thus, schools of education in taking over the role of training teacher educators also took with it the very criticisms and problems they had charged, the normal schools. The tradition of low admissions requirements and technical courses inherited from normal schools, has plagued teacher education in universities for the last ninety years.

State education agencies also openly supported redirecting teacher training from normal schools to universities. However, the state's role in helping to establish teacher education departments in universities, became a legitimate license to exercise power and control over the curriculum in schools of education. Intent on upgrading the qualifications of teachers, state education agencies began working intently with universities in the hopes that they would raise teacher certification requirements.[28] Although the state interest was on improving criteria, not necessarily on the content of what was taught, their involvement in specifying required subject areas for certification set a precedent of interference and dependency. Once schools of education relied on the support of state education agencies for recognition and approval of their teacher education programs, they were compelled to accept the role and authority of the state in order to justify their own existence.

Winning the teacher training market turned out to be a mixed blessing. The numbers of students seeking careers in education continued to increase through the 1920s. Professors were needed to instruct the courses. To meet this need, teacher education departments hired professors who received their graduate training in education. Education trained professors became the norm, philosophy professors an artifact of the past. From the perspective of schools of education, employing education trained professors added credibility and legitimacy to their programs. While it might have given legitimacy and credibility to the program in the view of potential student applicants, it did little but reinforce the negative perceptions the university community had previously acquired toward schools of education. Education professors suffered in prestige on two accounts. First, from the perspective of the liberal arts faculty, education professors lacked the pristine philosophical and psychological training which characterized their predecessors. Second, the graduate courses and experiences they were likely to receive in schools of education were already viewed as inferior, as a matter of history.

Perhaps the most critical problem that arose in the development of teacher education in universities centered on what knowledge and skills were going to be stressed in the programs. Although the very first schools of education developed programs which rejected the rote training methods engendered by normal school, within schools of education there were groups of professors who advocated a strictly professional school where the emphasis was on the acquisition of job specific skills.[29] At the other extreme were other groups of professors who supported a more liberal approach. Consistent with the university community's orientation, the more technically oriented perspective dominated through the 1900s. The value of this approach was that it was centered on delivering knowledge that was scientifically based. Building a systematically organized specialized knowledge base placed university trained experts in positions of authority for answering the full array of technical and social questions facing society at the time.[30]

Schools of education in universities chose early in their development to follow the research mode of experimentalization, quantification and classification[31] as a way to acquire a technical knowledge base. However, their successes were few, and this road of enquiry did little to increase the status or professionalism of the schools. Rather this press toward scientification led to a diffuse fragmented curriculum, and an ideologically divisive faculty. The major problem with schools of education in comparison to other professional fields such as medicine, was that the technological advances were less dramatic. No antibiotics were discovered to cure poor readers or operations to increase cognitive processing. The scientific bases of teacher education did not materalize. Educators were caught supporting a technical position without substance.

This technical approach to education continued through this century and was further strengthened during the progressive movement in education in the 1930s.[32] The progressive movement stressed that more was learned through direct experience, which was more consistent with a technical than liberal arts approach. It was during this period that 'practice teaching' and internships became a requirement in many teacher education programs.[33] The effect of this emphasis on direct experience further divided the faculty in schools of education as well as cast aspersions on the 'intellectual' value of teacher education programs.[34]

Universities, intensively competitive, prize institutional prestige. This prestige is gained through the research productivity of the faculty. As Trow states, 'Research confers elite status on an institution and a discipline, fields where research is done dominate the universities intellectually and politically'.[35] In the early 1900s when schools of education were first established, research was a central component of their programs. Many universities, both public and private, established research centers which were designed to conduct original studies on how to improve educational practice. These research centers published monthly and sometimes weekly 'Bulletins' devoted to solving educational problems through research. Some of the universities which published these 'Bulletins' were, *Series of Research Bulletins of the University Studies in Education, Bulletin of the State University of Iowa*, which in its second volume became *Studies in Education*, University of Iowa, 1911; *Studies in Education*, Bureau of Educational Research, University of Illinois, 1913; and the *Harvard-Newton Bulletins*, 1914. Harvard's bulletin is somewhat unusual in that it was a joint effort by the Newton public school system and Harvard University to develop a journal which sought the solution of educational problems through research in the schools. The first lead article by William Setchel Learned was titled, 'A school system as an educational laboratory'.[36] By 1928, nearly all the major research universities which had colleges or schools of education in the midwest — Indiana, Ohio State University, University of Michigan, University of Minnesota, and the University of Wisconsin, as well as other universities across the country such as Johns Hopkins, were publishing such bulletins on educational research. Audiences for these publications included state and local educational personnel, graduate students and university education professors.

These bulletins and journals published at the University of Chicago and Teachers College Columbia, formed an extensive corpus of educational research. Walter Monroe, in a booklet, *Ten Years of Educational Research* (1928), prepared for the Bureau of Educational Research at the University of Illinois, identified at that time the existence of 3650 educational research reports.[37] Many of these early studies in the field of education, focused on teacher instruction, student evaluation, teacher preparation and curriculum (for example, 'Teacher difficulties in arithmetic and their correctives', 'determination of a spelling vocabulary based on written correspondence'; 'measurement of linguistic organization in sentences'; 'a comparison between general and specific methods courses in the teaching of high school subjects'; 'practice teaching in the school of education University of Illinois 1893–1911'; and 'a study of supervised study'.[38] These writings by the first professors of teacher education in research universities, on topics uncannily similar to those found in the leading educational journals of today, established the foundations of educational research. Although teacher educators had a major role in developing the field of educational research, over time their influence and participation in the conduct of research was greatly diminished.

As educational research became increasingly valued in the university, it became less and less available to teacher educators. By the end of World War II, with the growing demand for school personnel, the role of teacher educators in universities became almost entirely one of training. Educational psychologists took over the research role previously performed by teacher educators. Freed from training responsibilities, educational psychologists ardently pursued research activities which emphasized quantification and experimentation. This mode of inquiry which dominated the sciences gave educational psychologists status and legitimacy in the university community. Although educational psychology did not have the status of psychology, the university community tended to perceive of it as a more pristine intellectual area than teacher education because of its historical link to the social sciences.[39] Thus, educational psychology not only filled the research role of teacher educators but achieved status and legitimacy within the university because of its history and research methods. By the 1950s, the university and education research community viewed educational psychology as the area where credible educational research was conducted.

This brief history of teacher education in research universities indicates that the problems of teacher education today are not the results of recent changes in schools of education. The status and prestige surrounding teacher education has always been a problem, even when the faculty were productive researchers. Standards regarding admission to teacher education have been of constant concern. Professors of teacher education have a continuous history of low status, and their subject area has repeatedly been perceived as devoid of content which has intellectual coherence. This historical context of teacher education has been somewhat neglected by researchers who have tended to trace some of the problems of the field to the characteristics of the faculty members who work in this area. By concentrating on the problems of individual faculty, some researchers have overlooked the relationships between the quality of teacher education and the institutional context in which teacher education departments were created and exist.

Teacher Educators and Their Work Environments

Evidence of low prestige, power, and research productivity among teacher educators can be linked to the structural properties and social behaviors characteristic of the schools of education and universities in which they work. Administrators and faculty members in schools of education share certain perceptions concerning the quality of teacher education departments which are sometimes shared in the larger university community.[40] Moreover, these perceptions have affected how teacher education departments are organized and function in the schools and university. For example, in a recent study of schools of education in research universities, forty-two deans were asked to identify their 'best' and 'weakest' programs.[41] The deans identified educational psychology more than any other specialization as the 'best program', in contrast to teacher education which was nominated most often as one of the 'weakest'. The deans' reasons for the poor quality of teacher education departments were similar to problems cited in other recent reports which have severely criticized teacher education departments.[42]

Criticisms of the deans and other regarding teacher education departments in research universities have focused on low admission standards[43], intellectual content of professional knowledge courses[44], adequacy of field experiences[45], low prestige and power of teacher education faculty[46] and research productivity.[47] These critiques share a common theme in that they trace many of the problems in teacher education to the faculty members who work in this area rather than the institutional norms, attitudes and policies which influence their behaviors. This focus is evident when examining the type of studies that have been conducted on teacher educators.

Characteristics of Teacher Education Faculty

Empirical research on teacher educators has been limited in quality and number. Several studies over the last twenty-five years have tended to examine the socio-economic characteristics of those who elect to go into the field of teacher education[48], faculty responsibilities outside of research[49], research productivity[50], and the perceived status and power of teacher education departments within the university.[51]

Research on the demographic characteristics of teacher education faculty indicate that the majority of the faculty are men, white, and middle aged.[52] Although females constitute the majority of elementary and secondary teachers they are disproportionately under-represented among teacher education faculty in research universities. This under-representation of females is consistent with other academic fields such as sociology, biology, and physics. Similar characteristics regarding race, sex, and age of teacher education faculty have also been found among masters level institutions.[53] A commonly held assumption is that one reason for the low scholarly productivity in teacher education is that the majority of teacher education professors are females and are less likely to have been socialized into the scholarship norms of the university. Some scholars such as Evelyn Beck have argued that these norms were intentionally established and upheld to exclude women from becoming professors at elite research universities. It would seem that attributing issues of low quality in teacher education to the over-representation of females in that field is questionable.

As for the socio-economic characteristics of education faculty, Prichard, Fen and Buxton found that education faculty in public comprehensive institutions were proportionately underrepresented by those coming from the homes of professionals, executives, and business proprietors.[55] While the Prichard, Fen and Buxton data are comparable to the socio-economic characteristics of elementary and secondary teachers it is unclear what the socio-economic characteristics are of education faculty in research universities or how they compare to professors in other disciplines. Some researchers have attempted to link the low socio-economic backgrounds of education professors in public comprehensive universities to their orientation to theoretical and cognitive skills.[56] The validity of this relationship is specious when considering the type and conduct of research characteristic of those in many fields of education. Broudy and Schneider have challenged this assumption and link research productivity of education professors to how the field has been defined and the value and institutional support it has among the academy.[57]

Other types of studies which have examined status and research productivity of teacher education faculty have tended to be more holistic in their investigations and interpretations. Judge and Ducharme have shown that teacher educators in universities continue to have little status in the academic community.[58] One recent explanation of low status among teacher educators has been attributed to their work responsibilities. Fuller and Bown found that the demanding supervisory responsibilities of teacher educators are unparalleled in any other type of professional school.[59] Because their responsibilities are not directed toward research, these faculty have difficulty adjusting to the norms of the university.[60] As they are not actively involved in research, teacher educators tend not to publish as much as their colleagues in other areas.[61] Two recent reports, by Raths, and Raths and Ruchkin compared the norms, attitudes, and research activities of teacher education faculty in research universities and in other more comprehensive institutions. Their findings indicate that teacher education faculty who received their training in research institutions and were employed in institutions which had competitive student enrollment policies were more likely to have a stronger scientific attitude toward their work.[62] However, Raths found that only 21 per cent of those faculty surveyed who are actively involved in teacher education are doing research in that field. The majority of teacher education faculty more strongly identify with their discipline field, such as history, or English, rather than teacher education. This self-selected identification with fields outside of education may explain why they are reluctant to conduct research in teacher education.

One might conclude from these studies that the majority of teacher educators in universities are in conflict with the research mission of universities which highly value research productivity and publication. However, Schneider, *et al.*, found that teacher education faculty share the same research and scholarship goals as faculty members in other specialization areas.[63] Conditions within schools of education, such as the formal time assignments teacher educators have to pursue research, as well as the lack of status and value university academic community confers on the knowledge base of professional training in education seems to contribute significantly to the problems of scholarly productivity in teacher education.

The Goals and Working Conditions of Teacher Educators in Research Universities

Differences between the goals and working conditions between faculty members who identify themselves as being in the area of teacher education and faculty members who identify themselves in other areas of specialization such as educational psychology were revealed in a study designed to examine variations in graduate program quality in schools of education. The schools were assessed on the bases of eight factors commonly identified as 'quality indicators',[64] i.e., program goal consensus, student admissions requirements, course content, faculty responsibilities, faculty and student research activities, quality of instruction, and administration and governance. Schools of education were selected by reviewing several major studies that rank schools of education according to measures such as faculty productivity, library resources, amount of external research funds[65]. Those schools of education that appeared in the top fifteen three or more times were labelled level one institutions, and those that appeared in the top fifteen no more than once and only once were labelled level two institutions. Institutions not mentioned in the top fifteen were listed as level three institutions. From this sample of schools of education, forty-two schools agreed to participate in the study.

To obtain information on quality indicators, thirty-one schools of education were visited by a member of the research team. During these on-site visits, deans, graduate deans and faculty were interviewed. Interviews were taped, transcribed, and coded. Responses were coded according to a scheme that permitted those parts of the transcript which were relevant to the interview to be further analyzed.[66] In addition to these interviews, each of the universities selected to be part of this study was asked to provide the number of full-time tenure-track faculty at their institution. If there were over seventy-five faculty members at a particular school, twenty-five full professors, twenty-five associate professors and twenty-five assistant professors were identified and sent questionnaires. If there were fewer than twenty-five assistant professors, they were all included in the study; and the remaining number was assigned randomly across the two remaining categories of associate or full professors. If an institution had fewer than seventy-five faculty, they were asked to include all of their faculty in the study. Total of 1410 faculty questionnaires were returned from thirty-seven institutions. Dean interview data were also obtained from these thirty-seven institutions.

Graduate students and alumni were also contacted. The sampling scheme was designed to obtain responses from doctoral students evenly distributed across three categories of students. Twenty-five questionnaires were randomly distributed to full-time doctoral students who had completed at least nine courses; twenty-five to students who had passed their preliminary exams, presented their proposals, and were admitted to candidacy within the 1982–83 academic year; and twenty-five to students who had completed all requirements with the exception of the final defense of their dissertations. Questionnaires were distributed randomly to twenty-five of their alumni who had graduated during 1979–82, twenty-five from 1975–78, and twenty-five from the 1971–1974 years.

Student and alumni data were obtained from only sixteen institutions. Costs and management problems associated with trying to locate alumni and students in different stages of their doctoral program made it more difficult to obtain the student data than originally anticipated. Consequently, the number of institutions that participated in this part of the study was smaller than the thirty-seven schools that contributed faculty and dean data. A total of 740 questionnaires were received from students and 698 questionnaires were received from alumni.

Responses from deans, faculty, students and alumni constitute the data set upon which the analysis was conducted. Questions asked to these three groups focused on assessing their view of the school of education's normative environment, and their activities and involvement in graduate training. All of the instruments were designed so that comparable questions were asked of all three groups. Respondents were asked about their backgrounds, admissions requirements in the doctoral program, research and teaching activities they were engaged in, the status their school of education had within the university community and other policies governing doctoral study. Faculty were questioned about the definition of their job, the time they spent on their job, their teaching load, the instruction or type of instruction they were involved in, advising, what type of dissertation committees they served on, the amount of mentoring they provided and what they believed to be the criteria for promotion. Faculty were also asked to identify what they contribute in an intellectual sense to their fields and their institutions through their publications, grants, awards, scholarships, membership in organizations, and participation as reviewers or editors for journals and books.

Although the data base in this study was targeted at doctoral training in various areas in schools of education, it has important relevance to issues of prestige and faculty research productivity in teacher education. The institutions in this study are responsible for the majority of teacher training in the country. Faculty who work in these schools of education produce the majority of educational research literature. As the intellectual and training leaders in education, they set the standards, expectations, and norms, for other less prestigious institutions. The activities of teacher educators in these schools of education and how they are perceived by their university communities are likely to mirror, to some extent, other types of institutions.

Differences in Goals

Although schools of education are often viewed by the university community as the place where they train teachers, only a proportion of faculty members, students and alumni identify themselves as teacher educators. Among the faculty responses, over seventy different areas of program specialization were cited. There are several explanations as to why faculty members maybe reluctant to identify themselves in the area of teacher education. First, issues of low status have continued to be associated with teacher education, and perhaps identifying with such an area creates problems of low self-esteem. Then it may be that the actual number of teacher educators has decreased as a result of declining student enrollments in the area. And finally, education as a field has greatly expanded within the last ten years to include many new areas which faculty can identify as their area of program specialization. Whatever the reasons, there were several striking differences among faculty within specialization areas in regard to goals, research activities, and expected levels of student performance and placement. Contrasts were sharply distinguishable between specializations closely linked to professional preparation for teachers, administrators, and counselors and those more closely linked to established social science disciplines such as economics, history, and psychology.

Although the deans perceive the goal of the PhD program to be the pursuit of scholarship and research training, faculty members within some specializations are not committed to these goals, or necessarily training or placing students in careers compatible with these expectations. For example, all faculty maintain that they pre-pare doctoral students to be employed as university professors emphasizing research. However, when asked if they should prepare individuals for these careers, over half of the respondents in policy (57 per cent), nearly half the respondents in technology (47 per cent) and 40 per cent of those in elementary education indicated that they should not. Perhaps, these professors did not believe that this type of preparation should be stressed because so few students actually matriculate to faculty positions in research universities. Fewer than twenty-five per cent of the alumni representing the eighteen speciali-zations responded that they were employed in faculty positions in research universities.

Contradictions between research goals and reality were also evident in the item responses of the students and alumni pertaining to their research experiences as graduate students. The majority of doctoral students responded that they were in programs which emphasized the acquisition of research skills. Over 50 per cent of the students also responded that they would like to be employed as professors in research institutions. Even though the majority of students, deans, and faculty responded that the purpose of graduate training was to train individuals for university positions in research universities, student participation in research activities other than the dissertation process is practically non-existent. Less than 20 per cent of the students had research experiences prior to the disserta-tion in problem conceptualization, instrument design, reviews of literature, data collection, and analysis. Alumni responses were similar, although they did tend to be, on the average, slightly higher (5 per cent). Variations across specializations were not significant.

The importance of research was also evident in the faculty responses concerning the comparative value of research and teaching for determining promotion and salary raises. When asked how much weight teaching, research and service are given in determining pro-

motion and salary raises for faculty members having similar responsibilities, nearly all of the faculty in the various specializations
responded that research activities were weighted approximately 52
per cent. There was slightly more variation pertaining to teaching
and service. Overall, the mean response for teaching was 31 per cent
and 19 per cent for service.

Although the majority of faculty acknowledged the significance
research productivity has to their careers, they are not necessarily
satisfied with this reward system. The relative value research,
teaching and service have in the reward structure is quite different
compared to how they should be weighted according to faculty in
various specializations. Only faculty responses in specializations
such as educational economics and measurement were consonant
with how faculty perceive the reward structure. Faculty in teacher
education and administration maintained that teaching, research, and
service should be weighted quite differently than presently determined. Rather than weighting research activities at 50 per cent, they
indicated that research should account for only 35 per cent. As
expected, faculty in these specializations also selected higher
percentage weights for teaching activities. Faculty in teacher education gave service 25 per cent weight, which was 7 per cent higher
than service is presently rewarded. Moreover, they ranked service
higher than any other specialization. Educational economics, philosophy, and measurement gave service the lowest rankings, which
were slightly under the mean ratings of total faculty responses.

Based on the dean data, research productivity is the most highly
valued institutional activity, and according to faculty the most
highly rewarded. Faculty in specializations other than educational
psychology, measurement, and educational economics are dissatis-
fied with this reward structure. Conflict over these goals is seen by
administrators and some faculty as the obvious result of the inability
of faculty in preparation specializations to conduct research. There
is some evidence to support this perception. According to faculty
self reports, the research productivity (for example, number of
publications in refereed journals, numbers of books published,
numbers of scholarly papers presented, number and type of research
grants, participation and involvement on editorial boards for
refereed journals, awards, fellowships, number of dissertations
chaired which were published) of teacher education faculty compared to other specializations is among the lowest.[67] However,
when examining the total data set, including the dean interviews, it
appears that certain constraints such as the supervisory respon-

sibilities of teacher educators seem to limit the time and resources these faculty can allocate toward pursuing an active research agenda. Problems with teacher education research productivity do not entirely reflect on the initiative and competence of the individual faculty members.

Teacher Education Faculty: Differences in Activities and Outcomes

When examining how faculty spend their time, those in teacher education areas are assigned to do more teaching than faculty in other specializations. Nearly 50 per cent of teacher educators are expected to allocate over 50 per cent of their assigned time to teaching. In contrast, only 29 per cent of the faculty in measurement are expected to allocate over half of their assigned time to teaching. Teacher educators are also formally assigned less time for research than any other specialization. Over 86 per cent of teacher educators are assigned less than 50 per cent of their time of research. In contrast, 45 per cent of the faculty in educational psychology are formally assigned to devote more than 50 per cent of their time to research.

Variations among program specializations were also apparent when faculty were asked to describe how they typically spend their time in a regular week. Again, the differences are more pronounced between teacher education and other specializations. Although 61 per cent of the faculty in measurement spend over 25 per cent of their times on dissertation advising, only 34 per cent of the faculty in teacher education spend similar amounts of time on advising. Forty-one per cent of the faculty in measurement spend over 50 per cent of their time on research, while only 19 per cent of the teacher educators devote similar amounts of time to research. Thus, it is hardly surprising that 37 per cent of teacher educators spend over half their time teaching while only 15 per cent of the measurement faculty spend equal amounts of time on teaching.

The difference between how teacher educators want to spend their time and how their formal time is assigned is the most discrepant among all faculty in other specializations. Teacher educators want to devote more hours to dissertation advising and research, and less time to classroom teaching. Even though they desire to spend less time teaching, however, they still have one of the highest percentages of faculty who want to teach.

Types of teaching activities teacher educators engage in are also the least consistent with doctoral training. They teach fewer doctoral seminars and graduate courses than practically all other specializations. Yet, they teach more undergraduate classes than do faculty in any other specialization. Results for faculty in measurement and educational psychology are almost completely reversed. Faculty in these areas teach more doctoral seminars and graduate courses and fewer undergraduate classes. In contrast to their heavy load, teacher educators have the lightest responsibilities in the dissertation process. They have the smallest number of active doctoral students, they chair and serve on the smallest number of dissertation committees.

Given how faculty spend their time, it is not surprising that faculty in educational psychology have more total publications than any other specialization. They also publish more articles in referred journals, spend more time as reviewers for refereed journals and attend more national conferences. During the last five years, they brought in more research and development funds than any other program specialization. As for their students, they chair more dissertation committees for students whose work is eventually published than any other specialization and they place more students in university positions.

Faculty in educational psychology as compared to faculty in three other program areas reported the highest indicators of faculty productivity as well as socializing and mentoring doctoral students into researchers (see Table 1). From the total sample of forty-two schools of education, a second sample of twenty-nine schools which had programs in teacher education, education foundations, administration, and educational psychology was selected. An analysis of variance was used to determine if among these twenty-nine schools of education, educational psychology faculty differed from faculty in the other three specialization areas on selected criteria (for example, numbers of articles published in the last five years, total publications, and number of dissertations that were published as books or articles). Information on these criteria were based on self reports.

As Table 1 indicates significant effects were found when the dependent measures were number of articles published in the last five years, $F(3, 908) = 3.83$, $p \leq 001$, total publications in the last five years, $F(3, 904) = 4.02$, $p \leq 01$, and number of dissertations chaired which were published as books or articles, $F(3, 737) = 3.55$, $p \leq 01$.

Table 1: *Faculty Research Productivity in Selected Areas of Specialization*

Criteria	Specialization area	M	SD	No. of faculty in area of specialization	F
Number of articles published in the last five years	Teacher education	4.44	3.38	335	3.83**
	Educational foundations	4.37	3.13	172	
	Administration	4.11	3.29	157	
	Educational psychology	5.13	3.20	244	
Total publications	Teacher education	14.70	9.41	333	4.01*
	Educational foundations	15.15	8.97	172	
	Administration	14.51	8.95	156	
	Educational psychology	17.15	9.59	243,	
Number of dissertations chaired which were published as books or articles	Teacher education	4.56	6.86	262	3.55*
	Educational foundations	4.24	5.35	139	
	Administration	6.16	7.49	135	
	Educational psychology	6.59	11.55	201	

* $p \leq .01$
**$p \leq .001$

The issue then became whether faculty in educational psychology would demonstrate these same characteristics of faculty productivity regardless of the type of institution i.e., one, two or three, in which they were located. (For description of distinctions between levels of institutions, see page 222). Similarly, would faculty in teacher education demonstrate low measures of faculty productivity regardless of the type of institution in which they were located? Examining faculty in those schools of education which had teacher education, educational foundations, administration, and educational psychology specialization areas, revealed significant effects for institutional type. A nested MANOVA design indicated considerable variation between faculty responses within specialization areas among the three levels of institutions, $F = 1.11$, $p \leq .05$. (see Table 2).

Results in Table 2 indicate that there is considerable variation between specialization areas among the three levels of institutions for total publications, number of articles in refereed journals in the last five years, formal time assigned for research, and actual time involved in research. At level two and three institutions, faculty in foundation or administration programs fared better on certain criteria than educational psychology (see Table 2). However, faculty in educational psychology at level one institutions probably exemplify more of the criteria associated with quality (i.e. publica-

Table 2: Nested Manova Results for Selected Faculty Productivity Criteria

Criteria	Area of specialization	Type of institution			
		Level 1 M	Level 2 M	Level 3 M	F
Total publications	Teacher education	15.21 (51)a	17.67 (46)	13.42 (131)	2.84**
	Educational foundations	17.31 (37)	19.46 (25)	14.36 (52)	
	Administration	18.34 (19)	16.04 (23)	14.90 (93)	
	Educational psychology	22.22 (31)	13.91 (44)	16.46 (94)	
Number of articles in refereed journals over last five years	Teacher education	3.96	4.59	4.32	2.10*
	Educational foundations	4.90	5.54	4.10	
	Administration	4.93	5.01	4.23	
	Educational psychology	5.64	3.89	5.35	
Formal time assigned for research	Teacher education	2.16	2.25	1.93	2.23*
	Educational foundations	2.38	2.41	2.12	
	Administration	2.14	1.92	1.78	
	Educational psychology	2.69	2.19	2.24	
Actual time involved in research	Teacher education	2.08	2.19	1.90	2.63**
	Educational foundations	2.22	2.36	2.01	
	Administration	2.05	1.76	1.91	
	Educational psychology	2.74	2.20	2.13	

[a] Number of respondents per cell
* $p \leq .05$
** $p \leq .01$

tion) than any other specialization area. Level two institutions tended to have more productive faculty in educational foundations and teacher education, at least with respect to certain indicators of faculty productivity, i.e., primarily publication, than level one institutions. In summary, it appears that most productive faculty in teacher education are located in level two institutions.

Teacher Education in Research Universities: Some Explanations for the Anomalies

Contrasts between teacher education and educational psychology can be explained from organizational management and social cultural perspectives. The organizational structure of schools of education in research universities places teacher education faculty at a resource disadvantage. Schools of education are commonly structured so that faculty in educational psychology have more time for research, teach more graduate courses, and chair and serve on more dissertation committees than faculty in other specialization areas. Teacher educators are assigned less time for research, teach more undergraduate courses, and chair and serve on fewer dissertation committees.

Organizational Perspective

Demands on the time of teacher education faculty for labor intensive activities such as supervision of apprentice teachers results in less time being available for scholarly pursuits. Restricted in their interactions with graduate students, often because of their undergraduate course loads, participation of teacher education faculty in research-related activities, such as conducting doctoral seminars or chairing dissertations has been limited. These research-related activities provide other faculty members with opportunities to sustain and strengthen their enquiry skills and research agenda. Thus, the organizational structure of schools of education hampers the research and scholarly activities of the teacher education faculty. Changing this structure is very problematic because of the attitudes and values faculty and deans have regarding teacher education.

Results from the dean data revealed that most of the deans described all of the program specializations within their schools as at least as good as any other school. A little less than half of the deans responded that their programs were of very high quality. When asked about the weakest specialization areas, the deans mentioned teacher education, curriculum and instruction, and secondary education most often. As one dean states, 'The strength of our school, the big over-arching strength is in psychology.... It's the strongest doctoral program that we have in terms of faculty resources; in terms of students generally ... The rest of them aren't terribly weak. It just means that there is such an overriding strength here. In psychology we are still able to be very selective and the student body is very good. In some respects I'd say it is better than it was ten years ago.... In fields like curriculum and instruction, it's a more difficult comment to make. I don't know whether the student body is as good as it was ten years ago. I know that it's not as numerous. The numbers have not held up. We are not probably as selective. By selective I mean the number that you draw from a pool. For example, in psychology we probably have three applicants for every one selected and of the three applicants, almost all of them, two-and-a-half on the average, meet all the criteria. We are selecting from a pool of people, all of whom are very, very, strong. That same thing is not true in other fields.... In terms of faculty I think that the potential contributions to research and scholarly enterprises is very high because they were recruited quite carefully.' Another dean states, 'The reputation of our most successful program is in educational psychology.' And from another dean, 'I think that surely two programs stand out. The higher education program has exceptionally good students who are already on a ladder leading to better positions. They take about twenty-five students per year in a program with six FTE faculty members, so that's a student faculty ratio of about four to one, and the students are primarily doctoral, there only are a few masters' students, so they can focus their efforts. The other program is the combined program in education and psychology, which is an interdisciplinary program, therefore it reports technically to the graduate school.... They take small number of students ... a substantial number get assistance grants from the federal government which has allowed them to take only those students who had full support. Another factor in their success is that the program requires a research effort prior to dissertation.... They have a committee that judges that effort ... it's part of the qualifying exam.... On the other hand, the curriculum and instruction program suffers from having the largest faculty cuts, from thirty-three FTEs in 1976 to about sixteen now.... That's where the enrollment declines have taken place too. I think the tension in that program exists because they do the majority of the teaching in the undergraduate program, as well as a masters program. The faculty members' energies are always con-flicting. The people who are doing the undergraduate teaching feel that their loads are too heavy because they have a lot of travel and supervision responsibilities for these undergraduate students. Working with doctoral students is the most the desirable thing to do, but these faculty are burdened with the undergraduate students, consequently they complain a lot and they don't do much research. The whole thing leaves the program with an ethos of having a faculty which doesn't conduct research on any substantive topic.... They do some good things, but essentially the research tends to be centered around how do you produce good teachers, rather than the questions that might be focused in the classroom about how students learn ...'

These quotes illustrate several points. From the deans' pers-pective, weak programs are linked to unselective admissions standards, low faculty research productivity, and in the instance of the last example, how teacher educators have defined the field. If these programs are so weak, it is hard to understand why the deans are not undertaking major initiatives to strengthen them. For example, the amount of assigned time for research allocated to teacher educators could be increased. Perhaps one reason why the deans are not making program changes is that they have little structural authority to implement new policies. When asked how much structural authority the dean had in their school, an overwhelming majority responded they had modest or low authority. It is not surprising, therefore, that they also perceived their influence in the schools as low to modest.

Even if the deans had more structural authority, it is questionable whether they would direct their efforts toward strengthening teacher education. If an educational psychology program is rated the best program in the school, and certainly comparable to educational psychology programs in other schools, diverting resources from this area would require a strong rationale. Moreover, it is unreasonable to assume that educational psychologists would take on the traditional responsibilities of teacher educators, particularly supervision, because of its technical nature and heavy time commitment. Educational psychology derives legitimacy from the university community because of its historical link to the social science areas. Because of this, it is more likely to have higher status within the university community than would a preparation area not rooted in a discipline. Undermining a program that has legitimacy and status in the university community seems hardly prudent.

Cultural Perspective

Schools of education continue to face problems of status and legitimacy within the academic community.[68] Teacher education still is viewed by the academy as a second status discipline. The cultural perspective of the 1890s continues today. In the following example a dean describes the problems of trying to change perceptions of the graduate school toward education by supplying data which would breakdown sterotypes, 'Education is the one department that is usually spoken about . . . I think there's a lot of folklore about what the school doesn't do, and in fact we find that our grants per faculty member are higher than some of the other highly touted departments, our students are more prestigiously placed, and nobody ever put that data together before. We have a bibliography of all of our publications ... that we update every year. I can supply the graduate school with every published article that our faculty has done, but no one else in the university admits to having the same. I tried to get the Vice President to do the same for all other departments on campus. Forget it! Why destroy the folklore.' In another instance, a dean also relates the problems of education's image, '... Education has an over representation on a per capita faculty basis of people, you know, holding distinguished professorships, named chairs, and so on and so forth, which are not endowed for education but distributed university-wide and you will still run into here from time to time the faculty member who looks down his or her nose at education.... Now we are trying to figure out what in the world to do with teacher training and I'm trying to talk to department chairs in science and mathematics. For example, I called up the chairman of the chemistry department and said we ought to have lunch and try to figure out what to do about teacher training because there are a whole bunch of things that are wrong and he said, "there's one thing for sure. There shouldn't be any education courses in it." ...' Over 100 years later, the criticisms of teacher education expressed by the President of Yale University in 1876, continue to be directed at the substance of professional knowledge in education courses (see page 214).

Teacher education programs, particularly within research universities have continuously had to justify their existence to the academy. External support has also been a problem, as the media and national and state policy reports have identified teacher training as one of the major sources contributing to the poor quality of teaching in some schools. Alumni of teacher education departments also have tended not to support the value of teacher education programs, and often assail their training experiences as trivial. Teacher educators often find themselves unable to respond to criticisms over the content of what is being taught, as state departments of education in their efforts to upgrade certification requirements are increasingly determining the courses and content offered in teacher education programs. Spuriously viewed by the academy, criticized in the media, and constantly in negotiation with state departments of education over course offerings for certification, it is hardly surprising that teacher education is not well respected among university administrators. It is ironic that the weakest program identified in these forty-two institutions is the one most closely tied to the very core of education. Without a strong graduate training program which encompasses training and research in teaching, how defensible is the existence of a school of education?

In contrast to teacher education, there are other program specializations which fall in the mid-range of faculty and student criteria. However, they are less defensible, from several of the deans' perspectives, as central to the mission of a school of education. Counseling psychology is an example of this type of specialization. At one time, the major responsibility of counseling programs was the training of school counselors. Today, most of the programs in these schools are training students to be clinicians. Many of these students seek the PhD not for a research career but to meet state licensure requirements for clinical psychologists. According to several of the deans, these programs are costly because of practicum requirements. Faculty in the counseling area are prolific, maintain mentor relations with their students, and support strong programmatic requirements for doctoral study. Yet the work they publish and the students they place have, in many instances, little relation to the mission of schools of education.

The institutional culture of research universities demands high levels of scholarship and research productivity. Based on the data it appears that the 'research press' often associated with high quality institutions does not apply to teacher education departments, although it does apply to other areas such as educational psychology. Second level institutions are more likely to have teacher education programs which demonstrate higher levels of faculty research productivity than level one institutions. The consequences of level one institutions' disinterest and low productivity in teacher education is likely to affect perceptions concerning the entire field. If teacher education is not a top rated specialization at Harvard, Stanford or other top ranked schools of education, university administrators and faculty are likely to question how good can it possibly be anyplace else?

When examining the data, it is the deans from second level institutions rather than level one institutions that indicate strong support for the field of teacher education. Level one deans tend to focus on the problems of training teachers, such as admissions standards in teacher education programs, but tend not to consider 'issues of practice' as a legitimate field of enquiry. Deans from second level institutions, which had faculty with high records of research productivity in teacher education placed a high value on the study of teacher education and practice. For example, a dean at a second level institution discussing what the purpose of graduate study should address makes this comment, 'Well, doctoral study, in my view, is to prepare people who can help us become better informed about the problems of education and things that might help its application ... I wouldn't rule out basic kinds of enquiry but eventually I think for doctoral study in education I want persons prepared along those lines to be concerned about education's eventual application and practice whether it's to further enquiry in research or it's to professional practice.... I want people to become smarter to the concerns of education, the practice of education.' Another dean with similar concerns about the role of graduate training in education makes the following remarks, '... I don't think we're like Stanford, Chicago, Harvard, or Northwestern, because I don't think that those schools, however good they are — and they are — however well they study problems related to education, haven't, at least for me, exhibited the kind of commitment to field problems, field issues and training ... I consider our school much more like the land grant types of state universities that, in some fashion, have had to develop the research and scholarship for their disciplines and their fields, as well as serve the people as a school that is committed to serving the field of education.... We have a mission in education which is connected with children and schools and real problems — that's why we're a professional school.'

Recent attention on the problems of teacher education has tended to focus on the symptoms of a field which is not highly valued both within the university or external community. Some of the reforms that have been suggested such as raising admissions standards address only part of the problem. Raising admissions standards for students desiring to enter the field of teacher education will bring people into the area who are expected to do better than average work in post secondary school; but what content and activities are students likely to receive in the programs, or what norms and values are these students likely to become socialized into? What will be the interests and concerns of faculty in the area, and how much time and resources will these faculty receive which they can direct toward improving knowledge in the field?

Some research universities have teacher education departments where faculty members demonstrate high levels of productivity, conduct research activities with their students, and are recognized as making substantive contributions to the study of teaching. Their efforts are likely to have only a minimal effect on the field because of the history and attitudes the academy has toward teacher education. If changes are to occur in the field of teacher education both organizational and perceptual issues will need to be considered. In many universities there is little institutional support to alter the organizational structure which contributes to the problems in teacher education. However, even if teacher educators had more time for research, were more actively involved in graduate programs, and produced numerous scholarly publications on teaching, only part of the problem would be resolved. Teacher educators and their respective schools of education are faced with having to change how the academy has viewed, thought and felt about teacher education for over 100 years. Problems in teacher education center not only on the students who decide to study teaching or the faculty members who work in this area, but in the university context in which teacher education departments were created and exist.

Notes

1. See, for example, SCHWEIBEL, M. (1985) 'The clash of cultures in academe: The university and the education faculty', *Journal of Teacher Education*, 36, Fall, pp. 2–7.
2. See, SCHNEIDER, B. *et al.*, (1985) 'The quality of the doctorate in schools of education', Final Report to the Ford Foundation, Evanston, Ill., Northwestern University.
3. See, SCHNEIDER, B. (1984) 'Some explanations for variations among specializations in schools of education', paper presented at the Wing-spread Conference Center, Racine Wisconsin, Johnson Foundation.
4. For critiques on the content of teacher education courses see, BUCHMANN, M. and SCHWILLE, J. (1983) 'Education: The overcoming experience', *American Journal of Education* 92, pp. 30–51. See also, Holmes Group, Report No. 1 (1985) *Chronicle of Higher Education*, and POPKEWITZ, T. (1985) 'Ideology and social formation in teacher education', *Teaching and Teacher Education*, 1.
5. For studies on the socio-economic characteristics of teacher educators see, LANIER, J. (1985) 'Research on teacher education', in WITTROCK, M. (Ed.), *Handbook on Research on Teaching* New York, Macmillan, pp. 527–69. See also PRICHARD, K. *et al.* (1976) 'Social class origins of college teachers of education', *Journal of Teacher Education*, 22, pp. 219–28.
6. For studies focused on the work responsibilities of teacher educators see FULLER, F. and BOWN, O. (1975) 'Becoming a teacher', in RYAN, K. (Ed.), *Teacher Education: Seventy-fourth Yearbook of the National*

Society for the Study of Education, Chicago, University of Chicago Press, pp. 25–52; and SCHNEIDER, B. (1984) *op cit.*

7. For studies which examine the norms and expectations of teacher educators toward research see, RATHS, J. (1985) 'Scholarly activities of teacher educators', paper presented at the annual meeting of the National Meeting of the American Association of Colleges for Teacher Education, Denver, Colorado; and RATHS, J. and RUCHKIN, J. (1984) 'Contexts affecting methods instruction in selected teacher education institutions', paper presented at the annual meeting of the American Association of Colleges for Teacher Education, San Antonio, Texas.

8. For the most comprehensive study on research productivity on teacher educators see, CLARK, D. and GUBA, E. (1977) 'A study of teacher education institutions as innovators, knowledge producers and change agencies', Final Report, ERIC Document Reproduction Service No. ED 139 805.

9. For studies which examine issues of status see, JUDGE, H. (1982) *American Graduate Schools of Education: A View From Abroad*, A Report to the Ford Foundation, New York, Ford Foundation; DUCHARME, E. and AGNE, R. (1982) 'The educational professorate: A research-based perspective', *Journal of Teacher Education*, 33, pp. 30–6; and SCHNEIDER, B. (1985) 'Underneath the panoply: Doctoral training in schools of education', *Proceedings of the Midwestern Association of Graduate Schools*, 41, spring, pp. 69–81.

10. See MATTINGLY, P. (1975) *The Classless Profession*, New York, New York University Press, and POPKEWITZ, T. (1985) *op cit.*

11. POPKEWITZ, T. (1985) *op cit.*

12. KOERNER, J. (1963) *The Miseducation of American Teachers*, Boston, Houghton-Mifflin.

13. See HALL, G.S. (1891) *The Pedagogical Seminary, International Record of Educational Literature, Institutions and Progress*, Mass, J.H. Orpwa; and HASKINS, C.H. (1923) *The Rise of the Universities*, New York, Henry Holt and Company.

14. BURHAN, 'The higher pedagogical seminaries in Germany', in HALL, G. *op cit.* pp. 390–408.

15. WOODRIDGE, P. (1975) 'The development of teacher education', in RYAN, K. *op cit.* pp. 1–24.

16. POPKEWITZ, T. (1985) *op. cit.*

17. AUERBACH, E. (1957) 'Aspects of the history and present status of liberal arts opposition to professors of education', *The Educational Forum*, pp. 83–94; and POWELL, A. (1976) 'University schools of education in the twentieth century', *Peabody Journal of Education*, pp. 3–20.

18. LEARNED, W. and BAGLEY, W. (1920) *The Professional Preparation of Teachers for American Public Schools. A Study Based Upon An*

Examination of Tax-Supported Normal Schools in the State of Missouri,
New York, The Carnegie Foundation for the Advancement of
Teaching.

19. AUERBACH, E. (1957) *op cit.*
20. BLAIR, A. (1938) *Henry Barnard*, Minneapolis, Educational Publishers,
    Inc.
21. See BORROWMAN, M. (1956) *The Liberal and Technical in Teacher
    Education: An Historical Survey of American Thought*, New York,
    Teachers College Press.
22. SHULMAN, L. (1986) 'Those who understand: Knowledge growth in
    teaching', *Educational Researcher*, 15, January, pp. 4–14.
23. BORROWMAN, M. (1956) *op cit.*
24. See LEARNED, W. and BAGLEY, W. (1920) *op cit.* and MERIAM, J. (1906)
    Normal School Education and Efficiency in Teaching, New York,
    Teachers College.
25. MERIAM, J. (1906) *op cit.*; LEARNED, W. and BAGLEY, W. (1920) *op. cit*;
    and JOHNSON, C. (1913) 'Progress of teacher training', *Report of the
    Commissioner of Education*, New York, pp. 5–20.
26. JUDD, C. (1918) *Introduction to the Scientific Study of Education*,
    Boston, Ginn and Company.
27. *Ibid.*
28. POWELL, A. (1976) *op cit.*; and CONANT, J. (1963) *The Education of
    American Teachers*, New York, McGraw Hill.
29. BORROWMAN, M. (1956) *op cit.*
30. See, CHURCH, R. (1974) 'Economists as experts: The rise of an
    academic profession in America 1870–1917', in STONE, L. (Ed.) *The
    University in Society, Europe, Scotland and the U.S. From the 16th
    Century to the 20th Century*, Princeton, NJ, Princeton University
    Press, pp. 571–610; and SILVA, E. and SLAUGHTER, S. (1984) *Serving
    Power: The Making of the Academic Social Science Expert*, Connecti-
    cut, Greenwood Press.
31. KOERNER, J. (1963) *op cit.*
32. RAVITCH, D. (1984) *The Troubled Crusade*, New York, Basic Books.
33. FLOWERS, J. (1948) 'Recommended standards governing professional
    laboratory experiences and student teaching', in *The American Associa-
    tion of Colleges for Teacher Education First Yearbook*, Washington,
    American Association of Colleges for Teacher Education; and RUGG,
    H. (1952) *The Teacher of Teachers*, New York, Harper and Brothers.
34. SARASON, S., DAVIDSON, K. and BLATT, B. (1962) *The Preparation of
    Teachers An Unstudied Problem in Education*, New York, John Wiley
    & Sons, Inc.
35. TROW, M. (1975) *Teachers and Students Aspects of American Higher
    Education*, New York, McGraw Hill Book Company, p. 57.
36. LEARNED, W. (1914) 'A school system as an educational laboratory',
    Harvard Newton Bulletin.

37. DENNY, T. personal correspondence to Dennis Gooler, Dean, College of Education, Northern Illinois University, 1984.
38. The full citations of these articles are as follows: STREITZ, R. (1924) 'Teacher difficulties in arithmetic and their correctives', *Studies in Education*, University of Illinois; ANDERSEN, (1912) 'Determination of a spelling vocabulary based upon written correspondence', *Studies in Education*, University of Iowa 2, pp. 7–66; GREENE, H. (1923) 'Measurement of linguistic organization in sentences', *Studies in Education*, University of Iowa, pp. 5–36; FRANZEN (1923) 'A comparison between general and specific methods courses in the teaching of high school subjects,' *Studies in Education*, University of Iowa; MOREHOUSE, F. (1920) 'Practice teaching in the School of Education at the University of Illinois 1893–1911', *Studies in Education*, University of Illinois, 10, pp. 1–15; BROWNELL, W. (1925) 'A study of supervised study', *Studies in Education*, University of Illinois.
39. BORROWMAN, M. (1965) *Teacher Education in America: A Documentary History*, New York, Teachers College Press.
40. SCHNEIDER, B. (1985) *op cit.*
41. SCHNEIDER, B. *et al.*, (1985) *op cit.*
42. Holmes Group (1985) *op cit.*; and GIDEONSE, H. (1984) *In Search of More Effective Service*, Cincinnati, University of Cincinnati.
43. WEAVER, W. (1979) 'In search of quality: The need for talent in teaching', *Phi Delta Kappan*, 61 pp. 29–32.
44. BUCHMANN, M. and SCHWILLE, J. (1983) *op cit.*
45. Holmes Group, (1985) *op cit.*
46. JUDGE, M. (1982) *op cit.*
47. GIDEONSE, M. (1984) *op cit.*
48. PRICHARD, K. *et al.* (1976) *op cit.*; LANIER, J. (1985) *op cit.*
49. FULLER, F. and BOWN, O. (1975) *op cit.*
50. RATHS, J. (1985) *op cit.*; RATHS, J. and RUCHKIN, J. (1984) *op cit.*; and CLARK, D. and GUBA, E. (1977) *op cit.*
51. JUDGE, M. (1982) *op cit.*; DUCHARME, E. and AGNE, R. (1982) *op cit.*; and SCHNEIDER, B. *et. al.* (1985), *op cit.*
52. DENNY, T. (1984) 'Selected characteristics of study participants', paper presented at the Wingspread Conference Center, Racine, Wisconsin, Johnson Foundation.
53. *Ibid.*
54. McCONNER, S. (1986) 'A study of graduate training in masters institutions', doctoral dissertation, Evanston, Ill, Northwestern University.
55. PRICHARD, K. *et al.* (1976) *op cit.* For socio-economic characteristics of public elementary and secondary teachers see, LORTIE, D. (1975) *Schoolteacher: A Sociological Study*, Chicago, University of Chicago Press.
56. PRICHARD, K. *et al.*, (1976) *op cit.*

57. BROUDY, H. (1980) 'What do professors of education profess?' *The Educational Forum*, 44, pp. 441–51; and SCHNEIDER, B. (1985) *op cit.*

58. JUDGE, M. (1982) *op cit.*, and DUCHARME, E. (1985) 'Establishing the place of teacher education in the university', *Journal of Teacher Education*, 36, pp. 8–11.

59. FULLER, F. and BOWN, O. (1975) *op cit.*

60. DUCHARME, E. and AGNE, R. (1982) *op cit.*

61. CLARK, D. and GUBA, E. (1977) *op cit.*

62. RATHS, J. (1985) *op cit.* and RATHS, J. and RUCHKIN, J. (1984) *op cit.*

63. SCHNEIDER, B. *et al.*, (1984) *op cit.*

64. BROWN, L. 'The doctorate in teacher education: Implications for the preparation of college teachers of education', *Frontiers of Teaching*, AACTE Yearbook, pp. 264–92; CLARK, M. (1974) *The Assessment of Quality in Ph.D. Programs*, Princeton, Educational Testing Service; and CLARK, D. and GUBA, E. (1977) *op cit.*

65. EASH, M. (1983) 'Educational research productivity of institutions of higher education', *American Educational Research Journal*, 20, pp. 5–12.

66. To check the reliability of the coding scheme, a subset of interviews were coded by the same raters. Raters had to classify the deans' responses into specific item categories and assign numerical weights to selected items. There was a 70–90 per cent agreement across raters on categorizing and assessing the value of selected items. Disagreements were resolved by conferring with the interviewer who conducted the original interview and obtaining his or her ratings on disputed items.

67. See, SCHMIDT, W. (1984) 'On what basis shall we judge quality?' paper presented at the Wingspread Conference Center, Racine, Wisconsin, Johnson Foundation.

68. See, BROWN, L. (1984) 'The structure and context of doctoral study in education from the perspective of students, alumni, faculty and deans', paper presented at the Wingspread Conference Center, Racine, Wisconsin, Johnson Foundation; MATHIS, B.C. (1984) 'The many roads to quality for schools of education', paper presented at the Wingspread Conference Center, Racine, Wisconsin, Johnson Foundation; SCHNEIDER, B. (1984) 'Graduate programs in schools of education: Facing tomorrow, today', in PELCZAR, M., JR. and SOLMAN, L. (Eds) *Keeping Graduate Programs Responsive to National Needs*, San Francisco, Jossey-Bass; SCHNEIDER, B., BROWN, L. DENNY, T., MATHIS, B.C. and SCHMIDT, W. (1984) 'The deans' perspective: Challenges to perceptions of status of schools of education', *Phi Delta Kappan*, 65 pp. 617–20.

9 Clinical Supervision and Power: Regimes of Instructional Management

The 'clinical' method of instructional supervision is examined in historical and philosophical contexts. Analyses of the principal theoretical writings on clinical supervision portray the relations between supervisors and teachers in terms of social and political power 'regimes'. Some general implications for practitioners are presented.

Introduction

This chapter is about the power relations incorporated in encounters between classroom teachers and their supervisors. The 'clinical' model of supervision widely invoked by American educators will be examined for evidence of those relations. The writings of Cogan, Goldhammer and others that advocate this model will be reviewed in terms of their discourse of power. What they say, and what they choose to leave unsaid, can begin to outline some contexts in which much of contemporary American education takes place.

The context which informs power relations has been called a 'regime' by Foucault. Regimes of power — and the regimes of truth that are linked to them — are embedded in every social, political, and economic transaction that characterizes a culture, its place and time. Regimes are implicit power relations that generate the common-sense codes and rules which, unquestioned and accepted as natural, make hegemonies possible. These regimes, their codes and the hegemonies they serve often are not problematic until their context may be viewed historically, or 'archaelogically', in the strata of their time. Foucault offers the following historical vignettes of regimes of power:

> In feudal societies power functioned essentially through signs and levies. Signs of loyalty to the feudal lords, rituals, ceremonies and so forth, and levies in the form of taxes, pillage, hunting, war etc. In the seventeenth and eighteenth centuries a form of power comes into being that begins to exercise itself through social production and social service. It becomes a matter of obtaining productive service from individuals in their concrete lives. And in consequence, a real and effective 'incorporation' of power was necessary, in the sense that power had to be able to gain access to the bodies of individuals, to their acts, attitudes, and modes of behavior. Hence the significance of methods like school discipline, which succeeded in making children's bodies the object of highly complex systems of manipulation and conditioning.[1]

I will look at the regimes implied in the methods of clinical supervision for evidence of incorporation of power in the 'acts, attitudes and modes of behavior' of teachers and supervisors, in service of America's social and political economies.

The term 'clinical supervision' was coined at the Harvard School of Education during the early 1960s. At the time, the Federal government's active role in school policy was growing. The Harvard School of Education, never in solid fiscal or academic shape, obtained an increasingly larger share of its expanding budget from Federally-funded programs: from 5 per cent of its income from government sources in 1955, to over 65 per cent by 1967.[2] The Master of Arts in Teaching (MAT) program, administered as a preliminary step in a ladder preparing an educational elite, sought private and Federal support for efforts to 'improve' teacher education through social science research and development. Cogan and other Harvard faculty promoted programs that would distinguish graduate students from the 'mass' of teachers, setting them on a route to 'professional leadership'.[3]

The model of supervision that emerged has become widely publicized among American teacher educators. It is often cited as a model for practice in teacher education courses.[4] Critiques of this model have focused on its technical limitations, not its power relations.[5] The following brief definitions of clinical supervision are listed by Cogan's colleagues, Goldhammer, Anderson, and Krajewski:

> Morris Cogan defines clinical supervision as: 'the rationale and practice designed to improve the teacher's classroom performance. It takes its principal data from the events of the classroom. The analysis of these data and the relationship between teacher and supervisor form the basis of the program, procedures and strategies designed to improve the student's learning by improving the teacher's classroom behavior'.
>
> Sergiovanni and Starratt say that clinical supervision: 'refers to face-to-face encounters with teachers about teaching, usually in classrooms, with the double-barrelled intent of professional development and improvement of instruction'.
>
> Flanders sees clinical supervision as: 'a special case of teaching in which at least two persons are concerned with the improvement of teaching and at least one of the individuals is a teacher whose performance is to be studied. [I]t seeks to stimulate some change in teaching, to show that a change did, in fact, take place, and to compare the old and new patterns of instruction in ways that will give a teacher useful insights into the instructional process'.
>
> . . . Clinical supervision as we see it, then, is: that phase of instructional supervision which draws its data from first-hand observation of actual teaching events, and involves face-to-face (and other associated) interaction between the supervisor and teacher in the analysis of teaching behaviors and activities for instructional improvement.[6]

These four definitions all speak of 'improvement'. Three prominently mention 'data' and 'analysis'. I will pose then these questions: 'What is made into data, for whose purposes? Whose power and truth are implicit in the analyses? What do their notions of improvement mean to the teacher, the supervisor, and the regimes under which they live?'. In the following sections, I propose to investigate some of the ways this method of instructional management springs from and serves three regimes: the clinical, the personal, and the professional.

Clinical Regimes: The Gazes of Power

According to Cogan, despite its connotations of mortal illness,

> *clinical* [author's italics] was selected precisely to draw atten-
> tion to the emphasis placed on classroom observation,
> analysis of in-class events, and the focus on teachers' and
> students' in-class behavior.[7]

Cogan sought an empirical basis for educational value judgments,
even at a time and place where the scientific community was
questioning the relation of fact and value.[8] Cogan's 'observation and
analysis of behavior' depend on faith in positive empirical science as
a route to transcendent certainty. His behaviorism continues a long
tradition of belief in inductive methodologies.[9] Clinical traditions
depend on a myth of an 'objective reality' superior to 'subjective
feelings'. Consider this statement by Garman:

> *clinical* [author's italics] has been associated with the act of
> administering to the patient in close proximity and the
> curative process was 'empirical,' based on actual observa-
> tion and treatment. A contemporary definition of clinical
> includes as one notation, 'extremely objective and realistic'.[10]

The data that clinical supervisors analyze is discussed with the
teacher during private conferences, but is always defined and categorized by the supervisor. As Goldhammer *et al.* state, the 'patterns'
of a teacher's behavior may only be visible to a trained supervisor,
not the teacher: 'Supervisor must organize the data into appropriate
categories. To some extent this process requires invention, or at least
imaginative treatment of the available data. Much depends on the
conceptual repertoire of Supervisor (*sic*), and also Supervisor's
analytical versatility'.[11]

In admitting 'inventive versatility', Goldhammer *et al.* reveal
the process by which clinical methods build facades of objectivity
and neutrality. In a transaction crucial to the maintenance of a
regime of truth, arcane terms mask the clinician's self-interest, as he
creates 'appropriate categories' that appear disinterested. As can
be seen in the history of eugenics, scientists' deep and explicit
prejudices are readily sanctified by complex words and complicated
numbers into 'objective' analyses. Science remains the source of
'appropriate' knowledge, and scientists solely possess 'objective and
neutral' methods.

The clinical approach Cogan proposed for 'improving' instruction emulates the methodology of clinical medicine. The teacher is asked to interact, but as a reclining patient in submission to the power of words, symbols, and tools that examine and claim to cure what may or may not be simply seen and felt. By first dissecting instruction into behaviors, then diagnosing the causes and treatments for events lived by the teacher and students, the clinical supervisor exercises an exclusive authority to name what goes on in classrooms. A face-to-face encounter with these clinicians is stacked in favor of the face that claims expert knowledge, its own language and system of symbols, and tools that convey the power of truth.[12] A medical clinician might pronounce to a waiting patient, 'The lab data says you're diabetic', just as a clinical supervisor pronounces in conference with a teacher, 'This observational data shows that you are reinforcing time off-task'. The offer of assistance and improvement is cloaked in symbols of power. These symbols confer superhuman capabilities on the clinician, to the benefit of the clinic and the regimes it serves. Foucault investigated the birth of the modern French medical clinic and its regime of truth, stating,

> The clinic — constantly praised for its empiricism, the modesty of its attention, and the care with which it silently lets things surface to the observing gaze without disturbing them with discourse — owes its real importance to the fact that it is a reorganization in depth, not only of medical discourse, but about the very possibility of a discourse about disease.[13]

The clinical 'gaze' with which clinical supervisors analyze a teacher in the classroom is no more real than the gaze of a parent, child, or teacher. The superior realism claimed by clinical supervision derives from a regime of power. The clinical gaze is that of an eye of power: facing it, the subject becomes an object, quantified into data, categorized, and judged. The eye, with its attendant symbols, language, and rituals, empowers the clinician, establishing the common structure that reduces lived events to behaviors, and places spontaneous actions into patterns.

The gaze of power reduces lived experience to positive knowledge for manipulation by symbol and word. The gaze is assymetrical: the subject-as-object may seem powerless to gaze back and question its majesty and authority: to do so would be called inappropriate, unrealistic, and against improvement. Such resistance, and the invasive responses reserved for it by the eye of power, must be investigated elsewhere. At this point, it is enough to say that recognizing the gaze of power, and calling it by name, is the vital first step towards opposition.

Personal Regimes: The Guises of Power

The beneficent vision of the clinical regime promises improvement and health. Not only do Cogan, Goldhammer, and associates borrow its positivist methods and its arcane system of symbols, they make beneficent promises as well. Clinical supervision claims to differ from other supervisory methods, which, according to Cogan,

> psychologically, ... (are) almost inevitably viewed as an active threat to the teacher, possibly endangering his professional standing and undermining his confidence.[14]

Cogan evokes an image of Simon Legree as a non-clinical instructional supervisor. This 'snoopervisor' fires helpless teachers for minute violations of a lengthy, detailed code of behavior. While the demise of this management style and its mode of power may be a step towards more open and equitable power relations in schools, teachers would be wise to judiciously question their self-proclaimed liberators, asking if they have only changed the appearance of the relationship and the language of the threat.

In this section, I will examine what could be a 'psychologically active threat', what clinical supervision would offer instead, and what constitutes the personal regime of power embedded in the encounters between a clinical supervisor and a teacher. Cogan and Goldhammer claimed to have synthesized concepts and practices from clinical psychology and psychotherapy and applied them to the supervision of instruction. They promise mutual interaction between supervisor and teacher, saving that supervisors should be less distant and abstract in their dealings with teachers. Cogan said

> clinical supervision is conceptualized as the interaction of peers and colleagues. It is not unilateral action taken by the supervisor and aimed at the teacher. On the contrary, the teacher is called on to assume almost all the roles and responsibilities of a supervisor ...[15]

Two factors, however, seem to militate a supervisor-centered power relationship: first, the on-going domination of a male hierarchy is not directly addressed, but rather, the recruitment and selection of 'clinical supervisors' was, and remains, dominated by males. This absorption and tacit endorsement of an unbalanced social power relation dims optimism for significant change in schools through clinical supervision. The writings on clinical supervision are silent about the imbalance of power along gender lines in American schools. The regimes of social and economic power in American education have practically dictated a predominantly female teacher population subordinated to a male managerial elite.[16] It is significant that Harvard's MAT program sought to recruit male teachers from privileged classes to join the elite of clinical supervisors.[17]

Furthermore, Cogan's use of clinical psychology as a model indicates the kinds of control that the clinical supervisor would employ. While it is beyond the scope of this essay to delineate the history of 'human relations' methods of managing labor, this investigation warrants a brief look at some ways that the science of psychology has affected personal relations among educators. Recent reports by teachers from inside the classroom provide vivid testimony that teachers' power is not in balance with their supervisors', even those who share 'almost all their roles and responsibilities'.[18] These imbalances are not the results of oversights by harried administrators, but rather the articulations through 'human engineering' of regimes of bureaucratic power.

In their work on the sociology of knowledge in modernized, technological and bureaucratic life, Berger, Berger and Kellner state the issue as follows:

> The production process ... necessitates 'human engineering', that is, the technological management of social relations. Although this management may involve attention to highly personal idiosyncracies of individual workers and may even contain a positively therapeutic dimension, its fundamental purpose is to control the unfortunate intrusions of concrete humanity into the anonymous work process. Individuals become organized in accordance with the requirements of production.[19]

The technology of clinical supervision explicitly subordinates human relations to effective instruction. These priorities clearly dominate the above definitions, and the precisely defined 'cycle', with its detailed specifications of goals and objectives. In these regimes, human beings do not live or create, they produce. They are not valued for themselves, but for their effective roles. Their usefulness is defined in terms of their social and economic roles, expressed in euphemisms, and out of their control, even in their face-to-face encounters with their most benign and helpful supervisors.

Silent regimes of power are no less powerful, nor is self-effacing and modest power less effective. The regimes of truth that are attached to them lead the subordinate to accept her role, rationalize it, and internalize the vision. The clinical psychotherapy of Rogers is an example of human engineering at its most subtle. His model of 'client-centered therapy' is adopted by many advocates of clinical supervision. He takes great pains to emphasize the mutuality and equity of this form of helping relationship, as follows:

> ... a helping relationship might be defined as one in which one of the participants intends that there should come about, in one or both parties, more appreciation of, more expression of, more functional use of the latent inner resources of the individual.[20]

If a relationship between a teacher and her supervisor were to be as balanced as Rogers supposes, any economic, class and gender disparities between them would magically disappear, leaving only two individuals and their mutual capacities for growth. While the advantages of this magic may be clear to supervisors, teachers know the disadvantages at first hand; their tacit submission to the 'realism' of the supervisor maintains the 'mutual' facade. The construct of 'latent inner resources' sounds like a miner's description of a mineral deposit and hints at the 'functional' purposes in 'non-directive' regimes of power and truth.

The 'psychologically active threat' Cogan referred to twenty-five years ago is no less threatening when made psychologically inactive, inert, and as benign-sounding as Rogers' definition. Teachers who resist the gaze and analysis of the supervisor may seem unreasonable, as might teachers who ask for too much attention. Blumberg refers to a 'role conflict' between helping and evaluating, proposing the following 'clinical' strategy:

> It is a question of creating an interpersonal climate between supervisor and teacher in which a productive balance is reached between the demands for freedom and creativity and for control and evaluation. When both parties can talk about the bind they are in, the possibility exists that the conflict can be managed to the satisfaction of both. As long as the overtly obvious constraints of the situation remain beneath

the surface, acknowledged individually but not mutually, the conflict will be avoided unproductively, so that one, ostensibly, wins, and the other, therefore, loses.[21]

The key to this passage is the verb 'manage', which Blumberg explicitly states elsewhere is the supervisor's sole responsibility. The adjective 'productive' indicates whether human or technological values are in question. To Blumberg, mutual acknowledgment of the supervisor's need to 'control and evaluate' presumably brings about the teacher's willing constraint on her own 'freedom and creativity'. This mutual and open process may avoid 'unproductive conflict', but is there any doubt about who wins?

Another threatening aspect of traditional supervision which clinical supervision claims to remove is the personalization of evaluation. Traditionally, a supervisor assessed all aspects of a teacher's personal life.[22] The proponents of clinical supervision offer open and mutual discussion between supervisor and teacher, but within an elaborate cycle whose etiquette proscribes topics deemed 'too personal'. Mosher and Purpel call this aspect of clinical supervision 'the notion of the sector', explaining:

the focus [of supervision] is held on the job, on the present, and on [the teacher's] performance, rather than on recapitulation or reorganization of who she is as a total person. The 'line' is reasonably clear and permits significant exploration of personal attitudes, feelings, and experience as a teacher.[23]

This alleviated threat of active intervention in a teacher's life, however, is accompanied by a depersonalized and anonymous bureaucracy. The threat by supervision to a teacher's self-esteem is not removed, but instead made more complex. According to Berger *et al.*, modern workers encounter bureaucracy as an 'explicit abstraction', which contains the following contradiction:

The individual expects to be treated 'justly.' . . . there is considerable moral investment in this expectation. The expected 'just' treatment, however, is possible only if the bureaucracy operates abstractly, and that means it will treat the individual 'as a number'. Thus the very 'justice' of this treatment entails a depersonalization of each individual case. At least potentially, this constitutes a threat to the individual's self-esteem and, in the extreme case, to his subjective identity.[24]

The bureaucratic forms of management remove direct personal threats, but replace them with an unfeeling, impersonal abstraction. Supervisors adopt guises of personal concern over their positivist omniscience, deferring the nasty business of visible power to the invisible 'system', which cannot be helped, or questioned. The psychological threats posed by supervision, whether articulated in 'active' hierarchy or 'inactive' bureaucracy, may be seen as different expressions of the regimes of power that hold the workplace in sway. The shift away from detailed lists of behaviors overseen by 'snoopervisors' to detailed analyses of behavioral data by 'clinicians' is a change of the guises of managerial power, not its redistribution.

Since Cogan sees preceding methods of instructional supervision as psychologically threatening to teachers, how does he claim clinical supervision could alleviate or even explicate those threats? He and others promoters point to its 'dynamic' and 'ethical' nature, in which teachers and supervisors become 'connected' and 'collegial'. Here again, the collegiality is not equal, but has its limit right at the point where empirical 'realism' must take over. As Garman concludes, 'Ultimately, a person becomes a clinical supervisor when he/she can use the method, act through the metaphor, and thereby sort out the nontrivial from the trivial in order to bring meaning to educational endeavors'.[25] The verbs of that sentence do not imply an open discussion of social contexts, and an even distribution of social power between supervisor and teacher. Rather, casting aside the 'trivial', each teacher would accommodate that power in her classroom through 'method and metaphor' used, acted, and defined by the supervisor.

Clinical supervision deals with the threats to teachers' identities in anonymous bureaucracies not by disassembling the bureaucracies, but by placing veneers of personal contact over the abstract relationships between teachers and their supervisors. Clinical supervision deals with the threats to teachers' self-esteem from technological standards of efficiency, not by examining the standards' linkages to larger social systems and questioning their educational value, but by asking that each teacher internalize and rationalize them. This method of supervision, by its silence, endorses the long-standing dominance of a male elite over a female majority. Wearing the guises of clinical beneficence, empirical certainty and hearty collegiality, the regimes of power retain control. Only by lifting the guises can educators obtain the power to describe and analyze instruction in their own ways.

Professional Regimes: The Classroom Struggle

In this section, I will bring to light some contradictory implications of clinical supervision in the American educational labor practices. Cogan proposed clinical supervisors could do much to alleviate what he called teachers' 'endangered professional standing'. Goldhammer *et al.* said

> we share with Cogan (in particular) and others [the conviction] that many of the weaknesses in American schools today stem in large part from the near-universal neglect of supervision, through which teachers could be assisted toward better performance and a clearer vision of what improvements are possible.[27]

I will investigate whether American schools have neglected supervision, as said above, or whether Goldhammer *et al.* are ironically pointing out that supervisors have already promised too much to teachers and are looking for scapegoats.

Seen in the contexts of political and economic power regimes, the history of the American teaching 'profession' is a story of laborers whose skills were defined entirely by management, in markets controlled by management, struggling for power in classrooms under the eye of supervisors empowered to describe and judge every aspect of their work. Compared to the professions of law or medicine, teachers in classrooms had little leverage for gaining economic independence and negotiable working conditions. Although the conservative elite of white middle-class males called education a profession, it was an uncertain one.

During the Progessive era, a transition from traditional hierarchical supervision to bureaucratic methods occurred in American public schools.[28] The cult of efficiency grew at the same time and the same rapid pace. Organically attached, both regimes of power in the American workplace were rooted in positivist empirical science and utilitarian capitalism. Clinical supervision, as I have said about the clinical and personal regimes, is made up of positivistic and bureaucratic elements. I contend that the clinical supervisor's observation and analysis of classroom life limits the discourse to behavioral terms defined by the supervisor and serving the interests of management.

The 'active threat' of the 'snoopervisors' was derived from the power regimes of religious dominance in early American education. As modernization and industrialization transformed American life in the past century, lay school boards took over responsibility for the supervision of teachers. New roles for principals and superintendents emerged, more analogous to industrial engineers and managers of capital than to deacons or slave-drivers. This transformation of industrial management methods has been called 'the decay of hierarchical control' and 'the institutionalization of bureaucratic control'.[29] In the traditional hierarchy, 'close supervision amounted to an intensification of the oppressive power of the firms and, as would be expected, created an intensified militance among the oppressed'.[30] As we have seen in the personal regimes, a change in method served the interest of the regime, smoothing over dissension at no cost in power, recapitulating the power of truth into bureaucratic and behaviorist terms.

The story of the rise of scientific management methods in America documents another metamorphosis of modern regimes of truth and power. Springing from the laboratories, universities, and factories, proclaimed as a route to secular salvation, scientific management transformed the discourse of American life: educators were fervent converts. Responsibility for scientific standards of efficiency in schools was centered on educated experts, to whom teachers were explicitly subordinate. Administrators who did not embrace quantitative standards of efficiency in the first two decades of the century were pressed by reformers citing progressive business and industrial practices.[31] Eventually, supervisors, along with principals and superintendents, learned to use the languages of psychology and scientific management to justify their continued and consolidated control of classrooms.

By 1960, when Cogan wrote the phrase about 'endangered standing', after decades of labor strife and collective bargaining the teaching profession still adhered to a process-product paradigm dependent on empirical measures.[32] Promoters of a 'scientific basis to the art of teaching' do not ask why schools run like they do and why educators work like they do, but only that research improve 'the way teaching is'.[33] Although there are many cases of teachers taking labor actions over wages and workplace conditions, control over curriculum and instruction has rarely been a central issue of overt political dispute.[34] Teachers' frequently acrimonious struggles with administrations over classroom authority and creativity end up quantified on bargaining tables as contract requests for dollars, hours, days, and 'class loads'. The bureaucratic cult of efficiency defines the terms at the table, just as the clinic defines the diagnosis. In the American workplace, many other semi-professions (for example, nurses, secretaries, and engineers) have similarly lost creative control and have become wage-labor.[35]

The teacher, unlike professionals such as doctors or lawyers, has little autonomy of design. Managers tell her what to teach, how to teach it, and how they evaluate her work. She not only dispenses reified knowledge, she is controlled by it as well. The paradoxical promise of clinical supervision is that 'improvement' is entirely defined by the regime, and so can only serve the regime. The regime sets the terms of work, makes the job hard, and then asks the workers to say why they like it. Teachers know why clinical supervisors feel neglected: people living under a bridge don't like conmen selling it to them. The status quo uses words that people cannot understand, unequally treats their point of view, and takes ultimate control of the classroom out of the teacher's hands. To the teacher, 'improvement' means further subjugation to bureaucratic control. Clinical supervision offers a 'clearer vision' of what teachers can already see when they give standardized tests, fill out forms for the office, or get the textbooks and lesson plans handed to them.

Just as bureaucratic control overcame the shortfalls of hierarchical control in expressing the regime of power, so 'human relations' management methods are used to boost efficiency in American industrial and educational enterprises. Cogan's words in 1961 were both physically and philosophically close to the methods of Harvard Business School, where Elton Mayo and associates had long been advocating industrial uses of motivational psychology to foster cooperative attitudes among workers, supervisors, and managers. Their classic Hawthorne experiments in the 1930s had been disseminated to managers during the crisis of capitalist society in the Depression, and Mayo's teachings had become widely adopted by the era of war production. As Mayo wrote in 1945,

> In matters of mechanics or chemistry the modern engineer knows how to set about the improvement of process or the redress of error. But the determination of optimum working conditions for the human being is left largely to dogma and tradition, guess, or quasi-philosophical argument. In modern large-scale industry the three persistent problems of management are:
>
> 1 The application of science and technical skill to some material good or product.
> 2 The systematic ordering of operations.

3   The organization of teamwork — that is, of sustained cooperation.

The last must take account of the need for continual reorganization of teamwork as operating conditions are changed in an *adaptive* society.[36]

Mayo clearly spells out the goal of 'improvement' that characterizes all definitions of clinical supervision. He and phalanxes of managerial disciples plainly advocate the same 'objective' positivism as the clinic. 'Teamwork' is a guise for efficiency: Mayo's modern managers leave no doubt that their regime is not one dedicated to symmetrical power relations between worker and manager, but rather one devoted to the most efficient production of maximum profits.

The contrast between 'efficiency' and 'human relations' perspectives on management[37] is really a matter of different roads to the same Rome: efficient application of managerial power. Consider the similarity of Mayo's passage above to the following passage by Goldhammer *et al.*:

We require a supervision that is basically analytic and whose principal mode of analysis comprises highly detailed examination of teaching behavior. We require a supervision whose precepts and methods are basically rational and unmysterious and in which teachers may participate with all of their faculties intact and without intellectual offense. We need a supervision whose effect is to enhance and to actualize and to fulfill, in degrees that are appreciable and sensible in the teacher's own experiential frameworks. Teachers (like anyone) must be able to understand what they are doing and the goals and process (sic) that govern their behavior, and supervision must provide adequate illumination for such understanding. We require a supervision that is basically teacher-initiated and consistent with independent, self-sufficient action. Our supervision must result, regularly and systematically, in palpable technical advancement; it must have methodological and conceptual rigor and it must produce real and measurable accomplishments.[38]

This passage summarizes the contradiction between what clinical supervisors say about teachers as persons and what they do about teachers as workers. Teachers are encouraged to initiate the process and understand what the supervisor sees and does, even as the supervisor defines the rigorous method and reality of its results. Are the benefits of this process equally distributed among educators when the results must be 'palpable technical advancement', defined by supervisors? In the last sentence above, we are told that teachers and supervisors require 'technical advancement, rigor, and measurable accomplishments', in terms that admit no disagreement. Where is the humanity in this method of supervision, if not wholly subordinated to the clinician's gaze and bureaucrat's management? Through 'rational, unmysterious' methods, 'sensitive to the teacher', regimes of power and truth impose themselves on classroom life for the explicit purpose of the 'real and measurable' results they alone require.

Despite the claims of 'open, humane and creative' methods, and stated emphases on teacher initiative and teacher growth, the method of supervision required by Goldhammer *et al.* solves management's problems as the first priority. In their incorporation of management's regime of truth, supervisors and teachers both come to see this priority as the real and natural order. As Nichols states,

> Managers' thinking may be ideological, in that they assume capitalism is a 'natural' system, is necessarily here to stay, and in that the truths it expresses are partial truths only. But what others call their 'ideology,' managers call 'common sense.' And 'common sense' tells them that they must not forfeit control; that the business of business is profit; and that, whatever ideas they might have in their heads, and whatever enriching or participatory ventures they may institute, there are limits — not of their making — of what they can 'sensibly' do.[39]

Cogan refers to 'endangered professional standing' that teachers faced in the heavy hands of non-clinical supervision past, as if clinical supervision defends teachers' struggles to wrest their social and economic autonomy from a patriarchal system. Yet, Cogan and his successors in this literature do little if anything to analyze the contexts of old-line supervisors, or scrutinize the contexts of their 'new approach'. Instead, inferring the same ideology of profit-centered capitalism, the same utilitarian moral values, and the same positivistic science, they proclaim a new relationship among the individual teachers and supervisors, as in Goldhammer *et al.*:

Because it is more specific, and because of the greater amount of interaction on the part of the teacher and the supervisor, it is probably easier for the parties to understand and accept their respective roles.[40]

Human-relations management methods claim to develop team-work among workers, so that they 'understand' and 'accept' the workplace conditions dictated by profit. Just as with the harder-to-understand previous methods, however, these managers don't include workers in 'unreasonable' decisions, like who gets the profit. Teachers' 'semi-profession' is subject to total control by management. They are not protected by licensing or royalty structures from management intrusion. The most creative teaching may not suit the regime of power, just as the most efficient production of goods by workers and engineers may be contravened by the requirements of capital.

The professional standing that clinical supervision would defend for teachers would still not empower them in major curricular decisions, nor would it allow teachers who meet professional certification and contractual requirements the same latitude for creativity that lawyers, doctors, scholars, and artists pursue in less tightly controlled marketplaces. Instead, each clinical supervisor promises 'empathy' and 'mutuality', but leaves the great imbalance of political, social and economic power intact along the lines of class, race, and gender. The regime of clinical and bureaucratic power remains incorporated in the daily lives of each teacher and student. As The Who sing, 'Meet the new boss, same as the old boss.'[41] In looking at the power relations in the American work-place, Whyte may have been blind to gender, but saw the regimes as follows:

> ... the behavior of men in industry is shaped to important degrees by money, technology and workflow, organization structure, and the social environment of the community in which the organization is located. This does not mean that the individual human being is simply a pawn of these forces. It does mean that his powers of changing the situation are severely limited if he can only operate on a face-to-face basis and without any control over money, technology, organization structure, and community environment.[42]

It is the task of educators who would analyze instruction to seek ways to obtain more control over the contexts in which the regimes of truth and power operate in the schools. Doing any less severely limits the prospects for growth by any standard. Promising more but doing less, as do the writings on clinical supervision, limits the prospects most of all.

Towards Whose Utopia?

Clinical supervision is said to inspire the teacher living under the regimes of power in America's schools, even though she may be subject to the supervisor's objective gaze and positivist language, coaxed to assume a strictly 'sectored' personal relationship with him. Her creativity and spontaneity may be further circumscribed by a depersonalized bureaucracy. As if these conditions are not already uninspirational, clinical supervisors also avow that they offer teachers collegial respect and professional autonomy, even as they regiment instructional efficiency and educational labor. Then, having already sold teachers most of the invisible new suit, clinical supervisors seem to say, 'But that's not all! There are visionary aims!'. Consider the inspirational utopianism of this passage by Goldhammer:

> The aims of clinical supervision will be realized when, largely by virtue of its own existence, everyone inside the school will know better why he is there, will want to be there, and, inside that place will feel a strong and beautiful awareness of his own individual identity and a community of spirit and enterprise with those beside him.[43]

What kind of utopia is Goldhammer conjuring up? Foucault describes two types: a classical utopia is a 'fantasy of origins', presenting the classes from which humanity and knowledge sprang, as the Trees of Life and Knowledge in the Judeo-Christian Eden. A modern humanist utopia, like Goldhammer's 'community of spirit',

> is concerned with the final decline of time rather than with its morning: this is because knowledge is no longer constituted in the form of a table but in that of a series, of sequential connection, and of development . . .[44]

Goldhammer's community of spirit aims for progress towards some fulfilled end of history, a mirage that civilized societies have regularly created and enforced for the immediate benefit of the regimes of power, holding out hope for deferred benefits to those doing the dirty work. Teachers and bureaucrats who might sneer at elysian visions of the Big Rock Candy Mountain still sign up for instructional improvement through clinical supervision. The enticing visions have been around for too long to resist or ignore. Gold-hammer's utopian vision, in this long tradition, may also be one more appropriation from clinical medicine's regime of truth, for, according to Foucault,

> the years preceding and immediately following the [French] Revolution saw the birth of two great myths with opposing themes and polarities: the myth of a nationalized medical profession, organized like the clergy, and invested, at the level of man's bodily health, with powers similar to those exercised by the clergy over men's souls; and the myth of a total disappearance of disease in an untroubled, dispassionate society restored to its original health. But we must not be misled by the manifest contradiction of the two themes: each of these oneiric figures expresses, as if in black and white, the same picture of medical experience. The two dreams are isomorphic: the first expressing in a very positive way the strict, militant, dogmatic medicalization of society, by way of a quasi-religious conversion, and the establishment of a therapeutic clergy; the second expressing the same medicalization, but in a triumphant, negative way, that is to say, the volitization of disease in a corrected, organized, and cease-lessly supervised environment, in which medicine itself would finally disappear, along with its object and raison d'etre.[45]

For modern regimes of power and truth, these 'corrected, cease-lessly supervised' paradises stand at the end of the clinic's history. It is not impossible to envision different futures, in which humans interact mutually and equally, sharing power and constituting truth from analyses of their history and common interests. Such premonitions of the future do not terminate in sterile, supervised utopias, but can leave growing room for imagination, mutation, and the unmediated power of life.

Conclusion

It would be cynical to end my deliberations, having examined the regime of power in instructional supervision, without implying that

I have prescriptions of my own for teachers and supervisors. I really don't endorse any general prescriptions that would go beyond Foucault's caution that

> It's not a matter of emancipating truth from every system of power (which would be a chimera, for truth is already power) but of detaching the power of truth from the forms of hegemony, social, economic and cultural, within which it operates at the present time.[46]

Cherryholmes compares Foucault's 'detaching the power of truth' to Habermas' 'critical discourse', Derrida's 'deconstruction' and Rorty's 'edifying philosophy', saying,

> Power structures, it seems, will always be around, but they can be made explicit, criticized, justified, and rearranged.[47]

In order to effect these rearrangements, critical discourse must be face-to-face, and must shun both obsequiousness to the status quo and nihilism which abandons the field to the status quo. The absence of metaphysical or empirical certainties does not void our responsibilities, but intensifies them. Without a fixed horizon, the boat we are all in deserves more attention, not less. A world with advanced technologies and instant communications requires our best efforts to respect its physical, social and spiritual natures, in infinite variety of form. Foucault said,

> The essential political problem for the intellectual is not to criticise the ideological contents supposedly linked to science, or to ensure that his own scientific practice is accompanied by a correct ideology, but that of ascertaining the possibility of constituting a new politics of truth. The problem is not changing people's consciousness — or what's in their heads — but the political, economic, institutional regime of truth.[48]

Foucault's analyses do not offer a system of hope for teachers, physicians, managers, or any of us who makes or effects social policies. Any system of hope would be yet another set of postulates for a metaphysical horizon at which truth is fixed, and towards which clerics, scientists, and politicians have been dragging or pushing their fellow humans in all directions for centuries. Hope, if there is to be any, may be embedded in the community of enquiry in which we all share our analyses and critiques, live with each other and our ambiguities, and constantly rebuild our horizons in the light of our discourse, 'the monotony of a journey, which, though it probably has no end, is nevertheless perhaps not without hope'.[49]

For us educators, face-to-face critical encounters can make possible new politics of truth only by assuming as much control over their contexts as we can mutually and equitably grasp. There have been recent proposals for 'critical' practices of educational administration and instructional supervision.[50] Confronting the power relations of schooling in their contexts is no easy task: no technology or ideology exists that can detach truth from power. Critical analyses of the regimes of truth and power must proceed case-by-case, with undisguised mutual respect among all parties and careful inspection of the terms of each encounter. The fault lines of class, race, and gender must be mapped again and again.

The daily epiphanies of classroom life can be shared through critical analyses among educators regardless of rank. The body of literature on educational supervision can be revived from the coma of empiricist subservience, and become alert to the many ways, large and small, that schools serve exploitation without question. Collegiality and growth, promised by the theories of clinical supervision but withheld by the politics of its practice, won't wait for a utopian apotheosis but are made through hard, open-minded and responsible work in each classroom encounter in every school, every day. In these encounters, in these struggles for open discourse, power is made, not granted to us; truth is not mediated from any distant source, but we make it, in what we think and say, incessantly and immediately.

Notes

1. FOUCAULT, M. (1980) *Power/Knowledge: Selected Interviews and Other Writings.* GORDON, C. (Ed. & Trans.), New York, Pantheon Books, p. 125. It may be said that for women this 'new form of power' had emerged long before.
2. POWELL, A. (1980) *The Uncertain Profession: Harvard and the Search for Educational Authority*, Cambridge, MA, Harvard University Press, p. 274.
3. *Ibid*, p. 266.
4. See: SERGIOVANNI, T. (1982) 'The context of supervision', in SERGIOVANNI, T. (Ed.), *Supervision of Teaching*, Alexandria, VA, ASCD pp. 82–90; SERGIOVANNI, T. and STARRATT, R. (1983). *Supervision: Human Perspectives*, New York, McGraw-Hill; GLATTHORN, A. (1984). *Differentiated Supervision*, Alexandria, VA, ASCD;

GLICKMAN, C. (1985). *Supervision of Instruction: A Developmental Approach*. Newton, MA, Allyn & Bacon.

5. HARRIS, B. (1975) *Supervisory Behavior in Education* (2nd ed.), Englewood Cliffs, NJ, Prentice-Hall, p. 94; GOLDSBERRY, L., MAYER, R. and HARVEY, P. (1985) 'Principal's thoughts on supervision', paper presented to the Annual Meeting of the American Educational Research Association, Chicago, 1–5 April.

6. COGAN, M. (1973). *Clinical Supervision*, Boston, Houghton Mifflin, p. 9; SERGIOVANNI, T. and STARRATT, R. (1983) *op cit.*, p. 305; FLANDERS, N. (1976). 'Interaction analysis and clinical supervision', *Journal of Research and Development in Education*, 9, winter, p. 47–8; GOLDHAMMER, R., ANDERSON, R. and KRAJEWSKI, R. (1980). *Clinical Supervision: Special Methods for the Supervision of Teachers* (2nd ed.), New York, Holt, Rinehart and Winston, Inc, pp. 19–20.

7. COGAN, M. (1973) *op cit.*, pp. 8–9.

8. See KUHN, T. (1962) *The Structure of Scientific Revolutions*, Chicago, University of Chicago Press.

9. See: GOULD, S. (1981). *The Mismeasure of Man*, New York, W.W. Norton & Co.

10. GARMAN, N. (1982). 'The clinical approach to supervision', in SERGIOVANNI, T. (Ed.), *Supervision of Teaching*, Alexandria, VA, ASCD, p. 36.

11. GOLDHAMMER, R. *et al.* (1980) *op cit.*, p. 86.

12. See EDELMAN, M. (1977). *The Political Language of the Helping Professions: Words That Succeed and Policies that Fail*, New York, Academic Press.

13. FOUCAULT, M. (1975). *The Birth of the Clinic: An Archaeology of Medical Perception*, SMITH, A. (Trans.), New York, Vintage, p. xix.

14. COGAN, M. (1961) *Supervision at the Harvard-Newton Summer School*, Cambridge, MA, Harvard Graduate School of Education, p. 7.

15. COGAN, M. (1973), *op cit.*, p. xi.

16. APPLE, M. in this volume reports that two-thirds of American teachers are women and three-fourths of the supervisors and managers are male. See also MATTINGLY, P. in this volume.

17. POWELL, A. (1980) *op cit.*, pp. 249–50.

18. See FREEDMAN, S., JACKSON, J. and BOWLES, K. (1983). 'Teaching: An imperilled "profession"' in SHULMAN, L. and SYKES, G. (Eds) *Handbook of Teaching and Policy*, New York, Longman, pp. 280–95.

19. BERGER, P., BERGER, B. and KELLNER, H. (1974). *The Homeless Mind*, New York, Vintage, p. 32.

20. ROGERS, C. (1958). *On Becoming a Person*, Boston, Houghton Mifflin, p. 3.

21. BLUMBERG, A. (1976) *Supervisors and Teachers: A Private Cold War*, (1st ed.), Berkeley, CA, McCutchan, p. 170.

22. See APPLE in this volume, (p. 72).

23. MOSHER, R. and PURPEL, D. (1972). *Supervision: The Reluctant Profession*, Boston, Houghton Mifflin, p. 148.
24. BERGER, P. *et al.* (1974) *op cit.*, p. 55.
25. GARMAN, N. (1982) *op cit.*, p. 52.
26. Exemplars of this supervisory power abound. See HUNTER, M. (1984) 'Knowing, teaching and supervizing', in HORSPORD, P. (Ed.) *Using What We Know About Schools*, Alexandra, Va., ASCD.
27. GOLDHAMMER, R. *et al.*, (1980) *op cit.*, p. 186.
28. See KESSLER-HARRIS, A. *Out of Work*. New York, Oxford University Press; LARSON, M. (1977). *The Rise of Professionalism: A Sociological Analysis*, Berkeley, CA, University of California Press, p. 184.
29. EDWARDS, R. (1979). *Contested Terrain: The Transformation of the American Workplace*, New York, Basic Books, p. 20.
30. *Ibid*, p. 53.
31. See CALLAHAN, R. (1962) *Education and the Cult of Efficiency*. Chicago, University of Chicago Press; KARIER, C. (1982). 'Supervision in historic perspective', in SERGIOVANNI, T. (Ed.), *Supervision of Teaching*, Alexandria, VA, ASCD, p. 2–15. For an interesting perspective on Taylorism and the class struggle, see also MEIKSINS, P. (1984) 'Scientific management and class relations: A dissenting view', *Theory and Society*, 13, pp. 177–209.
32. See POPKEWITZ, T. (1984). *Paradigm and Ideology in Educational Research. The Social Functions of the Intellectual*. London and Philadelphia, Falmer Press; POPKEWITZ, T., TABACHNICK, B. and ZEICHNER, K. (1979) 'Dulling the senses: Research in teacher education', *Journal of Teacher Education*, 30, 5, pp. 52–60.
33. GAGE, N. (1978). *The Scientific Basis of the Art of Teaching*, New York, Teachers College Press, p. 94.
34. MITCHELL, D. and KERCHNER, C. (1983). 'Labor relations and teacher policy'. in SHULMAN, L. and SYKES, G. (Eds), *Handbook of Teaching & Policy*, New York, Longman, pp. 214–38.
35. See WALKER, P. and WALKER, P. *Between Capital and Labour*, Montreal, Black Rose Books.
36. MAYO, E. (1945). *The Social Problems of an Industrial Civilization*, Boston, Harvard University, p. 10.
37. See SERGIOVANNI, T. (1982). *op cit.*
38. GOLDHAMMER, R. *et al.* (1980) *op cit.*, p. 206.
39. NICHOLS, T. (1980). 'Management, ideology, and practice', in ESLAND, G. and SALAMAN, G. (Eds), *The Politics of Work and Occupations*, Toronto, University of Toronto Press, p. 300.
40. GOLDHAMMER, R. *et al.* (1980) *op cit.*, p. 20.
41. DALTREY, R. and TOWNSEND, P. (1970). *Won't Get Fooled Again*, New York, Track Music/BMI.
42. WHYTE, W. (1961). *Men at Work*, Homewood, IL, R.D. Irwin Inc, p. 13.

43. GOLDHAMMER, R. (1969). *Clinical Supervision: Special Methods for the Supervision of Teachers*, New York, Holt, Rinehart & Winston, Inc, p. 56.
44. FOUCAULT, M. (1970). *The Order of Things: An Archaelogy of the Human Sciences*, New York, Vintage, p. 262.
45. FOUCAULT, M. (1975), *op cit*, p. 31–32.
46. FOUCAULT, M. (1980), *op cit*, p. 133.
47. CHERRYHOLMES, C. (1985). 'Theory and practice: On the role of empirically based theory for critical practice', *American Journal of Education.* November, p. 67.
48. FOUCAULT, M. (1980), *op cit*, p. 133.
49. FOUCAULT, M. (1970), *op cit*, p. 314.
50. See BATES, R. (1984). 'Toward a critical practice of educational administration' in SERGIOVANNI, T. and CORBALLY, J. (Eds), *Leadership and Organizational Culture*, Urbana, IL, Univ. of Illinois Press, pp. 260–74; FOSTER, W. (1984). 'Toward a critical theory of educational administration', in SERGIOVANNI, T. and CORBALLY, J. *op. cit.*, pp. 240–59; SMYTH, W. (1985) 'Developing a critical practice of clinical supervision'. *Journal of Curriculum Studies*, 17, pp. 1–15.

Part IV
Alternative Perspectives to
Professional Education

10 Teacher Education as a Counter-public Sphere: Notes Towards a Redefinition

Henry Giroux and Peter McLaren

Abstract

The authors attempt to locate teacher education within a peda-gogical model that stresses the primacy of cultural analysis, teach-ing for democracy, and active citizenry. The authors begin by analyz-ing the reasons why teacher education programs have failed to take seriously the concept of schools as sites for self and social transfor-mation, what the authors refer to as 'counterpublic spheres'.

Leftist educators are criticized for working primarily within forms of ideology critique while failing to provide alternative approaches to teacher education or what the authors call 'a language of possibility'. The lack of a well-articulated, emanci-patory political project defining current approaches to teacher education is linked, in part, to the failure of leftist educators to critically appropriate new advances in social theory into a pro-grammatic discourse.

The authors conclude by providing an emancipatory approach to teacher education through the development of a curriculum as a form of cultural politics. Such an approach centers around creating the conditions for student self-empowerment and social trans-formation.

Introduction

In the early and middle part of the twentieth century, John Dewey, C. Wright Mills, and Jurgen Habermas, among others, argued strongly that with the rise of mass society the community of publics that made up alternative public spheres throughout the industrial countries of the West were in danger of being eliminated.[1] With the development and expansion of the culture industry, the encroachment of the state into ever increasing aspects of everyday life, and the concentration of political and economic power into fewer and fewer groups, alternative public spheres such as church associations, trade unions, neighborhood alliances and social movements in which communities of people debated, struggled and fought for self and social determination, were slowly being eroded. For theorists such as Dewey, the public sphere provided the nexus for a number of important pedagogical sites where democracy as a social movement represented an ongoing effort by numerous subordinate groups to meet and produce a social discourse and to ponder the implications of such a discourse for political action.[2] In effect, the public sphere not only served to produce the language of critique, it also kept alive the hope for subordinate groups to create their own intellectuals, or in Gramsci's terms, to create organic intellectuals who could bridge the gap between academic institutions and the specific issues and workings of everyday life. That is, such intellectuals could provide the moral and political skills necessary to fund institutions of popular education and alternative cultures and beliefs.

Part of our intention in this chapter is to argue that teacher education institutions need to be reconceived as public spheres. In effect, we wish to argue that teacher education institutions are damagingly bereft of both social conscience and social consciousness. As a result, programs need to be developed in which prospective teachers can be educated as critical intellectuals who are able to affirm and practise the discourse of freedom and democracy.[3] As counter public spheres teacher education programs would create a public space in which prospective teachers would learn through dialogue, debate, and social engagement to articulate their own sense of moral and political purpose as future teachers. Such a program would create intellectuals who could translate the risks of discovery and learning into pedagogical practices that defend and extend democratic discourse and social practices in schools as well as in the wider society. Within this perspective, the notions of pedagogy and culture can be seen as intersecting fields of struggle. As such, the contradictory character of pedagogical discourse as it currently defines the nature of teacher work, everyday classroom life and the purpose of schooling can be subjected to more radical forms of interrogation.

More specifically, the problem we want to address centers around the issue of how the education of teachers can take place within a public space that illuminates the role schooling plays in the joining of knowledge and power. In short, we want to explore how a radicalized teaching force can provide for empowering teachers and teaching for empowerment.

We believe that one of the great failures of North American education has been its inability to seriously threaten or eventually replace the prevailing paradigm of teacher as a form of classroom manager with the more emancipatory model of the teacher as a critical theorist. Furthermore, teacher education has consistently failed to provide students with the political means and moral imperative for fashioning a more critical discourse and set of under-standings around the goals and purposes of schooling. Teacher education has rarely occupied a critical space, public or political, within contemporary culture, where the meaning of the social could be recovered and reiterated so that teachers' and students' cultural histories, personal narratives and collective will were permitted to coalesce around the development of a democratic, counterpublic sphere.

Despite the early efforts of John Dewey and others to shape schooling in the interests of a radical democracy[4] and the recent critical attempts by leftist educational theorists to connect the ideo-logy of schooling to the logic of the capitalist state,[5] the political space which teacher education occupies today continues to de-emphasize the struggle for teacher empowerment and generally serves to reproduce the technocratic and corporate ideologies that characterize dominant societies. In fact, it is reasonable to argue that teacher education serves primarily to create intellectuals who operate in the interests of the state, whose social function is to sustain and legitimate the status quo.

There are many reasons why educators have failed to seize whatever theoretical possibilities were available to them in order to rethink democratic alternatives and foster new emancipatory ideals. We believe that one major reason lies with the failure of leftist groups and other educators to move beyond the language of critique. That is, radical educators have remained mired in a language that links schools primarily to the discourse and social relations of domination. From this view, it follows that schools serve mainly as agencies of social reproduction producing obedient workers for the state; knowledge is generally considered to be part of the fabric of 'false consciousness'; and teachers appear trapped in a no-win situation. The agony of this position has been that it has prevented left educators from developing a programmatic language in which they can theorize *for* schools. Instead, radical educators have theorized primarily *about* schools, and, as such, seldom concern themselves with the possibility of constructing new, alternative approaches to school organization, curricula, and classroom social relations. Absent from their discourse is what we want to call a language of possibility, one which, as Laclau and Mouffe point out, suggests the 'constitution of a radical imaginary'.[6] In our case, a radical imaginary represents a discourse that offers new possibilities for democratic social relations; it traces out a link between the political and the pedagogical in order to foster the development of counterpublic spheres that seriously practise a form of radical democracy. Our purpose here is not to rehearse the failures of leftist politics and educational reform, but to address our concerns towards the development of a new discourse through which a more critical approach to teacher education might emerge.

Teacher Education and the Devaluing of the Political Project

Our own experiences in teacher training institutions — both as student teachers and eventually as instructors of both student and experienced teachers — has confirmed for us what is generally agreed to be commonplace in most schools and colleges throughout North America: that these institutions continue to define themselves essentially as service institutions generally mandated to provide students with the requisite technical expertise to carry out whatever pedagogical functions are deemed necessary by the various school communities in which students undertake their practicum experiences.[7]

Under the shadow of the present neo-conservative assault on education, the esteemed model of the teacher has become that of the technologist, technician or applied scientist. There is little talk within this view about the need for teachers to make critical and informed judgments with respect to both their own practice and what they consider to be the meaning and purpose of education. What is missing from neo-conservative discourse is the image of the teacher as a transformative intellectual who defines schooling as fundamentally an ethical and empowering enterprise dedicated to the fostering of democracy, to the exercise of greater social justice, and to the building of a more equitable social order. This situation perilously recaptures Braverman's claim that the capitalist imperative has proletarianized workers to the extent that they have become deskilled and reduced to merely executing the commands of management.[8]

This is not to imply that school critics have not put forth proposals for radicalizing teacher education programs. The problem has been that when such proposals appear they generally are either confined to a celebration of more refined methods for teacher educators or they stay within the language of critique we mentioned previously. Of interest here is that both liberal and radical forms of discourse share the inability to constitute a new theory and social space for redefining the nature of teacher work and the social function of teaching. In other words, absent from the political project that informs these discourses is an attempt to view schools as part of a wider struggle in the fight for radical democracy. Clabaugh, Feden and Vogel (1984) typify the liberal perspective when they write:

> teacher education must be restructured to develop in students a sufficient knowledge base for methodical problem solving. Students must also develop the attitudinal set to look to research findings for help in solving problems. We believe that students trained in this fashion will be superior teachers well-versed in content and able to create instructional programs that meet the needs of all age groups. They will also be able to use relevant and efficient problem-solving strategies to adjust instruction and thus maximize the probability that learning will occur.[9]

Needless to say, educators on the more radical left do not fall into the trap of attempting to reform teacher education in order to make teachers more efficient puzzle solvers or merely more technically competent in their mastery of subject matter. On the contrary, these educators generally invoke the language of critique, self-reflexivity and the linking of theory to practice. For instance, Landon E. Beyer (1984) reiterates a common leftist position on teacher education. Discussing his proposal for reforming teacher education, he writes:

> A part of this program ... seeks to connect critical analysis with experiences of actual classroom phenomena. By seeing schools as a sort of 'cultural laboratory,' available for

270

critique, interpretation and discussion, students begin to understand both why schools operate the way they do, and who benefits from this method of operation. Instead of schools and classroom activities being presented as pre-defined and given, this approach promotes the view that schools offer socially organized arenas susceptible to critical, reflective analysis and intervention.[10]

In spite of its call for making knowledge problematic and for linking theory to practice, this type of analysis falls afoul of the same oversight as the more conservative theories in its studious refusal to conceptualize teacher education as part of a wider political project. In other words, it fails to define teacher preparation programs as part of a potential counterpublic sphere that might work in some coordinated and concentrated fashion to create intellectuals, who, as part of a wider social movement, can play a central role in the fight for democracy.

The programmatic impetus of much radical educational reform remains fettered within the limited emancipatory goal of making the everyday problematic. But calling into question the arbitrary, relativistic, ideological and hegemonic dimensions of classroom transactions, while certainly commendable as a starting point, cannot further the project of democratizing our classrooms unless that approach is sutured to the larger goal of reconstituting schools as counterpublic spheres. In actuality, the language of critique that informs a great deal of radical theorizing is overly individualistic and reproductive. Radical educators trapped within this language fail to acknowledge that the struggle for democracy in the larger sense of transforming schools into counterpublic public spheres is logically and ethically prior to making teachers more reflexive thinkers or more critical problem solvers. That is, this language fails to grasp and employ the concept of counter-hegemony as a moment of collective struggle because its programmatic suggestions are locked into the limited posture of resistance theories. The distinctions between these two categories is worth elaborating.

Teacher Education as a Counterpublic Sphere

The term 'counter-hegemony'[11] as distinct from the term 'resistance', is one which we feel better specifies the political project we have defined as the creation of counterpublic spheres. As it is often used in the educational literature, the term 'resistance' refers to a type of autonomous 'gap' between the widespread forces of domination and the state of being dominated. Moreover, it has been defined as a personal 'space' where domination, contested by agency, is frozen or bracketed due to a concerted or even unconscious effort on the part of the active subject to subvert the process of socialization. Viewed as such, resistance functions as a type of negation or affirmation placed before ruling discourses and practices. Of course, resistance often lacks a political project and often reflects social practices that are informal, disorganized, apolitical and atheoretical in nature.[12] In some instances, resistance can constitute an unreflective and defeatist refusal to acquiesce to different forms of domination; furthermore, resistance can occasionally be seen as a cynical, arrogant, and even naive rejection of oppressive forms of moral and political regulation.

The concept of counter-hegemony, on the other hand, implies a more political, theoretical and critical understanding of both the nature of domination and the type of active opposition it should engender. More importantly, the concept of counter-hegemony expresses not simply the logic of critique but the creation of new social relations and public spaces that constitute counter-institutions, lived relations and ideologies that embody alternative forms of experience and struggle. As a reflective domain of political action, counter-hegemony shifts the characteristic nature of struggle from the terrain of critique to the collectively constituted terrain of the counterpublic sphere.

We have dwelled on this distinction because we believe that it points to ways in which teacher education programs have been and continue to be removed from a vision and set of practices within a political project that takes seriously the struggle for democracy and social justice. Over the years numerous theorists have rightly argued that teacher education programs rarely address the moral implications surrounding inequalities that exist within our present form of industrial capitalism and the ways in which schools function to reproduce and exacerbate these inequalities. Not surprisingly, little attention has been given to considerations of how power, ideology and politics work on and in schools to erode emancipatory democratic ideals. Zeichner underscores this concern when he writes:

> It is hoped that future debate in teacher education will be more concerned with the question of which educational, moral and political commitments ought to guide our work in

the field rather than with the practice of merely dwelling on which procedures and organizational arrangements will most effectively help us realize tacit and often unexamined ends. Only after we have begun to resolve some of these necessarily prior questions related to ends should we concentrate on the resolution of more instrumental issues related to effectively accomplishing our goals.[13]

Student teachers are generally introduced to a one-dimensional conception of schooling. Rather than viewing the classroom as a cultural terrain where a heterogeneity of discourses often collide in an unremitting struggle for dominance, schooling is often encountered in teacher training programs as a set of rules and regulative practices which have been laundered of ambiguity, contradiction, paradox and resistance. Schools as public sites are presented as if they are free of all vestiges of contestation, struggle and cultural politics.[14] Classroom reality is rarely presented as socially constructed, historically determined and mediated through institutionalized relationships of class, gender, race and power. At the existential level, this dominant conception of school vastly contradicts what the student teacher actually experiences during his or her practicum, especially if the student is placed in a working-class school. Yet student teachers are overwhelmingly taught to view schooling as an ontologically secured or metaphysically guaranteed neutral terrain. It is within this transparent depiction of school that student teachers are taught to view their own cultural capital and lived experiences as constituting some kind of standard cultural and political referent against which student meanings are objectified and measured.

In mainstream schools of education, teaching practices and methods are all too often linked to a menu of learning models which are to be employed in the context of particular stipulated conditions[15] — conditions in which questions of culture and power are either completely annulled or else shunted to the margins of pedagogical concern in favor of questions having to do with learning strategies and behavioral outcomes. Within this model of teacher training, '*performance* at a prespecified level of mastery is assumed to be the most valid measure of teacher competence ... the desire to have teachers critically reflect upon the purposes and consequences in terms of such issues as social continuity and change are not central concerns ...'[16]

As we indicated earlier, many of the problems associated with teacher preparation today signal an unhealthy absence in the curriculum regarding the study of critical social theory. Heavily influenced by mainstream behavioral and cognitive psychology, educational theory has been constructed around a discourse and set of practices that esteem the immediate, measurable and methodological aspects of learning.[17] Absent from this perspective are questions concerning the nature of power, ideology and culture and how these function to constitute specific notions of the social and to produce and legitimate particular forms of student experience.

While a new interest in social theory has played a major role in influencing radical educational theory, it has failed to make serious inroads into teacher education programs. This lack of attention to critical forms of social theory has deprived student teachers of a theoretical framework necessary for understanding, affirming and evaluating the meanings which their students socially construct about themselves and school, thereby silencing the possibility of granting them the means to self knowledge and social empowerment. For many student teachers who find themselves teaching working-class or minority students, the lack of a well-articulated framework for understanding the class, cultural, ideological and gender dimensions of pedagogical practice becomes an occasion for the production of an alienated defensiveness and personal and pedagogical armor that often translates into a cultural distance between 'us' and 'them'.

Teacher Education and Critical Social Theory

Over the years, left educational theorists have increased our understanding of schooling as essentially a political enterprise, as a way of reproducing or privileging particular discourses, along with the knowledge and power they carry, to the exclusion of other discourses or signifying systems. As a result of this effort, it has been possible for many educators to recognize schooling as a practice that is both determinate and determining. The conceptual core of the analysis undertaken by radical scholarship over the last decade has been strongly influenced by the rediscovery of Marx and has involved unpacking the relationship between schooling and the economic sphere of capitalist production. We are certainly sympathetic with this position, and especially with Ernest Mandel's[18] argument that we are now entering a form of corporate capitalism in which capital has prodigiously expanded into hitherto uncommodified areas. We are also in agreement that forms of power and control have become more difficult to uncover because they now saturate almost every aspect of the public and private dimensions of everyday life (Brenkman, 1979). But here we must sound a caution since we believe that this position has failed to escape from the economic reductionism that it attempts to press beyond. Moreover, such a reductionism in its more sophisticated forms is evident in the continuing work of radical educational theorists who overly stress the relationship between schools and the economic sphere at the expense of interrogating the role of signs, symbols, rituals, and cultural formations in the naming and constructing of student subjectivities and voice.[19] Our position stems from the observation that state capitalism is more than a purely economic phenomenon and that the intervention of the state in the economic process has eventuated the evolution of new symbolic and cultural discourses which give rise to and sustain important dimensions of modern social life. This is particularly evident in the ways in which the state mandates the form and content of teacher education programs through the legislation of certification requirements for prospective teachers. The ideology that underlies these requirements is generally drawn from the technocratic approaches at work in the natural sciences, though with much less theoretical sophistication.

While it is clear that economic forces and the intervention of the state are important determinants in shaping school policy, they need to be integrated into a new theory in which the role of culture plays a mutually constitutive role in effecting how teachers learn and act within their own classrooms. Thus, questions surrounding how students make meanings and create their cultural histories cannot be answered with sole recourse to discussions of social class and economic determinism but must begin to address the ways in which culture and experience intersect to constitute powerfully determining aspects of human agency and struggle.

Burgeoning interest in the realm of the cultural sphere as a mediator and generator of subjectivity and discourse is currently leaving its stamp on the theoretical project of critical pedagogy, both in the United States, Canada and Great Britain. In recent years, radical educators in the United States have attempted with varying degrees of success to appropriate into their work key concepts made by Continental European philosophers and social theorists. Theorists such as Derrida, Saussure, Foucault, Barthes, Lacan, Gadamer and Habermas and finding their way into North American educational journals and have had the cumulative effect of marshalling a massive assault on dominant modes of educational theorizing and practice.

Extrapolating from the deconstructionist campaign of Derrida, the hermeneutical combat of Gadamer and Ricoeur, Lacan's psycho-analytic reconstitution of the subject, Barthes' textual anarchy and Foucault's commentaries on power and historical inquiry, critical educators are beginning to construct a new theoretical vocabulary. It is not uncommon today to encounter attempts at 'deconstructing' the curriculum, reading the 'text' of classroom instruction, and articulating the 'discursive formations' embedded in educational research.[20] While it is impossible in this space to unravel and explain in detail the complexities of the language and concepts used by these theorists, we can point in a general way to some of the implications of their work.

Some educators have used these advances in social theory to help strip conventional thinking about schooling of its status as an objective, scientifically grounded discourse. Much of this work challenges the ideological view of the student as author and creator of his or her own destiny by describing how student subjec-tivity is inscribed and positioned in various pedagogical 'texts'. Such work constitutes an ebullient and a critical idiom through which oppositional behavior may be examined, political contestation problematized, and 'lived meaning' understood. Indeed, much of this new social theorizing can prove useful for examining how students fashion their constructions of self and school through the politics of student voice and representation. To understand student voice, for instance, is to grapple with the human need to give life to the realm of symbols, language and gesture. Student voice is a desire, born of personal biography and sedimented history; it is the need to construct and affirm oneself within a language that is able to rebuild the privatized life and invest it with meaning and to validate and confirm one's lived presence in the world. Inversely, to render a student voiceless is to make him or her powerless.

At the most general level, new advances in social theory have shifted the focus from the economistic logic of the Marxist tradition to the mutually determining categories of culture, ideology and subjectivity. Student subjectivity, struggle and lived experience are now being interrogated as social practices and cultural formations that embody more than simply class domination and the logic of capital. On the other hand, new theoretical approaches are now available for unravelling the complex relations among economic, cultural and ideological productions.

But there are a number of serious precautions that a radical pedagogy must take before it begins to weave these new strands of social theory into a programmatic discourse that can inform a more critical view of teacher education. Rather than endorse these movements in an unqualified manner, the task of radical pedagogy is to selectively and critically appropriate key concepts in discourse theory, reception theory, post-structuralism, deconstructionist hermeneutics and various other new schools without becoming trapped in their often impenetrable language, arcane jargon and theoretical cul-de-sacs. A radical pedagogy must usurp the critical potential of these movements but at the same time press them to account for their frequent apolitical, ahistorical and overly structuralist undercurrents. To quote Nancy Fraser in her paraphrase of Gayatri C. Spivak, 'the discourse of deconstruction cannot continue to exclude that of political economy'.[21] Like Fraser, we believe that these new movements must employ a viable, alternative political project. In other words, radical educators must continue to search within the new semiotic theories for a critical language that will enable relevant theoretical elements to be appropriated for the purpose of creating an emancipatory teacher education curriculum. This task must be realized, however, without becoming sidetracked by marginal debates on issues tributary to the political project of providing self and social empowerment for students most subordinated by the system.

We applaud the emergence of post-structuralist and semiotic theories for bringing about a cross-fertilization and restructuring of disciplines which hitherto were only marginally or tenuously connected and acknowledged. Furthermore, these theoretical developments remain significant for the ongoing creation of a pan-disciplinary intellectual movement that has a fundamental theoretical investment in analyses of the production and representation of meaning within contemporary cultural formations. But we must nevertheless insist that whatever new developments these discourses generate, they must continue to speak to the central problems of power and politics, particularly as these are expressed in the domination and subordination of peoples within society. The development of new theoretical trajectories within radical pedagogy must be buttressed by an acknowledgment that the necessary power to transform the social order cannot be brought about merely through the exercise of a particular critical discourse or a synthesis of discourses. Reform cannot exist *outside* the lived dynamics of social movements. Discourse alone cannot bring about fundamental social change. It is in this spirit that teacher education programs must commit themselves to issues of both empowerment and transformation, issues which combine knowledge and critique, on the one hand, with a call to transform social structures in the interest of democratic and just communities, on the other.

Teacher Education Curriculum as a Form of Cultural Politics

A curriculum as a form of cultural politics stresses the importance of making the social, cultural, political and economic the primary categories for understanding contemporary schooling.[22] Within this context, school life is to be conceptualized not as a unitary, monolithic and iron-clad system of rules and relations, but as a cultural arena characterized by contestation, struggle and resistance. Furthermore, school life is to be seen as a plurality of conflicting discourses and struggles, a terrain where classroom and streetcorner cultures collide and where teachers, students and school administrators accept, negotiate, and sometimes resist how school experiences and practices are named and accomplished. Within the context of a curriculum as a form of cultural politics, the overriding goal of education centers around creating the conditions for student self-empowerment and the self-constitution of students as political subjects.

The project of 'doing' a curriculum of cultural politics as part of a teacher education program consists of linking radical social theory to a set of stipulated practices through which student teachers are able to dismantle and interrogate preferred educational discourses, many of which have fallen prey to a hegemonic instrumental rationality that either limits or ignores the discourse of freedom. But our concern here focuses not just on developing a language of critique and demystification, one that can interrogate the latent interests and ideologies that work to construct subjectivities compatible with the logic of the dominant society. We are more concerned with developing a language of possibility that can address the issue of creating alternative teaching practices that are capable of shattering the syntax of the logic of domination both within and outside of schools. In the larger sense, as we mentioned in the beginning of this chapter, we are committed to articulating a language that can contribute to examining the realm of teacher education as a new public sphere, one that seeks to recapture the idea of critical democracy as a social movement that supports a respect for individual freedom and social justice. In effect, we want to recast teacher education as a political project, as a form of cultural politics, that defines student teachers as intellectuals who function in order to establish public spaces where students can debate, appropriate, and learn the knowledge and skills necessary to live in a real democracy.

We think that reconceiving teacher education in this way is one method of countermanding the retrograde practice within educational bureaucracies of defining teachers primarily as technicians, that is, as pedagogical clerks who are incapable of making important policy or curriculum decisions such as critically mediating state-mandated programs to the contexts and particularities of their own classrooms. The derision and contempt directed by professional bureaucrats towards teachers who demand and exhibit the right to link the practical with the conceptual in an effort to gain some control over their work, continue to haunt contemporary education. The hypostatizing of intellectuals as ivory tower theorists, removed from the mundane concerns and exigencies of everyday life, by both school administrators and the public is a grave political problem that radical educators must make greater efforts to understand as a necessary step toward rectifying it. A curriculum as a form of cultural politics encapsulates the belief that teachers *can* function in the pedagogical capacity as intellectuals and it is for this reason that a critical understanding of various commentaries on the role of the intellectual in the works of such writers as Antonio Gramsci, Mikhail Bakhtin and Paulo Freire remains indispensable for challenging the growing trend to assign teachers to roles of functionaries and technicians.[23]

We are concerned here with developing a program of studies that can serve as part of a counter-hegemonic discourse in the construction of schools as counterpublic spheres. We believe that a curriculum as a form of cultural politics should be centered around a set of core course concentrations which would include the study of language, culture, history and power. These courses are important precisely because they constitute the nodal points in the constellation of forces and relationships that both bear down on students yet simultaneously provide them with channels of possibility, that is, with means through which their subjectivities and identities can be affirmed and their life chances empowered.

The study of language is important because language 'embodies the ways by which we are inscribed by culture and how we try, literally, to make our mark in the world'.[24] As part of language studies, student teachers would be counselled 'to become more knowledgeable about and sensitive to the omnipresence and power of language as constitutive of their experience'.[25] As well, students would gain an introductory understanding of French post-structuralist traditions in discourse theory and the textual strategies that characterize their methods of critical enquiry; furthermore, through an introduction to semiotics, students will be encouraged to interrogate the numerous codes and significations that are constitutive of the texts of both their own personal narratives and cultural histories and those of their students.

The study of history is crucial and needs to play a larger and more critical role in teacher education programs.[26] A strong emphasis on history could provide student teachers with an understanding of how cultural histories are formed and could also bring to light the various ways literary texts have been 'read' throughout different historical periods. A focus on how specific educational practices can be understood as historical constructions related to economic, social, and political events in a particular space and time should replace conventional emphasis on chronological history 'which traditionally saw its object as somehow unalterably "there", given, waiting only to be discovered'.[27] In addition, it is through analyses of history that students can recover what Foucault calls 'subjugated knowledges'.[28] In this case, we are referring to those aspects of history in which criticism and struggle played a significant role in various attempts to define the nature and meaning of educational theory and practice.

Within the format of a curriculum as a form of cultural politics, it is necessary that the study of history be theoretically connected to both language and reading. Language can be studied as the bearer of history whereas history can be critically interrogated as a textual form. Reading can also be linked to history by emphasizing the fact that 'reading occurs within history and that the point of integration is always the reader'.[29] That is, students can come to understand how their own membership in particular class and social formations helps define the ways in which they, as members of a targeted audience, are meant to 'receive' various approved texts. Given this focus, student teachers will be better able to understand how reading occurs within a student's cultural history and in the context of their own concerns, beliefs and experiences. This will also assist student teachers to become more critically aware of how students from subordinate cultures bring their own sets of experiences to the reading act, as well as their own dreams, desires and voices.

The study of culture — or, more specifically, what has come to be known as 'cultural studies' — is a crucial component of any emancipatory curriculum because cultural studies can provide student teachers with a language by which to discern the various levels of power and privilege that inform the overall signifying system of the social order. Discursive classroom practices can therefore be seen as 'forms of power and performance'.[30] Within this context, questions can be raised as to how relationships of power and domination are inscribed not only in the various cultural codes of the school but also in the wider society so as to privilege particular groups of students and subordinate other groups. The study of culture would begin with an analysis of various discursive formations within and between the dominant and subordinate cultures. In part, this suggests an analysis not only of dominant school culture, with its attendant system of significations and discourses, but also an analysis of popular cultures — television, rock music, etc., which to a certain extent transcend class boundaries as foci of student interest — so as to provide meaningful contexts which can then be affirmed and interrogated.

The study of power is necessary in order to understand the crucial link between schooling, social control and culture.[31] First of all, it is important that the relationship between power and social control is redefined so that power is understood as possessing both 'positive' and 'negative' moments and thus its character will have to be viewed as dialectical, as both enabling and constraining. Ruling-class logic has traditionally defended schooling as part of the fabric of high culture and has therefore denied through omission, the cultural experiences and voice of oppressed groups. Our position is that the study of power must include not only affirming and dignifying particular formations of subordinate culture but also interrogating and criticizing them for their weaknesses (sexism, racism for example). Cultural power must therefore become a referent for examining what students and others need to learn outside of their own experiences.[32]

Language and Pedagogy as a Form of Cultural Politics

In this section we want to further elaborate on our claim that the education of teachers needs to be defined around a form of radical pedagogy as cultural politics. In doing so, we want to draw principally from the works of Paulo Freire and Mikhail Bakhtin and attempt to construct a pedagogical model in which the notions of struggle, student voice and critical dialogue are central to the goal of developing an emancipatory pedagogy. Bakhtin's work is important because it views language usage as an eminently social and political act linked to the ways individuals define meaning and author their relations in the world through an ongoing dialogue with others. As the theoretician of difference, dialogue and polyphonic voice, Bakhtin rightly emphasizes the need to understand the ongoing struggle between various groups over language and meaning as a moral and epistemological imperative. Accordingly, Bakhtin deepens our understanding of the nature of authorship by providing analyses of how people give value to and operate out of different layers of discourse. He also points to the pedagogical significance of critical dialogue as a form of authorship, and how it gives meaning to the multiple voices that constitute the 'texts' that are constitutive of everyday life. As Terry Eagleton rightly emphasizes, Bakhtin's work 'appeals to the language of the *people*' and can be used to de-familiarize 'the metaphysical truths of routine social existence.'[33]

Paulo Freire both extends and deepens Bakhtin's project. Like Bakhtin, Freire offers the possibility for organizing pedagogical experiences within social forms and practices that 'speak' to developing more critical, dialogical, explorative and collective modes of learning and struggle. But Freire's theory of experience is rooted in a view of language and culture in which dialogue and meaning are more strongly linked to a social project that emphasizes the primacy of the political, in which case the notion of empowerment is defined as central to the collective struggle for a life free from oppression and exploitation.

Both authors employ a view of language, dialogue, and difference that rejects a totalizing view of history. Both argue that a critical pedagogy has to begin with a dialectical celebration of the languages of critique and possibility, which finds its most noble expression in a discourse that integrates critical analysis with socially transformative action. Similarly, both authors provide a pedagogical model that begins with problems rooted in the concrete experiences of everyday life. In effect, Bakhtin and Freire provide valuable theoretical models from which radical educators can draw selectively so as to analyze schools as ideological and material embodiments of a complex web of relations of culture and power as well as socially constructed sites of contestation actively involved in the production of lived experiences. Inherent in these approaches is a problematic characterized by the way in which various pedagogical practices represent a particular politics of experience. Or, more specifically, it characterizes a cultural field where knowledge, language, and power intersect in order to produce historically specific practices of moral and social regulation.

This problematic points the need to interrogate how human subjectivities are produced, contested and legitimated within the dynamics of everyday classroom life. The theoretical importance of this type of interrogation within teacher education programs is linked directly to the need for beginning teachers to fashion a discourse in which a comprehensive politics of culture, voice and experience can be developed. At issue here is the recognition that schools are historical and structural embodiments of forms of culture that are ideological. They signify reality in ways that are often actively contested and experienced differently by various individuals and groups. Schools in this sense are ideological and political terrains out of which the dominant culture, in part, produces its hegemonic 'certainties'; but they are also places where dominant and subordinate groups define and constrain each other through an ongoing battle and exchange in response to the socio-historical conditions 'carried' in the institutional, textual and lived practices that define school culture and teacher/student experience within a particular specificity of time, space and place. In other words, schools are not ideologically innocent; nor are they simply reproductive of dominant social relations and interests. At the same time, as previously mentioned, schools do produce forms of political and moral regulation intimately connected with techno-logies of power that 'produce asymmetries in the abilities of in-dividuals and groups to define and realize their needs'.[34] More specifically, schools establish the conditions under which some individuals and groups define the terms by which others live, resist, affirm and participate in the construction of their own identities and subjectivities. Simon (in press) illuminates quite well some of the important theoretical considerations that have to be addressed with-in a radical pedagogy. He is worth quoting at length on this issue:

> Our concern as educators is to develop a way of thinking about the construction and definition of subjectivity within the concrete social forms of our everyday existence in a way that grasps schooling as a cultural and political site that (embodies) a project of regulation and transformation. As educators we are required to take a position on the accept-ability of such forms. We also recognize that while schooling is productive it is not so in isolation, but in complex relations with other forms organized in other sites ... (Moreover,) in working to reconstruct aspects of schooling (educators should attempt) to understand how it becomes

implicated in the production of subjectivities (and) recognize (how) existing social forms legitimate and produce real inequities which serve the interest of some over others and that a transformative pedagogy is oppositional in intent and is threatening to some in its practice.[35]

Simon rightly argues that schools are sites of contestation and struggle and as sites of cultural production they embody representations and practices that construct as well as block the possibilities for human agency among students. This becomes more clear by recognizing that one of the most important elements at work in the construction of experience and subjectivity in schools is language. In this case, language intersects with power in the way particular linguistic forms structure and legitimate the ideologies of specific groups. Language is intimately related to power and functions to both position and constitute the way that teachers and students define, mediate and understand their relation to each other and the larger society.

As Bakhtin has pointed out, language is intimately related to the dynamics of authorship and voice.[36] It is within and through language that individuals, in particular historical contexts, shape values into particular forms and practices. As part of the production of meaning, language represents a central force in the struggle for voice. Schools are one of the primary public spheres where, through the influence of authority, resistance, and dialogue, language is able to shape the ways in which various individuals and groups encode and thereby engage the world. In other words, schools are places where language is not only the medium of instruction but also a sphere of control and struggle. For Bakhtin, the issue of language is explored as part of a politics of struggle and representation, a politics forged in relations of power over who decides and legislates the territory on which discourse is defined and negotiated. The driving momentum of voice and authorship is inseparable from the relations between individuals and groups around which dialogue begins and ends. In Bakhtin's terms, 'the word is a two-sided act. It is determined ... by those whose word it is and for whom it is meant ... A word is territory shared by both addresser and addressee, by the speaker and his interlocutor.'[37] This serves to highlight the critical insight that student subjectivities are developed across a range of discourses and can only be understood within a process of social interaction that 'pumps energy from a life situation into the verbal discourse, it endows everything linguistically stable with living historical momentum and uniqueness'.[38]

With the above theoretical assumptions in mind, we want to argue in more specific terms for the development within teacher education institutions of a counter-hegemonic curriculum that embodies a form of cultural politics. In effect, we want to present the case for constructing a pedagogy of cultural politics around a critically affirmative language that allows potential teachers to understand how subjectivities are produced within those social forms in which people move but which are often only partially understood. Such a pedagogy makes problematic how teachers and students sustain, resist or accommodate those languages, ideologies, social processes and myths that position them within existing relations of power and dependency. Moreover, it points to the need to develop at this early point in a teacher's career, a theory of politics and culture that analyzes discourse and voice as a continually shifting balance of resources and practices in the struggle for privileging specific ways of naming, organizing and experiencing social reality. Discourse can be recognized as a form of cultural production, linking agency and structure through the ways in which public and private representations are concretely organized and structured within schools. Furthermore, it is understood as an embodied and fractured set of experiences that are lived and suffered by individuals and groups within specific contexts and settings.

In this view, the concept of experience is linked to the broader issue of how subjectivities are inscribed within cultural processes that develop with regard to the dynamics of production, transformation and struggle. Understood in these terms, a pedagogy of cultural politics presents a two-fold set of tasks for potential teachers. First, they need to analyze how cultural production is organized within asymmetrical relations of power in schools. Secondly, they need to construct political strategies for participating in social struggles designed to fight for schools as democratic public spheres.

In order to make these tasks realizable, it is necessary to assess the political limits and pedagogical potentialities of the different but related instances of cultural production that constitute the various processes of schooling. It is important to note that we are calling these social processes instances of cultural production rather than using the more familiar concept of social reproduction. While the notion of social reproduction points adequately to the various economic and political ideologies and interests that get reconstituted within the relations of schooling, it lacks a comprehensive, theoretical under-standing of how such interests are mediated, worked on and subjec-tively produced, regardless of the various interests that finally emerge.

A radical pedagogy that assumes the form of a cultural politics must examine how cultural processes are produced and transformed within related fields of discourse which we have chosen to call *the discourse of cultural production, the discourse of context*, and *the discourse of lived cultures*. Each of these discourses has a history of theoretical development in various models of leftist analysis, and each has been subjected to intense debate which we need not re-hearse at this time.[39] What we shall attempt to do is examine these discourses in terms of the fruitfulness of their interconnections, particularly as they point to a new set of categories for developing forms of counter-hegemonic educational practices that empower teachers and students around emancipatory interests.

Educational Practice and the Discourse of Cultural Production

The discourse of cultural production focuses on the ways in which structural forces outside the immediacy of the school help constitute the material conditions within which schools function. This strategic framework can provide us with illuminating analyses of the state, the workplace, research foundations, publishing companies and other embodiments of political interests that directly or indirectly influence school policy. Moreover, schools are examined within a network of larger social contexts that encourage a view of schools as historical and cultural constructions, embodiments of social forms that always bear a relationship to the wider society. A fundamental task of the discourse of production is to alert teachers to the primacy of identifying practices and interests that legitimate specific public representations and ways of life. To attempt to understand the process of schooling without taking into consideration how these wider forms of production are constructed, manifested and contested both in and out of schools is inconceivable within this discourse. This becomes obvious, for instance, if we wish to analyze the ways in which state policy embodies and promotes particular practices that legitimate and privilege some forms of knowledge over others, or some groups of individuals over others.[40] Equally signifi-cant would be an analysis of how dominant educational theory and practice are constructed, sustained and circulated outside of schools. For instance, radical educators need to do more than identify the language and values of corporate ideologies as they are manifested in school curricula, they also need to analyze and transform the processes through which they are produced and circulated. Another important aspect of this approach is that it points to the way in which labor is objectively constructed; that is, it provides the basis for an analysis of the conditions under which educators work and the political importance of these conditions in either limiting or enabling pedagogical practice. This is especially important for analyzing the critical possibilities that exist for public school teachers and students within specific conditions of labor to function as intellectuals or, in the words of C.W. Mills, as people who can generate, criticize and get 'in touch with the realities of themselves and their world'.[41]

We would like to stress that if teachers and students work in overcrowded conditions, lack time to work collectively in a creative fashion, or are shackled by rules or sets of institutionalized scruples that disempower them, then the technical and social conditions of labor have to be understood and addressed as part of the dynamics of reform and struggle. The discourse of production represents an important starting point in a pedagogy of cultural politics for evaluating the relationship between schools and wider structural forces against the ways in which such a relation contributes to a politics of human dignity; more specifically, it constitutes a politics fashioned around ways in which human dignity is realized in public spheres that are designed to provide the material conditions necessary for work, dialogue, and self and social realization in the interest of developing democratic and emancipatory communities. Accordingly, these public spheres represent what Dewey, Mills and Aronowitz have called the conditions for freedom and praxis, political embodiments of a social project that takes liberation as its major goal.[42]

Educational Practice and the Discourse of Textual Forms

Another important element in the development of a radical pedagogy, which we describe as a discourse of textual forms, refers to an enlistment of analysis capable of critically interrogating cultural forms as they are produced and used in classrooms. The purpose of this approach is to provide teachers and students with the critical tools necessary to analyze those socially constructed representations and interests that organize and validate particular readings of curricula materials.

A discourse of textual analysis not only draws attention to the ideologies out of which texts are produced, it also allows educators to distance themselves from the text so as to uncover the layers of meanings, contradictions and differences inscribed in the form and content of classroom materials. The political and pedagogical importance of this form of analysis inheres in its potential to open the text to a form of deconstruction that interrogates it as part of a wider process of cultural production; in addition, by making the text an object of intellectual enquiry, such an analysis posits the reader, not as a passive consumer, but as an active producer of meanings. In this view, the text is no longer endowed with a sacerdotal status; its authorial essence as received wisdom waiting to be translated or discovered becomes a matter of debate. Critical to this perspective are the notions of critique, production and difference, all of which provide important elements for a counter-hegemonic pedagogical practice. Belsey weaves these elements together quite well in her critique of the classical realist text:

> As an alternative it was possible to recognize it (classical realist text) as a construct and so to treat it as available for deconstruction, that is, the analysis of the process and conditions of its construction out of the available discourses. Ideology, masquerading as coherence and plenitude, is in reality inconsistent, limited, contradictory, and the realist text as a crystallization of ideology, participates in this incompleteness even while it diverts attention from the fact in the apparent plenitude of narrative closure. The object of deconstructing the text is to examine the process of its production — not the private experience of the individual author, but the mode of production, the materials and their arrangement in the work. The aim is to locate the point of contradiction within the text, the point at which it transgresses the limits within which it is constructed, breaks free of the constraints imposed by its own realist form. Composed of contradictions, the text is no longer restricted to a single, harmonious and authoritative reading. Instead, it becomes plural, open to re-reading, no longer an object for passive consumption but an object of work by the reader to produce meaning.[43]

Arguing against the idea that the various modes of representation in texts are merely neutral or transparent purveyors of ideas, the discourse of textual analysis underscores the need for a careful discernment of the way in which material is used and ordered in school curricula and how its 'signifiers' register particular ideological pressures and tendencies. At its best, such an analysis allows teachers and students to deconstruct meanings that are silently built into the structuring principles of the various systems of meaning that organize everyday life in schools. In effect, it adds an important theoretical dimension to analyzing how the overt and hidden curricula work in school.

At the day-to-day level of schooling, this type of textual criticism can be used to analyze how the technical conventions or images within various forms such as narrative, mode of address and ideological reference attempt to construct a limited range of positions from which they are to be read. Richard Johnson is worth quoting on this point:

> The legitimate object of an identification of 'positions' is the pressures or tendencies on the reader, the theoretical problematic which produces subjective forms, the directions in which they move in their force — once inhabited ... If we add to this, the argument that certain kinds of text ('realism') naturalize the means by which positioning is achieved, we have a dual insight of great force. The particular promise is to render processes hitherto unconsciously suffered (and enjoyed) open to explicit analysis.[44]

Coupled with traditional forms of ideology critique directed at problematizing the content of school materials, the discourse of text analysis also provides valuable insight into how subjectivities and cultural forms work within schools. The value of this kind of work has been exhibited in the analysis of structured principles used in the construction of pre-packaged curriculum materials, where it has been argued that such principles utilize a mode of address that positions teachers merely as implementers of knowledge.[45] Such a positioning is clearly at odds with treating both teachers and students as critical agents who play an active role in the pedagogical process. In a brilliant display of this approach, Judith Williamson has provided an extensive study of the way in which this type of critique can be applied to mass advertising.[46] Similarly, Ariel Dorfman has applied this mode of analysis to various texts used in popular culture, including the portrayal of characters such as Donald Duck and Babar the Elephant. However, it is in his analysis of *Readers Digest* that Dorfman exhibits a dazzling display of the critical value of text analysis. In one example, for instance, he analyzes how *Readers Digest* uses a mode of representation that downplays the importance of viewing knowledge in its historical and dialectical connections. He writes:

> Just as with superheroes, knowledge does not transform the reader; on the contrary, the more he (sic) reads the *Digest*, the less he needs to change. Here is where all that fragmentation returns to play the role it was always meant to play. Prior knowledge is never assumed. From month to month, the reader must purify himself, suffer from amnesia, bottle the knowledge he's acquired and put it on some out-of-the-way shelf so it doesn't interfere with the innocent pleasure of consuming more all over again. What he learned about the Romans doesn't apply to the Etruscans. Hawaii has nothing to do with Polynesia. Knowledge is consumed for its calming effect, for 'information renewal,' for the interchange of banalities. It is useful only insofar as it can be digested anecdotally, but its potential for original sin has been washed clean along with the temptation to generate truth or movement — in other words: change.[47]

Inherent in all of these positions is a call for modes of criticism that promote dialogue as the condition for social action, a dialogue, in this case, rooted in a pedagogy informed by a number of assumptions drawn from the works of Bakhtin and Freire. These include: treating the text as a social construct that is produced out of a number of available discourses; locating the contradictions and gaps within an educational text and situating them historically in terms of the interests they sustain and legitimate; understanding the text's internal politics of style and how this both opens up and constrains particular representations of the social world; recognizing how the text works to actively silence certain voices; and finally, discovering how it is possible to release from the text possibilities that provide new insights and critical readings regarding human understanding and social practices.

Educational Practice and the Discourse of Lived Cultures

We also want to argue that in order to develop a counter-hegemonic form of cultural politics within colleges of education, it is essential to develop a mode of analysis that does not assume that lived experiences can be inferred automatically from structural determinations. In other words, the complexity of human behavior cannot be reduced to merely identifying the determinants, whether they are economic modes of production or systems of textual signification, in which such behavior is shaped and against which it constitutes itself. The way in which individuals and groups both mediate and inhabit the cultural forms presented by such structural forces is in itself a form of production, and needs to be analyzed through a related but different mode of analysis. In order to develop this point, we want to briefly present the nature and pedagogical implications of what we call the discourse of lived cultures.

Central to this view is the need to develop a theory of cultural production that focuses on what we have termed a theory of self-production.[48] In the most general sense this would demand an understanding of how teachers and students give meaning to their lives through the complex historical, cultural, and political forms that they both embody and produce. A number of issues need to be developed around this concern within a critical pedagogy for teacher education. First, it is necessary to acknowledge the subjective forms of political will and struggle that give meaning to the lives of the students. Secondly, as a mode of critique, the discourse of lived cultures should interrogate the ways in which people create stories, memories and narratives that posit a sense of determination and agency. This is the cultural 'stuff' of mediation, the conscious and unconscious material through which members of dominant and subordinate groups offer accounts of who they are and present their different readings of the world. It is also part of those ideologies and practices that allows us to understand the particular social locations, histories, subjective interests, and private worlds that come into play in any classroom pedagogy.

If radical educators treat the histories, experiences and languages of different cultural groups as particularized forms of production, it becomes less difficult to understand the diverse readings, responses, and behaviors that, for example, students exhibit in the analysis of a particular classroom text. In fact, a cultural politics necessitates that a pedagogy be developed that is attentive to the histories, dreams and experiences that such students bring to schools. It is only beginning with these subjective forms that critical educators can develop a language and set of practices that both confirm and engage the contradictory forms of cultural capital.

Searching out and illuminating the elements of self production is not merely a pedagogical technique for confirming the experiences of those students who are often silenced by the dominant culture of schooling. It is also part of an analysis of how power, dependence, and social inequality enable and limit student self-empowerment within relations of class, race, and gender. The discourse of lived cultures becomes a valuable interrogative framework for student teachers as it illuminates how power and knowledge intersect to disconfirm the cultural capital of subordinate groups. This discourse can additionally be employed to develop a language of possibility, thereby creating a radical pedagogy that is ultimately capable of engaging the knowledge of lived experience through the dynamic of confirmation, interrogation, and hope.

The knowledge of the 'other' is accentuated in this instance not simply to celebrate its presence, but also because it must be interrogated critically with respect to the ideologies it contains, the means of representation it utilizes, and the underlying social practices it confirms. What is important here is to link knowledge and power theoretically so as to give students the opportunity to understand more critically who they are as part of a wider social formation and to help them critically appropriate those forms of knowledge that traditionally have been denied to them.

The discourse of lived cultures also points to the need for radical educators to view schools as cultural and political spheres actively engaged in the production and struggle for voice. In many cases, schools do not allow students from subordinate groups to authenticate their problems and lived experiences through their own individual and collective voices. The dominant school culture generally represents and legitimates the privileged voices of the white middle and upper classes. In order for radical educators to demystify the dominant culture and make it an object of political analysis, they will need to learn and master what we call the language of critical understanding. If radical educators are to effectively understand and strategically counter the dominant ideology at work in schools, they will have to interrogate and critically sustain those voices that emerge from three different ideological spheres and settings. These include the school voice, the student voice and the teacher voice. Each of these voices points to sets of practices that work on and with each other to produce specific pedagogical experiences within different configurations of power. The interests these different voices often represent have to be analyzed less as oppositional in the sense that they work to counter and disable each other than as an interplay of dominant and subordinate practices that shape each other in an ongoing struggle over power, meaning and authorship. This, in turn, presupposes the necessity for analyzing schools in their historical and relational specificity, and it points to the possibility for radical educational intervention. In order to understand and interrogate the multiple and varied meanings that constitute the discourses of student voice, radical educators need to affirm and critically engage, in a Bakhtinian sense, the polyphonic languages their students bring to schools. Educators need to learn 'the collection and communicative practices associated with particular uses of both written and spoken forms among specific social groups'.[49] Moreover, any adequate understanding of this language has to reach outside of school life into more encompassing social and community relations that give such a language meaning and dignity.

Teacher voice reflects the values, ideologies and structuring principles that give meaning to the histories, cultures and subjectivities that define and mediate the day-to-day activities of educators. It is the voice of common and critical sense that teachers utilize to mediate between the discourses of production, textual forms, and lived cultures as they are expressed within the asymmetrical relations of power that characterize potentially counterpublic spheres such as schools. In effect, it is through the mediation and action of teacher voice that the very nature of the schooling process is often either sustained or challenged; that is, the power of teacher voice to shape schooling according to the logic of emancipatory interests is inextricably related not only to a high degree of self understanding but also to the possibility for radical educators to join together in a collective voice as part of a social movement dedicated to restructuring the ideological and material conditions that work both within and outside of schooling. Thus, the category of teacher voice needs to be understood and interrogated critically in terms of its own values and political project as well as in relation to the ways it functions to mediate student voices.

In more general terms, the discourse of critical understanding not only represents an acknowledgement of the political and pedagogical processes at work in the construction of forms of authorship and voice within different institutional and social spheres, it also constitutes a critical attack on the vertical ordering of reality inherent in the unjust practices that are actively at work in the wider society.

To redress some of the problems which we have sketched out in the preceding pages, we believe that schools need to be reconceived and reconstituted as counterpublic spheres which are not co-extensive with the corporate needs of the bourgeoise state. These would be places where students learn the skills and knowledge to live and fight for a genuine democracy. As such, schools will have to be characterized by a pedagogy that demonstrates a strong commitment to engaging the views and problems that deeply concern students in their everyday lives. Equally important is the need for schools to cultivate a spirit of critique and a respect for human dignity that is capable of linking personal and social issues around the pedagogical project of helping students to become critical and active citizens.

Although we have been dealing in this chapter with developing a radical pedagogy within the field of teacher education and as such are calling for schools of education to place greater emphasis on the idea of teaching as a form of cultural politics, we acknowledge that the project we are describing is an ongoing one. Indeed, teachers need time in classrooms — more than is usually provided in one or two years of teacher training — to solidify the connections that we have been suggesting between schooling, subjectivity, voice, authorship and power. Understandably, a more sustained and protracted attempt must be made to link schooling to a concept of polity in which students debate and deliberate within a plurality of voices crucial issues surrounding the creation of a more just and equitable social order. Finally, we cannot underscore too strongly the importance of entering the teaching profession with a well-articulated grasp of the relationship among schooling, culture, voice and power.

In closing we suggest that teachers assume the role of the critic who, in Eagleton's (1984) words, engages 'through both discourse and practice with the process by which repressed needs, interests and desires may assume the cultural forms which could weld them into a collective force' (p. 123).

Notes

1. Some of the best writing on the public sphere can be found in DEWEY, J. (1927) *The Public and its Problems*, New York, Henry Holt and Company; MILLS, C.W. (1979) 'Mass society and liberal education', in HOROWITZ, I. L. (Ed.) *Power, Politics, and People: Collected Essays of C.W. Mills*, New York, Oxford University Press; MARCUSE, H. (1964) *One Dimensional Man*, Boston, Beacon Press; HABERMAS, J. (1962) *Strukterwandel der Offentlichkeit*, Neuwied, Luchterhand Publications; and EAGLETON, T. (1984) *The Function of Criticism*, London, Verso Books.
2. LOTHSTEIN, A. (1978) 'Salving from the dross: John Dewey's anarcho-communalism', *The Philosophical Forum*, 10, 1, pp. 55–111.

3. ARONOWITZ, S. and GIROUX, H.A. (1985) *Education Under Siege*, South Hadley, MA, Bergin and Garvey Publishers, Inc.
4. We want to make clear that there is a major distinction between the work of JOHN DEWEY, especially (1916) *Democracy and Education*, New York, The Free Press, and the hybrid discourses of progressive, educational reform that characterized the late 1960s and 1970s in the United States. Progressive educational reform bears little resemblance to Dewey's philosophy of experience in that Dewey stressed the relationship among student experience, critical reflection, and learning. In contrast, the call for relevance that has characterized the dominant quarters of progressive education generally surrenders the concept of systematic knowledge acquisition and uncritically privileges an anti-intellectual concept of student experience.
5. For an analysis of these positions, see GIROUX, H.A. (1983) *Theory and Resistance in Education*, South Hadley, MA, Bergin and Garvey Publishers, Inc.
6. LACLAU, E. and MOUFFE, C. (1985) *Hegemony and Socialist Strategy*, London, Verso Books.
7. GOODMAN, J. (1984) 'Reflections on teacher education: A case study and theoretical analysis', *Interchange*, 15, 3, pp. 7–26.
8. BRAVERMAN, H. (1974) *Labor and Monopoly Capital*, New York, Monthly Review Press.
9. CLABAUGH, G., *et al.* (1984) 'Revolutionizing teacher education: Training the developmentally oriented teacher', *Phi Delta Kappan*, May.
10. BEYER, L.E. (1984) 'Field experience, ideology, and the development of critical reflexivity', *Journal of Teacher Education*, 35, 3, pp. 36–41.
11. ADAMSON, W. (1980) *Hegemony and Revolution: A Study of Antonio Gramsci's Political and Cultural Theory*, Berkeley, University of California Press.
12. See GIROUX, H.A. (1983) *op cit.*
13. ZEICHNER, K.M. (1983) 'Alternative paradigms of teacher education', *Journal of Teacher Education*, 34, 3, pp. 3–9.
14. This is not true of all teacher education programs. For instance, Zeichner's work in elementary student teaching at the University of Wisconsin-Madison represents one exception to prevailing apolitical approaches to teacher education.
15. This position is clearly represented by BRUNER, J. (1985) 'Models of the learner', *Educational Researcher*, 14, 6, pp. 5–8.
16. See ZEICHNER, K.M. (1983) *op cit.*
17. One of the more sophisticated versions of this position can be found in GAGE, N.L. (1978) *The Scientific Basis of the Art of Teaching*, New York, Teachers College Press.
18. MANDEL, E. (1975) *Late Capitalism*, London, New Left Books.
19. A critique of this position can be found in McLAREN, P. (1986s)

Schooling as a Ritual Performance: Towards a Political Economy of Educational Symbols and Gestures, London and Boston, Routledge and Kegan Paul.

20. ALVARADO, M. and FERGUSON, B. (1983) 'The curriculum, media and discursivity', *Screen*, 24, 3, pp. 20–34; CHERRYHOLMES, C. (1983) 'Knowledge, power and discourse in social studies education', *Boston University Journal of Education*, 165, 4, pp. 341–58; and WEXLER, P. (1982) 'Structure, text and subject: A critical sociology of school knowledge', in APPLE, M. (Ed.) *Cultural and Economic Reproduction in Education*, London and Boston, Routledge and Kegan Paul, pp. 275–303.

21. FRASER, N. (1984) 'The French Derrideans: Politicizing deconstruction or deconstructing the political', *New German Critique*, 33, pp. 127–54.

22. GIROUX, H.A. and SIMON, R. (1984) 'Curriculum study and cultural politics', *Boston University Journal of Education*, 166, 3, pp. 226–38.

23. The works from which we will be drawing include: GRAMSCI, A. (1971) *Selections from Prison Notebooks*, HOARE, Q. and SMITH, G. (Eds. and Trans.), New York, International Publishers; FREIRE, P. (1973) *Pedagogy of the Oppressed*, New York, Seabury Press; FREIRE, P. (1985) *Education for Critical Consciousness*, New York, Seabury Press; FREIRE, P. (1985) *The Politics of Education*, South Hadley, MA, Bergin and Garvey Publishers, Inc.; BAKHTIN, M. (1981) *The Dialogic Imagination*, EMERSON, C. and HOLQUIST, M. (Trans), Austin, University of Texas Press; BAKHTIN, M. (1984a) *Problems of Dostoevsky's Poetics*, EMERSON, C. (Trans), Minneapolis, University of Minnesota Press; BAKHTIN, M. (1984b) *Rabelais and his World*, ISWOLSKY, H. (Trans), Bloomington, Indiana University Press; and VOLOSHINOV V.N. (BAKHTIN, M.M.) (1973) *Marxism and the Philosophy of Language*, New York, Seminar Press; VOLOSHINOV, V.N. (BAKHTIN, M.M.) (1976) 'Discourse in life and discourse in art', in *Freudianism: A Marxist Critique*, New York, Academic Press.

24. WALLER, G. (1985) 'Writing, reading, language, history, culture: The structure and principles of the English curriculum at Carnegie-Mellon University', Carnegie-Mellon University, unpublished manuscript.

25. *Ibid.*

26. *Ibid.*

27. *Ibid*, p. 14.

28. FOUCAULT, M. (1980) 'Two lectures', in GORDON, C. (Ed.), *Power/Knowledge*, New York, Pantheon Books.

29. WALLER, G. (1985) *op cit.* p. 14.

30. *Ibid*, p. 17.

31. ARONOWITZ, S. and GIROUX, H.A. (1985) *op cit.*

32. GIROUX, H.A. (1983) *op cit.*

33. EAGLETON, T. (1982) 'Wittgenstein's friends', *New Left Review*, 135, pp. 46–90.

34. JOHNSON, R. (1983) 'What is cultural studies?' *Anglistica*, 26, 1–2, pp. 7–81.

35. SIMON, R. (in press) 'Work experience and the production of subjectivity', in LIVINGSTONE, D. (Ed.), *Critical Pedagogy and Cultural Power*, South Hadley, MA, Bergin and Garvey Publishers, Ltd.

36. See SHUKMAN, A. (Ed.) (1983) *Bakhtin's School Papers*, Oxford, RPT Publications and VOLOSHINOV, V.N. (BAKHTIN, M.M.) (1973) *op cit.*

37. *Ibid*, pp. 85–6.

38. VOLOSHINOV, V.N. (BAKHTIN, M.M.) (1976), p. 106.

39. A major analysis of these discourses and the traditions of which they are generally associated can be found in JOHNSON, R. (1983) *op cit.*

40. Examples of this discourse can be found in CARNOY, M. and LEVIN, H. (1985) *Schooling and Work in the Democratic State*, Stanford, Stanford University Press.

41. MILLS, C.W. (1979) *op cit.*

42. DEWEY, J. (1917) *op cit.*; MILLS, C.W. (1979) *op cit.*; and ARONOWITZ, S. (1981) *The Crisis in Historical Materialism*, New York, J.F. Bergin Publishers, Inc.

43. BELSEY, C. (1980) *Critical Practice*, New York, Methuen.

44. JOHNSON, R. (1983), *op cit.*, pp. 64–5.

45. APPLE, M. (1983) *Education and Power*, Boston, Routledge and Kegan Paul.

46. WILLIAMSON, J. (1978) *Decoding Advertisements*, New York, Marian Boyars.

47. DORFMAN, A. (1983) *The Empire's Old Clothes*, New York, Pantheon Press.

48. TOURAINE, A. (1977) *The Self-Production of Society*, Chicago, University of Chicago Press.

49. SOLA, M. and BENNETT, A. (1985) 'The struggle for voice: Narrative, literacy and consciousness in an East Harlem school', *Boston University Journal of Education*, 167, 1, pp. 88–110.

11   Teacher Education in Cultural Context: Beyond Reproduction

Landon E. Beyer and Ken Zeichner

Abstract

This chapter places teacher education policies and programs within a larger social, political, and ideological context. By addressing the ways in which the dominant culture of teacher education in the US serves to support particular concerns and perspectives, the authors demonstrate the political nature of teacher education. In addition, this essay outlines an alternative approach to the preparation of teachers, based on reflection, critique, and personal and social enquiry. Instead of focusing on technical or procedural matters, this approach emphasizes the necessity of sustained political and moral debate. With the adoption of such a program, teacher education may become a progressive force — one aimed at overturning current patterns of social reproduction and reaffirming commitments to justice, equality, and non-exploitive social relations.

What is Teacher Education?

We have tended to forget in educational studies, and perhaps especially in those areas concerned with the preparation of teachers, that the solutions to problems and the possibilities for intervention depend to a significant extent on how we define those problems and interventions — on the questions we regard as appropriate, reasonable, and worth pursuing. There certainly are questions which seem to admit of no very clear answer, or perhaps no definitive answer at all. Yet a response to some set of ideas, and intervention into any intellectual and social arena, cannot take place apart from some question, problem or puzzlement which provides the necessary context. Put simply, there may be some questions that are unanswerable, but there cannot be answers unless there is some question to which that answer is a response. We have not paid sufficient attention to how such questions are formulated, nor which are excluded, within the conventional boundaries of teacher education.

Part of what is involved in the process of formulating and clarifying what question it is we're trying to articulate and respond to must include some assessment of what it is we're interrogating, and the traditions we may utilize in our response to that question — even if those traditions become modified or eliminated. If we are trying to respond to the general problem of how to justify moral judgments, for example, we must have some understanding — whether explicit or assumed — of what kinds of things moral judgments are, the possible justificatory schemes that might be employed in assessing their propriety, what moral reasoning is, and the like. We simply cannot proceed with any sort of analysis without at least some notion of what it is we are analyzing, and the processes by which the analysis may be reasonably carried out. Thus the matter of asking the right or appropriate question must logically be preceded by what it is we are analyzing.

Teacher educators have devoted too little time and attention to the question of what are teacher education curricula and preparation, as well as to what is the nature of those educational institutions for which we are preparing practitioners. We wish both to challenge the usual way teacher education is thought about and to suggest how we might begin to rethink questions and issues within the context of teacher preparation programs and practices. In particular, we will demonstrate in this chapter how the typical perspective in teacher education which sees our activities in apolitical, technical and procedural terms is conceptually mistaken, and how such a perspective may itself have certain problematic ideological consequences. Further, we will suggest that our efforts to provide preservice teacher education programs need to be analyzed in light of the economic, social, and political institutions within which both these programs and the public schools are embedded. This is not merely to suggest that our work in teacher education can be somehow enlivened by looking at the relationships between teacher preparation and the ongoing functioning of other social institutions that surround schools. It is, rather, to suggest that the process of preparing teachers is a necessarily and thoroughly political and ideological one and ought to involve complex ethical and ideological questioning and debate.

This chapter, then, will provide (i) a brief review and summary of some of the relevant literature which has gone some distance toward identifying the ties between schooling and the social order — especially the ways in which schools serve to perpetuate existing economic, political, and cultural practices, patterns, and arrangements; (ii) the theoretical linkages between teacher education and the wider society, including examples of how the form and content of teacher education in the U.S. is involved in the process of social reproduction; and (iii) an assessment of what this analysis implies for alternative practice and research in teacher education.

Throughout this chapter our efforts will be geared toward looking at the fundamental ideas that have generated our perspective of what teacher education programs are, and the questions or problems they are designed to provide solutions to. We will argue that more self-consciously critical analysis is essential in any attempt at reforming teacher education policies and programs. We will suggest that part of the failure of teacher education programs and curricula, and of the less than completely successful attempts at reform in these areas, is attributable to an inability or unwillingness to ask the proper questions. Laying the groundwork for asking these other, more ideological and political questions help us realize more clearly what teacher education is about and what its reformulation entails.

Education and Ideology

In an exceptionally important essay dealing with recurring issues in curriculum, Herbert M. Kliebard has argued that the field itself is 'characterized by an overwhelmingly ameliorative orientation'.[1] Such an ameliorative stance, Kliebard continues, may in part be created by 'the huge constituency of teachers, school administrators, and supervisors who exert continual pressure on those who conduct research for answers to such practical questions as, how can I improve my teaching, what are the best programs, and how can I recognize and reward a good teacher'.[2] Now as everyone is aware, teachers in classroom situations are continually confronted with such practical questions which, given the density and pace of classroom life, require or demand immediate, practical response. Frequently the requirement for some kind of action or intervention on the part of the teacher eclipses the opportunity for a more sustained, reflective analysis of educational issues and possibilities.[3] Yet in a large sense, as Kliebard again cogently argues, one problematic consequence associated with such an immediate, pragmatic model of teaching 'revolves around the effort to develop a kind of technology of teaching leading to the performance of certain presumably effective behaviors in the absence of any fundamental understanding or conception of what kind of activity teaching is'.[4] It is very easy to conceive of and confront teaching, within the dominant, pragmatic orientation Kliebard mentions, as a technical enterprise, with success and failure measured in rather technical and quantifiable terms (for example, as exhibited by scores on achievement tests or instruments used to identify 'exceptional children', ratings on supervisory evaluation forms, and so on). Another consequence of this pragmatic, technological orientation to teaching is an overemphasis on the techniques and methods of teaching, abstracted from any principled, well-grounded understanding of the educational ideas and ideals which stand behind and give such methods meaning.[5]

The field of curriculum for example, has been guided and informed, if not actually dominated, by such technical concerns. A substantial number of educators seem to limit their investigations into the nature and effects of schooling — into what counts as effective school practice — to two broad areas: those dealing with measures of (usually individual) academic proficiency on the one hand, and socialization effectiveness on the other. Though in many instances these two areas have been collapsed into a single pedagogical perspective, the traditions of academic achievement and socialization still form a good deal of the conceptual apparatus which underlies our collective sense of what schools are about.[6] Each of these traditions, in addition to being directed and dominated by technical concerns — for example, as evidenced in the move toward competency-based teacher education[7] — views the function or purpose of educational institutions as socially and politically neutral. In effect, technical concerns have served to defuse and displace more fundamental political and ethical debate within our educational discourse.[8]

Perhaps the most well-known analysis of the allegedly neutral socialization effects of schools may be found in Robert Dreeben's book, *On What is Learned in School*.[9] Much of Dreeben's explication of the hidden curriculum of schools[10] is concerned with how family life and school life each makes a contribution to larger social experience. The structural/functional view of socialization embraced by Dreeben moves the author to acknowledge what he labels an 'ideological caveat': he explains to the reader that, 'the main purpose of this analysis is to present a formulation, hypothetical in nature, of how schooling contributes to the emergence of certain psychological outcomes, and not to provide an apology or justification for those outcomes on ideological grounds'.[11] Indeed, in addition to not providing the reader with any such ideological justification, Dreeben also fails to examine the possible ideological functions of those 'psychological outcomes' he does consider. It is this tendency to construct a non-ideological, apolitical analysis of the socialization effects of schooling that has been influential in thinking about such educational ideas and issues. Socialization thus becomes a technical concern to discover the 'best way' or 'most effective methods' to promote the adoption of the correct or appropriate social norms in students; under such a technical rubric, those norms are, correlatively, conceived of as 'given' rather than socially constructed and to that extent problematic, open to critique, and changeable.[12]

In the achievement model, likewise, school knowledge has been typically thought of as unproblematic. Such epistemological and ideological questions as, what is the nature of knowledge and how is it to be verified, how is the selection process which produces 'school knowledge' itself governed, whose knowledge gets into schools, what is to count as an instance of having learned something, and the like, are often not considered; in their place, concerns about how best to structure, implement, package, and evaluate those forms of knowledge which find their way into classrooms become the central issues for educational investigation. Thus the achievement tradition becomes more and more given over to bureaucratic concerns for control, efficiency, and certainty, leaving the formal corpus of school knowledge largely unexamined.[13]

Both the achievement and socialization traditions may be viewed as important aspects of the technicist/functionalist perspective of schools, and as responding to the ameliorative and technological concerns outlined earlier by Kliebard. Each treats the respective body of content or organizational form as authoritatively pregiven, usually from 'outside' or 'above'. The possible latent functions of the selection processes themselves, and of schooling in general, go unrecognized and unnoticed, thereby confirming and legitimating the perception of schools as politically and ideologically neutral. Since only immediate, predominantly technical concerns are manifest, the less than immediately obvious effects of schooling become at best secondary, and the school's apparent status as politically neutral confirmed. Floud and Halsey point out the social consequences of such a position:

> The structural functionalist is preoccupied with social integration based on shared values — that is with consensus — and he conducts his analysis solely in terms of the motivational actions of individuals. For him, therefore, education is a means motivating individuals to behave in ways appropriate to maintain society in a state of equilibrium.[14]

Recently this assumption of equilibrium through political neutrality has come under increasing scrutiny and has been called into question from several quarters. Among others, this assumption has been seriously questioned by what has been called the 'new sociology of education' and by theorists of economic and cultural reproduction. This has led to extensive debate regarding the precise nature of the relationship between classroom activities and the larger social order. It is the assumption of social, political, and economic neutrality implicit in the traditions outlined above that theories of economic and cultural reproduction have challenged. By examining the outlines of the discussions surrounding these issues, we will be in a better position to see how the evaluation of curricular and pedagogical practices has been expanded to investigate such ideological concerns and perspectives. The expansion provided by these debates provides the context within which similar ideological concerns will be raised within teacher education.

It was with the publication of *Schooling in Capitalist America*[15] by Samual Bowles and Herbert Gintis that attempts to situate schooling as one of a number of important institutions which help perpetuate the current social structure gained respectability. These authors view the function of schooling as founded on the maintenance of social class distinctions, wherein schools respond to the needs of capital. This position is forcefully advanced in the authors' view of socialization:

> Our critique of education and other aspects of human development in the United States fully recognizes the necessity of some form of socialization. The critical question is: What for? In the United States the human development experience is dominated by an undemocratic, irrational, and exploitative economic structure. Young people have no recourse from the requirements of the system but a life of poverty, dependence, and economic insecurity.[16]

Schools, that is, serve to produce a 'finished product' that will have sufficiently mastered the requisite skills and dispositions to ensure the maintenance of American corporate capitalism; educational institutions function in a way that guarantees the production of a particular economic form. There are, in the authors' view, four main components to this relationship between educational and economic structure. These include (i) an adequate and appropriate labor supply provided by the educational establishment; (ii) social relationships within schools which can be used to 'facilitate the translation of labor power into profits';[17] (iii) a system of acknowledging, rewarding, and reinforcing personality traits which is shared by the school and the economic sphere; and (iv) a stratified and hierarchical way of thinking about one's relationship with others which is developed in schools through a differential system of status and distinctions and which has utility in the market place. Some specific examples from their own research may help in clarifying how, for the authors, a principle of correspondence exists which, in reproducing class structure and consciousness, perpetuates capitalist production.

Bowles and Gintis argue that the social relationships within schools correspond to the division of labor, along hierarchical lines, within the economic order. Within educational institutions, vertical lines of authority exist and become part of everyday classroom experience, with students at the low end of the power continuum, followed by teachers and administrators. This pattern of domination is in turn duplicated in many work places: individual workers stand on the bottom rung of the authority ladder, while the foreman or supervisor stands above them, with the manager/owner at the top looking down. Just as this pattern of social relations in the sphere of economic production creates alienated labor, and an alienated work force, so too is the student alienated from his or her own educational experience. By training students in the public schools to regard these patterns of dominance as 'normal' or necessary, students learn to habituate themselves to patterns of thought and ways of acting that assure the continuance of analogous relations of production in capitalist industry. As with many day-to-day decisions in the factory, the corporation, or the state bureaucracy, curricular and pedagogical decisions are made by those 'above', often with little or no input from students whose daily lives are informed if not defined by such decisions. As well, students are typically evaluated in terms of criteria over which they have little control. This way of making educational decisions, i.e., via people who in some way stand above and independent of the students themselves, serves to produce in each student, 'the types of personal demeanor, modes of self-presentation, self-image, and social-class identifications which are the crucial ingredients of job adequacy'.[18] In this way schools 'process' people who come to the market place equipped with the skills and attitudes requisite to the smooth, efficient operation of the economic machinery. 'By attuning young people to a set of social relationships in schools similar to those of the work place, schooling attempts to gear the development of personal needs to its requirements'.[19]

Bowles and Gintis further argue that schools function to prepare particular social groups for specific occupational slots, while reserving different occupations for other groups. Not only are alternative curricula devised, for example, for vocationally-oriented and college-bound high school students, but different behavioral norms are enacted and enforced as well. And as each curricular form develops its own set of dispositional rules, social relations of widely varying sorts are facilitated. It is in the correspondence between these social relations within each curricular track and the norms mandated by particular occupational slots that, the authors allege, the potency of our economic system for school settings may be seen. 'Thus in high school, vocational and general tracks emphasize rule-following and close supervision, while the college track tends toward a more open atmosphere emphasizing the internalization of norms.'[20] Just as supervised rule following in contrast to internalization of norms is a mark of stratification within schools, so these same differences may be seen in the subsequent job prospects for each group. Since the working class ethos of supervised rule following tends to recur in working class schools and classrooms, and internalization of norms within middle class schools and classrooms, social class distinctions and their perpetuation are fostered by different social relations within the educational establishment.

In contrast to the achievement and socialization traditions within education, theorists of economic reproduction view the activities of schools as intimately tied to the demands of a hierarchical, alienating economic system. School experience in this view furthers the interests of certain groups and classes while effectively curtailing those of others. Indeed, in arguing for a correspondence between schooling and economic form, Bowles and Gintis attempt to expose the perniciousness of the former by virtue of its complicity with the latter.

While we find the analysis provided by such theorists of

economic reproduction illuminating in its characterization of how school life may be tied to economic form, we need also to recognize the very real shortcomings of such a correspondence theory for understanding both curriculum and teacher education. There are several ways in which such an analysis may be misleading if not inadequate. For example, it does little in the way of clarifying how the day-to-day experiences of classroom life — the 'curriculum in use' of educational institutions — actually contributes to the continuance of an unequal distribution of goods and services within capitalist society; we are provided with little more than a 'black box' view here, making it difficult to situate even the latent functions of schooling the authors discuss within a larger, more coherent relational theory.

Two other shortcomings of this theory of economic reproduction are of special interest for this chapter. The correspondence view upon which the work of Bowles and Gintis is based (i) is too mechanistic in its portrayal of the relationship between schooling and economic form; and (ii) focuses too exclusively on the economic sphere in discussing the reproductive role of schools. The social and ideological functions of educational institutions are simply not fully revealed by addressing only their economic purposes and effects, at least when these are narrowly conceived. As well, the relationship between schools and the social order is not that of object to mirror image; the interconnections are more complex and subtle than Bowles and Gintis suggest. This is not to deny the ties which serve to bind schools and economic production. Rather, to expose the ideological commitments of our educational system and make them a subject for analysis, we need to go beyond 'merely' its relationship to economic form, without losing sight of this vital aspect of social reproduction.

Several studies have been extremely useful in extending the reproductive debate in precisely this way. We have found the work of several people, including Michael F.D. Young[21], Basil Bernstein[22], Bourdieu and Passeron[23], Michael W. Apple[24], and Walter Feinberg[25], helpful in clarifying our own understanding of these complex issues. It is, though, in Paul Willis' study, *Learning to Labor: How Working Class Kids Get Working Class Jobs*[26], that the flaws inherent in a correspondence theory of social reproduction can be most dramatically seen.

Divided into ethnographic and analytic segments, Willis' study details the interplay between the school and work lives of working class boys attending secondary school in an industrial town in

England. The relationship between this group's culture and the formal experiences and culture of the school is used by the author as an example of how working class ideology and cultural forms help reproduce class distinctions. In the process social control is maintained, not by overt intervention or 'outside' coercion, but by the development and solidification of what Antonio Gramsci referred to as cultural hegemony, or that 'range of structures as well as values, attitudes, beliefs and morality that in various ways support the established order and the class interests which dominate it'.[27]

The group of working class boys of which Willis writes, collectively referred to as 'the lads' by the author, forms its own counter-culture while being immersed within the 'official' or dominant culture of the school. They consciously exploit whatever 'cracks' or 'crevices' they can create within the existing culture of the school in ways that allow some measure of control over their own lives. Indeed, the lads define themselves in part at least on the basis of their rejection of and opposition to the established routines, activities, and culture of the school. 'This opposition', Willis writes, 'is expressed mainly as a style. It is lived out in countless small ways which are special to the school institution, instantly recognized by the teachers, and an almost ritualistic part of the daily fabric of life for the kids'.[28] Specific instances of such opposition are numerous — for example, silently mouthing words during instruction so as to create imaginary dialogue, derisively laughing as a teacher or another student passes in the hallway, cracking their knuckles during class, and so on. Now all of these can be seen as mere instances of deviant behavior from troublesome or delinquent students. Yet for the lads such gestures, Willis says, have another meaning: they become symbolic and almost ritualistic occasions which represent and solidify their rejection of the formal organization of the school and their correlative status as members of a select and, at least in their own minds, superior culture and social group.[29]

Another group of students within this secondary school, the 'ear'oles' (so termed because of their tendency to just sit and listen), accept and comply with the authority structure and culture of the school; these are the students who at least superficially agree with the rules and regulations of the school, who identify with the cultural activities and patterns embedded in the institution. Such students, as one might expect, help provide the day-to-day, concrete cultural symbols and artifacts which the lads make light of and reject. The ear'oles' acceptance of school rules, their dress, hair style, and mannerisms are equated with the established culture of the school, just as such cultural patterns and the formal curriculum become part of a broader perspective felt as distant and alien by the lads. That is, the formal organization of the school, including both overt and hidden curriculum forms, and the mode of culture which is engendered and embodied in the ear'oles, are rejected by the lads. Rejection of school rules and authority, and the social relations they produce, is thus seen by the lads as symbolizing their rejection of the dominant, middle-class culture of the school. Considering dress, for example, Willis says, 'It is no accident that much of the conflict between staff and students at the moment should take place over dress. [This conflict] is one of [the] elected grounds for the struggle over authority. It is one of the current forms of a fight between cultures. It can be resolved, finally, into a question about the legitimacy of school as an institution'.[30] Dress and personal attractiveness, as well as smoking and drinking, are used by the lads as cultural symbols, ways to define and substantiate their repudiation of the ear'oles and school culture generally. It also, of course, helps define membership in their group.

Yet the culture of the school is not rejected only because the lads find it alienating and foreign. An essential ingredient of this refusal to participate in the official culture is that in a significant sense it is not real for the lads; it has no relationship to the working class world which surrounds them, their families, and their friends. The lads respond to school, in a sense, by embracing the more familiar and meaningful cultural forms of the working class, with its emphasis on physicality and masculinity, while rejecting any notion of intellectual work which the school in part embodies. Here we can see one crucial ideological distinction being formulated and engrained in the lads' rejection of schooling and school culture. Mental and manual labor — 'book learning' versus the pedagogy of the shop floor — become separate categories for the lads and one of the central divisions which sustains their class identity. The reproductive function of schools is furthered by such distinctions and by the very rejection of official culture within the school. In rejecting mental labor, and the ear'oles as the personification of such labor, the lads maintain their own class standing and help cement class distinctions.

In this way what Willis terms the 'penetrations' made by the lads — this group's rejection of school culture as in some way ingenuine and its simultaneous utility in providing opportunities for 'having a laff' — has inherent social contradictions. In asserting the superiority of masculine working class jobs and culture, in preferring manual to mental labor, the lads also suggest or comply with the division of labor along sexual lines. Thus, in penetrating the dominant school culture, in exposing it as foreign and alienating to their own experience, the lads implicitly further such sexual and economic division. Though the lads act relatively autonomously in penetrating cultural forms established and practised in the school, social reproduction is actually enhanced in the very process.

Willis' study is important for several reasons and has clear implications for correspondence theories such as the one offered by Bowles and Gintis. Willis illustrates, in convincing detail, how and why such correspondence theories fail in their analysis of reproduction. It is simply not the case that the needs of capitalist production result in the imposition of certain dispositions, personality traits, and ways of thinking on students who acquiesce to and act on such economic needs. At least some important elements of the capitalist work force, as we can see from Willis' research, are produced in the process of rejecting the skills, propensities, and cultural symbols necessitated by capitalist production and perpetuated by schools; the contradictions built into the lads' penetrations of the official culture serve to solidify social class standing and working class ideology. The response of the lads within school gives them strength as members of a valued group while equipping them for employment in work that will ensure the continuation of their class history and social status.

Secondly, Willis shows how a particular set of economic realities is accompanied by various social and cultural forms which the lads find persuasive. A good deal of the lads' rejection of mental labor and book learning, for example, has to do with the discontinuity between the cultural symbols upheld by the school (voluntary rule following, specific styles of dress and personal appearance, a certain sense of sobriety, and the like) and the working class culture in which the lads themselves are immersed. The world of the lads contains its own network of cultural symbols and values, far removed from the dominant culture of the school. These cultural forms are not perceived as something other than, or in addition to, their economic and social standing. For the lads these cultural patterns are felt to be an essential ingredient of daily life, a part of their existential reality.

What we are urging here, in a more general way, is that we see cultural and economic forms — or, if you like, ideology and the relations of production — as intimately linked and conjoined. These areas are not as separable or isolated as many would have us believe, though thinking of culture as divorced from social relations and economic production may itself serve an ideological function in a society such as ours. That is, it may be politically useful for people to think of culture, especially those forms which potentially serve emancipatory interests, as abstracted from daily life and social exchange. If we can begin to see superstructure and infrastructure not as distinct levels with some causal relationship obtaining between them, but as different aspects of the same social forces, the linkages between schooling and the reproduction of social exigencies may become clearer. 'Ideology is not', Terry Eagleton has argued, 'a set of doctrines; it signifies the way men live out their roles in class-society, the values, ideas, and images which tie them to their social function'.[31] *Learning to Labor* provides an excellent example of how ideological forces persist in the day-to-day lived experiences we all share in. As ideological influences, the cultural images which tie the lads to their social function must be seen as contributing to the reproduction of social class divisions and the development of hegemony. No intervention by a 'repressive' or 'dictatorial' state is necessary to perpetuate the social order in its present form. Thus to understand the reproductive role of educational institutions requires a sensitivity to how cultural forms reinforce and interpenetrate ideological influences and economic 'needs'. Yet even this fuller understanding of social reproduction is not enough.

Beyond Reproductive Functionalism

As useful and illuminating as theories of economic and cultural reproduction have been, there is a serious danger in adopting un-critically the metaphor of reproduction as an explanatory device for understanding schools, curriculum, and teacher education. Part of the danger here can be understood in the context of the study by Paul Willis outlined above. The problem lies in assuming a kind of reproductive functionalism, with school practices and curricula becoming, in a sense, overdetermined. Schools can be seen, under such a guiding rubric, as bearing the brunt of capitalist ideology, and school people as relatively impotent in altering the dynamics of ideological imposition and domination. Consider again the analysis of Willis. If school practices are determined or at least shaped by social forces outside the school, and if even overt resistances to and mediations of these forces sustain the very ideological characteristics they were designed to modify, the temptation to regard any effort at overcoming such a dominant ideology as at best ineffectual, or at worst regressive, seems fairly powerful. These same reservations about the metaphor of reproduction as it pertains to curriculum hold with equal force for analyzing the ideological configurations which, as we will argue in the following section, pertain to teacher education.

Thus, the metaphor of reproduction may itself become, in an ironic way, the instrument of ideologically embedded ways of thinking that are less progressive than we might like.[32] Such a metaphor may, that is to say, have embedded within its ways of looking at schooling, curricula, and teacher education that are themselves less than emancipatory. Rather than seeing these activities as narrowly reproductive, hence, or even as reproductive but with potentially oppositional and mediational responses, we would suggest that the activities and exchanges which comprise the educational domain at all levels be seen as essentially contradictory, with at least the possibility that even those forms of curriculum and pedagogy which serve to maintain the status quo contain within them the seeds of social transformation. Such a position in fact calls into question the metaphor of reproduction and suggests that we need to concentrate, instead, on strategies for intervention, in part by exposing just those contradictory elements within extant practices and programs.[33] This emphasis on transforming current ideological configurations is precisely the direction we wish to ultimately focus on in our discussion of teacher education and its connection with other social institutions.

Ideology and Teacher Education

As Critenden correctly points out, the question of how teachers should be educated cannot be answered apart from taking a stand on how much of the existing institutional form and social context of schooling should be taken as given.[34]

> All teacher education is a form of advocacy. Each program is related to the educational ideology held by a particular teacher educator or teacher education institution, even though this relationship may not be made explicit. There is

no such thing as a value free teacher education, just as there is no such thing as a value free education for children.[35]

Specifically, every plan for teacher education is necessarily bounded by existing or proposed patterns of schooling and with the social, economic and political contexts in which schooling is embedded. Either a program has the consequences of integrating prospective teachers into the logic of the present social order or it serves to promote a situation where future teachers can deal critically with that reality in order to improve it. All curricular decisions in teacher education need to be considered and ultimately justified on the basis of which of these directions for educating teachers is the most desirable. Such decisions must, obviously, be accompanied by some axiological framework within which criteria for such a process of justification may be promulgated.

There is a misguided and unfortunate tendency prevalent among teacher educators to believe that curricular activities designed to help education students change the status quo are 'political' (and therefore inappropriate) and that activities tending to strengthen the status quo are neutral (and therefore desirable). This kind of thinking is unfortunate not only because it is illogical, but because it serves in the end to remove ethical and political debate over curricular and pedagogical issues from the discourse of teacher education. As we saw in the previous section dealing with issues in curriculum, technical problems are created which must be dealt with, usually in ameliorative terms; and the continuation of the current social order is enhanced because its particular form is thought to be irrelevant to curricular questions in teacher education.

It will be argued in the present section of this chapter that these claims to political neutrality in teacher education are illusory and that the process of teacher education is inherently a political and moral endeavor. Contrary to popular belief, it is not necessarily the case that the best program of teacher education is one that enables prospective teachers to function with the least friction in schools as they now exist. On the contrary, an integrative stance (i.e., one which seeks to prepare teachers to fit comfortably into schools as presently constituted) is less than defensible given the literature cited earlier that illuminates the powerful role that schooling now seems to play in the reproduction and legitimation of social and economic inequalities in a class-based, hierarchically structured society such as our own.

Popkewitz argues that we need to think of teacher education as more than the learning of the content and procedures of teaching.[36]

> Teacher education imposes work styles and patterns of communication which guide individuals as to how they are to reason and to act in their relationships to the setting of schooling. The language, material organization and social interactions of teacher education establish principles of authority, power and rationality for guiding occupational conduct. These patterns of thought and work are not neutral and cannot be taken for granted.[37]

The 'sacred' knowledge that is communicated overtly and covertly through the rituals and routines of teacher education are in fact value governed selections from a much larger universe of possibilities and, as Giroux points out, these traditions can be traced both contemporarily and historically to specific economic and social interests.[38] For example, as students participate in the activities of teacher education, they learn what types of roles are appropriate for teachers and pupils, how to classify and arrange school knowledge, how to assess what pupils have learned, and a language for thinking about educational problems and their solution.

All of the knowledge that is communicated to education students through both the form and content of teacher education curricula and through the social relationships of teaching and learning by which the knowledge is imparted do not represent neutral descriptions of how things are. They reflect, at least implicitly, answers to normative questions about the nature of education and the role of the school in society and represent commitments regarding either the maintenance or modification of cultural and social patterns. Given this 'dispositional' quality of teacher education, the question which needs to be raised is whose sets of meanings stand behind the choices that are made regarding the appropriate organization and content of a teacher education program and whose interests are served by the conceptions of knowledge and practice that are made available to education students through the dominant forms in US teacher education today. To answer these questions we need first to understand what these meanings and conceptions of knowledge and practice currently are.

Landon E. Beyer and Ken Zeichner

The Dominant Rationality in Teacher Education

There is a growing body of literature in teacher education that convincingly argues that the dominant forms of teacher education today embody a 'technocratic rationality' that serves to encourage acquiescence and conformity to the status quo in both schooling and society and, given the inequitable nature of our society, to serve the interests of those who benefit most from the current social order.[39] At one level we may acknowledge the apparent heterogeneous nature of the people, institutions and procedures involved in the education of teachers; yet at the same time we must recognize that there are certain common features in the orientations of teacher educators to their task and in the structural forms that have developed over time to perform that task that enable a distinctive subculture of teacher education to be identified. It will be argued in this section that, despite conflicting tendencies within US teacher education to reproduce and to modify traditional patterns of valuing, thinking and organizing the educational encounter, an individualistic, a political and technical orientation dominates the sub-culture of US teacher education, and given the political commitments embedded in these perspectives, teacher education in the US today represents a significant agency for the legitimation of the current social order.[40]

Van Mannen's analysis of three levels of rationality, each one of which embraces different criteria for choosing among alternative courses of practical action, is helpful in clarifying the quality of thought that dominates current debates about curriculum development in teacher education.[41] His discussion of the first level of rationality is of particular interest in the present context. This first level of rationality (technocratic rationality) has as its dominant concern the technical application of educational knowledge for the purpose of attaining given ends. The ends themselves are not questioned but are taken for granted as worthy of pursuance. Enquiry about practical action (for example, developing a curriculum for teacher education) is defined at this level solely according to the technical criteria of economy, efficiency and effectiveness. However, given the fact that educational research has failed to demonstrate the existence of universally superior curriculum principles either in teaching or in teacher education for attaining a given end[42] (i.e., there are always a multitude of technical recommendations available for achieving specific learning outcomes), Van Mannen argues that higher levels of deliberative

314

rationality become necessary. We shall have more to say about these higher levels of rationality in the final section of this chapter.

That teacher education in the United States today is dominated by forms of 'technocratic rationality' can be demonstrated by the widespread acceptance of newer forms of competency-based teacher education, the competency testing of teachers, apprenticeship-based clinical teacher education, systems management approaches to curriculum development and program evaluation, behaviorist psychologies and the nature of national accreditation and state licensing requirements.[43] For example, many approaches to competency-based teacher education (now presented under the new rubric of 'research-based teacher education') seek to foster the development of specific teaching skills (for example, asking higher order questions) or teaching strategies (for example, direct instruction) apart from considerations of the curricular context within which the skills are to be employed or the ends towards which they are to be directed. The effect of these programs has been to trivialize the relationship between teacher and learner by assigning to teachers the role of technical, value-free behavior manager. Education is viewed as a problem in human engineering and the solutions to the problems of teacher education are seen to lie within the grasp of 'science' and technology. The moral and ethical issues embedded in the ongoing processes of teacher education are obscured and teacher educators focus their attention exclusively upon procedures to attain ends which are not openly examined.[44]

Furthermore, there is a plethora of studies that demonstrate the consequences of the widespread and uncritical acceptance of apprenticeship-based clinical teacher education. For example, studies conducted on the development of pedagogical perspectives during the student teaching experience[45] consistently indicate that student teaching and other forms of field-based teacher education contribute to the development of 'utilitarian teaching perspectives' in which teaching is separated from its ethical, political and moral roots. According to these studies, as students spend time in the field, getting the class through the lesson on time in a quiet and orderly manner frequently becomes the primary basis for accepting or rejecting the use of a particular teaching activity. If a technique 'works', that is, solves the immediate problem at hand, it is often evaluated as good on that basis alone. Within this perspective that seems to characterize the majority of student teachers, technique of teaching often becomes an end in itself rather than a means towards some articulated, reasoned educational purpose. In fact, the issue of whether something should be taught and the possible latent and long-term consequences of a particular classroom action are typically not addressed by student teachers.

Consequently, student teachers tend to accept the practices they observe in their field placements as the upper and outer limits of what is possible. Katz[46] refers to this condition as one of 'excessive realism'. The knowledge structures that students confront and the ways in which knowledge is communicated to children are largely accepted as natural and right. The school serves as a model for practice and is not itself an object for scrutiny and challenge. There seems to be little sense of the socially constructed nature of the school and almost no searching for alternatives to what is taken to be natural within that world.[47]

Closely related to the almost exclusive focus on technique of teaching as an end in itself in both competency-based and field-based programs are general conceptions of knowledge and pedagogy that permeate virtually all aspects of American teacher education including campus-based experiences. Bartholomew[48] argues with regard to teacher education in the UK that in both the universities and schools the main form in which curriculum knowledge appears to prospective teachers is as a predefined set of 'worthwhile' activities to be mastered. Popkewitz[49] and Giroux[50] make the claim that this same externalized or objectivist conception of knowledge characterizes U.S. teacher education as well, and that as a result prospective teachers come to believe that knowledge is something that is detached from the human interactions through which it was constituted and by which it is maintained.[51] According to these authors, by ignoring the relationship between power and school knowledge, teacher educators often end up 'celebrating in both the overt and hidden curriculum, knowledge that supports the existing institutional arrangement'.[52] According to this scenario, the knowledge that is transmitted to education students in the US does not provide the explanatory power for prospective teachers to reflect upon how specific ideological and material conditions within and outside the schools shape and constrain what is offered for their pursuance. As a result, becoming a teacher becomes solely a problem in mastering the particular corpus of knowledge and skills that is distributed through the rituals of teacher education.

Furthermore, as Bartholomew points out, a transmission relationship is the only possible conception of pedagogy that can exist between teacher and taught within such a conception of knowledge.[53] Accordingly, the message that is communicated to prospective teachers is that being a teacher means identifying knowledge that is certain, breaking it into manageable bits, and transmitting it to students in an efficient fashion. Being a student means acquiring this knowledge and learning how to use it in a context which does not include criticism and has little patience with analysis. Friere has labeled this form of pedagogy as the 'banking concept of education'.[54] Although the rhetoric of teacher education institutions often encourages students to use liberal phases and to affirm liberal slogans about the education of people in places other than the university, the facts of social interaction in the colleges (for example, teacher-learner relationships) are similar to those found in the schools and the schools and universities work in consort to provide a powerful conservative force for defending existing institutional arrangements from close scrutiny and challenge.[55]

Another correlate of the technocratic rationality that dominates the thinking and debate in US teacher education today is an 'individualistic' orientation to problems of the field. This orientation is predominant in the debates over developing a curriculum for teacher education programs and is in turn imparted to education students through the curricula choices that result.[56] For example, one currently popular approach to the development of curriculum for pre-service teacher education is the 'personalized' approach that is based on the work of Frances Fuller and her colleagues at the University of Texas.[57] The essence of this approach is that the content of a teacher education curriculum be matched to the level of concerns that students are experiencing at a particular point in time. This approach further assumes that current concerns of students must be resolved (by a 'relevant' teacher education curriculum) *before* more mature concerns can emerge. Given the largely survival-oriented and instrumental perspectives described earlier and the results of Fuller's own empirical studies of teacher development[58], this would mean that the curriculum for teacher education would be constructed primarily with a view toward helping student teachers survive more comfortably within a context that is largely taken for granted.

There is nothing inherently wrong with suggesting that the content of teacher education be constructed with regard for the motives and purposes of prospective teachers or with the therapeutically oriented pedagogical methods that are recommended for use as part of a 'personalized' teacher education program (for example, counseling for student teachers). In fact, a teacher education program that does not take student motives into account is probably doomed to failure from the start. However, the apparent lack of 'mature' development during pre-service training is often used by advocates of this approach as a justification for excluding any non-survival-oriented content from the pre-service teacher education curriculum.

> On the basis of the evidence now available, it seems reasonable at least to offer survival training to pre-service teachers. Such training might be particularly welcome imme-diately after first contact with teaching when survival concerns seem particularly intense ... The thought even occurs to us that *only* survival training should be offered during pre-service education and that all of the sophisticated substance of professional education ought to be offered during the in-service years.[59]

The significant aspect of this approach to curriculum devel-opment in teacher education is that teacher educators evaluate their roles solely in terms of their impact on education students (for example, 'meeting individual needs') and not in terms of their impact on social systems. Along these lines it is important to remember that the 'survival concerns' of prospective teachers are not genetic endowments but are in fact concerns that are rooted at least in part in the current institutional contexts in which education students are expected to work. Just because teachers appear to develop in a particular way under present circumstances does not imply that this is the way we ought to help teachers develop. As Floden and Feiman correctly point out, 'change in the environment will change the sequence of changes through which teachers pass ... the search for commonalities in teacher changes will produce reflections of environmental regularities, not regularities of teachers'.[60] To attempt to prescribe a curriculum for teacher educa-tion solely on the basis of the teacher concerns literature or any other developmental literature for that matter is to legitimate the institutional contexts within which teachers now develop. Any approach to curriculum development in teacher education needs to consider the normative nature of the task itself and the social and political consequences of the decisions that result.

Closely related to the individualistic thinking that dominates the discourse over curriculum development in teacher education is the individualistic orientation that is imparted through the curri-culum to prospective teachers. Roger Dale argues that, teacher training has its most important effect at the level of cognitive style, in providing teachers with a particular way of looking at the world. This cognitive style can perhaps most adequately, though far from satisfactorily, be described as a cognitive style of individualism. It directs teachers to seek the sources of pupils' problems and the solution of those problems, in the individuals concerned, as well as providing a context for them to see their own failures and satisfactions as individual matters.[61]

The dominance of educational psychology in the curriculum of teacher education is one example of the way in which this individualistic orientation is imparted to prospective teachers. For example, in the state of Wisconsin, certification requirements for elementary teachers stipulate specific courses in the psychological domains of learning and development but are silent about the need for education students to consider educational problems through the lenses of other disciplines. The University of Wisconsin moves beyond these state stipulations and requires two credits of coursework in 'educational policy studies', but the effect of both of these policies is to place educational psychology and hence a psychometric epistemology in a superior position to other modes of analysis. Educational psychology has its own department and all of the other social sciences and humanities (philosophy, history, sociology, anthropology, etc.) are lumped together into a Department of Educational Policy Studies. A student cannot become an elementary teacher without a certain amount of coursework in educational psychology but can receive certification without ever having examined educational problems through, for example, sociological perspectives. The effect of the requirements and the structural arrangements that support them, given the epistemology that dominates current forms of educational psychology, is to mitigate against structural and relational analyses of curricular and pedagogical issues and to promote individualistic orientations to the solution of educational problems.[62]

It should be reiterated at this point that while certain claims are being made regarding what seem to be the dominant tendencies within US teacher education today, it is not being argued that all teacher educators and all teacher education institutions subscribe to this form of rationality.[63] Furthermore, despite the fact that much of the literature on teacher socialization seems to imply a strict correspondence between teacher education and schooling, in a way similar to Bowles and Gintis' analysis of the correspondence between schooling and society[64], there is another literature on the socialization of teachers which has been conducted from a conflict perspective that documents the same kinds of penetrations and resistances within teacher education that Willis has documented within schooling.[65]

This 'resistance' to the technocratic rationality of teacher education programs seems to take two major forms. On the one hand, there are some student teachers who outwardly comply with the dominant values and practices in their work settings but who retain private reservations about doing so. Lacey[66] refers to this tactic as a strategy of 'strategic compliance'. Pressures to receive favorable evaluations from supervisors and for getting a job are some of the reasons why students often understandably choose to exhibit a veneer of conformity in their public behavior. On the other hand, there are some prospective teachers who actively seek to change the range of acceptable behaviors within their classrooms and schools and who overtly engage in classroom practices and express opinions that are clearly contrary to the dominant norms in their work settings. Lacey[67] refers to this as a strategy of 'strategic redefinition'. In both cases, strategic compliance and strategic redefinition, the socialization of teachers is a more partial and incomplete process than often has been believed. However, even given the fact that the connections between teacher education, schooling, and society are of a dialectical nature, we still would argue that teacher education serves primarily to perpetuate existing educational, social and political forms.

That this is the case should not be surprising, given the history of teacher education in the US[68] and the current low status of schools of education both within the university and in relation to the public schools.[69] Given the role that current forms of teacher education play in the legitimation of the current social order, the question of how we should respond to this tendency in the development of teacher education curriculum becomes a matter of central importance.

In summary, we have argued in this section that a technocratic rationality dominates current debates within the teacher education community and have attempted to present examples of the way in which this rationality is represented in the curricula and instructional structures of teacher education. Specifically, the widespread and uncritical acceptance of newer forms of CBTE and apprenticeship-driven field-based experiences, individualistic orientations to curriculum development, and behavioristic conceptions of knowledge and practice illustrate the dominant characteristics of the sub-culture of U.S. teacher education. Now we will consider the implications of this analysis for research in teacher education and for the development of curriculum for teacher education programs.

Implications for Research and Practice in Teacher Education

Throughout this chapter we have pointed to the connections between curriculum, schooling, and teacher education on the one hand and the continued operation of a particular social, economic, and political system on the other. At the heart of our analysis is the view that teacher education is necessarily and thoroughly a political and ideological activity and that the forms of argumentation which take place over this area need to openly acknowledge and be sensitive to this fact. The terrain of the debates over programs, policies, and practices in teacher education needs to be reshaped so that, consequently, ethical and political considerations take precedence over the more technical ones which now dominate both research and practice.

We have also suggested that a sub-culture of teacher education exists in this country which gives form and substance to the current orientation toward teacher education. Although we feel there is ample evidence to support this contention of a dominant cultural form, some of which was presented in the previous section of this paper, we also are cognizant of the divergent traditions and cultures which serve as a counter to these dominant ways of thinking, seeing, and feeling within teacher education. In making claims about what seems to us to be the dominant forms, content, and themes of programs of teacher preparation in this country, it is clear that we must not slip into a kind of functionalism here and that further research be conducted to clarify the contradictions within the domain of teacher education. Just as a metaphor of reproduction may be oversimplified within the field of curriculum and may serve purposes which are less emancipatory than we would hope, we need to clarify as well how the very process of teacher education may contain within it the seeds of its own transformation.

What is crucially needed in order to expose and pursue such contradictory elements is more extensive critical research, both empirical and conceptual, that makes the existing categories of educational practice problematic.[70] We need to adopt a research position that approximates more closely the tradition of critical theory within sociology and philosophy. We need to assess, at a much more critical level than we usually do, the very categories and structures which we use to formulate and evaluate our efforts in teacher education.

Secondly, research efforts in this area must be directed at examining just those connections between schools, curriculum, and teacher preparation and the wider social structure that have been the focus of this chapter. What is needed in this regard is a more critical appraisal not only of the internal dynamics of teacher education culture but of the relationships between this culture and the dominant ideology of our society and the consequences of this for how we conduct programs and research in teacher education. Not only different methodologies for research may be required for the kinds of analysis we have suggested, but different questions must guide the efforts at understanding the problems and possibilities within teacher education. A good deal of extant research in teacher education either tacitly or overtly legitimates existing institutional arrangements and has either forgotten or neglected its generative and critical purpose.[71] Thus far, there has been little enquiry in this country into the question of how teacher education programs and curricula may be linked to ideological commitments within our social system and with the general phenomenon of cultural reproduction. The kind of critical analysis we are arguing for seeks to raise just these connections and that context to a conscious level and make it a subject for critical scrutiny and analysis.

The kind of critical research that is needed is not, however, without precedent. The sort of critique we are urging has perhaps most thoroughly been adopted and put into practice by James Lynch and H. Dudley Plunkett in their study of teacher education in England, France, and West Germany.[72] The authors argue in this monograph that,

> no sequence of social events can be fully apprehended by analysis from, as it were, the *inside*. Teacher education not only functions to produce teachers but, as a set of processes and institutions, reflects a mass of cultural and structural features both of the educational system to which it is most immediately linked and of the wider society and economy to which it owes its existence.[73]

Central to this study is the view that,

however obvious it may be, it is worth pondering that the existence of a teacher-education system and of the school system reflects the will of a political community to perpetuate itself. . . . We cannot therefore expect to understand educational policies and their formulation unless we are taking account of the structure of the distribution of power in the wider society.[74]

The isolated analysis of technical issues in teacher education needs to be supplemented if not supplanted by a more rigorous, complete investigation into how teacher education curricula, programs, and policies are related to this distribution of power in society and the ethical and political consequences of this relationship.

Moreover, we need to address the issue of whether or not the political consequences of teacher education are defensible and, if not, what our moral obligations are as moral agents who are also teacher educators. This requires, first, that we see more clearly that teacher education is a political act, as outlined above; secondly, it requires rethinking what our response should be to the political realities of our work and research. This latter phase is undoubtedly more difficult to deal with, considering where we are employed and the benefits we enjoy as a consequence. The fact that we as researchers and scholars and teacher educators derive certain benefits and privileges from an unequally structured, stratified social and economic system certainly makes the issues we are raising here more personally difficult to deal with; yet at the same time the very fact that we are the recipients of differential benefits serves to make such critique all the more pertinent and morally obligatory.

We have suggested throughout this chapter that part of what is involved in the adoption of such a critical posture — one that goes beyond a concern for technical rationality and efficiency — is the more general development of a critical, reflective spirit in teacher education aimed at open enquiry, critique, and investigation. Yet even the process of enquiry must be related to some larger process or aim; i.e., to what end or for what purpose do we undertake such enquiries. We would suggest that redirecting our efforts in teacher education will confront us with the issue of whether social conservation or transformation is to be forwarded as an educational aim. With Lynch and Plunkett, we would argue that:

> In so far as there is a teacher education which encourages reflective activity by teachers and teacher educators and which trains them in theories and methods of criticism of

their own roles in college, school and society, it enables them to enhance their roles so as to become conscious agents of social reform, not only as individuals but as members of a profession sensitive to the whole range of aims and expectations for education held in the community and alert to a broad educative society.[75]

Our own view is that efforts in teacher education, of whatever orientation or conviction, contain at least implicit ideological commitments. It is not that a political or idealogical purpose can be imposed upon or attached to a program of teacher preparation but that some such purpose is inherent in the very nature of what teacher education is and does.

Other examples of the more critically oriented research paradigm we are suggesting include the study by Bowden which analyzes the content and distribution of forms of knowledge in a philosophy of education class at the University of London[76]; the analysis by Ginsburg and Newman of 'professionalism' and its implications for the process of cultural reproduction within student teaching[77]; the sociological investigation into teacher education curricula by Renshaw[78]; and the chapter by Popkewitz which addresses the focus in teacher education on 'cultural deprivation' models and how this affected the formulation and resolution of educational problems by a group of Teacher Corps interns.[79] All of these investigations offer attempts at reorienting empirical research along the more critical, relational lines we have suggested in this chapter. Additional research of this sort is urgently needed.

The ideas presented also prescribe changes in the practice of teacher education programs. Perhaps the most striking need in this regard is for programs that, like the research we have suggested is necessary, help students become more critical, reflective participants in the process of becoming a teacher.[80] We need to develop programs that self-consciously foster in students the commitment to becoming active, informed critics of their own experiences and situations, rather than merely passive respondents to their professional and occupational circumstances. As Maxine Greene has put this point:

> The concern of teacher educators must remain normative, critical, and even political. Neither the teachers' colleges nor the schools can change the social order. Neither colleges nor schools can legislate democracy. But something can be done to empower teachers to reflect upon their own life situa-

tions, to speak out in their own ways about the lacks that must be repaired; the possibilities to be acted upon in the name of what they deem decent, humane, and just.[81]

Along these lines, we can utilize the experiences and perceptions of students, their own socialization, if you will, as one of the ways in which to talk about and explain the role of schools and teacher education as ideological apparatuses. We can explore with them the ways in which their own experiences can be reinterpreted within this context, and in a way which provides these students with a more complete disclosure of their political significance. By focusing on their own experiences, both in schools and colleges, critiquing them and offering them as subjets for analysis, in the process considering the moral dimensions of these experiences, we will retain the essentially normative character of teacher education. This is one example of what we can do to expose and exploit the contradictions within existing programs and the kind of exchange which may help us move beyond the metaphor or reproduction in teacher education.

It is not unusual to hear enquiry-oriented teaching being advocated as a valuable goal for programs in teacher education, yet the differences between the approach we are urging and more typical enquiry-centered proposals are of extreme importance and consequence. Though an enquiry-oriented approach has often been advocated in relation to the day-to-day activities of teachers, seldom has enquiry been forwarded as an ideal in connection with the social context in which teaching and schooling occurs.[82] In the previous section of this chapter we cited the work of Van Mannen, specifically his analysis of three 'levels of reflectivity' that operate within different approaches to enquiry. This analysis has considerable bearing on the present discussion.

Recall that first level of reflectivity discussed by Van Mannen, technocratic rationality, involves the application of knowledge to the pursuit of some desired goal or end point, on the basis of what is most efficient or effective. Basically, this level of reflectivity is central in the tradition of pragmatic or utilitarian ways of thinking which have been dominant among numbers of teacher educators for at least the last half century. This is the sort of enquiry that tends to dominate the concerns and perspectives of education students during pre-service teacher education and the level to which many enquiry-oriented teacher education programs have responded. An example applied to programs in teacher education is provided by the attempt of researchers at Ohio State University to establish a system of 'reflective teaching' through the adoption of a program of 'Reflective Teaching Lessons' (RTLs) in a program funded under the auspices of Exxon, Inc.[83]

A second level of reflectivity, according to Van Mannen, is based on a conception of practical action where the problem is one of explicating and clarifying the assumptions and predispositions underlying practical affairs and assessing the educational consequences to which action leads. Every educational action is seen as linked to particular value commitments and the debate is over the worth of competing educational goals. However, while this second level of enquiry enables one to transcend the purely instrumental concerns of a technocratic rationality, another level of reflectivity becomes necessary to enable one to decide the worth of competing educational goals and experiences. In other words, the value of diverse educational goals cannot be decided on the basis of educational principles alone.

A third and, in Van Mannen's view, final level of reflectivity (critical reflectivity) incorporates considerations of moral and ethical criteria such as justice and equity into the discourse of educational thought about practical action. This level of reflection legitimates a notion of enquiry where education students can begin to identify connections between the level of the classroom (for example, the form and content of curriculum, classroom social relations) and the wider educational, social, economic, and political conditions that impinge upon and shape classroom practice. The question becomes which educational goals, experiences and activities lead to forms of life that are mediated by concerns for justice, equality, and emancipation; within such a view, both teaching and the contexts that surround it are viewed as problematic.

While there is, of course, a great deal of debate over issues of justice and equality, for instance (the debate between Rawls and his critics may be representative here),[84] the level of this debate is what is of interest in the context of this chapter. Debates such as those over what constitutes equality and the just distribution of wealth and power are concerned with what is morally correct or ethically justifiable, and not with what is merely most efficient. It is not that technical questions of the latter sort are necessarily bad or always the wrong questions to ask; certainly there are times when deciding what is most efficient is a legitimate, even pressing concern. The point is that, given the inequitable nature of our current social system, and the role that schools play in the maintenance of such inegalitarian institutions and practices, there are more pressing, urgent questions which need to be seriously addressed by educators at all levels. A preoccupation with technical, pragmatic concerns prevents these more consequential issues from even being considered, much less debated and resolved. It is this third level of enquiry described by Van Mannen that represents an attempt to address these issues openly and that is being advocated in the present chapter as a basis for teacher education.

This kind of critical, enquiry-oriented research and practice in teacher education must have at least four components.[85] These include (i) analyzing the culture of teacher education itself — what assumptions, loyalties, values, and ideologies seem to permeate the work and lives of those involved in programs to prepare elementary and secondary school teachers; (ii) placing teacher education within the extant patterns and processes of schooling; (iii) becoming increasingly sensitive to and critical of the educational experiences within the university setting, especially regarding apparent contradictions between what we profess about education and what we do as educators;[86] and (iv) understanding historical, theoretical, philosophical, and sociological studies of the work of teachers. All of these facets will contribute to a broader, more encompassing perspective from which to judge the value and significance of teacher education programs, and further illuminate the extent to which we cannot separate the practices of teacher education from those social institutions like the economy and the political structure which surround the schools.

While we feel such an orientation for research and practice in teacher education is essential, we are also well aware of the context within which we work as teacher educators and the constraints which may serve to deflect the kind of critical perspective we are advocating. Indeed part of our recommendations in this regard is aimed at confronting and recognizing the political and social commitments which propel these constraints.

Certainly the policies of state departments of education, as well as national and regional accreditation agencies, represent two such constraining influences on the sort of research program we envision, and the corollary changes in practice we have recommended. We need to continue to counteract the kind of 'hyperrationalization' that is promoted by such agencies[87] and resist the movement of state departments of education to mandate course content and form within teacher education.

We need to bring the same critical framework and orientation discussed earlier to bear on such policies. Attempts to intimidate and coerce university teacher education programs into compliance with values and ideas that are politically laden and ideologically suspect must be resisted. A part of the resistance that is necessary here involves setting forth and arguing for alternatives to the dominant forms of accreditation and licensing, testifying at state legislative hearings, and so on.[88] Yet such resistances cannot be undertaken unless we are willing to engage in the kind of political and ethical debate which raises the sort of issues and problems we have presented in this chapter.

Certainly this will not be an easy task. More than good intentions and ample information about alternatives is necessary to change policies and practices in teacher education, and we must heed Whitty's warning about prematurely celebrating the power of critical thought to transform lived reality.[89] However, encouraging and legitimating open debate and critique over the moral issues surrounding teacher education and raising the kinds of political and ideological issues we have suggested are a fundamental part of teacher education will, we believe, begin the process of analyzing and evaluating teacher education programs and policies in terms of their ethical and political justifiability rather than exclusively in terms of their efficiency or utility. Unless we begin to think about the problem of teacher education in relation to the contexts within which it is embedded and in light of its historical roots, we will continue to be oblivious to the ways in which our actions as teacher educators help perpetuate a culture marked by inequality, domination and exploitation.

Notes

1. KLIEBARD, H.M. (1975) 'Persistent curriculum issues in historical perspective', in PINAR, W. (Ed.), *Curriculum Theorizing: The Reconceptualists*. Berkeley, CA, McCutchan Corporation, p. 41.
2. *Ibid*, p. 42.
3. See ZEICHNER, K. (1981–82) 'Reflective teaching and field-based experience in teacher education', *Interchange*, 12, 4, pp. 1–22.
4. KLIEBARD, H.M. (1975) *op cit.*, p. 43.
5. See DEWEY, J. (1904) 'The relation of theory to practice in education', *National Society for the Scientific Study of Education*, third yearbook, Part I, Bloomington, IL, Public School Publishing Co.; and BEYER, L. and ZEICHNER, K. (1982) 'Teacher training and educational foundations: A plea for discontent', *Journal of Teacher Education*, 33, 3,

May–June.

6. See in this connection, for example, WALLER, W. (1932) *The Sociology of Teaching*, New York, John Wiley & Sons; and EBMEIER, H. and GOOD, T.L. (1979) 'The effects of instructing teachers about good teaching on the mathematics achievement of fourth grade students', *American Educational Research Journal*, 16, 1, winter, pp. 1–16.

7. For an interesting treatment of the philosophical and legal issues involved here, see GOLDSTONE, P. (1979) 'A plea for incompetence', in Philosophy of Education Society, *Philosophy of Education*, Urbana, IL Philosophy of Education Society, pp. 44–61.

8. BEYER, L. (1984) 'Field experience, ideology and the development of critical reflectivity', *Journal of Teacher Education*, 33, 3, May–June, pp. 36–41.

9. DREEBEN, R. (1968) *On What is Learned in School*, Reading, MA, Addison-Wesley Publishing Company.

10. JACKSON, P.W. (1968) *Life in Classrooms*, New York, Holt, Rinehart and Winston Inc.

11. DREEBEN, R. (1968) *op cit.*, pp. 85–6.

12. See GREENE, M. (1979) 'The matter of mystification: Teacher education in unquiet times', in *Landscapes of Learning*, New York, Teachers College Press.

13. Recently, however, several studies have attempted to raise this kind of issue. For example, see APPLE, M. and WEIS, L. (Eds) (1983) *Ideology and Practice in Schooling*, Philadelphia, PA, Temple University Press.

14. FLOUD, J. and HALSEY, A.H. (1958) 'The sociology of education: A trend report and bibliography', *Current Sociology*, 1, p. 171.

15. BOWLES, S. and GINTIS, H. (1976) *Schooling in Capitalist America*, New York, Basic Books.

16. *Ibid*, p. 130.

17. *Ibid*, p. 129.

18. *Ibid*, p. 131.

19. *Ibid*, p. 131.

20. *Ibid*, p. 132.

21. YOUNG, M. (1971) *Knowledge and Control*, London, Collier-Macmillan Publishers.

22. BERNSTEIN, B. (1975) *Class, Codes, and Control, Volume 3: Towards a Theory of Educational Transmissions*, London, Routledge and Kegan Paul.

23. BOURDIEU, P. and PASSERON, J. (1977) *Reproduction in Education, Society and Culture*, R. NICE, trans., London, Sage.

24. APPLE, M. (1979) *Ideology and Curriculum*, London, Routledge and Kegan Paul.

25. FEINBERG, W. (1983) *Understanding Education*, New York, Cambridge University Press.

26. WILLIS, P. (1977) *Learning to Labor: How Working Class Kids Get*

Working Class Jobs, Lexington, D.C. Heath.

27. MacDONALD, M. (1977) *The Curriculum and Cultural Reproduction*, Milton Keynes, Open University Press, pp. 68–9.
28. WILLIS, P. (1977) *op cit.*, p. 12.
29. Willis says on page 12 of his study, 'the lads not only reject but feel *superior* to' other students.
30. WILLIS, P. (1977) *op cit.*, p. 18.
31. EAGLETON, T. (1976) *Marxism and Literary Criticism*, Berkeley, CA, University of California Press, p. 6.
32. BEYER, L.E. (1983) 'Aesthetic curriculum and cultural reproduction', in APPLE, M. and WEIS, L. (Eds) *op cit.*; and BEYER, L.E. and WOOD, G.H. (1986) 'Critical inquiry and moral action in education', *Educational Theory*, 36, 1, winter, pp. 1–14.
33. See BEYER, L. (1985) 'Aesthetic experience for teacher education and social change', *Educational Theory*, 35, 4, Fall, pp. 385–97; and BEYER, L. (1986) 'Critical theory and the art of teaching', *Journal of Curriculum and Supervision*, 1, 3, spring, pp. 221–2.
34. CRITTENDEN, B. (1973) 'Some prior questions in the reform of teacher education', *Interchange*, 4, 2–3, p. 1.
35. KATZ, L. (1974) 'Issues and problems in teacher education', in SPODEK, B. (Ed.) *Teacher Education*, Washington, DC, National Association of Education for Young Children.
36. POPKEWITZ, T. (1979) 'Teacher education as socialization: Ideology or social mission', paper presented at annual meeting of the AERA, San Francisco, April.
37. *Ibid*, pp. 2–3.
38. GIROUX, H. (1980) 'Teacher education and the ideology of social control', *Journal of Education*, 162, spring, p. 6.
39. For example, see POPKEWITZ, T. (1979) *op cit.*; GIROUX, H. (1980) *op cit.*; and GREENE, M. (1979) *op cit.*; also see POPKEWITZ, T. (1985) 'Ideology and social formation in teacher education', *Teaching and Teacher Education*, 1, 2, pp. 91–107.
40. William Taylor, in his description of the 'romantic infrastructure' in British teacher education, argues that the dominant values in the British subculture of teacher education also mitigate against political and structural change. See TAYLOR, W. (1969) *Society and the Education of Teachers*, London, Faber & Faber.
41. VAN MANNEN, M. (1977) 'Linking ways of knowing with ways of being practical', *Curriculum Inquiry*, 6, 3, pp. 205–28.
42. See TOM, A. (1958) 'The reform of teacher education through research: A futile quest', *Teacher College Record*, 82, 1, pp. 15–29.
43. See APPLE, M. (1972) 'Behaviorism and conservatism: the educational views in four of the systems models of teacher education', in JOYCE, B. and WEIL, M. (Eds) *Perspectives for Reform in Teacher Education*,

Englewood Cliffs, NJ, Prentice Hall, for a general discussion of the dominant instrumental rationality in teacher education. Also, as Kliebard points out, this form of rationality is not a new phenomenon within teacher education but has dominated the form of discussion and debate since the turn of the century. See KLIEBARD, H. (1973) 'The question in teacher education', in McCARTY, D. (Ed) *New Perspectives on Teacher Education*, San Francisco, Jossey-Bass; and KLIEBARD, H. (1975) 'The rise of scientific curriculum making and its aftermath', *Curriculum Theory Network*, 5, pp. 27–38.

44. See KEPLER ZUMWALT, K. (1982) 'Research on teaching: Policy implications for teacher education', in LIBERMAN, A. and McLAUGHLIN, M. (Eds) *Policy Making in Education*, Chicago, University of Chicago Press, for a discussion of the problematic aspects of CBTE. Also see CRONIN, J. (1983) 'State regulation of teacher preparation', in SHULMAN, L. and SYKES, G. (Eds) *Handbook of Teaching and Policy*, New York, Longman, for a discussion of the technocratic approach of state influence on teacher education programs.

45. For example, see IANNACCONE, L. (1963) 'Student teaching: A transitional stage in the making of a teacher', *Theory into Practice*, 2, pp. 73–80; TABACHNICK, B., POPKEWITZ, T. and ZEICHNER, K. (1979–80) 'Teacher education and the professional perspectives of student teachers', *Interchange*, 10, pp. 12–29; and POPKEWITZ, T. (1977) 'Teacher education as a problem of ideology', paper presented at the annual meeting of the AERA, New York.

46. KATZ, L. (1974) 'Issues and problems in teacher education', in SPODEK, B. (Ed.) *Teacher Education: Of the Teacher, By the Teacher, For the Child*, Washington, DC, NAEYC.

47. For a more detailed analysis of the obstacles to teacher learning associated with current forms of field-based teacher education see ZEICHNER, K. (forthcoming) 'The practicum as an occasion for learning to teach', *South Pacific Journal of Teacher Education*.

48. BARTHOLOMEW, J. (1976) 'Schooling teachers: The myth of the liberal college', in WHITTY, G. and YOUNG, M. (Eds) *Explorations in the Politics of School Knowledge*, Driffield, Nafferton.

49. POPKEWITZ, T. (1979) *op cit.*

50. GIROUX, M. (1980) *op cit.*

51. See ESLAND, G. (1971) 'Teaching and learning as the organization of knowledge' in YOUNG, M. (Ed.), *Knowledge and Control*, London, Collier-Macmillan, for a detailed discussion of the assumptions embedded in an objectivist conception of knowledge.

52. GIROUX, H. (1980) *op cit.*, p. 19.

53. BARTHOLOMEW, J. (1976) *op cit.*, p. 120.

54. FRIERE, P. (1970) *Pedagogy of the Oppressed*, New York, Seabury Press.

55. For a summary of the empirical evidence supporting this assertion see ZEICHNER, K. (1986) 'Individual and institutional influences on the development of teacher perspectives', in KATZ, L. and RATHS, J. (Eds) *Advances in Teacher Education — Volume 2*, Norwood, NJ, Ablex.

56. This should not be surprising given the fact that, as Cagan points out, 'Perhaps no other aspect of American social thought and culture is as widely acknowledged and deeply felt as that of individualism'. CAGAN, E. (1978) 'Individualism, collectivism and radical educational reform', *Harvard Educational Review* 48, pp. 227–66.

57. FULLER, F. (1971) *Relevance for Teacher Education: A Teacher Concerns Model*, Austin, TX, University of Texas R & D Center for Teacher Education.

58. For example, see FULLER, F. (1969) 'Concerns of teachers: A developmental conceptualization', *American Educational Research Journal*, 6, pp. 207–26.

59. FULLER, F., PARSONS, J. and WATKINS, J. (1973) *Concerns of Teachers: Research and Reconceptualization*, Austin, TX, University of Texas R&D Center for Teacher Education, pp. 46–7.

60. FLODEN, R. and FEIMAN, S. (1980) *A Developmental Approach to the Study of Teacher Change: What's to be Gained?*, East Lansing, MI Institute for Research on Teaching, Michigan State University, p. 22.

61. DALE, R. (1977) 'Implications of the rediscovery of the hidden curriculum for the sociology of teaching', in GLEASON, D. (Ed.), *Identity and Structure: Issues in the Sociology of Education*, Driffield, Nafferton, p. 51.

62. See DE LONE, R. (1979) *Small Futures: Children, Inequality and the Limits of Liberal Reform*, New York, Harcourt, Brace, Jovanovich, for a discussion of the dominant individualistic orientation of present day thinking in educational psychology.

63. For example, see ZEICHNER, K. (1983) 'Alternative paradigms of teacher education', *Journal of Teacher Education*, 34, 3, pp. 3–9, for one interpretation of the different subcultures of teacher education in the US today.Also see TOM, A. (1985) 'Inquiring into inquiry oriented teacher education', *Journal of Teacher Education*, 36, 5, pp. 35–45, for a somewhat detailed description of a subculture of teacher education at least some segments of which are in direct opposition to the dominant technocratic rationality of US teacher education.

64. For example, see HOY, W. (1967) 'Organizational socialization: The student teacher and pupil control ideology', *Journal of Educational Research*, 61, pp. 153–5; EDGAR, D. and WARREN, R. (1969) 'Power and autonomy in teacher socialization', *Sociology of Education*, 42, pp. 386–99; and COPELAND, W. (1979) 'Student teachers and cooperating teachers: An econological relationship', *Theory into Practice*, 18, pp. 194–9.

65. For example, see SHIPMAN, M. (1967) 'Theory and practice in the

education of teachers', *Educational Research*, 9, pp. 208–12; GINS-BERG, M. and LE COMPTE, M. (1980) 'Passive and active models of occupational socialization: The case of teachers', paper presented at the annual meeting of SW Sociological Association, Houston; and ZEICHNER, K. (1980) 'Key processes in the socialization of student teachers: Limitations and consequences of oversocialized conceptions of teacher socialization', paper presented at the annual meeting of the AERA, Boston, April.

66. LACEY, C. (1977) *The Socialization of Teachers*, London, Methuen.

67. *Ibid.*

68 For example, see Mattingly's analysis of teacher institutes in the nineteenth century, which documents the overtly integrative role played by nineteenth century institutions of teacher education in the US. MATTINGLY, P. (1975) *The Classless Profession*, New York, New York University Press.

69. For discussions of the weak position of schools of education in relation to both the public schools and the university community as a whole see FRIEDENBERG, E. (1973) 'Critique of current practice', in McCARTY, D. (Ed.), *New Perspectives on Teacher Education*, San Francisco, Jossey-Bass; and ZEICHNER, K. (1986) 'Social and ethical dimensions of reform in teacher education', in HOFFMAN, J. and EDWARDS, S. (Eds) *Reality and Reform of Teacher Education*, New York, Random House. For the outline of a revised conception of education and teacher preparation within the culture of the university, see BEYER, L.E. (in press) 'Beyond elitism and technicism: Teacher education as practical philosophy', *Journal of Teacher Education*, 37, 2, March–April.

70. See POPKEWITZ, T., TABACHNICK, B. and ZEICHNER, K. (1979) 'Dulling the senses: Research in teacher education', *Journal of Teacher Education*, September–October, pp. 52–60, for one view of the kind of 'critical' research that is needed in teacher education.

71. Peck and Tucker's analysis of research in teacher education offers a clear example of the ways in which research serves to legitimate existing institutional practices; see PECK, R. and TUCKER, J. (1973) 'Research in teacher education', in TRAVERS, R. (Ed.) *The Second Handbook of Research in Teaching*, Chicago, Rand McNally.

72. LYNCH, J. and PLUNKETT, H.D. (1973) *Teacher Education and Cultural Change*, London, Allen and Unwin.

73. *Ibid*, pp. 50–1.

74. *Ibid*, p. 51.

75. *Ibid*, p. 186.

76. BOWDEN, T. (1979) 'On the selection, organization and assessment of knowledge for teachers: A case study', *Education for Teaching*, 89, autumn, pp. 12–18.

77. GINSBERG, M. and NEWMAN, K. (1981) 'Reproductive and transforma-

tive implications of preservice teachers' views on professionalism'. paper presented at the annual meeting of the Comparative and International Education Society, Tallahassee, March.

78. RENSHAW, P. (1971) 'The objectives and structure of the college curriculum', in TIBBLE, J.W. (Ed.) *The Future of Teacher Education*, London, Routledge and Kegan Paul.

79. POPKEWITZ, T. (1977) *op cit.*

80. See the following sources for examples of the programmatic implications of adopting the stance that we advocate: ZEICHNER, K. and LISTON, D. (forthcoming) 'An inquiry-oriented approach to student teaching', *Journal of Teaching Practice*; BEYER, L.E. (1984) *op cit.*

81. GREENE, M. (1979) *op cit.*, p. 71.

82. As GREENE, M. (1979) *op cit.*, p. 54, correctly points out, 'even where emphasis has been placed on critical thinking or experimental intelligence, there has been a tendency to present an unexamined surface reality as natural, fundamentally unquestionable'.

83. CRUICKSHANK, D. and Associates, (1981) *Reflective Teaching*, Bloomington, IN, Phi Delta Kappa.

84. RAWLS, J. (1971) *A Theory of Justice*, Cambridge, MA, Harvard University Press.

85. POPKEWITZ, T., TABACHNICK, B. and ZEICHNER, K. (1979) *op cit.*

86. BARTHOLOMEW, J. (1976) *op cit.*

87. WISE, A. (1979) *Legislated Learning: The Bureaucratization of the American Classroom*, Berkeley, CA, University of California Press.

88. The following represent examples of the kind of world we are advocating here. TOM, A. (1980a) 'NCATE standards and program quality: You can't get there from here', *Kappan*, 62, October, pp. 113–6; TOM, A. (1980b) 'Chopping NCATE standards down to size', *Journal of Teacher Education*, 31, pp. 25–30; and PEKERSKE, S. (1978) 'The knowledge legitimation crisis and competency-based teacher education curricula', *Journal of Educational Thought*, 12, pp. 37–47.

89. WHITTY, G. (1977) 'Sociology and the problem of radical educational change', in YOUNG, M. and WHITTY, G. (Eds) *Society, State, and Schooling*, Lewes, Falmer Press.

12 Knowledge and Interest in Curriculum Studies[1]

Thomas S. Popkewitz

> The organization of teacher education is involved with interrelating three concerns: (i) problems and paradoxes of knowledge; (ii) the institutional quality of schooling; and (iii) social and cultural interests that influence school knowledge. These concerns raise issues about the social functions of the intellectual, the meaning of 'rationality' and the politics that underlie the sciences and discourses of professional life.

The curriculum for educating teachers has become part of the public debate about schooling. Recent federal, foundation and state reports have focused upon the organization and content of professional programs. Legislators, state departments of public instruction, university presidents, deans of schools of education and teachers unions are intervening to change certification requirements at all levels of professional activity.

Most often, the responses have been instrumental. Issues of schooling and curriculum are thought related to increased administrative or organizational efficiency. Increased time in schools or student-teaching, reduced student electives, increased grade points for admission into teacher education programs or 'product' control through testing are seen as solutions to problems of program quality. The instrumental quality of the proposed reforms assumes what Marcuse called a one dimensionality: change, progress and social reform are considered as intricately bound to the correct application of a rational organization.

The one dimensionality filters out issues of political agendas and social interests embedded in our social affairs. The act of teaching 'carries' more than questions of cognition. Children are taught how to organize social phenomena, ways of considering the legitimacy of social institutions and conceptions of 'self' that have broad and profound implications. The politics of schooling evolves around not only the public debates about desegregation, evolution or computer 'literacy' but through the manner in which knowledge and social interactions are structured.

The interrelation of school knowledge with social and political issues compels us to ask about how might we think about problems of curriculum education or pedagogy.[2] What issues, dilemmas and contradictions are involved in the constructions of schooling? What are the social, political and ethical implications of the selection and organization of school knowledge? I believe these questions provide a way to consider the organization and evaluation of teacher education. The questions can be explored by focusing upon at least three concerns:

1 The problems and paradoxes of knowledge.
2 The institutional quality of schooling.
3 Social and cultural interests that influence school knowledge.

Some parameters to these concerns will be discussed as issues of teacher education. The concerns will be then be related to issues of the social functions of the intellectual and the meaning of 'rationality'. The intent is to provide a method for teacher educators to consider the larger context in which issues of organization and procedures exist. How we answer the above concerns provides a way of considering the obligations of study, the interrelation of theory and practice and the problem of politics that underlies the sciences and discourses of professional life.

The Problems and Paradoxes of Knowledge

Let me begin with what might seem obvious and non-controversial. Schools are places that deal with knowledge. By knowledge, I refer to not only the 'facts' or content that become part of the curriculum. Underlying the words and practices of curriculum are dispositions that have the potential to fashion and shape our consciousness. Clyde Kluckhohn, an anthropologist, expressed this view of knowledge when he talked about 'culture' as a word that enables us to select from the vast array of events that confront us in our everyday life. That selection, however, is not just related to the cognitive elements of life. Culture provides a way of thinking, feeling, acting and talking about the world. Thomas Kuhn, focusing upon the context of the history of science, also gives focus to the ways in which our cognitive lenses are more than 'descriptio.s' of affairs; the perspectives of science become elements in our interpretation and valuing of the world that confronts us.

A French school of historiography, The Annales, enables us to consider in greater depth the idea that knowledge is 'more' than content or fact.[3] What we know, our organization of facts in our daily life, the language of our conversations and our conceptions of individuality are seen as containing a structure. The structure enables people to interpret and make plausible their participation in the world.

The structure of consciousness does not emerge from thought or ideas alone but from our historical participation in social relations. LeGoff for example, focuses upon the medieval period to understand how theologies, the development of commerce and the geographical situation interrelate with intellectual writings to produce a collective psychology and a basis for rationality.[4] The development of a new consciousness was related to a conflict between the merchants' and church's conception of time. Merchants were involved in a network of commerce. They sought to make time an object of measurement. The church, in contrast, defined time as eternal, with no temporal hiatus. As the bourgeois gained ascendancy, their conception of time and space dominated the public and private space of society. Their codes of discourse came to govern perception, its exchanges, its techniques and hierarchies of practice.

The measurement of time, a new sense of space and conception of embodiment were not just cognitive inventions. The new knowledge about the world was also knowledge about how to effect change and which elements were to be most valued. Languages of psychology, political theory and epistemology began to emerge to reflect the new perceptions of self. The new consciousness enabled people to think about the world as socially constructed and individuals as actors. The mental structures become a basis for modern science and positivism. It also underlies much of our current pedagogical talk about teacher competencies, testing, academic learning time and the ideologies of progress that underlie models of school change.[5]

The relationship between our social arrangements and consciousness would not be a problem if it was straightforward and uni-dimensional. However, that is not the case. Our daily life contains different sets of values, sensitivities and awarenesses that have their origins in social struggles and transformations. Science, social science, literature and art are social and political endeavors. Each contains implicit theories of cognition, sociality, individuality and political community. In certain ways, we can see the different theories as offering tribal views in which there is controversy about the 'nature' of human affairs, the role of human agency and the relation of community, work and individuality.

Art, Science and Social Interests

We can explore the problematic quality of knowledge by considering more directly the social values that give organization to art and social science. Our 'logic' tells us that art is both a matter of individual creative genius and its formal qualities, such as the use of color and shape. In reading the history of aesthetics, art appears as social production. There is an interplay of art, general philosophical thought, institutional practices and changing cultural consciousness. Aristotle's and Plato's views of aesthetics are understood in relation to the different cosmologies that underlie their writing. Their ideas also need to be considered in relation to the political and cultural conditions of Greek society that they sought to sustain and transform. The development of the first uniquely American style of painting, Abstract Expressionism, as well, responded to social tensions and transformations. It was originally an avante-garde movement during the 1930s that sought to combine socialist commitments with urban experiences. A new ideological orientation to Abstract Expressionism developed by the 1950s with the influence of the Cold War and the movement of the production of art into the academy. A view of art was emphasized that drew upon bourgeois theories of individualism and cognition, emphasizing objective aesthetics and personal expression.[6] The new ideologies were made part of the school curriculum but argued as neutral and universal theories of art.

The social sciences are also social productions, being neither neutral, disinterested nor unrelated to their political context. Enquiry methods, procedures and findings contain visions of social systems and definitions of problems that are culturally located and historically formed.[7] The discourses of social science are secondary abstractions drawn from the everyday strains, tensions and conversations of the world in which scientists participate. Many of the major concepts of sociology, for example, come from literature and poetry rather than science itself.[8] The concepts provide ways by which particular social groups give expression and confront the strains and contradictions of living in dynamic societies. The idea of anomie was taken from poetry to express the tensions created by industrialization among the middle class.

The methods and procedures of science are produced often in response to particular social agendas. The modern testing and measurement industry has its origin in a political movement of eugenics to improve the quality of racial 'stocks'. A current school research interest in ethnography can be viewed in relation to the conflict of the 1960s.[9] Issues of loss of community, lack of efficacy to control one's life and the importance of pluralism were raised. The themes of ethnography reassert these beliefs through the methodological assumptions. The ethnographies provide a symbolic means of asserting individual involvement in the larger political process.

The values underlying our science helps us to understand that there is not one notion of science but multiple traditions for understanding and interpreting. Our social sciences contain paradigms or different constellations of value, commitment, methods and procedures. One can juxtapose behavioral, marxist and phenomenological research in the various social and educational disciplines to understand the deeply rooted and conflicting cognitive interests that guide research. The research traditions offer different vantage points for focusing upon the possibilities of our social conditions.

To recognize the *social* embeddedness of our *social* sciences is to raise issues about the structure of power in our forms of rationality. The concepts, methods and procedures of a social science affirm certain values, yet remain silent about others. While much intellectual work accepts existing traditions, some resist and some seek to reform. What values are sustained or denied remains problematic.

Social Knowledge, Interest and Curriculum

The socially constructed quality of science raises profound and complex issues about the formation of curriculum. Our models of curriculum and teaching often fail to recognize that our discourses are dynamic in construction, multiple in interests and value laden. The discipline-centered curriculum movement of the 1960s, for example, made concepts things to be taught. But to fix the findings of science ignored the debate about knowledge in the disciplines, the different ways concepts are defined by various intellectual traditions, and the social values that underlie the scholarly debates. For example, the concept of power in behavioral and critical traditions in political science 'asks' different questions about politics and imposes different restrictions upon the claims of knowledge.

Rather than exploring the various ways the social sciences interpret our social arrangements, curriculum designs crystalized the concepts and made existing arrangements seem 'natural' and inevitable.[10] These curriculum designs are 'carried' into teacher education through methods textbooks and practicum experiences.[11]

To select a story, a concept or a way of talking about learning or thinking is to engage in a discourse about the world. To 'teach' history is to select someone's history out of the total array of possibilities. To choose a concept for children to learn is to incorporate prior values and interests which are expressed in the way that a concept is given definition. Strategies for teaching impose ways children are to give shape and organization to their social consciousness. No choice is free of assumption or value. Discourse places value upon the disparate events that confront us in our social situation.

The issues of knowledge in art and science provide a way of considering curriculum studies. Central to a curriculum discourse are social/philosophical and political questions about knowledge: What is knowledge? How is it made? In whose interest is knowledge selected, organized and evaluated? How can its tensions, contradictions and limitations be considered by children? I believe that in these questions lie the foundations of curriculum studies in teacher education. What knowledge is chosen and how it is organized involves profound and complex questions about our human conditions and patterns of social conduct.

The Institutional Quality of Schooling

The social quality of knowledge leads us to consider curriculum study in relation to the institutional patterns of schooling.[12] The knowledge of schooling is related to particular sets of rules, patterns of conduct and roles. It is typical only in school to accept a decorum by which conversation is controlled by the raising of hands, sitting in rows of desks and reading of standardized texts for literacy. It is also peculiar to the practices of teaching to set aside a specific time to be 'creative' or to do 'enquiry'. The ethos of politeness and civility in schooling are more than manners or conveniences of organization. The institutional patterns of schooling have identity-forming potential through the way in which behaviors, attitudes and emotions of those who participate are channelled.

The identity forming potential of schooling develops through the specializations and differentation in the knowledge needed to participate. Teachers 'know' different things than children. Principals 'understand' the context of schooling in ways that are in contrast to parents or teachers. As important, the knowledge distributed by schools varies not only by role but also by social location and cultural circumstances. While more about the distribution of school knowledge will be discussed later in this chapter, it is important to note that there is not one common school but schools that are different in their social assumptions, implications and consequences.

The peculiar quality of school knowledge developed historically in relation to a number of social issues and pressures. Among these issues have been the use of the schools to Americanize immigrants, to create a viable democracy and to help in labor selection. The multiple social functions of schooling produce strains and contradictions in which the actual consequences of schooling are often different than that expressed in the public language of teaching or learning.

At least three institutional dimensions can help us understand the tensions and contradictions in curriculum study: (i) achievement, competence and learning as social constructions; (ii) the ways in which school patterns alter the meaning of science and other disciplined practices; and (iii) professionalization as ideological practice. Often the assumptions, implications and consequences of these three dimensions of institutional life are obscured in school discourse.

Thomas S. Popkewitz

The Meanings of Learning, Achievement and Competence are Developed in the Everyday Patterns of Work and Communication in Schools

To participate in the world of schooling is to participate in a social world which maintains particular lines of reasoning, action and values. The organization of classrooms establishes standards about how children should consider their personal competence and achievement. To do social studies, for example, provides students with definitions of which social problems are important, with instruction involving criteria for judging the truth and validity of social statements, and with assumptions about the elements of the social world and their interrelations. The learning of schooling orients the students toward situations and the appropriate form in which to cast the academic knowledge.

To understand the accomplishment of schooling is to understand how the everyday activities and discourse give definition to school life. Criteria of subject-manner learning are mediated by social interaction in which issues of gender, social class and cultural expectations held by teachers are important. Ethnographies of classrooms illustrate the manner in which social characteristics influence the nature of social interactions between teachers and children, the quality of assignments and evaluation given, and the expectations placed upon the school work.[13]

What is learned in schooling is made more complex as there is not one common school but different forms of schooling. The differences were most poignantly expressed for me in a study of an elementary reform program which introduced a management program to make instruction more efficient.[14] The research focused upon the culture of six schools defined as exemplary in the reform implementation. While public language and organization projected a consistency among the different schools, the social patterns reflected different expectations, demands and definitions of pedagogy. These differences were referred to as Technical, Constructive, and Illusory schooling. I would like to explore these findings as a way of focusing upon the socially constructed quality of teaching, learning, achievement and competence.

The definition of competence in the three schools giving Technical schools was related to administrative criteria: a teacher's ability to keep records and monitor children's pace as they moved through a prepackaged curriculum. Children's competence was overtly defined in relation to mastery of the particular behavioral objectives, though mastery was often related to a second criterion of success: students were to look industrious in doing the school work if their efforts were to be judged worthwhile. There were no criteria of excellence of quality except related to quantity. The school called 'Constructive' focused upon knowledge as problematic, children's inter- and intrapersonal skills, and the integration of the arts, sciences and language arts.

Illusory schooling, as shown in two of the studied schools, had cultural patterns in which the social characteristics of the children's background was seen as pathological. The task of the school was to enforce what teachers saw as a universal morality. The illusory quality of these schools had a double edge. Children were not being taught the subject matter of schooling. There was little teaching of reading, mathematics or language, although the formal rituals of subject-matter organization and departmentalization made it seem that the teaching was occurring. The social interactions contained messages, however, that blamed the failure to learn on the individual children rather than on institutional patterns.

Rituals of homogeneity obscured the differences among the schools. Tests of achievement of competence projected an image of objectivity that made the social values seem to occur as judgments external to the life of schooling. Yet the tests are derived from notions of competence that originate in the categories, assumptions and power arrangements of schooling. Test items are built upon socially derived criteria about achievement and intelligence. The test items are mediated by classroom interactions and receive meaning within a world that involves interpretive competence.[15]

The details of everyday life in schools help us understand how the patterns of work and communication in schools transform the texts of curriculum into social texts that have identity-sustaining potential. The patterns of school work offer both a knowledge 'about' and a knowledge of 'how to' effect the content. The 'how-to' knowledge is not the same for all children. The variations in school cultures have significant implications for how children are to view their 'self' in relation to their world.

Curriculum study, then, involves not only questions about the selection and organization of knowledge for schooling. It must also direct attention to the ways in which that knowledge is mediated and differentiated by the ongoing institutional patterns of schooling.

Thomas S. Popkewitz

*The Particular Patterns of School Conduct are Often
Different in Assumption From the Discipline From Which
They Draw Their Labels*

What is taught as science, social studies, art or literature in schooling has a greater relation to the particular history and culture of schooling than to the practices of the disciplines from which the subject matter is drawn.

Science is illustrative for it is considered our most cognitive activity. The knowledge generating quality of science can be seen in relation to its communal and craft qualities.[16] All disciplines contain patterns of social interactions and communication that guide practices. These patterns create shared ways of 'seeing' the world, of working and of testing each other's findings. A discipline is guided by preferred forms, a sense of appropriateness, aesthetics and conceptual structure. The norms, attitudes and dispositions, however, are not static and involve conflict and competition.

In seeming contradiction to its communal nature is the craft-like quality of science. The craft quality gives focus to the combination of practical skills, aesthetic feelings and conceptual order by which individuals generate scientific knowledge. In a way that a chisel becomes an extension of a sculptor's hand and imagination, the concepts and techniques of science are an extension of a researcher's attempt to give meaning and imagination to the work of enquiry.

The communal organization and craft-quality of science are dialectically related. The community organization of norms and practice bestows autonomy upon the individual to develop individual imagination and craftsmanship. The ambiguity, tentativeness, playfulness as well as conflicting visions necessary for the craft quality acts back upon the communal norms and conceptual schemes in a way that alters both craft and community.

Methods of science reflect the interplay of community and craft. Concepts and techniques of science do not stand alone. They are interrelated with purposes, social visions and the existential experiences of study. The interplay of 'self' and world is not one that proceeds by formal logic, hierarchy or taxonomies of tasks. There is always a critical interplay between a theorist and community, society and the phenomena of the world investigated.

In what is perhaps an irony of schooling, the models of curriculum design posit a view of science in which methods of teaching are strategies to uncover and explain predetermined

order.[17] The process of science is a logically ordered set of procedures. Our psychologies of instruction assume there are universal
qualities or states that exist as external to children. Knowledge is
made distinct from method. Content is unambiguous and hierarchical in quality. Thought is viewed as logical, and unrelated to
culture and social conditions. The craft and communal elements of
the construction of science are lost as rational procedures and
abstract qualities are made objects of instruction. As one reads
teacher education method textbooks, a mythic structure is offered in
place of science: the organization of content portrays an image of
science as an objective activity that brings progress to society,
democracy to our political system and the resolution of questions of
fact and value.

Studies of curriculum need to give attention to the manner in
which we borrow from the disciplined fields of enquiry. Our
language and practices need to consider the relation of community, craft and knowledge. Further, teaching needs to take into
account how the imperatives of the social organization of schooling
deny or create possibilities related to the practices of scientific
communities.

A Third Dynamic of Institutional Life is the Professionalization of Occupational Work

Everett Hughes suggests that a profession should be viewed as a
special occupation licensed to act upon clients in ways not permitted
by other forms of social interaction.[18] The label 'professional' is
used by occupational groups to signify a highly trained, competent,
specialized, and dedicated group that is effectively and efficiently
serving the public trust.

But the label 'professional' is more than a declaration of public
trust. It is a category that gives status and privilege to an occupational group. Professionals involve social authority built upon the
recognition that a group's definitions are legitimate according to
prevailing rules of society. There is also cultural authority related to
assigning the realm of meaning by which particular definitions of
reality and judgment prevail as valid and true.

An occupational's authority lies in its claims to scientific
expertise. The 'helping' professions use scientific technology and
language to orient, describe and legitimate their activities. Terms
used to describe mental illness, forms of delinquency or educational

capabilities imply scientific knowledge and justify professional actions.

The idea that science provides the professions with moral authority has both formal and public qualities. The formal language calls attention to an image of inner control, respect for rules and proven experiences. The public language of science occurs through the introduction of the concepts and generalizations into the events of schooling, helping to create beliefs about the nature, causes, consequences and remedies of institutional practices. To talk of diagnosis, to give a technical name (dyslexia) to a child's inability to read, or to prescribe a behavior modification for a child who does not behave has a symbolic effect: they imply that the causes of the problem are known, and that all that is needed is the correct treatment. The use of technical language, specialization and hierarchical ranking of school personnel tend to separate the initiated from the uninitiated. Teaching is made to seem professional, that is, esoteric, technical in purpose, and not amenable to outside influence.

An important element of the sciences of teaching and learning is the interjection of therapeutic language. The language of therapy is part of the public and political context of schooling. The language justifies the status, power and authority of professions. Attention is concentrated on procedures within the institution and failure is rationalized in advance.[19] The application of deviant categories, however, depends more upon the social situation and values in the school than it does upon any perceived, objectively defined criteria. Often, the categories involve highly unreliable diagnoses and prescriptions.

Professionalization poses contradictions: by shaping clients' understanding of their experience, techniques of social manipulation are introduced into professional activity that influence moral conduct and direction of will. Professional knowledge rationalizes experience and offers categories by which to examine one's 'self' in relation to others. While the purpose of professional knowledge is to introduce social and personal autonomy, a form of dependency is introduced as people are to rely on professionals to define and solve their problems.

Some authors have argued that the culture of professionalism may have consequences for the capacity of individuals to provide for themselves.[20] Individual ability and personal competence have been progressively diminished through schemes controlled, disseminated, and evaluated by particular occupational groups. To help its clients, for example, the teaching profession is faced with the necessity of identifying classes of needy or deficient persons to serve. Thus, reading readiness produces unreadiness, computer literacy has unliteracy, and so on. Professional practice creates a contradiction between helping the deficient and maintaining a pool of deficient subjects to help.

Social and Cultural Interests in Schooling

The previous discussion highlighted certain political dimensions of schooling. The politics of curriculum is not one of brute force or power. It is the ways in which ideas and sensibilities of particular groups in society are made dominant in schooling, the range of debate that exists at any one time about that hegemony, and the ways in which these larger debates and struggles filter into and influence pedagogy.

The history of pedagogical debates reflects the relationship between school, society and consciousness. What is defined as school knowledge reflects interests that have the power to structure definitions and communication patterns available in a society. Durkheim (1936/1977), for example, focused upon the development of the French secondary school as involving an interplay of Christian purpose, secular developments of the state and bourgeois, and factors of geography.[21] He argues that the Reformation and Counter Reformation developed 'individualized' pedagogies to mold character. The pedagogies responded to beliefs of those in the larger society who sought to exercise power through the formation of consciousness. The idea of a 'classroom system', as well, was related to the issues and struggles of the Scottish Enlightenment.[22] Pedagogy formed in relation to philosophical, economic and social practices of the time. The class, like the factory, was to be systematically organized and controlled in ways similar to the organization of material life by science and technology. The basis of the classroom system was a moral economy, drawn from the ideas of the political economy of Adam Smith but modified by the social conditions and circumstances of change occurring in eighteenth-century Scotland.

The relation of our contemporary school to culture and society has a particular complexity embedded in its construction. Our world is differentiated by, among others, class, ethnicity, gender and religion. Differences are not presented in the form of carefully articulated arguments or forcefully documented concerns. Cultural expectations provide background assumptions that are absorbed into the discourse of school in a variety of ways. Teachers' perceptions of a community's lifestyle, patterns of school work and selection of curriculum content mediate the conditions and dispositions related to larger social and cultural patterns. Technical, constructive and illusory schooling, discussed earlier, were plausible in relation to the social, cultural, geographic and religious elements of their communities.

What is taught *as* teaching methods or criteria of student learning are categories that are mediated by larger social and cultural power relations. Schools take the experiences and expectations of particular groups and refocus them through abstractions that make the categories seem a universal part of the education of all in society. Theories of learning and teaching, for example, are based upon the conceptions of time, space and embodiment that emerge from bourgeois experience. Time is a commodity that is logical, can be rationalized, 'spent', and put into distinct relations with elements of space. Providing special help for children also emerges from power relations. The category of learning disability, Sleeter argues, was created in the 1960s to distinguish middle class children from other special education categories for the children of the poor and racial minorities.[23] She hypothesizes that the category of learning disabilities emerges to help the middle class prepare their children for the 'new' science and mathematics curriculum that was becoming important to school success.

Professional discourse tends to hide the social assumptions of schooling. The recent proposals for teacher educational reforms, for example, maintain a public language that obscures the social interests that are actually represented. Requests for university/school collaboration, the effort to introduce minimum competencies and admission criteria, and changes in course content represent a ten-year trend of increased power by state educational authorities. The increased control and standardization are labelled, ironically, local control.

The latent implications of reform can be illuminated in computer literacy, a major slogan of the current discourse. The slogan suggests that the school is preparing children for the new worlds of science and technological innovation. The innovations are seemingly neutral yet holding the promise of a better life. Computer literacy 'makes sense' if we focus upon an emerging meaning of science and technology. Three social trends make the idea of computer literacy plausible. The first is the drastic increase in industrial and military R&D since the last years of the Carter administration. The idea of 'science-for-its-own-sake' has been devalued and replaced by a more limited notion. Science is seen as a commodity, its products are to be related to the profit-motive of industry.[24] The second is the commodification of schooling itself. Schools are multi-billion dollar commercial markets. Computer companies have engaged in a large scale effort to introduce the technologies into classrooms. The third is a general cultural belief that change can be brought about instantly. For many in schooling, computer literacy is related to a computer 'revolution' that will bring the millennium.

What is socially significant about the current reforms is the manner in which the symbols of change obscure the political interests served. Concerns with equity and excellence are replaced with a singular call for excellence. The notion of excellence assumes an objective knowledge and differences based solely upon individual effort and merit. The discussion about 'excellence' hides the ways in which the experiences of particular groups in society are given advantage through the development of particular dispositions, tastes, sensitivities and awareness. The dispositions provided by middle class groups make it more likely that these groups will be able to take advantage of the 'opportunities' provided by school in ways that others cannot — Bourdieu called the advantage 'cultural capital'. The current reforms in schooling and teacher education decontextualize the nature of science and technology to be taught by refocusing the problem as one of a universal, abstract quality of literacy. The discourse obscures economic interests that provide direction to the reform proposals. The proliferation of computer literacy courses in teacher education makes the practices seem neutral yet productive towards school reform.

How different cultural knowledge is established, modified and transformed through school practice is subject to debate and to be considered as part of curriculum studies in teacher education. The decontextualization of school experience as abstract categories of learning, teaching or computer literacy dulls our sensitivities to the manner in which the social constructions of schooling favor and handicap certain interests in society. In significant ways, methods of teaching, theories of instruction and practices of student teaching are part of a discourse that responds to tensions and power arrangements underlying our social conditions.

Thomas S. Popkewitz

A Critical Perspective and the Problem of Practice

My concern in this chapter is to suggest an orientation to the discourse of curriculum studies and teacher education. It has focused upon a method to approach the organization of teaching and the issues of learning. I have used the notion of pedagogy to give focus to the complexities of occupational practices. Skills, practices and methods of teaching should emerge as efforts to consider questions about the social construction and production of knowledge.

The discussion reflects my belief in a critical quality to scholarship. My usage of 'critical' goes beyond a concern with understanding the internal logic and consistency in an argument, methods, or findings. 'Critical' gives reference to an intellectual outlook and tradition that has its origin in the development of nineteenth-century European social science. The problematic quality involves interrelating questions of social philosophy with politics, history and 'unmasking' motifs of social enquiry, such as found in the sociology of knowledge and Marxism. 'Critical' means moving outside the assumptions and practices of the existing order. It is a struggle against our cultural givens. The categories, assumptions and practices of everyday life of an institution are to be made problematic.

The argument for a critical view to curriculum studies poses a way of approaching the relation of theory and practice. Knowledge about schooling should provide a way of considering the constraints and possibilities of our pedagogical situation. Our world is continually offered as one of ready-made customs, traditions and order-to-the-things of daily life. Yet, the natural order is not natural or inevitable, but constructed historically, socially and with political interest. Professional education should enable us to consider the possibilities of our social conditions by making fragile, to some extent, the causality in which we live. To make our social situation problematic, not as an order of things but as outcomes of the collective actions of men and women, is to make these situations potentially alterable and amenable to human agency. It is out of such consideration that methods of teaching, student-teaching and the commonplaces of schooling need to be framed and an order to professional educational shaped.

The Social Functions of the Intellectual and the Problem of Practice

The obligation of study has two further qualities. There is a concern for the social function of the intellectual. The notion of 'intellectual' directs us to consider the central role of teachers in creating forms of reasoning that enable students to work towards an integrity in practice. The education of teachers should involve a self-reflective stance to the role of 'science' and the social position of those who serve as the 'intellectuals' of schooling.

Alvin Gouldner focused upon the contradictory quality of the intellectual.[25] The work of intellectuals seems to be transcendent, having no boundary of time or place. This characteristic of enquiry can help to unmask the pretentions, deceptions and self-deceptions that fashion our existence. Yet a social scientist's work is also socially located. The discourse of science provides symbolic canopies that can serve tradition, legitimate existing social relations and maintain power structures. This contradictory quality of intellectual life is inherent in the work of educational researchers, curriculum workers and teachers, and cannot be ignored.

I believe the consideration of the social function of the intellectual provides a way of further broaching the relation of theory and practice. Practice, in this context, refers not as much to the ongoing relations of schooling itself but to enquiry as a form of practice. Intellectuals have historically affiliated with political and social movements, although their relationship to social movements is obscured by ideologies of disinterest found in contemporary sciences.[26] How pedagogical research responds to larger social movements and the ways in which curriculum 'theories' are realized in ongoing power relations are central features of the problem of theory/practice.

A second concern of the intellectual is the problem of rationality. There is no one method for 'being rational'. Our contemporary situation seems to offer us a pluralism of rationalities by which to 'make sense' of our daily life. Yet, one dominates in American social and intellectual life. It is one that is instrumental in focus, giving attention to administration, procedures and efficiency as criteria of change and progress.

An instrumental rationality assumes there is a common framework of experience for all people. The problem of social affairs is to identify the most appropriate means towards defined goals. The instrumentality of culture is embedded in our behavioral and cognitive models of teaching, learning and evaluation.

An instrumental discourse is inadequate to the tasks of understanding schooling or teacher education. The language of systems of instruction, models of teaching or competencies flatten the reality of schooling. The values and interests that underlie pedagogy are obscured and the power relations made to seem natural and legitimate.

Not understanding administrative problems as existing within contexts of power and authority removes from scrutiny the social assumptions and implications of professional actions. We need to recognize that all practice contains implicit epistemologies. Facts exist only in relation to some general theory which enables us to make phenomena interpretable. Further, being without a method of understanding how behaviors are structured within culture and social interest leaves us with no guiding theory and undisciplined practice. Our conventional dichotomies of theory and practice or the liberal and technical mystify the existing social and power relations in schooling. The technical and practical are intricately bound to the norms, values and ideologies of our situation.

A multiplicity of perspectives is important when we recognize intellectual traditions as socially constructed and containing interest. Each provides a vantage point for considering the complexities of our human conditions. When practised well, the different intellectual traditions or paradigms can enable us to 'see' and think about various elements of our social world in ways that can increase our understanding of the whole. The problem of contemporary research is not a lack of a single paradigm to guide enquiry or, as some would say, the youth of the endeavor to collect data. Rather, it is what Feyerabend focused upon when he spoke of professionalized incompetence; that is, the tendency to reify knowledge, to make procedures central to enquiry, and to deny the relation of science to history. A consequence is to produce 'professionals' who profess efficiency and rigor but who obscure the profound and complex quality of our human condition.

Notes

1. 'What is curriculum: The project and its prospects', paper prepared for the annual meeting of the American Educational Research Association, Chicago, 1–5 April 1985.

2. I will use the notion of pedagogy as interchangeable with curriculum. Pedagogy is used most often in European contexts to give reference to the complex relationship between teaching, learning and the contextual elements of schooling. It is that meaning that I wish to emphasize in this chapter.

3. BRAUDEL, F. (1979) *The Structure of Everyday Life, Civilization and Capitalism, 15th–18th Century.* Vol, New York, Harper and Row; LE GOFF, J. (1980) *Time, Work and Culture in the Middle Ages,* GOLDHAMMER, A. (trans) Chicago, University of Chicago Press.

5. POPKEWITZ, T. and FREEDMAN, K. (1984) 'Culture, art and consciousness: On social transformation and the production of myths in science and curriculum', *Contemporary Education Review*, 3, 1, pp. 269–80.

6. FREEDMAN, K. (1985) 'Art in exile: Formalism and self-expression as curriculum ideology', paper presented at the Art Educational Association meeting, Dallas, April.

7. POPKEWITZ, T. (1984) *Paradigm and Ideology in Educational Research: Social Functions of the Intellectual.* London, Falmer Press.

8. NISBET, R. (1976) *Sociology as an Art Form*, New York, Oxford University Press.

9. See POPKEWITZ, T. (1984) *op cit.*

10. APPLE, M. (1972) 'Community, knowledge and the structure of the disciplines', *Educational Forum*, 37, November, pp. 75–82; POPKEWITZ, T. (1976) 'Latent values of the discipline-centered curriculum', *Theory and Research in Social Education*, 4, 1, pp. 57–79.

11. POPKEWITZ, T. (1983) 'Methods of teacher education and cultural codes', in TAMIR, P., PERETZ, M. and HOCKSTEIN, A. (Eds) *Preservice and Inservice Education of Science Teachers*, Rehovot, Israel's Balabon Press.

12. BERGER, P. and LUCKMANN, B. (1967) *The Social Construction of Reality: A Treatise in the Sociology of Knowledge*, Garden City, NY, Anchor Books.

13. CUSICK, P. (1983) *The Egalitarian Ideal and the American High School, Studies of Three Schools*, New York, Longman; KEDDIE, N. (1971) 'Classroom knowledge', in YOUNG, M. (Ed.). *Knowledge and Control: New Directions for the Sociology of Knowledge*, London, Collier MacMillan.

14. POPKEWITZ, T., TABACHNICK, B. and WEHLAGE, G. (1982) *The Myth of Educational Reform: A Study of School Responses to a Program of Change*, Madison, University of Wisconsin Press.

15. CICOUREL, A., JENNINGS, K., JENNINGS, S., KEITER, K., MACKAY, R., MEHAN, H. and ROTH, D. (1974) *Language Use and School Performance*, New York, Academic Press.

16. The use of these metaphors for curriculum is discussed in

POPKEWITZ, T. (1977) 'Community and craft as metaphor of social inquiry curriculum', *Educational Theory*. 5, 1, pp. 41–60.

17. See POPKEWITZ, T. (1983) *op cit.*
18. HUGHES, E. (1958) *Men and Their Work*. Glencoe, IL, Free Press.
19. EDELMAN, M. (1977) *Political Language: Words that Succeed and Policies that Fail*. New York, Academic Press.
20. LASCH, C. (1977) *Haven in a Heartless World: The Family Besieged*, New York, Basic Books; BLEDSTEIN, B. (1976) *The Culture of Professionalism: The Middle Class and the Development of Higher Education in America*, New York, W.W. Norten Co.
21. DURKHEIM, E. (1936/1977) *The Evolution of Educational Thought: Lectures on the Formation and Development of Secondary Education in France*, COLLINS, P. (trans.,) London, Routledge and Kegan Paul.
22. HAMILTON, D. (1980) 'Adam Smith and the moral economy of the classroom system', *Journal of Curriculum Studies*, 12, 4, pp. 281–90.
23. SLEETER, C. (1987) 'Why is there learning disabilities? A critical analysis of the birth of the field in its social context' in POPKEWITZ, T. (Ed.) *The Formation of School Subject Matter: The Struggle for Creating an American Institution*, Lewes, Falmer Press.
24. DICKSON, D. (1984) *The New Politics of Science*, New York, Pantheon.
25. GOULDNER, A. (1979) *The Future of the Intellectual and the Rise of the New Class*, New York, Seabury Press.
26. OFFE, C. (1981) 'The social sciences: Contract research or social movements', in McNALL, S. and OWHE, G. (Eds). *Current Perspectives in Social Theory*. Vol. 2, Greenwich, Conn. JAI Press; GOULDNER, A. (1979) *op cit.*

Notes on Contributors

MICHAEL W. APPLE is Professor of Curriculum and Instruction and Educational Policy Studies at the University of Wisconsin-Madison. He has been concerned with the relationship between curriculum and teaching practices and inequalities in the larger society.

LEN BARTON taught at Westhill College before becoming Principal Lecturer in Education Studies at Bristol Polytechnic, where he is exploring alternative approaches to teacher education through the idea of the teacher-as-researcher. He is interested in the political and social aspects of special educational needs, and is editor of *Disability, Handicap and Society* journal and chairperson of the *British Journal of Sociology of Education* journal.

LANDON E. BEYER is an Assistant Professor of Education, University of Rochester. He is interested in curriculum theory, social foundations and teacher education.

CATHERINE CORNBLETH is Professor of Education at Suny, Buffalo. She is active in social studies curriculum and classroom process research while extending her interests to questions of teacher education and school reform in relation to larger social structural contexts.

KATHLEEN DENSMORE is Assistant Professor of Educational Studies at the University of Utah. She is currently engaged in research on how both gender and the ideology of professionalism have influenced teacher unionism in the U.S.A.

MARK GINSBURG is an Associate Professor in the Comparative Sociology of Education, Department of Educational Leadership and Cultural Studies and a Research Affiliate in the Institute of Higher

Education Law and Governance, University of Houston — University Park. His research interests focus on how everyday processes in educational settings serve to reproduce or contradict the legitimacy of unequal social structures.

HENRY GIROUX is a Professor of Education and Distinguished Scholar in Residence, School of Education and Allied Professions, Miami University, Oxford, Ohio. His work primarily centers around an interest in cultural studies, the sociology of education and curriculum theory.

PAUL MATTINGLY is a Professor of History at New York University. He has written extensively about the development of teacher education in the United States, considering the social and political issues in institutional history. Professor Mattingly was the editor of the *History of Education Quarterly*.

PETER McLAREN is Assistant Professor, School of Education and Allied Professions, Miami University, Oxford, Ohio. He is interested in the sociology of education.

ANDREW POLLARD has taught and researched in English primary schools for many years. He was centrally involved in the development of an enquiry-based initial teacher education course at Oxford Polytechnic, before becoming Reader in Primary Education at Bristol Polytechnic. Amongst his recent publications is *The Social World of the Primary School* (Holt, Rinehart and Winston, 1985).

THOMAS S. POPKEWITZ, Professor of Curriculum and Instruction, University of Wisconsin-Madison, is concerned with the social, political and economic interests that underlie the discourse of schooling. He has written about the social function of the intellectual, the myths of educational reform and the issue of professionalization in teaching and teacher education.

HENRY A. ST. MAURICE is a doctoral student at the Department of Curriculum and Instruction, University of Wisconsin-Madison. He has taught in varied settings, including secondary English and vocational rehabilitation programs. His current teaching and research are concerned with the education of elementary-school teachers.

BARBARA SCHNEIDER is an Assistant Professor at Northwestern University. Her area of interest is the social organization of schooling.

GEOFF WHITTY works in the field of education policy studies and has a particular interest in the sociology and politics of the curriculum. After teaching in primary and secondary schools, he taught in two university departments of education before taking up his present post as Head of the Department of Education at Bristol Polytechnic. His most recent book is *Sociology and School Knowledge* (Methuen, 1985).

KEN ZEICHNER is a Professor of Curriculum and Instruction, concerned with the interrelation of biography and institutions in the socialization patterns of teacher education.

Index

education
education
banking concept 3, 4, 317
conflict in 130–1
politicization 179
professional 110
professionalism and 95–6,
111–12, 116
Education Act 1944 161, 166
education courses
attitudes to 214
professional knowledge in 234
education professors 216
educational administration 47
educational administrators 89, 115,
116, 117–18
educational goals, values and 326
educational policy studies 319
educational practice 285–94
educational practices, as historical
constructions 279
educational psychology 219, 235
curriculum dominance 319
research productivity 228–30
research status 218–19
university view of 212
educational reform viii–ix
educational research 217–19
educational system, meritocratic
111
educational value judgments 245
Edwards, R. 44, 136
efficiency 254, 255
cult of 252, 253
elementary school teachers 72
elementary school teaching 71
elementary schools, male-female
ratio 61–3
elementary teaching, womens' work
61, 63
Elsbree, W.S. 63
emotional engagement, teachers role
90, 116, 118
empiricism 9, 10

employees
identification with job 138–9
teachers as 140–1
enquiry oriented courses, school
experience 175–7
enquiry oriented teaching 325
epistemology, psychometric 319
equality 326
Erasmus, D. 347
Erickson 23
ethnography 21, 339
eugenics 339
eugenics movement 9
evaluating, teachers 249–50
evaluation, personalization 250
evangelism 39, 40
excellence 349
expertise
professional 133, 153–4, 345–6
experts
curriculum design 143
role of 7, 8
explanations, myths as 204–5

Feden 270
Feiman, S. 318
Feinberg, W. 306
females, teacher education faculty
220
femininity, idealization of 69
feminization
occupations 136–7
teaching 42–4, 61–8, 88, 100–1
Fenn, 220–1
field-based teacher education
315–16
Flanders, N. 244
Floden, R. 318
Floud, J. 303
formal language, science 9–10
formal operations stage, Piagetian
195, 196
formal preparation, professionalism
and 95–6